futurecasting digital media

futurecasting digital media

Bob Cotton

PEARSON EDUCATION LIMITED

Head Office
Edinburgh Gate
Harlow CM20 2JE
Tel: +44 (0)1279 623623
Fax: +44 (0)1279 431059

London Office:
128 Long Acre
London WC2E 9AN
Tel: +44 (0)20 7447 2000
Fax: +44 (0)20 7240 5771
Website: www.business-minds.com

First published in Great Britain in 2002

ISBN 0 273 65348 2

British Library Cataloguing in Publication Data
A CIP catalogue record for this book can be obtained from the British Library.

10 9 8 7 6 5 4 3 2 1

Designed by Sue Lamble
Typeset by Pantek Arts Ltd, Maidstone, Kent
Printed and bound in Italy

The Publishers' policy is to use paper manufactured from sustainable forests.

contents

1 introduction

'TODAY IN THE ELECTRONIC AGE of instantaneous communication, I believe that our survival, and at the very least our comfort and happiness, is predicated on understanding the nature of our new environment, because unlike previous environmental changes, the electric media constitute a total and near instantaneous transformation of culture, values and attitudes. This upheaval generates great pain and identity loss, which can be ameliorated only through a consciousness of its dynamics. If we understand the revolutionary transformations caused by new media, we can anticipate and control them; but if we continue in our self-induced subliminal trance, we will be their slaves.'

Herbert Marshall McLuhan, 'Making contact with Marshall McLuhan', interview by Louis Forsdale, 1974, quoted in McLuhan: Forward Through the Rear-view Mirror

going digital in the year zero-one The non-linear future is getting closer. This book is for all of us riding the shockwave of the present – for everyone involved in the new media business, and for everyone who will be affected by it.

Now that new media are front-page news, raising issues of concern to the popular press and hinting at a future that is frightening and fantastic at the same time, and now that we are on the cusp of a century whose first decades will be characterized by digital media, it's time to take stock of all these developments, and ask where they are going and how we might best use them in our lives.

We are in the process of building a vast information and communication machine that interlinks individuals, organizations, government and business in a global network. This network will become the primary tool for communicating with our friends and relatives, it will become the means of accessing whatever we think of as 'entertainment', of continuing our education, and of conducting our business in the world, whether this is commercial, financial, political, cultural or philosophical. Networked digital technology is also transforming the way we work, the machine tools and manufacturing processes we use, and the means of distributing, marketing and selling our products and services. As such the new media are affecting every aspect of our culture.

By the middle of the year zero-one, these new media of digital, computer-mediated communications had already spread their binary lingua franca through the worlds of business, finance, banking, share trading, telecommunications, television, music and publishing. During the next decade these new media will come to dominate the retail and entertainment sectors, changing the global 'web/net' from a department store, credit card market to a (digital) cash-payment global village street-market along the way, and Silicon Valley will eat Hollywood just as it is in the process of eating Tin Pan Alley. The web/net is becoming the primary means by which we communicate, and through which we access *all* our information and our entertainment. In this decade, as the web becomes wireless and truly worldwide, new media will affect every aspect of our lives. While we can only guess as to the extent of this impact, we can prepare ourselves somewhat by understanding the range and nature of the technologies involved. We can ask how we might use or direct these new media to the advantage of us all. And as businessmen, we can ask how best we can understand this new global marketplace, and how we can operate successfully in this wholly new environment.

This book is about the information you need to design new products, plan new businesses and grow new organizations for the computer-mediated networks that we call 'new media'. It is about how you can build a big picture – a conceptual model – of what's going on in this rapidly developing, constantly changing e-environment. It is designed to help you understand the main development vectors that have emerged as a product of the extraordinary intellectual, cultural and technological ferment of the latter half of the 20th century. And most importantly, it is about developing the 'look-ahead' tools you need to plan for the future.

defining new media

Asked about new media, most people will mention computers, the internet, and perhaps e-commerce and digital television. But the new media mean much more than this, much more than the convergence of telecommunications, media and the computer (as though this is not spectacular enough!), and they promise all kinds of radical developments in every aspect of our lives, from the study of the nature of consciousness itself, to the development of new kinds of symbioses between man and machine; and from new ways of communicating between people, to the possibility of new forms of social organization and governance. The fertile mix of technological innovations developed since World War Two – emerging from telecommunications and computer science, and from that wide range of activities that cluster under the heading of 'artificial intelligence' (including expert systems, pattern recognition, robotics, encryption, natural language recognition, software agents, artificial life, etc) – is driving a revolution in finance, in communications, in manufacturing, and in business in general, and is just starting to impact on the entertainment and education sectors.

For me, the term 'new media' doesn't just mean 'new publishing media' (such as online newspapers) or 'new broadcasting media' (such as digital television). Sure, it includes these reiterations of older media, but it is broader than that. I mean 'media' in the sense that Marshall McLuhan meant media – as 'extensions of Man' – that is, including all the various ways in which we extend our sensory apparatus and our central nervous system into the world. Seeing further and in more detail than ever before, 'seeing' wave lengths outside the visible, speaking to and hearing others all around the world; extending our sense of smell; extending the reach of our hands and feet, and augmenting our memory and our very thought processes with new means of recording and storing our knowledge for the future, and of processing and disseminating our knowledge for the present.

So 'new media' also include the new media of communication – between people (extensions of the postal and telephone systems), and between people and machines (software design, telematic control and feedback), and between machines and machines (robotics, wireless networks of embedded processors and sensors). And they also include all the technologies we are developing to facilitate such communication, to create more natural ways of interfacing with machines, and of interfacing with others (and sometimes multiples of others) over vast distances using the full range of gesture, touch, sight and sound – even smell if we want. But for me, the real fascination of the new media is that they provide both a networked system for ordinary people-to-people communications *and* a new publishing and 'broadcasting' system for traditional media-makers.

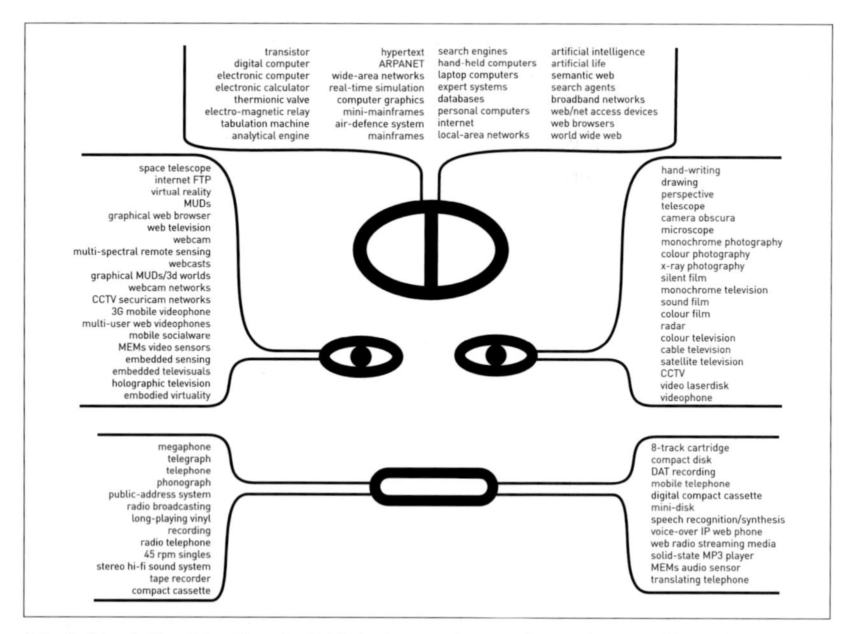

'Media' is defined by Marshall McLuhan as 'extensions of man'. 'E-media' includes all the ways in which electronic and digital technologies are extending our central nervous system around the world. Together they have the potential of transforming every aspect of our lives.

It is both people – and the communication tools they need – and publishing that will dominate the development of new media.

In toto, these new media will gradually subsume most of our older media, and will continue to impact directly upon our financial and commercial practice. They will become the main means by which we educate ourselves, by which we organize ourselves both socially and politically, and as I hope to illustrate through some of the scenarios in this book, I believe they hold the promise of helping us to meet some of the many challenges facing us as a species in this new century.

“YOU IGNORE WHAT'S HAPPENING HERE AND NOW AT YOUR PERIL”

Two things: first of all, new media aren't going to go away. In fact, they are extending their reach and their usefulness exponentially. They are not a passing fad akin to the Hula-Hoop or Furbies. So you ignore what's happening here and now at your peril. Secondly, this is not an easy area to understand. It's an amazingly rich agglomeration of different technologies, and these technologies are still really immature, the product of sciences that are at most only 50 years old (information theory, computer science, cybernetics, systems theory, ecology, genetics, artificial life, chaos theory and the science of complexity, etc), so they are still developing rapidly.

feel the width As an example of how rich an agglomeration these new media are, these are just a few of the innovations and inventions they include: artificial intelligence, CADCAM, CD-ROM, compression, computer graphics, corporate intranets, data encryption, digital money and micropayment schemes, digital television, digital video, distance learning, DVD, e-commerce, electronic publishing, fibre optics, film and video special effects, geographical information systems, handheld computers, home banking, infra-red and microwave networks, microprocessor design, mobile cellular networks, motion capture, MP3, MPEG2, PC cards, remote sensing, satellite communications, set-top boxes, simulation, smart cards, software design, speech recognition, video games, virtual reality, wearable computers, wireless communications and wireless networking.

Then of course, there are all the established and newly formed companies that are the big players in the digital domain, from the gigantic 'super verticals' and content giants such as AOL/Time Warner, Sony, CBS-Viacom, News Corp, Disney and Vivendi Vodafone, down to dot com start-ups and success stories like Amazon.com. Then there are a plethora of new companies aiming to fill the niches in all kinds of developing sectors in the new media web/net: new broadband solutions, new online services, new portals technologies, new peer-to-peer networks, new mobile services, new video and 'internet TV' channels, new net-radio and MP3 channels, avatar and motion-control interfaces, multi-player games sites, and many of the other areas we survey in 'The next big thing'. As these technologies develop, they hybridize, cross fertilize and synthesize, and sprout new off-shoots at an ever-increasing rate.

At the same time the corporate and entrepreneurial response to this rapidly developing electronic eco-system is itself dynamic, with some companies completely re-engineering themselves, some girding their loins for rapid

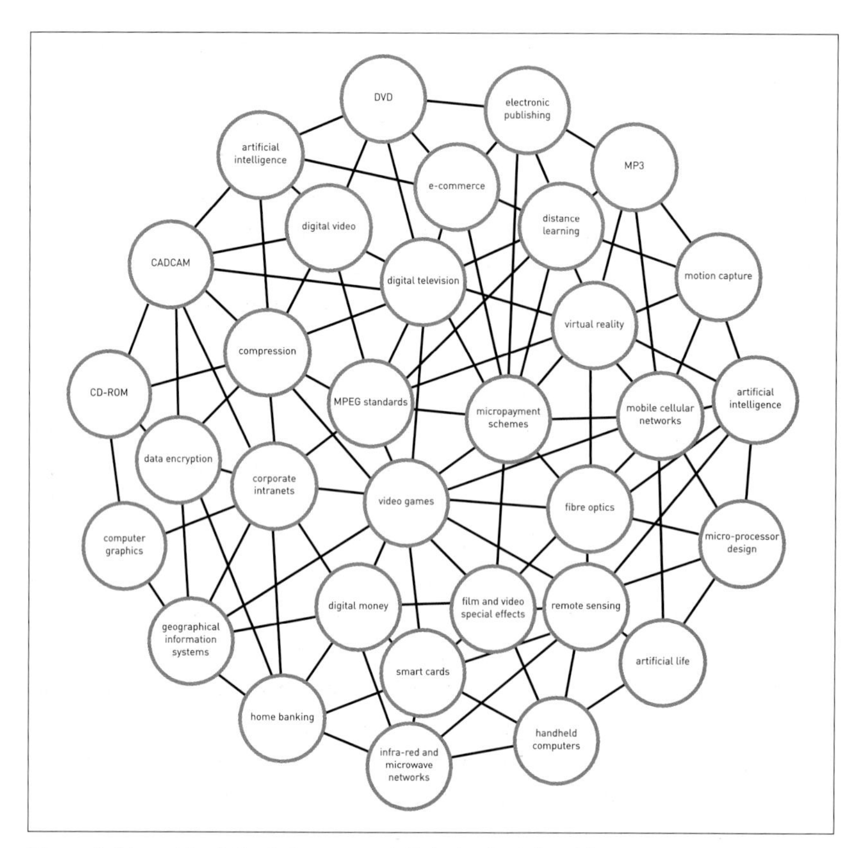

'E-media' is not just the internet and digital television. The scope and pace of 'e-media' developments is bewildering – new technologies, new services, new software, new businesses – and new business models – appear almost daily. Meantime the number of internet users doubles every year. How can we develop a 'big picture' of what's going on?

change, others developing strategies for change, and some frozen in denial or disbelief as their familiar marketplaces disappear or are radically transformed by the web/net.

planning in a chaotic environment These developments are already happening really fast, and look likely to continue to accelerate as we progress through this first decade. By the end of 2000, the web had encompassed nearly half a billion people (332 million in July 2000, according to NUA – *www.nua.ie*) and was extending its embrace at a rate of about 10 per cent per month. As a result of this diversity and pace, the cyberspace that these new technologies both create and inhabit can appear to be a confusing, seething, chaotic mess. Their range, their technological complexity, and their phenomenally rapid rate of development appear to mitigate against rational analysis and strategic thinking, just when the need for such planning becomes overwhelming.

Of course, planning ahead in an apparently chaotic situation like this, where new technologies, new products, new businesses, even new business models are appearing weekly, and where yesterday's start-up is tomorrow's market leader, is extremely difficult. How can you plan ahead successfully in what appears to be an inherently *unpredictable* environment? There's no doubt about it, the 'new media' can present a very confusing picture, leading some observers to conclude that it is totally unpredictable. For example, the writer and digital artist Peter Small argues in *The Entrepreneurial Web* that since normal business planning techniques (projected cash flows and other spreadsheet-based predictive modelling) are rendered useless in this unpredictable environment, the businessman should adopt the entrepreneurial approach of working without plans, letting the solutions evolve – in other words, not bothering with predictive analysis at all.

This is a problem faced by everyone involved in 'planning ahead': all those writing a business plan, preparing market analyses, planning new product developments, designing new services, preparing a marketing campaign, investing in R&D (research and development), buying stock, making investments in the dot com companies, or planning an education or a career. However, there are many ways of making sense of what is happening right now in the new media, and even some techniques for 'looking ahead' into the future, and successfully predicting the directions these important new technologies are likely to take.

Essentially, this is what I do, and what I have done for nearly 20 years. I help designers and project developers, planners and businessmen, all kinds of new product developers, build as accurate a model as they can of the future technological and technology-related developments that are likely to affect their design, their product, their campaign or their business, during its anticipated life span.

Of course designers, in a very real way, are always 'predicting the future' – they know that the products and programmes they are designing now will impact on the real world to some greater or lesser extent at some future time. But the specialized art of the new media strategist – the role of providing detailed context, forecasting and interpretation for the designer – although new as a discipline, has become central to the practice of design, just as it is now becoming central to every aspect of business planning.

While I have a great deal of sympathy with the 'bottom-up' approach proposed by Peter Small, I also know that the 'business plan' is still a central requirement of any business venture (and for any venture capitalist or bank), and despite the apparently chaotic nature of the digital-technology marketplace, I know there are several techniques we can use to help build adequate predictive models of the new media environment. At the very least, these techniques and approaches offer the possibility of providing evidence to your investors of 'best endeavours' at predicting the likely success of your venture. At best, they become a valuable tool that forms an integral and iterative component in your strategic planning or product development planning.

Of course, when you're planning a new business, developing or marketing a new product, providing new services or information/entertainment channels, you need to acquire as much of this kind of competitive intelligence as possible. Essential intelligence at this stage of planning might include what your competition is doing or likely to do, which new or upcoming technological developments might affect your business model, which new business models might affect your business model, which new distribution and marketing channels might affect your plans, how much your market is going to grow and, of course, any possible changes in legislation that may affect your plans.

In order to focus and amplify these questions, the designer or strategist will try to map the 'problem space' – the arena in which the client's planned developments are mapped onto the existing situation, and where the potential or possible effects of new developments in any of the relevant underlying technologies can be taken into account. This map may take the form of a 'spider' diagram, a set of lists, or often literally a pictorial 'route map' illustrating all the factors to be considered.

Extracting strategic intelligence from a large and dynamically evolving problem space is not difficult, but it is essential that you have first interiorized a 'big picture' of what is going on – have developed a conceptual model of the system's dynamics, know what is driving this gigantic wealth-making engine, know what the underpinning 'enabling technologies' are, and know how to detect the emerging developments that may impact on your plans. In other words, before we start planning ahead, and 'looking ahead', we need to develop and interiorize a big picture of the present, of what is happening right now. From this overview, we will be able to detect several interesting vectors of probable development – we will know where to look for our competitive intelligence.

"BEFORE WE START PLANNING WE NEED TO DEVELOP A BIG PICTURE OF THE PRESENT"

Building a big picture of the present is what this book aims to help you with. And there are two main functions we will expect from our big picture: a map of what is happening now, and an indication of where it is all going – how this map might develop over time. We need enough of an indication of how things may develop to predict the likely success of our plans, or to change or modify them in the light of this information, and also, of course, to demonstrate 'due diligence' to our investors and shareholders.

Like all design, planning is an iterative process. The plan is subjected to intensive 'what if?' questioning, and the answers to these questions are ploughed back into the planning procedure. The plan is gradually modified and perfected through a series of iterative exercises: preparing the proposal or plan; exposing it to 'what if?' questions; performing the research to determine the answers to these questions; folding this new information back as refinements to the original proposal.

predicting the present

'(McLuhan) never predicted the future, never tried to. That was one of the things that irritated people. He said: 'No. There are a lot of people busy predicting the future. I'll leave them to it, the futurologists and certain sociologists. That's their job, to look at the future. Historians take care of the past. I'll tackle the really tough one: the present. Let me see if I can predict the present.' So he spent his time trying to 'predict' the present, not the future. He often remarked that 'the future is easy; it is anybody's game. But looking at the present and predicting that – that's difficult. That's what I want to do.' Everything he said wasn't a prediction of what would happen but of what was just happening at the time. But if you take these techniques and turn them on the world and use them just as a means of finding out what is going on around you, then you've got McLuhan's whole technique. He didn't romanticize about the future or sentimentalize about the past. He just worked on the present and found that a full-time occupation.'

Eric McLuhan, 1997, quoted in McLuhan: Forward Through the Rear-view Mirror

The central idea of 'predicting the present', *pace* McLuhan, is that in the process of developing a multi-perspective view of the present, the vectors of development into the future will become clear. The difficulty is in developing a holistic awareness of exactly what is happening here and now – how the various technologies, scientific disciplines, new discoveries and inventions, market trends, fashions, R&D programmes and theoretical work can be interpreted to 'predict the present'. In this book, I have tried to create a montage or mosaic of data, information and interpretation to help construct a big picture of what's happening, and to identify and interpret trends of development into the future.

This montage will include data from some unlikely sources of competitive intelligence, including indications of how cyberpunk writers, and cybernetic artists and designers, are already working with the new networked media, and how they are performing a unique R&D role in the exploration of our perception of these new interactive spaces.

In his prescient interpretations of the present, McLuhan points to the unique role of the artist as an observer and interpreter of the present – the present that the rest of us find really hard to perceive, as we are constantly fixated on our 'rear-view mirror' vision of what is going on. Artists are as important to 'reading' the present as R&D imagineers and futurists are to predicting the future:

'The artist is the only person – his antennae pick up these messages before anybody. So he is always thought of as being way ahead of his time because he lives in the present. There are very many reasons why most people prefer to live in the age just behind them. It's safer. To live right on the shooting line, right on the frontier of change, is terrifying.'

Marshall McLuhan, 'The New Majority with Ed Fitzgerald, CBC Television, 1970, quoted in McLuhan: Forward Through the Rear-view Mirror

information, extrapolation, interpretation So this book is designed to help you acquire an insight into how digital media strategists work, and the techniques and tools they use to build the best possible insights into the present and into our emerging future. With this book we hope to provide you with some of the essential tools for strategic planning in the new media: information for building a holistic and dynamic model of what is happening now, and ways to constantly update this model; the means of extrapolating current trends, and forecasting probable futures; and an understanding of the role that the imagination plays in the development of cybermedia, and how you might use this understanding to critically assess and interpret how new, and even unexpected, developments might impact on your business, your products and your plans.

what this book is about This book has three objectives:

- to describe what is happening right now in the world of new media, and to help you acquire an overview – a 'big picture' of these developments;
- to outline how digital media technology is likely to develop in the next ten years or so (using several perspectives, including extrapolation, tracing development vectors, aggregating R&D developments, watching the futurists, the imagineers, the cyberpunks, the artists, etc);
- to provide some pointers as to the means by which you can dynamically and critically update your 'big picture' in the light of new developments.

The book and website are organized to reflect these objectives. The first sections are about technology forecasting – the various means deployed by futurologists and strategists to mine enough information from the present to make reasonable predictions about the future. We illustrate the power of

Moore's Law in extrapolating developments in processing power, and the resources we can use to develop an aggregate of opinion from professional futurists, academics and think-tanks worldwide. Not surprisingly, most of these resources are online. The web/net itself provides the means to decode the future of the web/net.

the vision thing The bulk of the book is about constructing a mental model – a 'big picture' – of current developments, beginning by examining the ideas and aspirations, the 'visions' that underpin and define the new media. Surprisingly perhaps, some of the main drivers of new media turn out to be grand, altruistic visions of how man and computers might co-evolve, of how we might use the new media to help solve global problems, to develop better forms of governance, more open and fluid markets, and to augment every aspect of our thinking and our lives. These visions not only resonate through the entire history of new media (from 1945, and even earlier), they still inspire and enthuse new media developments, especially in the critical melting pot of the programmer and developer community, and still serve as 'conceptual lenses' to focus lines of development. Understanding the visions that underpin the web/net is a crucial step in building our 'big picture'. These visions are periodically revised, revisited and reiterated, and occasionally they are prototyped and productivized into practical tools that help all of us to 'see' the vision.

> “H.G. WELLS' 1936 IDEA OF A 'WORLD BRAIN', INSPIRED SEVERAL GENERATIONS OF COMPUTER SCIENTISTS”

To my mind, this is the real key to building a useful mental model of how all these technological and cultural creations will develop. Acquiring an understanding of the visionaries that conceived them, and the visions that defined – and still help determine – the directions they will take, you begin to 'see' the present, and perceive possible future directions. H.G. Wells' 1936 idea of a 'world brain', and Vannevar Bush's 1945 description of a 'memory-expansion' system that he called 'Memex', inspired several generations of computer scientists, and sparked visions of how non-linear media might more ably assist our thinking, our creativity and our communications. In part, the 'central vision' was how the potential symbiosis of mankind and smart machines might enable us to create a better world for all. An underpinning aspiration was that by providing the means to access information in the forms that make most sense to individuals, and creating the means to enable people to freely communicate, we would create a global network of empowered individuals – a network that would be the best defence against overweening government, intransigent bureaucracy, monopolistic practices or tyrant dictatorships. Many of the network pioneers envisioned new forms of social and political organization, and even new evolutionary routes for mankind, emerging from the gigantic, world-encompassing electronic network we have constructed over the past 150 years.

And these visionaries, who were mapping the future that we can see already sketched out before us, came not just from the scientific and engineering sectors, but included cybernetic artists, media philosophers and science fiction writers. Concepts such as 'cyberspace', 'the global village', 'virtual communities' and 'co-opetition' appeared in the literature of new media often well in advance of the technological developments they related to.

It is visions of this kind that drive technological innovation. Several important 'development vectors' emerge from an analysis of these visions, and provide us with another tool with which we can interpret developments and accommodate them into our dynamically evolving 'big picture'. Perhaps the most important vector stems from the relatively young sciences of systems dynamics, complexity theory and ecology. This has led to a re-conception of the marketplace as a massively interconnected, self-organizing and co-evolving 'business ecosystem'. This ecosystem is seen by many evangelists as the natural product of laissez-faire capitalism, by some as the natural destiny of communism, socialism, libertarianism and even anarcho-syndicalism; and thinkers from the extreme right and extreme left are drawn to the networked economy by these exciting potentials.

building a big picture Then, we go on to explore the background to the new media: the convergence of media, telecoms and computing that was the inevitable result of the development of the microprocessor and the digitalization of media, and look at some of the directions it is taking in media production, delivery and storage; in disk, and solid-state technology, in the web/net, in digital television, in mobile networking and in networked games consoles. Here we also try to develop a picture of how people are reacting to these developments, and how the notions of 'audience' and 'consumer' are already in flux as people adopt, and become empowered by, the new media.

We build on this emerging big picture by mapping the main areas of new media development in web/net technologies. For example, in 'content and software' we look in some depth at the development of the technologies and the applications that are likely to play important roles in the development of the web/net. These include the important genre of 'socialware' – the kind of software that encourages social intercourse and social discourse, both in the usual sense of communications between people, and in the cybernetic sense of discourse with the machines and sensors that can mediate between us and our environment. The 'media matrix' section focuses on the diversity of the new digital technologies, looking at the current state of the art and developments in processing, memory, bandwidth, access devices, content and software.

In 'the next big thing' we review the short but varied history of how new media technologies have been rolled out onto the world stage in a series of triumphant product announcements heralded as 'the next big thing'. The story of new media technologies is not just determined by cold, scientific logic and common sense. Far from it. The 'best' technologies don't always score in the marketplace, and developers and investors alike are swayed by greed, by rumour, by fashion, and by hype and spin. We look at the record of this process over the past ten years or so, as manufacturers and developers have searched for the 'killer application' that will market itself, and tried to identify the 'next big thing' that will turn a mega-profit and help define the market. Considering that 'new media' is about 20 years old, the surprisingly long list of 'next big things' indicates that the new media sector – and the market itself – is still far from sure exactly what all this new technology is for, or where it is heading. But these 'next big things' can be powerful indicators, helping us define some of the main development vectors in new media, and rounding out our big picture.

the foresight saga The last section aggregates forecasts from many sources focusing on developments during this decade. By 2010, for example, we will have cheap, high-powered microprocessors; a wireless world wide web that is mostly accessed by machines other than personal computers; and we could have automatically translating telephones, wearable miniature internet access, and communication devices controlled by voice-user interfaces and monitored by half-frame 'augmented reality' spectacles, we may have thousands of accurate replicas of ourselves (or cosmetically adjusted representations if we want) to act as our avatars in cyberspace. It's likely that we will routinely use mobile videophone networking, and that by 2010, most of our entertainment and information media, if not themselves interactive, will be accessed by us through an interactive interface. By the end of the decade, we may be doing half of our shopping online, and we will be routinely transacting business through a variety of smart software mediators: agents and avatars that represent us and work for us in the networked cyberspaces of business, commerce and entertainment.

'The future of the past is in the future. The future of the present is in the past. The future of the future is in the present.'

John McHale (cyberneticist), 1969.

'A friend has said the future of the future is the present. If you are really curious about the future, just study the present. Because what we ordinarily see in any present is really what appears in the rear-view mirror. What we ordinarily think of as the present is really the past. Modern suburbia lives in Bonanzaland. It looks back nostalgically and sentimentally to the frontier as a safe and, at the same time, admirable and desirable world. This habit of seeing back one stage when thinking one is looking at the present is an age-old human habit. And it may be that we are the first to discover a means of overcoming the limitations of this habit.'

Herbert Marshall McLuhan, 'The Best of Ideas', CBC Radio, 1967, quoted in McLuhan: Forward Through the Rear-view Mirror

The intent throughout this book is to provide a concise briefing on the present state of the art in e-media for all those who work professionally in the world of communications. Whether this is to encourage people to buy their produce or products, to propagate ideas, to tell stories, to organize or to manage, to work together or to meet like-minded people and to learn, socialize or play together, or to provide information, education or entertainment services, the world of communications will be dominated by new media, and this book intends to provide an essential overview of developments in this area.

In providing such an overview, I hope thereby to provide a glimpse of the many synergies, symbioses and other hybrids that become possible as our culture adapts to the common language of binary code. You might consider this book as a new product development tool, an attempt to provide a map of some of the principal features of the binary territory we are exploring. We will look at some of the new businesses, new business models, new products, new services, and many kinds of hybrid forms of media, social, economic and political discourse that will emerge from the interactions of people with the hardware and software of this digital domain.

2

inventing the future or predicting the present?

competitive intelligence and how to get it In periods of relative stability, it's safe for businesses and organizations to follow well-tried and proven routines that 'guarantee' their continuing success. In these periods, because technological change is slow, these 'environmental' conditions are not noticed – they become a familiar feature in the landscape. As Marshall McLuhan observed: 'If you want to know about water, don't ask a fish.' In these conditions, businesses and organizations don't notice the early-warning signs of the emergence of new society-transforming technologies. This has been the case in much of world industry until very recently. Indeed, it is only when these signs have been around for a while, and the impact of the new technology is becoming obvious, that organizations suddenly notice them, and (in most cases) perceive them as a threat or even a catastrophe.

> “MANAGERS START FLOUNDERING AROUND 'LIKE FISH OUT OF WATER'. THEY LOSE FAITH IN THE 'TRADITIONAL' WAYS OF DOING BUSINESS”

Then, when the true impact of the technologically-induced change is felt, all the well-tested and proven theories and methodologies of business success become instantly obsolete. Faced with these unpredictable and apparently threatening circumstances, managers start floundering around 'like fish out of water'. They lose faith in the 'traditional' ways of doing business, feel out of control, and find it very difficult to understand what is going on and how they should respond.

Some companies and organizations are still in this unhappy situation, unsure of their direction, or of how to respond to the threats and opportunities that face them, scared of arrogant young start-ups stealing their business, worried by security issues, anxious about the corporate transformation that seems inevitable if they are to come to grips with, and compete successfully in, the new transforming technologies.

Some companies have jumped the paradigm shift, and are now operating in the real-time, just-in-time, networked world of the new technology. And of course, some young companies and dot com start-ups stepped straight in, mobile network-savvy, their real-time, head-up, wearable computer displays seething with data, fully aware of the potential of the new digital media.

But companies and organizations in all three of these categories have one thing in common: the desire for the best competitive intelligence, for the best forecasting tools, for ways of understanding exactly what is going on and how it's likely to develop. On such intelligence they can map their business objectives and derive strategic pathways to their goals.

fin de siècle transformations

From the late 1980s, there was a discernibly different atmosphere of excitement in the design schools where I taught interactive media and computer graphics. For the first time, it was possible for students working in this new digital media to graduate, venture out into the big wide world with a great starting salary, and straightaway step into the leading edge of design developments. By the mid-1990s, it was no longer the expectation of a mere well-paid job that was driving graduates and post-grads, by then it was the expectation of becoming a dot com millionaire that put a glint in the eye. The reason for this? The web/net, of course. During the early 1990s, the market for interactive media designers had been growing steadily as businesses and publishers explored the new media of interactive video disks, compact disks, information kiosks, enhanced CDs, and the like. But the sudden spurt of growth in the mid-1990s, was occasioned by the phenomenal success of the WWW.

It was great to watch this giant wealth-making machine emerge out of the esoteric networked world of science and academia and, much more suddenly than we had ever imagined, become the real-time commercial world where our skills in communications and information design, interface design, animation, programming and all those things taught more as an article of faith in the 1980s (faith in the idea that the 'new media' must eventually flourish) became the lingua franca of the biggest mass market ever created.

Even in those early days, the range of technologies folded into the web/net, and the pace at which software and hardware were being developed and improved, meant that an increasing amount of a designer's 'downtime' was spent staying abreast of the technical news, and checking out online developments – new design and authoring tools, new compression algorithms, better video and animation software, push technology, webcasting, virtual-reality tools, new business and e-commerce developments, new business models, content management systems and the like. These developments came thick and fast in this new real-time, global marketplace. And designers had to be on the cutting edge of technology in order to do their job properly. Inevitably, they became expert new media advisers to their clients, and pretty soon their input reached right up into the boardroom. Designers knew more about what was going on in new media, and how it might affect their clients' business, than the clients did themselves. Designers began to play major roles in strategic planning operations. They became suppliers of crucial competitive intelligence, the critical elements of which include describing the present state of the art ('explaining the present'), assessing the technological capabilities of competitors, and 'explaining the future' – forecasting the direction and rate of technological advance – especially in those areas directly relevant to the client's business or plans.

Pretty soon, the business of research, analysis and strategic consultancy became a full-time role, and designers like myself, aware of the holistic effects the digital media networks would have at every level of the supply chain, in every facet of business operations, and in every corner of the marketplace, began to marry creative problem solving with strategic analysis, and to offer clients integrated solutions.

Providing well-thought-through solutions to particular problems – whether this was in the design and development of a new product or service, or the design and provision of corporate intranets or extranets, new advertising or marketing techniques, new interface design, online branding, entertainment software and games design, or simply a brilliant corporate website – meant that analysts were much in demand, especially for their skill in 'looking ahead' and detecting or predicting the emergence of new technologies, new business models, and even new socio-cultural phenomena that might in some way affect the client's plans.

Clients wanted to present themselves as 'new media savvy' and develop leading-edge online services, with as much fore-knowledge as possible of the factors that might affect these services during their planned life span, so increasingly they turned to the new media analysts, strategists or creative consultants for help. That this process of adopting new media channels was a can of worms, and dictated a total rethink or re-engineering of organizational structures and the adoption of radical new ways of thinking about what business was in an online, networked marketplace, caused much friction at the time, and spawned a new wave of radical business thinking (more of that later). At the time there was an obvious mismatch between the kind of 'online thinking' as understood by designers and web practitioners and the understanding of the middle managers who so often had to make – or duck – the decisions relating to these issues.

A rather bizarre artefact of this mismatch was that while industrial leaders such as Sumner Redstone (Viacom) and Rupert Murdoch (News International) and articulate industry spokesmen such as Andrew Neil (then editor of *The Sunday Times*) quickly grasped the import of the global network marketplace and defined general strategies to future-proof their businesses, their middle managers still failed to get it and were caught in the uncomfortable position of being harangued by designers and business consultants who were quoting their bosses' new media insights back at them in support of an online marketing idea.

the foresight saga: a history of the future Of course for designers, getting to be professionally involved in technological forecasting meant not only checking out the techniques used by other professionals – mainly the academics and researchers involved in the relatively new discipline of technology forecasting – but also looking at the work of the acknowledged masters or gurus in this field (people such as Nicholas Negroponte and George Gilder).

The history of the art and science of technological forecasting is relatively short, emerging from the awareness, after six years of high-tech warfare in the Second World War (radar, atomic fission, sonar, cryptography, the jet engine, rocketry, digital computing, cybernetics, etc), that scientific research and development was going to continue to play a decisive role in national defence. As a response, the US War Department set up Project RAND in December 1945, dedicated to 'furthering and promoting scientific, educational and charitable purposes for the welfare and security of the United States'. RAND quickly developed a broad interdisciplinary team of researchers and experts, and they in turn developed methodologies for research and forecasting. Their first report, 'Preliminary design of an experimental world-circling spaceship' (concerned with the potential design, performance and uses of man-made satellites), appeared in May 1946, just seven months after Arthur C. Clarke's now famous article proposing communications satellites, 'Extra-terrestrial relays', appeared in *Wireless World* magazine, and clearly illustrated RAND's role (and, incidentally, confirmed the important role of the 'visionary' in technology forecasting).

Apart from research into capacities, projecting statistics and extrapolating numerical growth curves, the breakthrough in 'future-casting' was that of scenario development, a technique developed by the Business Environment Department of Royal Dutch Shell in the mid-1960s and much influenced and inspired by the work of Herman Kahn at the Hudson Institute. The art and science of forecasting has developed rapidly. 'Futures research' is the umbrella term that encompasses forecasting and other activities that improve understanding about the future consequences of present developments and choices.

The aim of technological forecasting is described by R. Amara and G. Salanik in *Forecasting: from conjectural art towards science* (1972) as the following progression:

'Forecasting is:

A statement about the future
A probabilistic statement about the future
A probabilistic reasonably definite statement about the future
A probabilistic reasonably definite statement about the future, based upon an evaluation of alternative possibilities.'

W. Ascher, in his 1979 book *Forecasting*, says that technological forecasting includes 'all efforts to project technological capabilities and to predict the invention and spread of technological innovations.'

But apart from the scientific definitions and rationale, just how effective is this new science? Even one of the UK's foremost technology forecasters, Ian Pearson (British Telecom's futurologist), admits that 'accuracy is impossible for all but the most trivial question' (and adds the important rider, 'but blurred vision is better than no vision at all'). And most of the (pre-)history of scientific or technological forecasting is peppered with predictions that in retrospect are laughably wide of the mark. Consider, for example, Thomas Watson, chairman of International Business Machines, who in 1944 suggested that there was a market for perhaps five computers in the whole of the United States (it turned out he was at least 100 *million* short)*.

"MOST OF THE (PRE-)HISTORY OF SCIENTIFIC OR TECHNOLOGICAL FORECASTING IS PEPPERED WITH PREDICTIONS THAT IN RETROSPECT ARE LAUGHABLY WIDE OF THE MARK"

*Adding up PCs, mobiles, laptops, games [illegible] set-top boxes, mainframes, supercomputers, minis, handhelds, etc.

There are other major difficulties that the forecaster has to contend with, not least the uncertainty and unreliability of the collected data, the projection into forecasts of personal ideologies, emotions or just plain wishful thinking, and the danger of trying to force facts into pre-conceived patterns. But perhaps the most difficult issue is the very complexity of the real and virtual world of the digital domain: understanding the present can be difficult enough, let alone predicting the future, and that's why a fair chunk of this book is devoted to developing a 'big picture' of what's going on right now.

To offset these problems, forecasters have developed a set of methodologies which taken together provide a suite of powerful forecasting tools. These include the major categories of forecasting technique (which I explain more fully below):

- Aggregating expert opinion: the Delphi procedure
- Trend extrapolation
- Historical analogy
- Scenario building
- Modelling and simulation.

However, the subtext to all these is the 'scanning/monitoring' process – the equivalent to a continuous and ongoing academic 'literature search' – developing and evolving an holistic overview of the digital communications network media arena. Of course, this was how we designers got into this forecasting business in the first place: reading technical literature, checking out specialist and trade magazines, science and technology journals, and research papers and books, except now we were applying more logical research techniques, more intellectual rigour and discipline, to what had been a serendipitous and ad hoc activity.

However, bringing the 'scanning/monitoring' process together with access to human expertise, trend extrapolation, and relevant historical analogy, and using this information and data to develop probabilistic scenarios of possible futures, has resulted in credible, proven methodologies and has led to the growth of future-casting enterprises such as the Global Business Network. So let's look at these techniques first, before I explain more fully how I work as a technological forecaster and introduce some other useful approaches to this area.

the Delphi procedure This is a procedure designed at the Rand Corporation in the 1950s for the systematic soliciting of expert opinion about likely future developments – a procedure characterized by anonymity, iteration with controlled feedback, and statistical group response. A questionnaire on aspects of future technology is sent to a selected group of experts in the relevant technologies. Anonymity protects the source of the expertise – experts can feel free to speculate without being taken to task by their peers. The results of these questionnaires are then summarized by the forecaster and sent back to the experts so that they have a chance to review their own comments in the light of other opinions. This process might be repeated several times and the final result is 'an intuitive consensus of group expert opinion': Delphi – what you get when you ask the oracular experts.

trend extrapolation This is the simple basis of most forecasting, including profit-loss and cash-flow projections. It entails looking at current and recent developments and trends and forecasting future development on the basis of past and current performance. Usually expressed numerically, in terms of unit sales over time, price-performance ratios over time, etc, trend extrapolation is essentially a medium- to long-term forecasting technique which tends to even out temporary fluctuations in order to develop an overview of a trend. The most useful trend extrapolation tool for technology forecasters is Moore's Law, formulated by Gordon Moore of Intel in 1965 to describe the performance increases of each new generation of integrated circuits and microprocessors. On the basis of his observations, and his knowledge of the microprocessor design business, Moore predicted that processing power would continue to double every 18 months, while price would remain steady. Using Moore's Law means we can predict some decades ahead what computing power will be available, and roughly what it will cost. For example, the AI (artificial intelligence) expert Ray Kurzweil has predicted, on the basis of Moore's Law, that by 2019 we will have the ability to build a $1000 computer that has the processing capability of the human

“USING MOORE'S LAW MEANS WE CAN PREDICT SOME DECADES AHEAD WHAT COMPUTING POWER WILL BE AVAILABLE” brain. And in late 1999, Intel technology strategist Paolo Gargini estimated that memory chips would contain 64 *billion* transistors by 2014 (compared with the 64 million per chip in 1999). He also predicted that we would solve the problem of squeezing ever more components onto silicon chips (components are now only 0.15 microns apart – about $\frac{1}{800}$ of the width of a human hair – and eventually components will be packed so closely that unwanted quantum-tunnelling effects will occur as electrons jump through the few atoms of insulating silicon) by creating alternative processor technologies and ever-smaller components (such as the FinFET transistor from the University of California announced in November 1999, which is 400 times smaller than current transistors).

There are problems with trend extrapolations of course, the key one being that you may be analyzing the wrong trend. For example, in the 1950s and early 1960s US television manufacturers were making bigger and bigger sets, responding to a market trend for bigger screens, and grander cabinets, while the Japanese electronics companies had already starting using the new technology of transistors to make sets that were smaller, and even portable. So while the US firms acted on the perceived extrapolated trend, the actual trend was towards television sets that were variable in size, portable, and more relevant to the emerging 1960s lifestyle. The lesson here: reliable extrapolations require the forecaster to have an understanding of the factors which determined trends in the past, and have confidence that these factors will continue to influence trends in the same way.

Another philosophical objection to linear trend extrapolation is that often technology developments are non-linear. New products and new core technologies can arrive with little or no advance warning. The world wide web is the classic example here: its sudden emergence as a 'global standard' in the early 1990s caught many of the big media and software players (including Microsoft) on the hop. Suddenly all the trend extrapolations – previously pointing towards cable, fibre and ISDN networks – had to be radically redrawn.

historical analogy These are forecasting arguments based on historical precedent, for example, the mid-2000 assumption that the take-up of WAP-enabled and third-generation mobile phones will follow the compounded growth curves of cell phones and of internet access itself.

There have been some spectacularly expensive examples of the mis-application of historical analogy in the recent past: Philips Electronics projecting that sales of its Cdi (compact-disk interactive) – an early digital video disk format – would follow the growth curve of the compact disk audio, or that its digital compact cassette (DCC) would catch on in the same way that its original compact cassette did in the 1960s and 1970s. Inappropriate analogy, or just plain wishful thinking, are real dangers here. But the main problem with historical analogy in the current climate is simply finding analogies that are relevant. Things are moving so fast that many developments are literally unprecedented. No historical analogies exist. Of course, the same rate of change will quickly establish sets of precedents for media-watchers and forecasters, but these won't strictly be 'historical' – more like 'parallel' or 'real-time' analogies.

Scenario building

'Scenario planning is a discipline for rediscovering the original entrepreneurial power of creative foresight in contexts of accelerated change, greater complexity and genuine uncertainty.'

Pierre Wack, Royal Dutch Shell, 1984

This forecasting technique has its origins in war games. As mentioned above, it was conceived as a tool for policy planning by Herman Kahn at the Hudson Institute in the early 1960s and refined and developed as a commercial forecasting technique by Pierre Wack at the Business Environment Department of Royal Dutch Shell in the mid-1960s. Scenarios are descriptions of possible futures and ways of 'deconstructing' or 'reverse engineering' these futures in order to examine the planning necessary to create them – or to avoid them. Scenario building therefore is goal-oriented, as opposed to trend extrapolation in which the existing situation is examined and developing tendencies are extrapolated to create a forecast. But combining these two techniques, we can base our scenarios on extrapolated forecasts, and we can then identify the strategic decisions necessary to lever advantage from this probable or possible development.

According to scenario development pioneer Herman Kahn: 'The normative (or goal-oriented) approach, by contrast, involves first setting up some future context or scenario that is either desirable to achieve or to avoid, and then asking what sequence of events might lead to the realization of this objective.' ('Choosing a perspective on the future,' Hudson Institute online at *www.hudson.org*.)

There are two approaches to scenario development: the synthetic technique, where several technologies or technology-related issues are examined separately then synthesized into a big picture; and the 'morphological' approach, where a general holistic description is developed, from which specific issues can be extracted for more detailed analysis. 'In other words the synthetic begins with actors and situations and then creates a suitable environment for them, the morphological approach begins with the environment itself, and then seeks the most appropriate actors and situations,' says Herman Kahn.

Scenarios are built from a variety of sources, including results from the other forecasting methods mentioned here, and infused with a mix of data projections, intuitive insight, creative imagining, and empirical knowledge – much the same, in many respects, as science fiction. There is also a more theoretical approach, in which an abstract model of the real situation is constructed, then the variables of this model are examined. This approach is also taken in the computer modelling and simulation of real-world events.

The foremost practitioner of scenario development in the new media context is the Global Business Network (GBN) a loose organization of experts created by Peter Schwartz, Stewart Brand and others (including many scenario-development pioneers from Shell), with the laudably idealistic aim of creating a worldwide learning community of organizations and individuals in order 'to encourage companies to question and change their maps, to embrace uncertainty, and to stop forecasting the future based on the past'. GBN believes that 'the business community – not government – is most likely to translate emerging opportunities into sustainable growth and a better future'.

'Scenarios are tools for ordering one's perceptions about alternative future environments in which today's decisions might be played out. In practice, scenarios resemble a set of stories, written or spoken, built around carefully constructed plots. Stories are an old way of organizing knowledge; when used as a strategic tool, they confront denial by encouraging – in fact requiring – the willing suspension of disbelief. Stories can express multiple perspectives on complex events; scenarios give meaning to those events.'

GBN: 'Scenarios', www.gbn.org

If this talk of 'stories', 'carefully constructed plots' and 'multiple perspectives' rings a bell, you're right; they sound like science fiction. In fact hundreds, maybe even thousands, of future-tech science-fiction scenarios have been prepared over the past 50 years, many of which are detailed descriptions of the future. Now these are not 'scenarios' in the sense I've been talking about here, but they still play an important role in technology forecasting, as I point out later in 'The vision thing'.

modelling and simulation Ever since Visicalc and Lotus 1-2-3 hit computer screens in the early 1980s, spreadsheet-based numerical modelling and simulation of future business performance have become so commonplace as to be ubiquitous.

The computer-based simulation of complex real-world processes goes back to the work on system dynamics initiated by Jay Forrester at MIT in the early 1960s (including his work on 'urban dynamics', 1959, 'industrial dynamics', 1961, 'world dynamics', 1969, and 'limits to growth', 1972). Forrester had had extensive experience working on feedback control systems and gun-laying servomechanisms in World War Two, and later he worked on flight simulators, the Whirlwind digital computer, and the SAGE air-defence early-warning system. Along the way he invented 'magnetic core memory' – the breakthrough in digital storage that underpins a lot of our computer memory technology. At MIT's Sloan School of Management, Forrester developed system dynamics from an attempt to create an inventory control system with paper and pencil. Of course, the more variables a problem has, the more you need a computer to do the problem solving. Fortunately, Forrester had access to the latest computers like the Whirlwind. The Whirlwind was developed as a result of the inadequacy of analogue computers to tackle the many simultaneous, real-time variables involved in flight simulation, and later in SAGE.

The idea of computer simulation itself however lies in John von Neumann's work with the ENIAC and EDVAC computers in the mid-1940s, first for the simulation of the hydrogen-fusion bomb at Los Alamos, then for the simulation and prediction of weather at Princeton's Institute for Advanced Studies. Despite the fact that early simulations with ENIAC took 24 hours to predict the weather pattern 24 hours ahead, the results were good (if untimely), and by 1955 national weather forecasting using computer simulation (NWP – numerical weather prediction) was routine, though it took another decade for NWP to approach the accuracy of human meteorological forecasts.

“EARLY SIMULATIONS TOOK 24 HOURS TO PREDICT THE WEATHER PATTERN 24 HOURS AHEAD”

It was during this period (1950s) that Jay Forrester developed the SAGE early-warning, real-time, command-and-control system to detect invasions of US air space, and to direct defences against the invader. Such large systems required a constant stream of data from a network of radar stations encircling the US. During the 1960s the SAGE concept was gradually extended to create a world-encompassing surveillance, communications and control system (the WWMCCS – world-wide military command and control system). With this ‘global’ background, it was not surprising that Forrester turned to modelling the development of the world itself.

SAGE and NWP together had proved the value of using computers both as simulation and as command-and-control systems – NWP for near real-time simulation of immensely complex physical processes, and SAGE for real-time data analysis and control of complex human-machine systems.

In the late 1950s Jay Forrester left the SAGE project and at the Sloan School at MIT began to apply systems thinking to the study of industrial processes. This resulted in his development of ‘industrial dynamics’ where he argued that a company should be regarded ‘not as a collection of separate functions but as a system in which the flows of information, materials, manpower, capital equipment, and money set up forces that determine the basic tendencies toward growth, fluctuation and decline’.

According to the Systems Dynamics Society at the University of Albany, New York (*www.albany.edu/cpr/sds/*), Forrester's systems dynamics methodology involved:

- identifying a problem;
- developing a dynamic hypothesis explaining the cause of the problem;

- building a computer simulation model of the system at the root of the problem;
- testing the model to be certain that it reproduces the behaviour seen in the real world;
- devising and testing in the model alternative policies that alleviate the problem;
- implementing this solution.

Simulations are the result of testing various assumptions, changing the variables, and inputting new data into computer 'models' that have been constructed to accurately reflect a real-world situation or process. The accuracy of the model of course determines how useful the simulations are. And faithfully 'mapping' the maze of interactions involved in your business, the market and your distribution channel is a job for the professionals.

There are a number of commercial products that offer rich business modelling and simulation, from established corporate strategy tools such as SAP AG's Enterprise Resource Planning software to, for example, Powersim's Business Planning Simulation tools, which is based on the systems dynamics model created by Forrester. Managers can experiment with different strategic pathways, understand the consequences of their decisions in advance of budget spend, and experiment with new strategies to prepare for a variety of scenarios (you can download a free copy of Powersim Constructor Lite from *www.powersim.com*).

See also Optima! and ithink.

The process of designing and building simulations of complex systems such as the web/net is of course complicated and presents many difficulties, including those of dealing with the essentially non-linear nature of this vast interacting system of people and machines.

As an example of just how difficult, let's briefly consider the work of Lewis Fry Richardson, who devised a numerical weather forecasting methodology* during the World War One. He used equations of motion and state to build a model of atmosphere dynamics (essentially a problem in fluid dynamics), and when his model was initialized with data from met stations to provide values for key variables such as wind speed and direction, and barometric pressure for different regions, Richardson predicted that it should be able to

*This delightful example is from 'The World in a Machine: Origins and Impacts, by Paul N. Edwards of the University of Michigan, in **Systems, Experts and Computers: The systems approach in management and engineering, World War II and after** by Thomas P. Hughes and Agatha C. Hughes (eds), MIT Press, 2000.

simulate the evolution of weather patterns. Thousands of calculations would have to be made to produce this simulation, and of course Richardson's only means of testing his model at that time was with the only computers around – human mathematicians.

Now humans have great brains, but they just don't have the numerical processing speed of digital computers. Faced with the problem of how he could perform all the calculations necessary to produce a weather simulation in time for it to be useful as a forecasting device, Richardson imagined a device he called the 'forecast factory' which was designed to perform these calculations for the whole world. This involved getting 64,000 human computers together in a big stadium, giving them each slide rules or mechanical calculators, and splitting the computational work by parcelling out calculations so that each person would perform just a small part. Participators would communicate their results to others by means of flashing lights, vacuum tube networks, and telegraphy. The entire forecast factory 'performance' would be led by a kind of conductor, who would orchestrate the calculation by means of more flashing lights. Even using this fantastic example of parallel processing, Richardson reckoned he could only calculate changes in the weather about as fast as they happened.

Modelling complex non-linear systems, such as the weather, depends on massive amounts of raw data. The more measurements of what is actually happening, from as many 'weather cell' locations as possible, the better the model and the simulation, and the more accurate the prediction. One of the earliest problems systems scientists had to deal with was how to turn a variety of analogue and digital (numerical) raw data from various kinds of weather sensors into a common data format ready for computer processing.

The latest approach in this kind of modelling echoes the cyberspace developments of 'virtual worlds': it is that of simplifying the complex system to create artificial worlds or 'agent-based models'. These use object-oriented programming approaches (based on Sun's Java language) to construct simulation systems comprising thousands of compatible and reusable simulation components. The advantages of this approach include (a) low-cost, 'open-source' development tools, (b) web-based, (c) browser (with Java virtual machine)-driven, (d) potentially thousands of developers producing reusable 'plug-in' components (see: the Silk Java library (collection of Java classes for discrete-event simulation) from *www.threadtec.com*), and (e) Java's multi-threaded approach gives much more realistic simulation performance.

the web as forecasting tool Of course, as you will have realized already, the web/net provides many of the means and tools we need to make 'a probabilistic reasonably definite statement about the future, based upon an evaluation of alternative possibilities'. In the last few years of the 20th century the web/net started to become what the internet had long promised to be: an immense, distributed library of information. It reached 'critical mass' between 1997 and 2000. Quite suddenly during this period, the gaps and interstices between the islands of specialized information available on the web/net began to infill, and more and more information, statistics, embodied knowledge in the form of scientific research papers, digitized archives, databases and encyclopaedias were uploaded and published, often for free. By mid-2000, the amount of data on the web/net exceeded 210 terabytes* (about 2.1 billion pages at an average of 10kb/page, according to Cyveillance.com). With 7 million new pages being uploaded to the web/net daily, Cyveillance estimated that by early 2001 there would be around 4 billion pages. The average number of external links in each page was 5.6, giving a rough total of 11.8 billion hyperlinks. And these billions of hyperlinks that together we were creating through and between these information nodes started to look like new neuronal pathways networking their map of memories through the learning brain.

*Of course, the web/net is nowhere near the size and complexity of the human brain – yet! The brain, with its 100 billion neurons, and each neuron with an average of 1000 interconnections to other neurons, is still the most sophisticated network on the planet, indeed in the universe as we know it, but is far from the fastest in computing terms.

Hand in glove with this tangible expression of the exponential information explosion came the development of the tools we need to explore, search, and classify the information embodied in this vast amount of data. So in theory we now have enough data, and adequate means to explore this data, to use the web/net as a 'prediction machine'. And that's what the classified links on our parallel website are for. Matched to the structure of this book, we provide links to *all* the information you need to use the web/net as a forecasting tool. But this collection of useful links is of limited use on its own. To make them really useful, you will need to develop a 'big picture' of what is going on in the world of new media – and that is what this book is designed for.

“YOU WILL NEED TO DEVELOP A 'BIG PICTURE' OF WHAT IS GOING ON IN THE WORLD OF NEW MEDIA”

However, before we start examining the information we need to help develop this big picture, let's look at a few ways we can use the web/net as a forecasting tool.

aggregating the futurologists There has always been a remarkable 'generosity' in the way people have used the web/net. After all (as we discuss later), the internet grew from the tradition of sharing knowledge that is a hallmark of scientific study. An instance of this generosity is the number of futurologists and researchers who make their work (or some of it) openly available on the network.

Using our collected links resources, you can check out several of the foremost forecasters, analysts and researchers on the web/net, tracing interesting forecasts and vectors of development though these multiple perspectives that we have aggregated.

the R&D direction Of all the information that forecasters can source on the web/net, there is one source that is not based on opinion, nor even on the objectively researched opinion of expert forecasters. It is based on Alan Kay's idea that 'the best way of predicting the future is to invent it'; it is one of the few sources of 'hard' information about the future available to us, and it reflects the billions of dollars that national governments and global businesses are investing in the core sciences, and in the development of new digital technology. Of course, these worldwide academic research and industrial R&D programmes reflect the range and diversity of digital technologies indicated in this book, but by collating and comparing R&D work across a wide range of technology developers, we can spot the main vectors of development – those vectors to which several institutions or companies contribute.*

*Included in our list are Apple Computer (Advanced Technology Group) Research Labs, Sun Microsystems, Lucent, Cisco (81 per cent of the router market, optical networking, vo/IP, DSL, cable modems, mobile wireless, etc), Nortel, Juniper, BT, Chello, IBM, Hewlett-Packard, Microsoft ($3.8 billion in R&D for 2000), Tellabs, Bell, Intel, Palm, Motorola, Nokia, Ericsson, Symbian, NEC, Hitachi, Sony, AT&T, NTT (information processing is the largest single R&D sector in Japan – 10.4 per cent compared with 9.8 per cent in life sciences), ICL, Fujitzu, Logica, NCR, Vodafone, Cable & Wireless, Orange, France Telecom, Deutsche Telekom, Mannesmann, Telecom Italia, Xerox PARC and Disney Imagineering.

Then there are the 'generalist' new media R&D outfits such as MIT Media Lab and Paul Allen's Interval research (*www.interval.com*), Xerox PARC and EuroPARC, Bell Labs, etc.

corporate strategic indicators 'No man is an island' and no company can develop in isolation, especially in the real-time, globally networked, hyperlinked economy of today, where even major multinationals need to work in co-operation with other companies to develop the global standards that are the basis of global technologies, to produce tools and products for the widest possible constituency, and to invest in the common infrastructure of the web/net itself. Monitoring and tracking developments in these corporate alliances, acquisitions, joint ventures, takeovers and mergers provides a set of valuable indicators for the forecaster.

During the 1980s and the early 1990s, the main accent in corporate strategic thinking was on achieving ever greater efficiencies, lower costs, and greater productivity. The resulting wave of down-sizing, re-engineering, restructuring and quality improvement characterized the era dominated by Thatcher and Reagan. But these changes on their own weren't enough in the networked 1990s. The new network thinking demanded even more radical change. And in an era of instant – even automatic – price comparison, companies had to define very carefully exactly what it was they were bringing to the table. 'The pure efficiency approach did very little to generate distinctive competitive advantage,' says Dwight Gertz of Mercer Management Consulting Inc.

The way that the web/net exploded into the world took lots of people – often people who should have known better – by surprise. The 'steady-state' theories of traditional business gave way to 'big bang' thinking as firms tried to catch up with the furious pace of change forced by digital convergence. Microsoft was initially caught on the hop. When Marc Andreeson launched the browser revolution, Microsoft had no 'net-ready' products, but within two years Bill Gates had completely redefined the company's strategy – this was big bang thinking writ large.

In 1996, explaining Microsoft's realization that the internet should be the main focus of the company's future strategy, Bill Gates explained rather ruefully: 'Every new change forces all the companies in an industry to adapt their strategies to that change.'

In 1996, Microsoft wasn't the only company radically reappraising its strategy: 'At one company after another – from Sears to Hewlett-Packard to

Searle – strategy is again a major focus in the quest for higher revenues and profits. With help from a new generation of business strategists, companies are pursuing novel ways to hatch new products, expand existing businesses, and create the markets of tomorrow.' (*Business Week*, August 1996)

The impetus was of course the rapid development of the networked marketplace, and the extraordinarily rapid rate at which new communications and computing technologies were developing. The necessity of including technological forecasting in any strategic planning is explained by Kent C. Nelson, the chairman of UPS: 'Because we're making bigger bets on investments in technology, we can't afford to spend a whole lot of money in one direction and then find out five years later it was the wrong direction.'

What was interesting about this new direction in strategic planning was that it wasn't based on what *Business Week* called the 'abstraction, sterility and top-down arrogance' of the older models of strategic planning. In the past five years, the direction has been towards the decentralization and democratization of the planning process. This is a direct response to the new 'network thinking' of the new wave of management consultants.

This decentralization of strategic planning amounts to much more than just involving lower tiers of management and front-line employees in the planning process. In the common pursuit of staying closer to the evanescent and evolving realities of the marketplace, the planning process now extends much further than that to include the intricate network of stakeholders in which every company operates: its shareholders, suppliers, distributors, retailers and customers. This new strategic thinking is derived from the work of people who had made a lifetime's study of complex systems, specifically the 'network' or 'systems' thinking of cyberneticists and ecologists, and deals in some key observations derived from these disciplines, observations to do with feedback loops, co-evolution, stakeholding, 'business eco-systems', emergence, evolutionary processes, decentralization, self-organizing systems, flocking mechanisms and the rest (we take a closer look at network thinking in 'Networking' later in this book).

“THE STORY IS NO LONGER COMPETITION, IT'S CO-OPERATION”

The central idea emerging from this new look at strategic thinking is the impossibility of isolation. The story is no longer competition, it's co-operation. Companies must learn how to operate in this deeply interconnected 'ecosystem', where the major objective, as Kevin Kelly puts it, is to 'feed the network' – to create the opportunities for other players, even your competition, to join together in a co-evolution which optimizes the aims and objectives of all players: a 'win-win' strategy.

'Maximizing the value of the net itself soon becomes the number one strategy for a firm. For instance, games companies will devote as much energy to promoting the platform – the tangle of users, game developers, and hardware manufacturers – as they do their games. For unless their web thrives, they die. This represents a momentous change – a complete shift in orientation. Formerly, employees of a firm focused their attention on two loci: the firm itself and the marketplace. Now there is a third horizon to consider: the network. The network consists of subcontractors, vendors and competitors, emerging standards for exchanges, the technical infrastructure of commerce, and the web of consumers and clients.'

Kevin Kelly, New Rules for the New Economy

Shared strategic objectives – where two or more companies perceive a mutual benefit, or even synergy, from some overlap in their plans – create indicators of great interest to forecasters. For example, the group of companies, including Nokia, Ericsson, Motorola, Philips and Psion, which perceive a common interest in creating new standards, new technologies, and new products for wireless data communications, are now involved in the Symbian alliance; and more than 40 companies became members of the WAP (wireless application protocol) when it was founded in 1998. (WAP is an interim wireless data protocol, the first step on the way to the broadband wireless web – see 'The big picture: the media matrix'). The kind of technologies (and standards) these two consortia are 'co-evolving' will largely determine the shape of wireless networking over the next few years, and perhaps even longer, so advance knowledge of these developments is key market intelligence. And of course, this is not difficult to acquire, as evangelizing and propagating this information is central to the growth of these co-evolved strategies: the more companies on board the better. Feed the net!

So another strand of forecasting that is accessible to all through the web/net is the abundant information published by companies in their annual reports, their press releases and product announcements, and in the promotional websites that are generally a feature of this kind of joint venture. There is a whole industry dedicated to the analysis and interpretation of this kind of information, but its usefulness of course depends on how well you have interiorized a 'big picture' of what's happening.

standards organizations As the web/net becomes ever more central to the development of global commerce, the organizations responsible for setting and maintaining international standards in telecommunications, the web, networking and other related sectors assume considerable importance as indicators of future developments. Organizations such as ISO (the International Standards Organisation – *www.iso.ch*), the ITU (International Telecommunications Union – *www.itu.int*), the IEEE (Institute of Electrical and Electronic Engineers – *www.ieee.org*), and especially the World Wide Web Consortium (*www.w3.org*) define the standards on which future developments of the web/net will be based. These organizations are important indicators for the forecaster, and new specialists standards bodies, such as the 3G Partnership Project (*www.3gpp.org*), the Moving Pictures Experts Group (*www.cselt.it/mpeg/* or *www.mpeg.org*), provide the technical details that underpin developments in the latest web/net technologies, such as interactive television, and mobile networking – though a fair degree of technical knowledge is needed to interpret these specifications in terms of their potential implementation.

regulatory indicators Despite the common perception that the web/net is an open, unregulated free market, and despite government protestations that they want to keep the web/net free of regulations (unless of course, there are perceived threats to national security, law and order, data protection, the moral health of our children, etc), there are already many ways in which the telecommunications infrastructure that supports the web/net is regulated, both in terms of internet service providers (ISPs), terrestrial and satellite telcos, and the licensees of broadcasting and cellular network spectrum. Awareness of these regulations, and knowledge of the possible impact of new regulations on the marketplace, is another indicator for forecasters.

Until 1991, the only major regulation of internet content was the restriction on the commercial use of the net. This was lifted in March that year by the then standards body overseeing the internet, the National Science Foundation (NSF). But as the web/net took off and digitally enfranchized a much broader spectrum of citizens (including women and children), governments began to take notice, and the first steps in nationally enforced content control were taken, starting with the US Communications Decency Act of 1996, which attempted to impose controls to limit access to pornography, paedophile rings and other socially undesirable traffic. However, in 1997 this law was successfully challenged on the grounds that it was an infringement of the constitutionally protected right to free speech and could not be enforced in a global environment. Thus a second stage of content control began, with the introduction of rating and filtering products that let users block unwanted material from their personal systems. The most widespread of these was the PICS (Platform for Internet Content Selection) system, introduced by the World Wide Web Consortium (W3C – the standards body for the web/net). This became the self-regulatory option preferred by most European countries, and by the EU itself.

But PICS applied mostly to the world wide web, not to the other internet communication channels (such as FTP* and newsgroups), and anyway was crude and tended to block too many sites (eg sex education sites as well as pornographic ones). In the late 1990s a third stage of content control began as nations conferred on how to co-operate internationally to regulate content. This followed the initiative of the Electronic Commerce and Consumer Protection Group, an organization that includes Microsoft, AOL/Time Warner, Dell, IBM and Visa, to establish internationally consistent rules governing e-commerce on the web/net. (The issues of regulation, censorship and internet access are covered in depth by organizations such as the Global Internet Liberty Campaign (*www.gilc.org*) and the Electronic Frontier Foundation (*www.eff.org*).)

*File transfer protocol: the means to copy data files to (upload) and from (download) any computer on the net configured for FTP (an FTP server). This was, and still is, the primary means of exchanging data files which are too large for e-mail attachments.

venture capital indicators During the 1990s venture capitalists invested billions of dollars in new internet and digital media-related companies. Information on their investments – the choice of businesses likely to succeed, and the type of technology development that venture capitalist companies back – provides a set of extremely useful indicators of likely future developments, especially when averaged from a large pool of investments. During the period 1987–1996, between 15 per cent and 33 per cent of all venture capital investment in the US was in computer and IT-related businesses. By 1996, total investments reached $9.4 billion in the US and $8.6 billion in Europe. How do you keep in touch with these developments? Check out the list of more than 300 online venture cap companies maintained at *www.columbia.edu/~alt12/vconline.html*, and for example look at Bill Gross's IdealLab! site (*www.idealab.com*) for indicators of developments in e-commerce, content provision and internet infrastructure and services.

pros and cons of technology forecasting It is important to realize that, no matter how brilliantly researched, how detailed, how all-encompassing, how credible a forecast is, it is still just a forecast not a prediction. The problems inherent in technology forecasting are manifest. Consider how Thomas Watts, the then chairman of IBM, must rue his 1944 comment that 'I believe that there is a market for no more than five computers in this country [the USA]'.

Essentially, you can't predict the future with any clarity, but this does not mean that we are helplessly at the mercy of events, unable to plan ahead in a world in which computing and communications technology is developing at a bewildering pace. What I have done in this book is to point to the various ways in which you can lever advantage from many sources of easily available information, and create a business or product development strategy that is as informed as possible about future developments relevant to your business and your strategy. Even a fuzzy picture of the future will give you competitive advantage over those with no picture at all.

Consider these other pros and cons:

- Linear extrapolation is a proven future-casting technique, but it can't predict the new – the unexpected.
- Our interpretation of developments will be coloured by our predelictions and desires. Make your forecast assumptions as clear and as transparent as possible. Consider the forecasts of other professionals, aggregate forecasts and average them to create an objective view.
- Identify the trends that are relevant to your aims and objectives. Identify the current position of the trend on the S-curve of innovation.
- The future is dependent on many variables. There are many possible futures. It is important that forecasters should consider a range of variables, and the range of possible futures that might emerge from them. A single-future prediction is just a gambler's hazard. Multiple, parallel futures – all of which are catered for in your strategy or detailed planning – are an essential tool in the planner's and designer's palette of options.
- Identifying the most important trends to forecast is not easy. Remember back in the early 1990s when the telcos, the computer manufacturers and most professional futurists were all predicting the imminent arrival of the superhighway? The superhighway was the expected broadband, fibre-optic network that would (eventually) be created by the telcos. Did anyone mention the internet? Had anyone heard of Tim Berners-Lee? Remember also how the TV industry was expecting the future to be dominated by high-definition television – at the time it was considered impossible to deliver this down telephone wires. But new broadcast technologies, new compression techniques, and new networking protocols were invented (largely to solve other problems), and satellite return-loop broadband delivery, MPEG and ADSL appeared, so that now the future of TV looks much more like it will be based on the broadband web model trailed by Hughes's DirecTV, Microsoft's WebTV, IchooseTV, and others.
- The best way to predict the future is to design it. Don't worry about what others are doing (but keep an eye on them). Develop a plan to put

you where you want to be, then research the technologies impinging on or relevant to your plan. Build an extrapolation of these developments, then fold back into your business plan and product design. In other words, 'don't follow trends, create them'.

- There are some central visions that drive many developments in new media (several are discussed in this book). Analyze these visions. How do they relate to *your* company's visions?
- Market research is retrospective, increasingly irrelevant in an environment of constant change and novelty, whereas technology forecasting, while still only informed guesswork, provides important competitive intelligence – it is 'advanced market research' or market research in advance of the market.
- Interpreting the social impact of new developments and how that impact will resonate (or not) with the fashion zeitgeist (as mobile messaging did at the turn of the millennium) is part of the role of the technology forecaster/design team as they help create new products and new markets (in the past few years: Palm-style handhelds, text messaging boxes, digital cameras, scooter-boards, solid-state portable digital music players (MP3)). Social factors, and especially fashion, play a major role in the success or failure of a technology. Predicting these psychic social changes is the role of the artist, ergo, watch the artists.
- Technology forecasting feeds back into business development, new product development, business strategy and investment strategy. It forms an essential part of the iterative design and planning process.

3 planning in the digital domain

NOW THAT THE WEB ENCOMPASSES nearly half a billion people and is extending its embrace at a rate of around 10 per cent per month, and new technologies and new businesses emerge every week, the 'new media' can present a very confusing picture, leading some observers to conclude that it is all totally unpredictable. But the business plan still seems to be a central requirement to any business venture (and to any venture capitalist or bank) and, despite the apparently chaotic nature of the digital technology marketplace, I believe there are several techniques we can use to help build adequate predictive models of the new media environment. At the very least, these techniques and approaches offer the possibility of providing evidence of 'due diligence' at predicting the likely success of your venture. At best, they become a valuable tool that forms an integral and iterative component in your strategic planning or product development planning.

So how do you begin to make sense of a complex techno-cultural arena which is developing so rapidly? We have seen that it is possible to stay in touch with a variety of indicators available on the web/net, and we have access to a plenitude of informed opinion in both print and online form.

understanding the present: mind mapping a 'big picture'

All these indicators that we use to build our forecasts are not, of course, processed and interpreted in a vacuum. The analyst and forecaster processes this constant stream of new opinion, new prediction, new developments, new discoveries, new strategies, new standards and new regulations as new data that modifies, extends or reinforces a conceptual model or 'big picture' of the digital domain. Building a useful big picture of course takes some time, but hey, no one said this was going to be easy! The various schema that I have found useful are presented in the 'The big picture', and a useful big picture is a model that helps *you* understand the complexities of the real world.

Developing a conceptual model like this is a highly personal task. Artists, designers and other visual thinkers find sketching, drawing and diagram making useful in analyzing complex systems, but visual thinking can be used by anyone, and can start from the simplest representations, such as the flow charts, Venn diagrams and 'spider diagrams'. Mapping a complex system implies simplification (by imposing some kind of editorial order) and clarification ('revealing the invisible') – delineating the inter-relationships between components of the system to be modelled. Visualizing and illustrating the complex system not only helps you build a conceptual model but provides you with the means to involve others in your model building too. In fact, this was the central idea in J.C.R. Licklider's famous paper on man-computer symbiosis, a paper that influenced much of the early work on the internet:

“VISUAL THINKING CAN BE USED BY ANYONE, AND CAN START FROM THE SIMPLEST REPRESENTATIONS”

'For modelling, we believe, is basic and central to communication. Any communication between people about the same thing is a common revelatory experience about informational models of that thing. Each model is a conceptual structure of abstractions formulated initially in the mind of one of the persons who would communicate, and if the concepts in the mind of one would-be communicator are very different from those in the mind of another, there is no common model and no communication.'

Joseph Licklider, Man-Computer Symbiosis

Designers call the first steps in the process of understanding complex systems or processes 'mapping the problem space'*. To do this, we often begin by listing all the relevant issues to be taken into consideration. This can quickly become unmanageable as an unclassified list, so for clarity it's best to start the visualization process with a simple diagram: perhaps mapping the problem space in which you or your business or organization operate vis à vis the new media. So, start with a 'box' in the centre of a largish sheet of paper, labelled 'mycompany' and start adding the 'key themes' as 'legs' to this spider's body. Key themes could include target customers, suppliers, supply chain, manufacturing, distribution,

*Of course you could use one of the many planning tools that work using spider diagrams, such as Inspiration, Visio, MindManager or SmartDraw, but pencil and paper are immediate and cheap! And a paper diagram can have a permanent physical presence in the workspace, and act as route map, project plan, workflow sheet and diary throughout the course of the project.

marketing, etc – all the principal elements in the value web in which you operate. You can then annotate these legs with relevant items from your list. Brainstorming this process with others ensures that a variety of perspectives are involved, and that you don't miss anything important. Links, one-way, two-way and feedback channels and parallels between real-life processes and departments can be inked in on the diagram. By materializing the problem in this way, you force the brain to consider exactly how all these factors inter-relate, and this is the start of creative strategic thinking.

In the late 1960s, about the same time that hypertext was being invented as a non-linear method of presenting ideas in text form, Peter Russell and Tony Buzan were developing their ideas on non-linear idea processing, through a diagrammatic technique they called 'mind maps'. The technique of developing a 'mind map' is explained on Peter Russell's website (*www.peterussell.com/mindmap1.html*) and listed below:

Use just key words, or wherever possible images.

- Start from the centre of the page and work out.
- Make the centre a clear and strong visual image that depicts the general theme of the map.
- Create sub-centres for sub-themes.
- Put key words on lines. This reinforces the structure of notes.
- Print rather than write in script. It makes them more readable and memorable. Lower case is more visually distinctive (and better remembered) than upper case.
- Use colour to depict themes, associations and to make things stand out.
- Anything that stands out on the page will stand out in your mind.
- Think three-dimensionally.
- Use arrows, icons or other visual aids to show links between different elements.
- Don't get stuck in one area. If you dry up in one area, go to another branch.
- Put ideas down as they occur, wherever they fit. Don't judge or hold back.
- Break boundaries. If you run out of space, don't start a new sheet; paste more paper onto the map. (Break the 8×11 mentality.)

- ▶ Be creative. Creativity aids memory.
- ▶ Get involved. Have fun.

What will emerge from your diagram-making activity will be a structured and focused map of the 'problem space'. Using this spider diagram as a shared conceptual model, you will be able to perceive areas of importance, and to begin to define the territory your solution will inhabit. You can use this diagram to trace the interconnections and influences between different sections of your organization, the various tasks they perform, and the tools and channels they need to perform them. But importantly, what is happening while this process is unfolding is that you are gradually interiorizing all the issues to be considered, and beginning to sort them into a schema or 'big picture' of the problem space. You can sketch different 'routes' through this problem space by proposing typical solutions already widely used by other companies: intranets and other virtual private networks, corporate

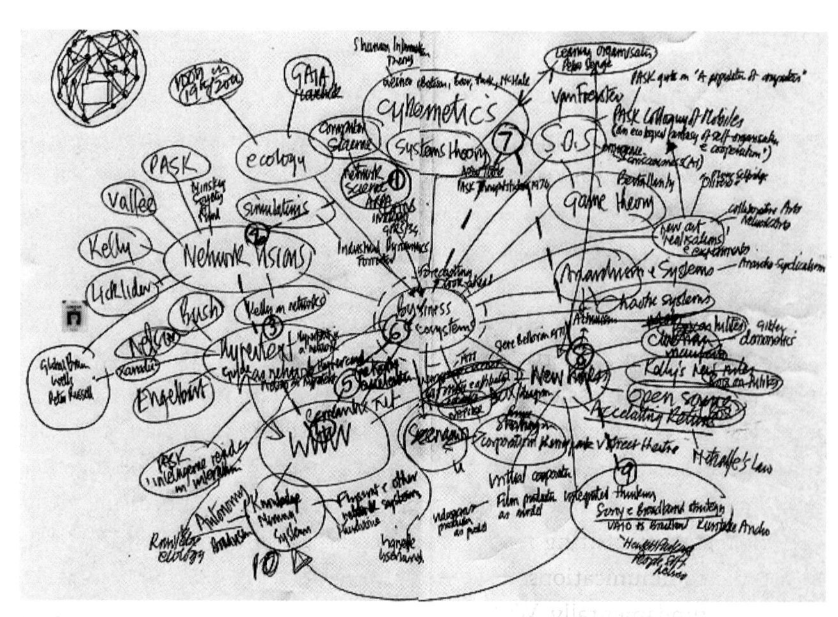

'Mind-maps' are a way of diagramming ideas and inter-relationships, and are a useful tool in the visualization of complex systems and processes. This is one of several such maps produced during the planning of this book.

websites, e-mail lists, webcasting, extranets, e-incentive schemes, consumer groups, stakeholder groups, vendor exchanges, helplines and help sites, a corporate communications channel, 'infotainment', joint ventures, structural corporate re-engineering, just-in-time manufacture, online recruitment, and all the other techniques, technologies and ploys that feature on your list as a result of researching your competition.

And this is where the 'problem space' becomes the 'solution space': using these routes through the spider diagrams or 'mind maps' that define the problem space, you begin to define several possible approaches to the 'problem'.

Now that you've attempted a simple mind map, it's time to sketch out some ideas as to how you can build a big picture of what's going on across the whole spectrum of new media. Why do we need to do this? Surely all I need to know and care about is how my company or organization operates or should operate in this media matrix?

business ecosystems

Well, yes and no. Sure, you need to develop a picture of how the new media (will) affect you and your business, but in this massively hyperlinked, real-time electronic marketplace we're entering, where your customers and your competition are only a click away, the rules are different. And the most important realization that has to occur for you to begin to operate successfully in this complex mesh of interacting elements and processes (a situation that Ted Nelson, the hypertext pioneer, described as 'deeply intertwingled') is that everything affects everything else. The new business environment, while sharing many characteristics with the old real-world business environment, differs in that it is both massively interconnected and physically or wirelessly networked together; and that commercial interactions (the purchases, orders, processing, delivery, even manufacturing itself) are accelerated to the speed of light by electronic communications. This changes the ball game not just quantitatively but fundamentally. We'll come back to this new ecosystem thinking in the next chapter, which outlines some of the singular visions that are driving new media developments.

Before we look at these visions, and the developmental vectors they have inspired and created, let's continue to build our conceptual models of this new networked media space.

the primary change enablers To name just a few of the innovations and inventions that constitute new media, consider the following: artificial intelligence, virtual reality, speech recognition, wireless application protocol, smart cards, digital television, set-top boxes, handheld computers, infra-red and

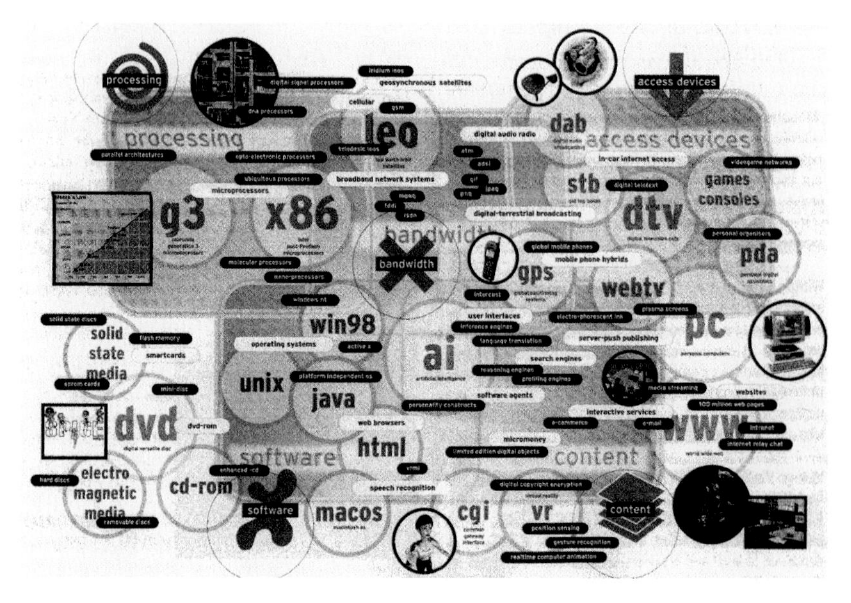

In this diagram, designed by Malcolm Garrett from my rough scribbles, we have begun to order the new media 'problem space' around the main areas of enabling technologies – the 'primary change enablers' that together will determine the future of all digital technologies. These are the enabling technologies that underpin computer processing, memory, bandwidth, access devices, and content and software. I find these sectors useful in my own analysis of new media developments, but you may want to organize and order this problem space in an entirely different way. The purpose of you working through your own mind-mapping diagram is for you to interiorize a useful working model of what's going on in this complex techno-socio-cultural-economic arena.

microwave networks, fibre optics, special effects, motion capture, computer graphics, simulation, software design, video games, satellite communications, digital money and micropayment schemes, home banking, e-commerce, electronic publishing, PC cards, microprocessor design, CADCAM, etc – *and* all the developments in content, software, online services, digital consumer electronics, and of course all the telecommunications technologies: DSL, FDDI, ATM, Frame Relay, ISDN, sub-millimetre radio, GPRS, 3G, etc.

And in the face of all these innovations and developments in order to give yourself the best chance of succeeding, whether you're planning a new business, developing or marketing a new product, providing new services or information or entertainment channels in this network marketplace, you need to acquire as much competitive intelligence as possible. Essential intelligence might include what your competition is planning, what technological developments might affect your business model, what new business models might affect your business model, what new distribution and marketing channels might affect your plans, how much your market is going to grow, and the answers to many more such questions.

> "THERE IS A PLETHORA OF NEW COMPANIES AIMING TO FILL THE NICHES IN ALL KINDS OF DEVELOPING SECTORS IN THE NEW MEDIA WEB/NET"

As I have said, extracting this kind of intelligence from a large and dynamically evolving solution space is not difficult if you have interiorized a big picture of what is going on – if you have developed a conceptual model of the system's dynamics, know what is driving this gigantic wealth-making engine, know what the underpinning 'enabling technologies' are, know how to detect the emerging developments that may impact on your plans. In other words, before we start planning ahead – and looking ahead – we need to develop and interiorize a big picture of the present, of what is happening right now. From this overview, we will be able to detect several interesting vectors of probable developments – we will know where to look for our competitive intelligence.

hands-on and in-touch

This is the importance of the mind mapping we mentioned earlier. But building a conceptual model – a big picture – isn't just a matter of pure intellection or mind-map diagram making. There are other physical ways that we can use to reinforce this process. Indeed, all the evidence from educational practitioners and cognitive psychologists is that we can enormously accelerate the process of learning by approaching the problem space from several different perspectives, and in several different learning modes. Artificial Intelligence (AI) guru Marvin Minsky has said: 'You don't understand anything until you understand it in more than one way.' And in this case, the 'more than one way' could include wide-ranging research (as we outlined in the previous section), mind mapping, brainstorming, and importantly, practical 'hands-on' experience – both as a user and as a *creator* of new media.

Now, I'm not suggesting that you start to design or redesign your company website from scratch, but you could tackle your own homepage, or family website. Several dozen free website design and construction tutorials are available on the web, and many low-cost software packages offer WYSIWYG web-page design, with absolutely no coding involved, unless you want to get down to the very essence of what drives the web, the Hypertext Mark-up Language (HTML) designed by Tim Berners-Lee as part of his WWW program. Indeed, whether you use a web-design application or not, it's worth just coding some simple HTML documents in a text editor or word processor and opening them in a browser window to get the feel of how easy this operation is.

Getting hands-on in designing and making objects and publishing them online, even in some small way, is one important visceral step you can make towards developing your big picture. Another is using the web a lot. While you're researching the factors to include in your mind maps, get hold of a good computer, a fastish connection, and try out some of the better search engines such as Google, Northern Lights or AltaVista, getting used to the various ways you can use these engines to refine and focus your searches. Collect data, build favourites/bookmarks, copy important facts and stats into a word-processing file or database. Start using the web in the several ways we listed in the previous section.

The bookmarks you collect as you build on your research, will create the means by which you can periodically build, modify and update your conceptual model, and its expression in your mind map.

As you can see, there are several stages in developing an understanding of what is happening in new media. The first stage is building an initial conceptual model or big picture, through the iterative process of research and mind mapping. The second stage has two facets – acquiring the practical, hands-on experience of building a website, buying or acquiring a domain name, and 'publishing' your work on the web; and starting to use the web on a daily basis: using a browser should be as natural and as easy as using a pencil to scribble a memo.

The third stage is rounding out your big picture by examining how e-media have been driven by the visions of the pioneers that developed them. This means delving through the short history of these technologies to discover what inspired the computer scientists, product designers, engineers, cyberneticists, artists and writers who first perceived the potential of computing, networking, hypertext and artificial intelligence.

From these explorations, we will detect some lines or vectors of development that still infuse and inspire the web/net of e-media. Awareness of these vectors will help us accommodate the constant stream of new developments pouring from these sectors.

4

the vision thing

UNDERSTANDING THE VISIONS that have driven developments in new media helps build a big picture and provides a framework within which to contextualize the plethora of new developments.

How do we assess the likely importance of the new developments that are emerging daily in the world of new media and the web/net? How do we fit these developments into our big picture? How do we determine their short-, medium- and long-term import? How do we divine into what form or direction they might catalyze, hybridize, mutate or transform as they begin to interlink, cross-fertilize, breed, absorb, contextualize and metamorphose with other new or existing elements? What gaps appear for new products, for new routes to market, for new markets, for new businesses, in the overlaps, in the interstices and the intersections of our dynamically developing big picture?

In order to begin to answer these questions, and to create for ourselves a big picture of what is going on and a schema of how things are likely to develop, it is useful – indeed essential – to know something of the aims and objectives of those individuals whose work has most influenced the development of the web/net and the digital media it carries. Understanding the drive and direction of these visions will also help us accommodate the constant stream of developments and more readily absorb these into our big picture.

'Leave it to specialists to discuss the latest developments (in computers and communications). The rest of us need perspective, and the most important elements of perspective are history, a vision of perfection, the reasons we haven't achieved it, some pitfalls, and a sense of humour.'

Mark Crispin Miller, Business Week, March 14 1994

'We cannot see the future; we do not know what lies around the next bend in the information superhighway; we cannot predict where, ultimately, the computer revolution will take us. All we know for sure is that, when we get there, we won't have enough RAM.'

David Barry Cyberspace

past visions of the present and present visions of the future

We are not driven by practicality or pragmatism, nor even by greed, but by foresight and vision. In our acquisition of knowledge, dreams and inspiration play a more important role than fixed investigative methods or 'scientific objectivity'. Understanding the visions that drove developments in computing and hypermedia in the pre-web days gives us an important insight into what is happening now, and exploring the visions that are emerging now will help us understand and contextualize the vectors of development spreading into the future. It is as if these 'big visions' are the lenses in our 'look-ahead' glasses – they focus and filter developments so that it is possible for us to construct, together with other information from extrapolations and industrial research developments, a set of plausible scenarios with which we can explore future developments and their consequences.

I'm not talking about mystical or drug-induced visions, by 'vision' I mean 'seeing something not present to the eye' – specifically, creating a mental picture of a way in which things may, could or should develop.

I mean 'vision' in two ways here: the 'big visions' that provide exceptional people with complete pictures of possible futures (Ted Nelson's vision of a global hypertext system he called 'Xanadu', Joseph Licklider's vision of 'man-computer symbiosis', or Roy Ascott's vision of networked culture, for example), and 'vision' in the sense of our personal insight and understanding when we are able to project ahead of the big picture we have interiorized, and come to an understanding of these big visions.

So here I want to present a collection of different 'big visions' – from scientists and technologists, from philosophers, writers, artists and designers – and I will argue that these visions of our computer-mediated future are the important intellectual and emotional drivers that together determine where we are heading.

I believe that these central visions actually still drive much of the development in new media, and many of the assumptions and aspirations of the original hypermedia and computer networking visionaries still resonate in the contemporary computer-science fraternity. Indeed, the ideology and objectives of these founding fathers, as well as the 'openness' of the scientific community in which they worked, still inform and guide the development of the web/net. These aspirations are manifesting most clearly in the 'open-source' movement, the fraternity that has evolved around the co-operative ideals of networked software development as illustrated in the past few years by the worldwide enthusiasm in the developer community for Linux and Java. This libertarian, communalistic, decentralized tendency underpinning the web/net with its connotations of anarchy and people-power (illustrated by notions such as shareware, consumer-centric, user groups, freeware, online communities, open standards, etc), sits rather uncomfortably alongside the blatantly materialistic and commercial aspirations of the more recent new media converts – the e-commerce and dot com entrepreneurs. In this zone of friction between communalism and commerce there is a fertile intermingling of ideas, where entrepreneurs learn from net-heads and net-heads learn from entrepreneurs.

“IN THIS ZONE OF FRICTION BETWEEN COMMUNALISM AND COMMERCE THERE IS A FERTILE INTERMINGLING OF IDEAS”

Many of the really interesting and influential developments that led to the web/net of today were initiated in the spirit of the early visionaries – men like Vannevar Bush, Douglas Engelbart, Ted Nelson and Alan Kay – while some of the most successful (but most counter-intuitive) 'business' ploys turn out to be reiterations of co-operative practices embedded deep in the culture of the internet. Radical web/net ideas – such as giving away your product for free – so alien to traditional business, were actually commonplace on the web/net. 'Free' was a word that 20th-century business in general didn't understand, but as Nathan Newman has pointed out in his paper on open-source software, the success of the internet (and indeed of its transformation into the web/net) is built upon the fact that the public space – the global commons – of the network harnessed the energies of universities, research labs and independent practitioners alike to provide a continuous flow of free 'open-source' software to improve and hone its functionality. The web/net was built on the concept of the free.

OPEN SOURCE SOFTWARE

See 'The Origins and Future of Open Source Software' by Nathan Newman at **www.netaction.org/opensrc/oss-whole.html#create.** Open-source software is so called because, unlike commercial software, its source code is published freely on the web/net and is accessible to hundreds of thousands of programmers, who can study it and improve upon it, with the provision that their improvements and amendments are published freely in return. Open-source software is therefore continuously tested and improved by an army of volunteer programmers, many more than could be employed by any single corporation. By 2000, many open-source evangelists were arguing that open-source was the future of the web/net, the only chance people had of competing with the monopolies of the giant software corporations.

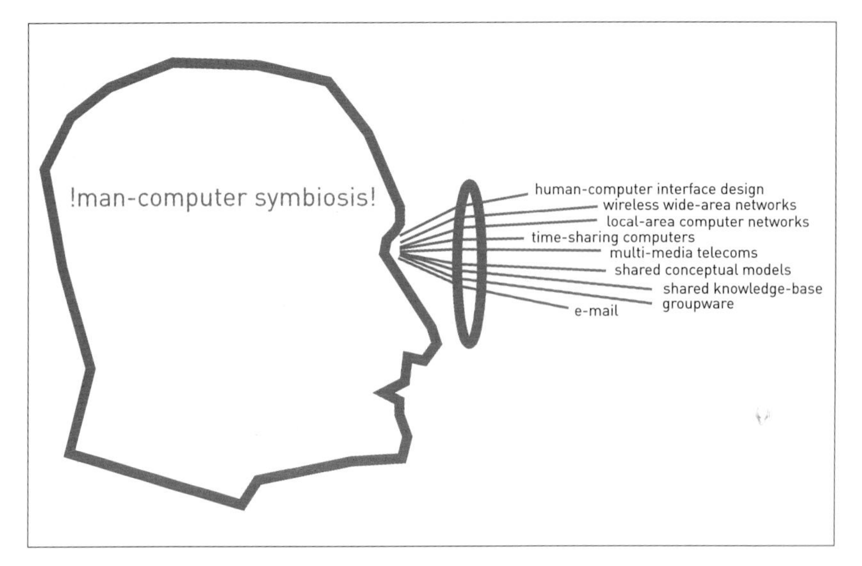

The visions of the early computing pioneers and cyberneticists still drive many of the developments in e-media. Knowledge of these visions helps us to understand the main 'development vectors' across a wide range of related technologies.

There is no doubt that the general spirit of academic co-operation, transparency, shared knowledge and openness still infuses the web/net and is at the root of these communalistic leanings. But there are other, more fundamental, reasons why the web/net fosters communalism and altruism. As influential cyberneticist Gordon Pask points out, networks consisting of an 'independent population of computers' – autonomous computers able to interact with each other – are capable of creating and to some extent resolving conflict; that is, of being co-operative. He cites an experiment by the British neurologist Grey Walter, who built a number of small battery-powered electro-mechanical robots (he called them 'tortoises') in the early 1950s.

'Each of them contained a simple but powerful computing system, basically analog in structure. They were able to move freely around the floor, and were able to sense light signals and solid objects as they did so. When their batteries ran low, they would head towards a recharging station, to which they were attracted by a light. They were quite independent of each other – their computing circuitry was not physically linked in any way – but they were capable of interacting. Although programmed to avoid solid objects, they occasionally bumped into one another. Their light sensors also occasionally confused the light of the recharging station with the flashing lights on their own heads which indicated that their batteries were running low. Within the frame of reference of their system, collisions and confusions counted as examples of conflict.

'It was particularly interesting to see what happened when two tortoises collided and were unable to escape from the situation. Typically, a third tortoise would move in and by its presence break the deadlock. In general the behaviour of the tortoises was co-operative, primitive though that may have been by human standards, and showed a richness difficult to reconcile with the simplicity of their structure.'

Gordon Pask and Susan Curran, Microman

There is evidence from other sources that co-operation is an emergent property of networks of individuals free to interact:

'Co-operation can emerge out of self-interest. In our post-industrial economy, spontaneous co-operation is a regular occurrence. Widespread industry-initiated standards (both of quality and protocols such as 110 volts or ASCII) and the rise of the internet, the largest working anarchy in the world, have only intensified interest in the conditions necessary for hatching co-evolutionary co-operation.'

Kevin Kelly, Out of Control

So it looks as if networks may 'naturally' foster co-operation.

understanding networks

But *why* do networks foster this spirit of co-operation and communalism? I believe that understanding why this tendency emerged is essential in building a deeper understanding of the digital domain and the web/net phenomenon. In *New Rules for the New Economy*, the network evangelist Kevin Kelly agrees:

'Networks have existed in every economy. What's different now is that networks, enhanced and multiplied by technology, penetrate our lives so deeply that "network" has become the central metaphor around which our thinking and our economy are organized. Unless we can understand the distinctive logic of networks, we can't profit from the economic transformation now under way.'

Kevin Kelly, New Rules for the New Economy, Fourth Estate, 1998

“THE POSSIBLE FUTURES OF COMPUTER NETWORKING WERE BEING MAPPED OUT IN THE BLUE-SKY PROJECTIONS AND FICTIONAL CREATIONS OF WRITERS AND FILM-MAKERS”

There are two main species of 'big vision' that I want to present here – visions of how computers can be used to enhance our learning and thinking, and visions of how computer-mediated networking may transform our world. We'll come back to Kelly's 'distinctive logic of networks' later because first I want to examine the various routes through which the visions of the future of networked media and computing have materialized.

the literary vision thing: inventing the future by imagination

During the 1970s and 1980s, while the internet and digital technologies were just starting to impact on the real world, parallel developments were taking place in the world of the imagination. While the nitty-gritty of networking – the wires and fibres, routers, servers, switches and all the other infrastructural components of the internet – were being laboriously designed and developed in research labs, corporate R&D divisions and universities throughout the real world, the possible futures of computer networking were being mapped out in great detail in the blue-sky projections and fictional creations of writers and film-makers*. And these science fiction and futurological essays didn't exist in some cultural space separate from the world of the engineers and scientists, the two arenas constantly intertwined and intermingled, symbiotically feeding from each other, gradually reaching a kind of consensus during the 1980s and early 1990s of 'where we should be heading'.

*The most avid readers of the cyberpunk genre, naturally enough, were the young hackers, programmers, students and computer-graphic artists who were real-life 'cyberpunks'.

This was happening not only in the US but in the UK too. From as early as 1975, sci-fi writer John Brunner was describing the future of computer networking and broadband media – what he called the 'data-net' and 'three-vee' – and describing the 'network effects' of large numbers of interacting people:

'It works, approximately, like this. First you corner a large – if possible very large – number of people who, while they've never formally studied the subject

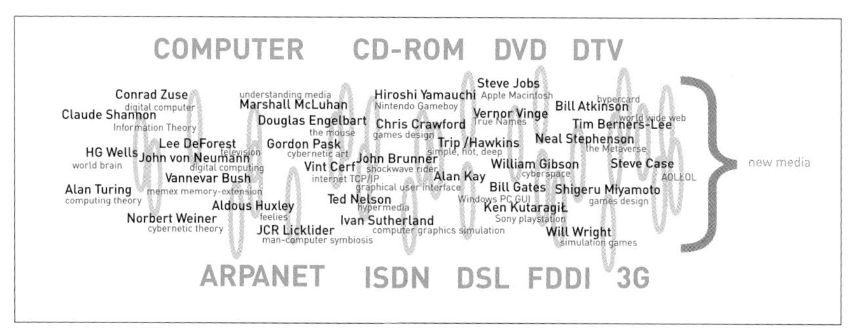

Creative thinkers from many disciplines help define the future of media. Science fiction writers, cybernetic artists, philosophers, ecologists, engineers and programmers have all contributed insights that have helped to direct and channel the development of computing and networking.

you're going to ask them about and hence are unlikely to recall the correct answer, are nonetheless plugged into the culture to which the question relates. Then you ask them, as it might be, to estimate how many people died in the great influenza epidemic that followed World War One, or how many loaves were condemned by EEC food inspectors as unfit for human consumption during June 1970. Curiously, when you consolidate their replies they tend to cluster around the actual figure as recorded in almanacs, year-books and statistical returns. It's rather as though this paradox has proved true: **that while nobody knows what's going on around here, everybody knows what's going on around here**. [my emphasis]

'Well, if it works for the past, why can't it work for the future? Three hundred million people with access to the integrated North American data-net is a nice big number of potential consultees.'

John Brunner, The Shockwave Rider

Cyberspace and the web/net matrix were being invented just as thoroughly in fiction at the same time as they were being created in reality. These imaginative envisionings of the potential of networking, computing and digital media were expressed in three main ways: through science fiction; in non-fiction (as a product of the critical analysis of our techno-culture), and in the written and audio-visual work of artists and film-makers and other creative practitioners. The media analyst Herbert Marshall McLuhan remains the constantly most surprising for me – more than a decade before Brunner's *Shockwave Rider* his *Understanding Media* was a revelation to artists and other creatives, and McLuhan's insights still resonate in the first decade of the 21st century. Indeed, we are now living in the 'global village' of his imagination.

'After three thousand years of specialist explosion, and of increasing specialism and alienation in the technological extensions of our bodies, our world has become compressional by dramatic reversal. As electrically contracted, the globe is no more than a village. Electric speed in bringing all social and political functions together in a sudden implosion has heightened human awareness of responsibility to an intense degree.'

McLuhan, Understanding Media

And indeed, through the web/net, we have telematically extended our nervous system around the world as he predicted:

'Men are suddenly nomadic gatherers of knowledge, nomadic as never before, informed as never before, free from fragmentary specialism as never before – but also involved in the total social process as never before: since with electricity we extend our central nervous system globally, instantly interrelating every human experience.'

McLuhan, Understanding Media

In critical essays and in fiction over the past 30 years, writers like McLuhan, Brunner, Herman Kahn, Richard Buckminster Fuller, Philip K. Dick and many others have gradually sketched a patchwork montage of the networked future. Starting with Vernor Vinge's *True Names* novella in 1981 (first published as a short story in *Dell Binary Star #5*) and later, with the arrival of William Gibson, Bruce Sterling and the cyberpunk authors of the mid 1980s, sci-fi writers began to flesh out more specific visions of the technofuture:

'powering up the portal'

'He powered up his processors, settled back in his favourite chair, and carefully attached the portal's five sucker electrodes to his scalp. For long minutes nothing happened: a certain amount of self-denial – or at least self-hypnosis – was necessary to make the ascent. Some experts recommended drugs or sensory isolation to heighten the user's sensitivity to the faint, ambiguous signals that could be read from the portal.

'... And just as a daydreamer forgets his actual surroundings and sees other realities, so Pollack drifted, detached, his subconscious interpreting the status of the West Coast communication and data services as a vague thicket for his conscious mind to inspect, interrogate for the safest path to an intermediate haven.'

Vernor Vinge, True Names

the invention of cyberspace

'Cyberspace: a consensual hallucination experienced daily by billions of legitimate operators, in every nation, by children being taught mathematical concepts ... A graphic representation of data abstracted from the banks of every computer in the human system. Unthinkable complexity. Lines of light ranged in the nonspace of the mind, clusters and constellations of data. Like city lights, receding.'

William Gibson, Neuromancer

the global metaverse

'Hiro is approaching the Street. It is the Broadway, the Champs Elysees of the Metaverse. It is the brilliantly lit boulevard that can be seen, miniaturized and backward, reflected in the lenses of his goggles. It does not really exist, but right now millions of people are walking up and down it. The dimensions of the Street are fixed by a protocol, hammered out by the computer graphics ninja overlords of the Association for Computing Machinery's Global Multimedia Protocol Group. The Street seems to be a grand boulevard going all the way round the equator of a clack sphere with a radius of a bit more than ten thousand kilometres. That makes it 65,536 kilometres around, which is considerably bigger than Earth.'

Neal Stephenson, Snowcrash

the vision thing – in prototype

'Demo or Die.' MIT Media Lab motto

And the vision thing isn't just *writings* about the kind of technologies we may or could or should develop, it's about the visualization, realization, or 'imagineering' of these ideas too. Some of the most influential insights in the history of new media weren't real. They existed in the halfway house between concept and realization – they were embodied in prototypes, in descriptions of prototypes, in movies about prototypes, and in movies about the future. From Vannevar Bush's description of a memory-extension machine (the 'Memex' – see below), to Alan Kay's cardboard model of the Dynabook, to Jeff Hawkins' wooden model of what would become the famous PalmPilot, to John Sculley's video of his Knowledge Navigator personal digital assistant, and on to Star Trek's 'Holodeck' virtual reality theatre, handheld tricorders and communicators, and to the megalomaniacal HAL 9000 in Kubrick and Clark's *2001*, part of the vision thing has always been about the materialization of an idea in an illustration, a demonstration, or a prototype. Since the mid-1950s, the Disney Corporation has labelled these activities 'imagineering'. A classic example of this kind of future projection was the 'Knowledge Navigator' video produced by John Sculley of Apple Computer in 1987.

the Knowledge Navigator In 1987 John Sculley was CEO (chief executive officer) of Apple Computer and was busy redefining the company's image. Inspired by Apple's brilliant software designers, product developers and resident experts – people like Bill Atkinson (MacPaint, Hypercard), Andy Hertsfield (MacWrite), and Alan Kay (who developed SmallTalk and the GUI at Xerox) – and driven by the ideas of hypermedia that we summarize in this section, Sculley decided to create a short video that would illustrate his vision of how computer technology, networking and artificial intelligence could be brought together and embodied in a really 'personal' computer, a personal digital assistant (PDA) he called the Knowledge Navigator. He worked with Apple team members Doris Mitsch and Hugh Dubberly and created a video that still acts as a defining illustration of what such a PDA could be. Although looking forward to the late 1990s and beyond, like all the great prototypes mentioned below the Knowledge Navigator was not so much about the future as about a present that hadn't quite got off the drawing board.

“THE KNOWLEDGE NAVIGATOR WAS NOT SO MUCH ABOUT THE FUTURE AS ABOUT A PRESENT THAT HADN'T QUITE GOT OFF THE DRAWING BOARD”

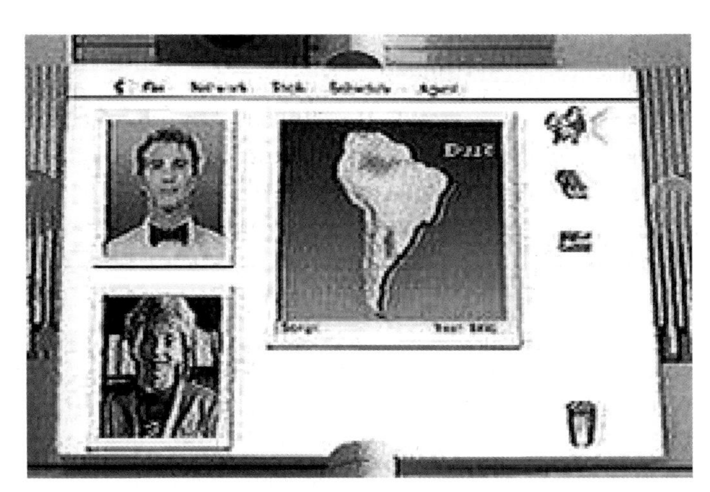

In 1990, John Sculley was CEO of Apple Computer. Inspired by the possibilities of powerful, easy-to-use, networked computers, Sculley worked with video producers and writers Doris Mitsch and Hugh Dubberly to produce this video 'vision' of the future of computing. Produced by Apple Computer and the Kenwood Group, 'The Knowledge Navigator' featured an artificial intelligence named 'Phil' who acted as a personal secretary and digital 'slave' to 'his' human owner. The video illustrated some of the ways that personal networking and clever programming will affect our lives 'in the future'. With synthespian news presenters like Ananova already commanding large fees, and with 3G mobile information appliances just around the corner, most of the components of the Knowledge Navigator are assembled and ready to go – only the product styling will be different.

The video showed a typical computer user, a college lecturer, planning his day, preparing reports, lectures and seminars, using the multimedia, networked Knowledge Navigator, which featured an anthropomorphic synthespian software agent called Phil who 'knew' his 'owner' really well (had built a detailed personal profile of the professor), could understand spoken 'natural language' commands, and was able to perform tasks such as arranging meetings, finding information, booking flights, etc, semi-autonomously. Pictured as a handheld pad-like device, the Knowledge Navigator video illustrated the kind of personal empowerment one might expect from a world that was just about to go online in a big way. In the real world, Knowledge Navigator prepared the ground for real products –

such as Apple's Newton PDA, the Sony MagicLink and the PalmPilot – and became a kind of inspirational benchmark or 'Platonic ideal' for assessing the usability and functionality of these devices. In a similar way, Alan Kay's cardboard prototype and written description of the Dynabook was the benchmark for assessing every new portable computing device manufactured over the past 30 years, from the first laptops and Grid-Pad to Powerbook and e-book.

'The best way to predict the future is to invent it.' **Alan Kay**

'imagineering' – creating the future by invention As you've probably gathered, here I am defining 'imagineering' as the 'imaginative application of engineering sciences'; Disney's definition is 'the blend of creative imagination and technical know-how'*. Take your pick. Essentially, it is the harnessing of three important creative processes to explore the possibilities of present and future technologies. These three main strands of creativity include:

*Walt Disney founded Walt Disney Imagineering in 1952 in order to design and develop ideas for DisneyLand. Since then imagineers have developed ideas for DisneyWorld, the EPCOT center, EuroDisney and many other Disney enterprises worldwide.

- Imaginative envisioning
  - the work of science fiction and (especially) cyberpunk writers;
  - the writings, and projections by media critics, artists and designers.
- Future-casting
  - linear extrapolation of recent and current technological developments;
  - the imaginative but 'credible' scenarios of futurologists;
  - simulating the future.
- Creative engineering: 'imagineering'
  - new product design and prototyping;
  - the product development work of engineers, computer scientists and designers.

When these three strands come together in a realized artefact – a product, prototype or 'artist's impression' – you get 'imagineering'.

Imagineering has punctuated the history of hypermedia. Some of the seminal developments in new media are products of small teams of 'imagineers', generally multi-disciplinary teams, comprising computer scientists, electrical engineers and product designers, and often including information designers, cognitive psychologists, graphic designers and other media creatives.

Examples such as Douglas Engelbart's Augmentation Research Center, the Atari Research Centre, Bell Labs, the MIT Media Lab, Xerox PARC and EuroPARC, the Viacom New Media Kitchen, the Apple Advanced Technology Group, and the Disney Studios spring readily to mind. The multiple disciplines included in these publicly or commercially funded teams have also included cognitive psychologists, telecoms engineers, AI experts, games designers, and designers and practitioners from the wide range of media disciplines that are now converging in this digital domain.

These imagineering teams have been responsible for many of the big breakthroughs in human-computer interface, networking, and many other aspects of computing and digital media.

'The mother of all demos'

'When I saw the connection between a television-like machine, an information processor, and a medium for representing symbols to a person, it all tumbled together in about half an hour. I went home and sketched a system in which computers could draw symbols on the screen and I could steer through different information spaces with knobs and levers, and look at words and data and graphics in different ways. I imagined ways you could expand it into a theatre-like environment where you could sit with colleagues and exchange information on many levels simultaneously. God! Think of how that would let you cut loose in solving problems!'

Douglas Engelbart, 'A Conceptual Framework for the Augmentation of Man's Intellect' (edited by Howard Rheingold in HyperAge, May/June 1988)

Douglas Engelbart's Augmentation Research Center (ARC), for example, gave us the mouse, screen windows, e-mail, office networking and groupware, and a working hypertext system, all back in 1967. A recipient of

DARPA* funding, ARC was the second host on the ARPANET – the earliest iteration of the web/net. During the 1960s Engelbart and ARC had been developing the tools that he figured were necessary components of a human augmentation machine. Central to the Augmentation project was the kind of hypermedia system imagined by Vannevar Bush (see below) some 20 years earlier. Engelbart had read Bush's article, 'As we may think', in 1945 while he was stationed in the Philippines as a radar technician. His NLS (oN-Line System), conceived and invented at ARC, was demonstrated live at the Fall Joint Computer Conference in 1968 in a remarkable and prescient 90-minute demonstration of the future of 'personal' computing and human-computer interface design that included a wooden mouse pointing device, screen displays in adjacent but separately addressable multiple windows, word processing (including outline processing), cross-file editing, context-sensitive help, e-mail and much more. And this wasn't a mock-up or simulation, Engelbart and ARC had built the essential ingredients of personal computing using the best computer he could get hold of at the time. His personal computing tools were running on a mini-mainframe pretending to be a personal computer of some 20 years later.

*The US Department of Defense Advanced Research Projects Agency.

There are many other examples of the importance of imagineering in the development of new media, notably including the Atari Research Centre, with Alan Kay, Brenda Laurel, Jaron Lanier and Thomas Zimmerman, who gave us lots of innovative video games, virtual reality and the dataglove. At MIT, the Media Lab produced a string of influential developments including the first interactive video disk, the 'Aspen Movie Map', gestural-recognition interfaces such as the 'Put That There' project, and all the other technologies so well reported by Stewart Brand in the mid-1980s. And look at Xerox PARC (Palo Alto Research Center): Alan Kay with the dynabook idea, the graphical user interface, and the object-oriented programming language Smalltalk, Bob Metcalfe with Ethernet, Larry Tesler (who went on to project manage Newton and many other products, including Hypercard, at Apple), John Warnock of Adobe, and many others. Outside the US, imagineering is alive and prospering at Nokia Research, Ericsson R&D, Sony Computer Science Labs, BT Martlesham Labs, and colleges and universities from Dublin to Darwin.

See biblography.

Lately Disney chief Michael Eisner has extended the 'imagineering' idea, creating Disney Imagineering Fellows – currently including some of the superstars of digital media: Alan Kay, Seymour Papert (developer of the LOGO programming language), Marvin Minsky (AI guru), Danny Hillis (developer of the Connection Machine supercomputer), as well as Jeff Katzenberg, George Lucas and others. Inventing the future is the best way to predict it.

rapid prototyping and digital visualization Of course, the end product of all these imagineering developments in computer science and networking over the past 40 years or so is our current highly networked, highly computerized environment. Not all the tools that the pioneers envisioned are here yet, but what we do have is a superb collection of tools for the realization of imagineered products. We have rapid prototyping tools to produce 'proof of concept' demonstrations, we have hugely powerful computers that can simulate virtually anything, we have superb 3D computer graphic modelling and animation tools to assist in the visualization of new products, we have very sophisticated CAD systems to turn ideas and drawings into plans and production tools, and we have multimedia telecommunications networks through which to bring together experts and expertise. One way of building our big picture of the future is to monitor this work, both in the R&D departments of the big multinationals, and in the public-sector research labs, where these rapid prototyping and visualization tools are already materializing possible futures.

> “NOT ALL THE TOOLS THAT THE PIONEERS ENVISIONED ARE HERE YET”

the information that we want, when we want it If we condense the visions that have driven 'hypermedia' from the very beginning, we envision a world of organized digital information, a world of accessible, manageable, just-in-time information, explorable information, multimedia information, a seamlessly and intelligently linked matrix of books, papers, journals, magazines, movies, archives, records, museum collections, statistical data, news streams, from which we can easily locate and extract the information we want, where and when we need it, in the form we want it, and with the tools we *personally* need to turn it into knowledge. All of us – decision makers, scientists, researchers, designers, writers, creatives – want an information matrix that we can plug into and quickly (instantly!) get the information we need, in the format we want, and with credentials and a publishing provenance we understand and trust, and a fair and equitable royalty scheme to reward intellectual endeavour. As well as this, we all need an extra-somatic memory, a virtual 'theatre of memory', a memory machine that intelligently absorbs the information we want to retain, lets us manipulate, manage, juxtapose, order, transmute, represent and edit it (while remembering the provenance, and the intellectual property audit trail back to the creator or rightful owner and to its source); provides us with the means of reassociating and revisualizing and illustrating it, and then the tools to repackage, redesign and republish it with our own intellectual endeavours recorded as linked glosses, amendments, additions, addenda, references, citations, footnotes, marginalia, superscriptions, or complete, self-contained works that spread their conceptual tentacles out through the web/net, tracing and labelling for verification and adjudication the routes to sources, quotations, notes, references, bibliographies, glossaries, indices and statistics.

We also want this self-same network to link us as people, providing the means to communicate in real time, preferably in our own language, with our peers, our friends, relations, business colleagues and others wherever they happen to be.

We don't really want much – just 'the best facts, and the best communications in the known world' and like Withnail, 'we want it here, and we want it now'.

the global knowledge base We are getting closer and closer to the realization of this vision – the invention of the computer, the development of information and communication theory, the study of artificial intelligence, the digitization of media, the creation of computer networks, the invention of the database and database-management techniques, the design of graphical-user interface, the embodiment of human expertise in 'rule-based systems' (expert systems), the invention of hypermedia and its application in the web/net, the development of sensors and webcams, wireless networking, embedded computing *et al.* – all of these are stages along the path to a global knowledge base.

In my experience, the web/net began to reach a kind of critical mass of useful information and data in the mid-1990s. By 2000, there was hardly any subject, no matter how esoteric, that was not represented, often in great detail, on the web/net. Already it is becoming the norm for scientific knowledge, traditionally published in journals and books, to be stored in digital form and made available to everyone through the web/net. For a more complete list of stepping stones to the global knowledge base, see the diagram 'World-Brain Timeline'.

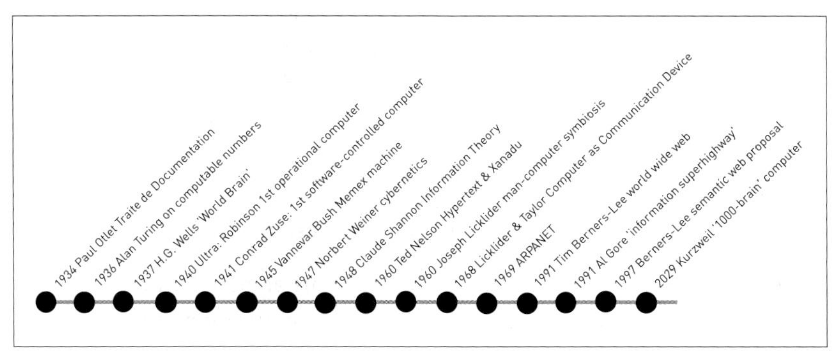

World-Brain Timeline –The ideas that drove the internet – and that still inspire and guide many of the programmers and engineers involved in 'e-media' – stem from the vision of providing everyone with easy access to mankind's accumulated knowledge. From H.G. Wells' 1936 idea of a 'global brain', through Vannevar Bush's 'As We May Think' to Licklider's 'Man-Computer Symbiosis', Nelson's 'Dream Machines', Alan Kay's 'Dynabook' vision of personal portable computing, and on to Berners-Lee's 'World Wide Web' and future global Artificial Intelligences – this vision still underpins many e-media developments.

But there's still some way to go along the path to what H.G. Wells called the 'World-brain': we are still developing the infrastructure, the tools, the natural language interfaces and all the other bits we will need for such a system, there is still no global standard for the interconnection of knowledge bases, no standard for the creation of knowledge base documents (such as a schema for the identification, synopsis, provenance, dating, copyright, citations), and so forth.

But this seems to be the direction in which we are heading. It is the central vision that lies at the core of the predictions and aspirations of most of the visionaries of networked media.

the central vision

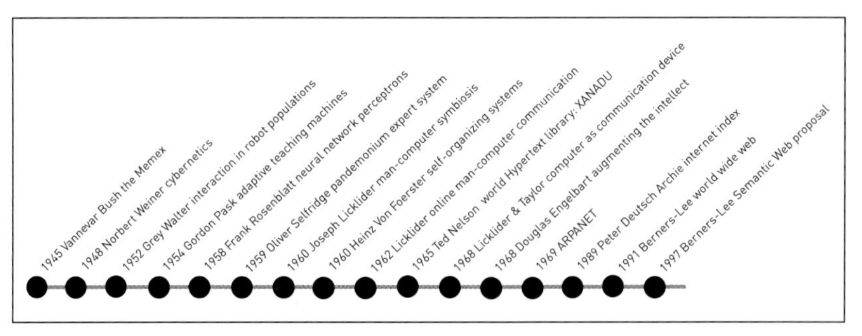

'The visions that drive the web/net and e-media technology iterate throughout the last fifty years, and emerged in papers, proposals, prototypes, projects and real products too. What's more, these ideas and visions will continued to steer e-media developments into the foreseeable future.'

'An important choice faces us: let the computer perpetuate archaic methods of publishing, or use it to vault our minds into a hyperspace of thought.'

Ted Nelson

'The computer is a tool for augmenting our intelligence.'

Douglas Engelbart

Right from the very beginning, the history of e-media (aka new media or hypermedia) has been driven by the vision that these new networked technologies were essential tools to help us manage the enormous flow of information presented to us daily, and that they would 'augment' our intelligence in all kinds of ways. There are many thousands of engineers and computer scientists who contributed to the development of digital media and the web/net, but I want to look at just half a dozen individuals whose insight and vision most shaped the future of e-media. By examining the following brief histories, we will discover for ourselves the basis of Kelly's 'new rules', and begin to absorb the elements of network thinking.

the Memex machine Vannevar Bush was chief scientific adviser to Franklin Delano Roosevelt during World War Two, and in this role was the recipient of thousands of scientific research papers, which he had to summarize, comment upon and circularize to the president and to other key decision makers in the government. At the time of the Manhattan Project, the development of advanced computation machinery, radar, encryption, new medicines, new chemical pesticides, microfilm, television and many other new technologies, Bush was appalled at the amount of information generated by researchers, and the danger of missing really important developments.

'Professionally our methods of transmitting and reviewing the results of research are generations old and by now are totally inadequate for their purpose. If the aggregate time spent in writing scholarly works and in reading them could be evaluated, the ratio between these amounts of time might well be startling. Those who conscientiously attempt to keep abreast of current thought, even in restricted fields, by close and continuous reading might well shy away from an examination calculated to show how much of the previous month's efforts could be produced on call. Mendel's concept of the laws of genetics was lost to the world for a generation because his publication did not reach the few who were capable of grasping and extending it; and this sort of catastrophe is undoubtedly being repeated all about us, as truly significant attainments become lost in the mass of the inconsequential.'

Vannevar Bush, 'As We May Think,' Atlantic Monthly, June 1945

After the war, he realized the necessity of coming to grips with this explosion of information, and in an article in *Atlantic Monthly* in June 1945 proposed some radical solutions to this problem. In his article, Bush described the Memex, a machine for the mechanical extension of human memory. Remember that this was in 1945 – in the early years of digital computing, three years before the transistor was invented, and 30 years before the development of the personal computer. So in Bush's vision, Memex was based on the use of microfilm, the then current state-of-the-art information storage and retrieval medium (before World War Two, Bush had developed a microfilm reader for Kodak). Bush realized the importance of data compression, and microfilm offered the means by which information could be stored in highly compressed form:

'Assume a linear ratio of 100 for future use. Consider film of the same thickness as paper, although thinner film will certainly be usable. Even under these conditions there would be a total factor of 10,000 between the bulk of the ordinary record on books, and its microfilm replica. The **Encyclopaedia Britannica** could be reduced to the volume of a matchbox. A library of a million volumes could be compressed into one end of a desk.'

But the overall importance of Memex was that this was the first time anyone had proposed an electro-mechanical device for extending human memory.

"THESE ASSOCIATIVE TRAILS WOULD ENABLE A READER TO FOLLOW AN ARGUMENT ACROSS AND THROUGH DISPARATE DOCUMENTS"

The central idea of Memex was that ideas, research papers and information could be stored on microfilm, and reviewed and viewed using a back-projection screen large enough to display two Memex documents (microfilm frames) side by side. Importantly, Bush suggested the means by which these documents could be annotated and cross-referred. In anticipation of the kind of hyperlinking that is the primary feature of the web/net, Bush came up with the idea of 'associative trails' – annotations and links that could be appended to microfilm frames in order to create trails for others to follow. These associative trails of links through stored Memex documents would enable a reader to follow an argument or discourse across and through disparate documents, while at the same time adding their own notes and cross-references, effectively building their own trails, that could in turn be saved and passed on for others to follow.

Bush contrasted his method of linking documents together – his associative trails – with the traditional alphabetical indices and classifications used by libraries and other information archives:

'The human mind does not work that way. It operates by association. With one item in its grasp, it snaps instantly to the next that is suggested by the association of thoughts, in accordance with some intricate web of trails

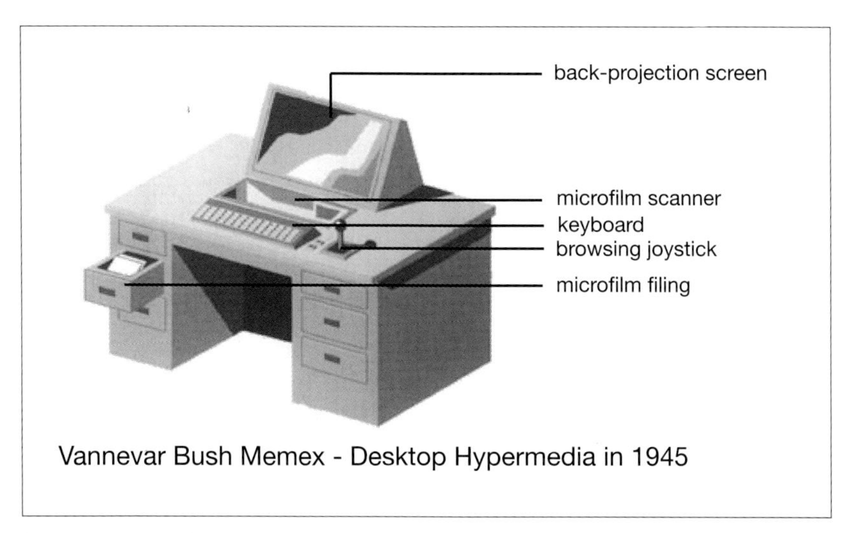

Vannevar Bush Memex - Desktop Hypermedia in 1945

'Memex' was an idea for a memory-extension machine, described by Bush in 1945. Twenty-five years before the personal computer, Bush described Memex in terms of the then state-of-the-art in information storage, microfilm, but his ideas of linking and indexing information were to influence the generation of computer scientists who invented the personal computer and the internet.

carried by the cells of the brain. It has other characteristics, of course; trails that are not frequently followed are prone to fade, items are not fully permanent, memory is transitory. Yet the speed of action, the intricacy of trails, the detail of mental pictures, is awe-inspiring beyond all else in nature.'

He goes on to describe how this associative indexing could be mechanized:

'Man cannot hope fully to duplicate this mental process artificially, but he certainly ought to be able to learn from it. In minor ways he may even improve it, for his records have relative permanency. The first idea, however, to be drawn from the analogy concerns selection. Selection by association, rather than indexing, may yet be mechanized. One cannot hope thus to equal the speed and flexibility with which the mind follows an associative trail, but it should be possible to beat the mind decisively in regard to the permanence and clarity of the items resurrected from storage.

'Consider a future device for individual use, which is a sort of mechanized private file and library. It needs a name, and, to coin one at random, "memex" will do. A memex is a device in which an individual stores all his books, records, and communications, and which is mechanized so that it may be consulted with exceeding speed and flexibility. It is an enlarged intimate supplement to his memory.'

The Memex was to be built into an office desk, with microfilm records stored at one end, and the machinery for searching and displaying the records at the other. The desktop contained a glass platen for 'photocopying' text documents and pictures onto microfilm, a keyboard for typing in notes and index codes for the retrieval of records, together with a joystick that controlled the rate at which images could be (back-)projected onto the slanted screen at the back of the desk. Pushing the joystick to the right or left displayed the microfilm records one after another. You could speed through hundreds of documents with an action similar to rewinding or fast-forwarding a video tape, but Memex would also provide the kind of 'random access' we associate with computer-based memory:

'There is, of course, provision for consultation of the record by the usual scheme of indexing. If the user wishes to consult a certain book, he taps its code on the keyboard, and the title page of the book promptly appears before him, projected onto one of his viewing positions. Frequently used codes are mnemonic, so that he seldom consults his code book; but when he does, a single tap of a key projects it for his use. Moreover, he has supplemental levers. On deflecting one of these levers to the right he runs through the book before him, each page in turn being projected at a speed which just allows a recognizing glance at each. If he deflects it further to the right, he steps through the book 10 pages at a time; still further at 100 pages at a time. Deflection to the left gives him the same control backwards.

'A special button transfers him immediately to the first page of the index. Any given book of his library can thus be called up and consulted with far greater facility than if it were taken from a shelf. As he has several projection positions, he can leave one item in position while he calls up another. He can add marginal notes and comments, taking advantage of one possible type of dry photography, and it could even be arranged so that he can do this by a stylus scheme, such as is now employed in the telautograph seen in railroad waiting rooms, just as though he had the physical page before him.'

Thus Bush described his vision of 'web browsing' and 'surfing' some 50 years before Tim Berners-Lee invented the world wide web. OK, it's expressed in pre-computer, photo-mechanical terms, but the vision in 'As we may think' influenced many of the key thinkers and inventors of the web/net and digital media, up to and including Berners-Lee himself. We're going to have a look at some of the ways that the Memex idea permeated the thinking of these new media innovators, extracting all we can of their shared vision of the future.

towards man-computer symbiosis In the 1960s the computer scene was in ferment. Although mainframe and mini-mainframe computers dominated the research and development sector throughout the decade, the core technology of these computers and the means of using these expensive machines was changing. Until the mid-1950s all computers employed thermionic valves as switching devices, and as a result were unreliable, consumed lots of power and generated lots of heat. They had to be kept in sealed, air-conditioned rooms, and were tended by white-coated operators. At the start of the decade mainframes supported only the batch processing of punch cards, a tedious way of working, where programmers had to prepare their program in advance ('off-line') and then encode it as a set ('batch') of punch cards. These were then processed through the computer and the results delivered back to the programmer some hours later. It took a long time to see whether your program worked.

However, with the introduction of the transistor, a new generation of smaller, cheaper machines, the so-called 'mini-mainframes' or just 'minis', emerged and by the early 1960s, new ways of using the computer had been introduced. Time sharing was one of these. Several 'dumb' terminals (screens and keyboards) could be attached to a mini and the computer shared by several programmers at once. Minis used paper tape to input and output programs and data, were much faster, and gave the programmer direct access to the computer.

But naturally, programmers wanted much more than this. The most influential computer visionary of this period, J.C.R. Licklider (a project director in the ARPA programme), had a dream of truly interactive computing:

'At present there are no man-computer symbioses ... The hope is that, in not too many years, human brains and computers will be coupled together very tightly, and that the resulting partnership will think as no human being has ever thought and process data in a way not approached by the information-handling machines we know today.'

J.C.R. Licklider, Man Computer Symbiosis

This was blue-sky thinking in 1960, but in his role as director of the Information Processing Techniques Office of ARPA, Licklider was in a position to fund the research necessary to turn this vision into reality. And it began to happen much sooner than he had imagined.

As early as 1965, Ivan Sutherland, then a PhD student working at the Lincoln Laboratory under Claude Shannon*, showed his work on Sketchpad, his program that demonstrated a radically new way in which people could interact with computers. It was a giant step in the direction of Licklider's dream of man-computer symbiosis.

*Claude Shannon invented Information Theory in the early 1940s.

Sutherland's work on Sketchpad not only signposted the direction the entire field of computer graphics and computer-aided design would take over the next three decades, but the implications of his insights into what real-time, interactive computing could be so inspired other computer pioneers, such as Ted Nelson and Alan Kay, that Sketchpad marked a defining moment in their own thinking.

Ted Nelson describes Sketchpad in his 1977 book *The Home Computer Revolution* in a chapter entitled 'The most important computer program ever written' (quoted in *Virtual Reality* by Howard Rheingold):

'You could draw a picture on the screen with a light-pen – and then file the picture away in the computer's memory (Sketchpad was running on the first transistorized computer – the TX-2, with a cathode-ray tube as a monitor). You could, indeed, save numerous pictures this way.

'You could then recombine the pictures, pulling copies from memory and putting them amongst one another. For example you could make a picture of a rabbit and a picture of a rocket, then put little rabbits all over the large rocket. Or little rockets all over a large rabbit. The screen on which the picture appeared did not necessarily show all the details; the important thing was that the details were in the computer, when you magnified a picture sufficiently, they would come into view.

'You could magnify and shrink the picture to a spectacular degree. You could fill a rocket picture with rabbit pictures, then shrink that until all that was visible was a tiny rocket; then you could make copies of that, and dot them all over a large copy of the rabbit picture. So when you expanded the big rabbit till only a small part showed (so it would be the size of a house, if the screen were large enough), then the foot-long rockets on the screen would each have rabbits the size of a dime. Finally, if you changed the master picture – say by putting a third ear on the rabbit – all the copies would change correspondingly.'

Courtesy Theodore Holm Nelson, quoted in Howard Rheingold's Virtual Reality (1991)

SKETCHPAD – THE REVOLUTION IN HUMAN-COMPUTER INTERFACE DESIGN AND THE ORIGIN OF INTERACTIVE COMPUTER GRAPHICS

In early 1960s, most computers were still room-size mainframes relying on thousands of thermionic valves to perform the complex switching operations necessary to run programs. But in 1962, the US Air Force commissioned Lincoln Laboratories at MIT to build two test-bed computers, the TX-0 and the TX-2. These were to demonstrate the use of the newly available transistors (invented 14 years earlier but only recently mass produced), which promised to be much more reliable, more energy efficient, much cooler, much cheaper and much, much smaller than valves. Later, Digital Equipment Corporation (DEC) was to productivize the designs of the TX-0 and TX-2 as its PDP-1 and PDP-6 mini-mainframes.

The TX-2 was an extremely advanced machine in its day. It boasted twice the 'fast' memory (nee RAM) of the biggest commercial computers, it had magnetic tape storage, an online keyboard terminal, paper-tape input, the first Xerox printer for hard-copy output, and importantly, a 9 inch cathode ray tube (CRT) for output and monitoring.

For his 1963 PhD thesis as a student of Claude Shannon (the pioneer of Information Theory), Ivan Sutherland wrote a paper on how the TX-2 and future iterations of similarly powerful computers could, with the addition of a light-pen and some clever software, be interactively 'programmed' by the user.

Up till then most computer programming had entailed the advance preparation of a program in the form of punched hole cards, stacks of which were then fed through the computer in batches, processed, then output in the form of a print-out on paper or paper-tape. This was a tedious process for programmers. They often had to wait several hours or even days for their program to be run, then wait for the print-out in order to see whether it had worked (or how much of it had worked).

Sutherland's breakthrough with Sketchpad was not only in designing software that would work in real time – that is interactively, with the programmer hardly having to wait for results – but it was **visual** – it used the CRT display both to input instructions and to output results in the form of computer graphics. The thesis was called 'Sketchpad: A Man-Machine Graphical Communications System', and the software was called simply 'Sketchpad'.

Sketchpad has been described as the most important computer program ever written. It was the beginning of computer graphics (the special effects and animations of **Titanic** and **Toy Story**, the 3D animation in **Tomb Raider**, and the 3D modelling of synthespian Ananova are all recent iterations of computer graphics work begun in 1963), and led Sutherland on to design flight simulators, virtual reality-style software, and to lay the foundations for a billion-dollar industry. Sketchpad also introduced the idea of the 'graphical user interface', some 30 years before it was perfected at Xerox (by Alan Kay, one-time student of Sutherland). It was also among the first interactive CAD (computer-aided design) programs.

With Sketchpad, Sutherland pioneered many computer graphics concept, such as the 'rubber-banding' of drawn lines, zoom-in and zoom-out (Sketchpad provided a scale of 2000:1, presenting the designer with a huge area of virtual space in which to create) the ability to easily create perfect corners and connections, and importantly, the ability to specify groups of lines and other structures as 'objects' that could then be replicated and iterated through the design process.

Sketchpad meant that designers and engineers could really use the computer as though it were a clever drafting table. The computer would memorize all the lines they drew on the screen, remember their structural relationship and display them. Designers could work with a familiar instrument – a pen, though in this case a light-sensitive pen – to create lines, move them and otherwise manipulate them directly on the CRT screen. It was a much more 'natural' way of programming, produced instant results, and sowed the seed of other 'natural language' and 'gestural' means of interfacing with a computer.

Sutherland went on to run the information processing programme at DARPA (from 1963), to form the flight simulation company Evans & Sutherland (1968), and later to develop much of the technology for virtual reality.

5 networking

THERE ARE JUST THREE FUNDAMENTAL visionary vectors that have driven and defined the web/net. These are the *potential* of computer networking, hypertext and artificial intelligence. Understanding the visions and aims of the pioneers of these three technologies will help us understand the potentials in these three areas – what the original vision was, how much we have achieved up to now, and what's likely to happen next – and build our big picture of what's happening in new media right now, and further to this, indicate the main development vectors we might expect in the immediate future. Hypertext with its complex web of interlinked words and media objects is, of course, a network, and the discipline of artificial intelligence will, during this decade, blossom and flower, producing a wide range of tools that will enhance and expand access to the hyperlinked information on this global network.

“THE DISCIPLINE OF ARTIFICIAL INTELLIGENCE WILL, DURING THIS DECADE, BLOSSOM AND FLOWER”

So much of our big picture is dominated by networks that it is worth spending some time in this area. Networking – of people (communications), of machines (device networks), of words (hypertext and knowledge structures), of neurones (human intelligence), of transistors (machine intelligence or AI) – dominates our 21st-century culture, as cybernetic artist Roy Ascott realized in 1989:

'Networking provides the metaphor for late 20th-century culture: it speaks of interactivity, decentralization, the layering of ideas from a multiplicity of sources. Networking is the provenance of far-reaching connectivity and, mediated, accelerated, and intensified by the computer, it leads to the amplification of thought, enrichment of the imagination, both broader and deeper memory, and the extension of our human senses. Computer networking means the linking of person-to-person, mind-to-mind, memory-to-memory regardless of their dispersal in space and their dislocation in time. In its global reach, in its complexity of idea processing, in its flexibility of output (image/music text and articulation of remote cybernetic systems, structures and environments) and in its capacity to accommodate a great diversity of input modes, all of which are digitally treated in universal dataspace, it is particularly suited to take on the challenge of late 20th-century art, which can be seen as the overarching project of our time: to make the invisible visible. That is, to bring to our senses, to make available to our minds, within the human constraints of space and time, what is otherwise beyond our reach, outside our perceptual range, the far side of our mind.'

'Gesamptkunstwerk: Connectivity, Transformation and Transcendence' (1989) from Ars Electronica Facing the Future

Networks are made up of 'nodes', the things connected, and 'connections', the links between nodes. Indeed, as Tim Berners-Lee points out in *Weaving the Web*, 'the world can be seen as *only connections*, nothing else'. The human organism is itself a triumph of the synergy of networks of not-so-dumb cells. Our knowledge of the world is embodied in the trillions of interconnections between the billions of neurons in our brain – and *only* in these interconnections. Fascinating video sequences have been shot of neural networks forming in the brain as new things are learned. The product of learning is networks – networks created, reinforced or (if they are not reinforced) neglected and 'forgotten'.

Human society has of course always thrived on networks – family, tribal, national and international networks of people, of information, of trade. The difference now, in our social, cultural and economic networks, is the speed and compass of these networks. Until the 19th century, the speed of social networks beyond the purely local was governed by the speed of the horse, and limited to the literate. In the 21st century, our communications networks operate at light speed, binding the entire world in McLuhan's real-time 'global village', are not confined to the literate – they carry voice-telephony as well as algorithms and multimedia information – and are potentially accessible to us all in our own language.

And the compass of these networks is growing exponentially – more and more of our world is being woven into the common web. Take e-mail as an indicator. Some experts have predicted that since e-mail is growing so fast, it is likely that, within a couple of years, there will be more e-mail accounts than television sets in the world. And the enabling technology underpinning this global communications revolution is networking – not just the microprocessor (the digital switches in our telecommunications systems, in routers and servers, in personal computers and other digital access devices) but the technology networking these devices together. Just as a pile of 100 billion separate neuronal cells doesn't constitute a brain, let alone a single human memory, 200 million (or so) *individual* computers don't have anything like the same impact on human society as this number of machines networked together.

Understanding how computers and other digital devices can be linked together into networks is central to an understanding of e-media. And understanding the visions that drive these developments will help us perceive the directions they are likely to take in the future.

understanding computer networks

Although remote-processing experiments were carried out at Bell Laboratories as early as 1940 (it invented the first computer 'terminal' at this time), computer networking did not become a practical reality until the 1960s. Up to then most digital communications were based on the concept of 'time-division multiplexing' (TDM)*, a technique invented for voice communications. The idea of creating a new universal standard for data communications was proposed in the 1960s by Paul Baran, Leonard Kleinrock and others. This came to be known as 'packet switching' (named by independent co-inventor Donald Davies in 1966).

*TDM is used in public telephone networks, as well as in T1 (and in Europe E1) digital transmission format, and narrow-band ISDN, and in SONET, the US optical media transmission standard. It works by taking data from many simultaneous users, splitting signals into a series of short time-duration segments, then sending them one after the other ('multiplexing' them together) down a single transmission line to the receiving computer, where they are de-multiplexed and sent on to their recipients.

Packet switching is the key idea that ensures that the internet is robust and fault-tolerant. It is the foundation of most modern digital networks and is important because it forms the basis of the TCP/IP protocols that underpin much of the web/net, in both its wired and wireless forms. Packet switching was conceived by Leonard Kleinrock, then independently by Paul Baran and Donald Davies, between 1962 and 1964.

Conventional point-to-point communications networks, such as the telephone network, rely on 'connections' – switching apparatus that literally creates a one-to-one connection through the many nodes in the network to carry your call. Perfect you say. But no. In this type of network only one node in the line connection has to go down and the communication is terminated. The more nodes (switches and relays, etc), the more chance of disruption. In pre-digital days, long-distance calls were very vulnerable to network failure.

Packet switching solves this problem by using a smart digital trick. The entire message to be communicated is divided up into many individual 'packets' of data, then sent through the network using clever routing protocols to ensure their delivery. Packets can take any route to reach their destination. If one node or router is down, packets can be re-routed or 'switched' through to other parts of the network.

A packet comprises of two main parts – the data (in chunks of about 1000 bits), and the packet header, the numbers that control the delivery of the packet. The header includes the important information: where the packet comes from (ie the address of the computer sending the packet), the destination, the length of the packet in bytes, the total number of packets in the complete message, and the sequence number of this particular packet.

The essential idea of packet switching is that it needs only one of the packets in a message to get through to the receiving computer. That computer reads the header, figures out which packets are missing, then sends a message back to the originating computer asking for the missing packets to be re-sent. Routers track packets and adjust their routes to avoid any glitches or unstable connections. For additional reliability, each packet header also contains an error-correction code, a number representing the total number of bits in the packet. Receiving computers use this to check that the message is complete. Of course, all the processing necessary for reading each packet and re-routing it through the network meant that routers and switches for digital telecommunications had to be computers. And it wasn't until the late 1960s that computers became suffiently available – and cheap enough – to warrant the implementation of packet switching over a wide-area network.

Networking several different types of computers together is not just a question of wiring them up. In addition to this, a set of formal conventions have to be developed, which govern how the computers send data to each other and how that data is interpreted. These conventions are called 'protocols'. Essentially, protocols determine how data is to be broken down into packets by the transmitting computer, and how those packets are sent and interpreted by the receiving computer. From 1971 to 1977, the ARPANET (the infant internet) had run on a protocol ('network control protocol' or NCP) devised by Stephen Crocker and his colleagues in the ARPA network working group from 1969. This protocol standardized the ARPANET network interface, making it easier for more and more sites to join the network. By 1971, there were 15 sites connecting to ARPANET using NCP. But by the mid-1970s the growth of sites and of other computer networks (including the French Cyclades network, CATENET, ALOHANET, SATNET, TELENET, and many others) led to the call for a new protocol that would provide the common technology by which networks designed by different developers could be linked to form a 'network of networks' – the internet. The successful solution was TCP/IP (transmission control protocol over internet protocol) designed by Vincent Cerf and Bob Kahn. In their 1974 paper on TCP/IP, they coin the word 'internet', and TCP/IP was so good that it went on to become a global standard, with IP still underpinning many of the developments in wide-band and mobile networking that characterize the first decade of the 21st century.

INTERNET PROTOCOL

Your computer (or phone, handheld, PDA, set-top box, etc) has a unique internet protocol (IP) address that enables other computers to find it on the web/net. Just like your street address enables the postal service to deliver your mail to the right place, this IP address gives the TCP/IP networking protocol the information it needs to route packets of data from one computer to another across the web/net and find its way to your machine. So whenever you use e-mail, the web, or another internet service to communicate with another computer (or phone, PDA, etc), the IP address of the destination computer forms part of the packet header. IP version 4 carried us into the new millennium, but it was obvious by the mid-1990s that the 'address space' of version 4 would restrict future developments. We would run out of IP addresses some time in the Noughties.

An Ipv4 address consists of four numbers: for example 155.18.234.68, each of which may be between 0 and 256. Hence there are more than 4.2 billion possible IP addresses in this 32-bit 'address space' (2^{32} eg 256×256×256×256 = 4,294,967,296). Depending on whether you are permanently connected to the internet or connecting via a phone line, your computer's IP address may be permanently assigned, or you may have a temporary number assigned to you when you log on (these temporary IP addresses are dynamically assigned from an available pool of addresses). IP version 6 (IPv6), the planned upgrade to IPv4, quadrupled the number of bits available to the IP address (from 32-bit to 128-bit), thereby creating a fantastically large number of possible addresses. It looks like we'll have enough addresses to supply several million for each square metre on the planet's surface.

Why on earth should we need so many? Well, we may not, but if the ideas of ubiquitous computing and 'smart dust' (tiny sensors) catch on, and we pepper our physical environment with intelligent sensors, effectors and other networked devices, if we build a machine-to-machine software network that looks after our safety and well-being in the real world as well as some visionaries imagine, then we'll need lots of unique IP addresses so that these smart items (including smart dust) can talk to each other. IP numbers are allocated to organizations, businesses and internet service providers, and thence to individual machines or access devices.

In an era of burgeoning networks based on various standards such as DSL (Digital Subscriber Loop), ATM (Asynchronous Transfer Mode), ISDN (Integrated Services Digital Network), FDDI (Fibre Distributed Data Interface), and Frame Relay, the value of a common internet protocol is obvious. Now mobile IP is being designed as a potential global standard that builds on, and is backwardly compatible with, IP. The aim of mobile IP is to create the situation where users are automatically connected and reconnected to different IP addresses as they move through the real world, such that you could continuously browse the web on the move without noticing the switch from one IP address to another. Mobile IP already forms the basis of much mobile networking research, including Cellular Digital Packet Data which is based on a draft implementation of mobile IP.

Packet switching and network protocols such as IP provided the means by which to format and transmit digital messages across large networks. By the mid-1970s, the proliferation of computers and computer peripherals occasioned by the invention of the microprocessor (computer on a chip) in 1971 meant that the issue of harnessing several computers together in a 'local area' (in a campus, a building or even a single room) had to be addressed.

local-area networks In the wake of the introduction of the microprocessor, significant amounts of R&D effort became focused on the potential of an 'electronic office' in which communications would be digital rather than paper-based. The paperless office was a chimera (though we are getting closer to this ideal now), but the immediate results of this kind of R&D were the creation of the tools and techniques that underpin much of our contemporary information technology.

XEROX PARC IN THE 1970S

Many of these core technologies were developed at the Palo Alto Research Centre (PARC), owned by Xerox Corp, which was established in 1970. During the 1970s and 1980s PARC invented or developed an astonishing range of the technologies we now take for granted in the office and at home. The graphical user interface, the mouse (the first commercially produced mouse), the personal computer, bit-mapped screen displays, flat-panel screens, the laser printer, page-description languages, client-server architecture – all these emerged from PARC (and it must be said, were mostly productivized and marketed by companies other than Xerox). Ethernet, the global standard used by most local-area networks, was developed by Bob Metcalfe at PARC. And PARC maintains its reputation for innovation with its work on information visualization, 'fluid documents', electronic paper, natural language technology, 'smart matter' and other developments.

The paperless office idea involved physically connecting computers, printers and other peripherals in a 'local-area network' (LAN), either by linking them with wires or by using radio as the transmission medium. The key development in LANs was the invention of Ethernet in the early 1970s by Bob Metcalfe and his Xerox PARC team.

Metcalfe had previously worked on another important 'wide-area network' that evolved outside the DARPA domain. This was Norman Abramson's 'AlohaNet', a packet-switched radio network that connected computers scattered through the Hawaiian islands. The Aloha protocol was the first multiple-access protocol, and Metcalfe was able to build on his experience of working with Abramson when he began to tackle local-area networks.

In late 1972, Metcalfe and his PARC colleagues constructed the first experimental Ethernet system – with a transmission speed of 2.94 Mbps – (later boosted to 10 Mbps) to link Xerox's new personal workstation, the Alto, to other Altos and to servers, and to the early laser printers that Xerox had developed. Initially this was called the Alto Aloha Network, but Metcalfe changed the name to Ethernet in order to differentiate it from AlohaNet (Metcalfe's system had evolved considerably from Abramson's) and because Ethernet was designed to work with any computer, not just the innovative Alto (the first 'personal' computer with a graphical user interface). The Ethernet protocol was refined, and Metcalfe's dissertation paper was published in 1973 – the year before Intel introduced the first 8-bit microprocessor, the 8088, which was to spark the development of personal computers. (Ethernet was eventually ratified as an international standard by the IEEE in 1985.)

With Ethernet protocols to handle local-area networking, and with ARPANET, AlohaNet and other systems to take care of the wide-area networks (WANs), 'networking' became the signature of digital developments during the 1970s. And networking of course became increasingly important as the invention of 4-bit and 8-bit microprocessor chips fuelled the development of personal computers.

The 1970s saw the development of many of the network software tools that we now take for granted. In 1972 Ray Tomlinson of the DARPA consultancy BBN invented an e-mail program to send messages across a distributed network (he is the man who decided to use the @ symbol in e-mail addresses). This first e-mail client was released onto the ARPANET at the same time as Abbay Bhushans' File Transfer Protocol (FTP) – used to copy data files from one computer to another around the network.

“NETWORKING OF COURSE BECAME INCREASINGLY IMPORTANT AS THE INVENTION OF 4-BIT AND 8-BIT MICROPROCESSOR CHIPS FUELLED THE DEVELOPMENT OF PERSONAL COMPUTERS”

A year later, Larry Roberts wrote the first e-mail managing software, which spread rapidly through ARPANET. And in 1974 John Vittal wrote MSG, an e-mail client that handled dozens of messages, and introduced the ANSWER (reply) command. As Katie Hafner and Matthew Lyon point out in *When Wizards Stay up Late*, their important history of the internet, MSG was the first 'killer app' (a must-have software application). It was completely 'unofficial' (remember ARPANET was a Department of Defense-funded project), but it had widespread grass-roots support and became the standard for e-mail through the 1970s and 1980s.

'More than just a great hack, MSG was the best proof to date that on the ARPANET rules might get made, but they certainly didn't prevail. Proclamations of officialdom didn't further the net nearly so much as throwing technology out on the net to see what worked. And when something worked, it was adopted.'

Katie Hafner and Matthew Lyon, When Wizards Stay up Late

The first commercial local-area networks were installed in 1977 (Datapoint Corp's ARCNET system, described by Ted Nelson at the time as 'the first and best of the lot' (Dream Machines) and over the next decade many thousands of LANs appeared in offices and laboratories all over the world, many of them based on Ethernet or on IBM's Token Ring network system (other LAN systems included FDDI (for fibre networks), ATM and Apple's Localtalk).

In 1979 Bob Metcalfe left Xerox to start his own company, 3Com, now one of the major network technology players. Subsequently he formulated his own law of networking, Metcalfe's Law, which states that *the value of a network grows by the square of the size of the network*. New additions to a network – new people and machines going online – amplify the value of the network for everyone. For example, if you are the sole owner of a fax machine, it is entirely useless – you have no one to fax things to. The more people who buy faxes, the more useful the fax machine is, and the more valuable the fax network becomes. So a network that is twice as large will be four times as valuable because there are four times as many things that can be done due to the larger number of interconnections.

the network visionaries Metcalfe wasn't the only one to realize that networks were something special. From as early as 1960, when Joseph Licklider wrote his paper 'Man-computer symbiosis', the new generation of computer scientists were fired with visions of what computer networking might mean to us all.

'It seems reasonable to envision, for a time 10 or 15 years hence, a "thinking centre" that will incorporate the functions of present-day libraries together with anticipated advances in information storage and retrieval. The picture readily enlarges itself into a network of such centres, connected to one another by wide-band communications lines and to individual users by leased-wire services.'

Joseph Licklider, Man-Computer Symbiosis

As we shall see, some of the central development vectors of new media cluster around the visions of the network, computer and hypertext pioneers working in the wake of Licklider's vision of the broadband information network.

During this period of the 1960s and 1970s, the great pioneers of our global web/net, and of the computing and software technologies that support it, were just beginning to glimpse the potentials. One of the most eloquent was French computer scientist and networking specialist Jacques Vallee:

'Many years and many computing generations ago, I had been told that there was no future in this field (computing) and that Man could not get out of his sphere. Today, computers were literally bending our entire culture out of shape, changing the way we interacted as individuals and in groups. There was a new social form, the network, with its methods of instant, unlimited access to information never before experienced by the human race. It was forcing us to choose between two forms of society: not along the obsolete lines of Marxism and Capitalism, but along lines of its own demands: for we are already out of our sphere. We cannot go back. We must choose: either to surrender our existence in a warm and cozy world of controlled memory frames, or to join the new networks, the new grapevines, to discover who we really are at the limit of an information space where we can learn to live.'

Jacques Vallee, The Network Revolution: Confessions of a Computer Scientist

And he wasn't about to stop there. Vallee seemed to realize (as early as 1982) that the 'network thing' was unstoppable and would soon expand so incredibly fast that it would even leave the experts behind:

'Then we'll create a brain for humanity by letting people link up. Some will do it out of loneliness and others will use the net to screw the others or to advertise or to steal or to go on their big ego trips, and they will reconstruct their male territories around the networks, that's already happening on ARPANET, the big shots go around defecating all over the software from MIT to Stanford so you know it's their turf, but don't worry, that's just a transition, the future will take care of that, the network will expand so fast even the big shots will soon be left sitting on their behind, they won't even know what's happening.'

“CYBERNETICS WAS THE FIRST SCIENTIFIC DISCIPLINE TO RECOGNIZE THAT A SYSTEM COMPRISED OF MACHINES AS WELL AS HUMANS WAS AS COMPLEX AS A PURELY BIOLOGICAL OR 'ECO' SYSTEM”

Obviously, you don't have visions about the potential of a highly technical development if you know little about it. The network visionaries of the mid-20th century emerged from two main areas: computer science and cybernetics. Cybernetics was the first scientific discipline to recognize that a system comprised of machines as well as humans was as complex as a purely biological or 'eco' system. The eccentric British cyberneticist Gordon Speedie Pask not only understood this but was quick to realize that such complex systems had emergent properties, not the least of which was self-organization:

'For the possibilities it opens up of co-operation, if for no other reason in this uncertain world, it would be wise to explore the idea of populations of computers. Co-operative systems of this kind constitute a sub-class of what Professor Hans van Foerster of the Biological Computer Laboratory, University of Illinois, has called "self-organizing systems". Though often loosely used to refer to systems that are adaptive, the term self-organizing accords in its strictest sense with an independent reinvention of van Foerster's definition by John Nicolis of the University of Patras, Greece: "If a system is self-organizing, then the rate of change of a suitable measure of its organization is positive." For our purposes a positive rate of change of "a suitable measure of organization" can be taken as meaning the active co-operation through interaction of the individuals constituting a computer population.'

Gordon Pask and Susan Curran, Microman

In a famous demonstration of this self-organizing potential, Pask created 'an ecological fantasy of self-organization and co-operation' for the seminal cybernetic art show 'Cybernetic Serendipity' organized by Jascia Reichardt and held at the Institute for Contemporary Art, London, in 1968.

Pask describes his 'Colloquy of Mobiles':

'It is a group of objects, the individual mobiles, that engage in discourse, that compete, co-operate and learn about one another. Their discourse evolves at several levels in a hierarchy of control and a hierarchy of abstraction. The trick is that if you find them interesting, then you can join in the discourse as well, and bring your influence to bear by participating in what goes on. It is a crude demonstration of an idea that could be developed indefinitely.

'Each individual mobile has a set of programmes that determine its motions and its visible state. Each individual learns how to deploy its programmes in order to achieve a goal: namely, to reduce an in-built drive. Its level of "satisfaction" is reflected partly in its behaviour and partly in a visual display. The mobiles are of two sorts. As a whimsy, we have called one sort male, the other female.

Gordon Pask combined his interests in cybernetics, self-organizing systems and the nature of co-operation in this work for the famous 'Cybernetic Serendipity' exhibition organized by Jascia Reichardt at the ICA, London in 1968. Photograph courtesy of Amanda Heitler

'Whereas males compete amongst themselves and so do females, a male may co-operate with a female and vice versa, for one possesses programmes that are not in the repertoire of the other, and jointly a male-female pair can achieve more than both individuals in isolation. Ironically, this property is manifest in the fact that a male can project strong beams of light but it cannot satisfy an urge to have them play on its periphery, whereas a female (who cannot shine light) is able to reflect it back to a male (and when she is competent, to reflect it on the right position). To co-operate or even to orient themselves and to engage their programmes, the mobiles must communicate. They do so in a simple but many-levelled language of light flashes and sounds. You may engage in this discourse if you wish to, though your goals may be alien to the goals of the mobiles; for example, you might be trying to achieve a configuration that you regard as pleasing.'

'The Colloquy of Mobiles' in Cybernetic Serendipity

The realization that networks of machines had the potential to become self-organizing 'ecosystems' was the contribution of early cyberneticists such as Pask and van Foerster and leads directly to our discussion of 'business ecosystems' later in this section. Nearly 30 years after Pask's demonstration at the ICA, business gurus began to apply cybernetic thinking to the newly webbed world of e-commerce and dot com business:

'No longer does any company, even one as powerful as Microsoft or Intel, succeed as a single entity. Rather, enduring success means companies must

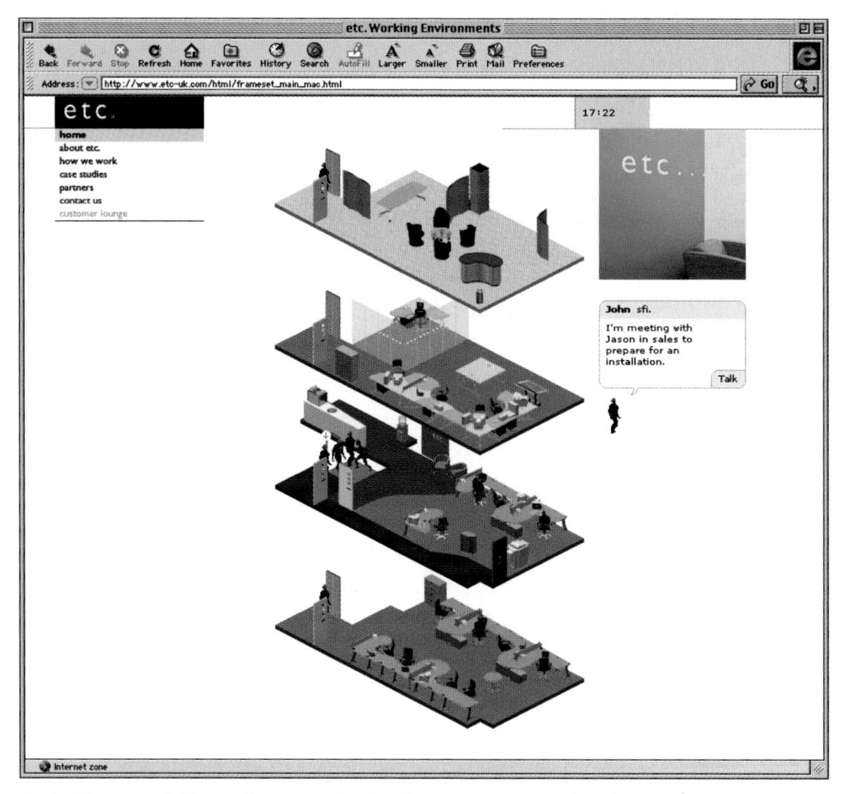

Tonic Design's delightful take on the 'business ecosystem' is this cutaway animation of etc-uk's office – it runs in real time – with people arriving in the morning, working through the office during the day, and leaving and turning out the lights in the evening. Designed and produced in Shockwave by Tonic Design (www.tonicdesign.uk)

be leaders and shapers of a voluntary organization of suppliers, customers and others who all mutually benefit from the association.'

James F. Moore, CEO, GeoPartners Research, Inc, 'The Advent of Business Ecosystems', The Death of Competition: Leadership and Strategy in the Age of Business Ecosystems

There was something about the network zeitgeist that permeated thinking in the late 1960s. The cyberneticist John McHale eulogized about communication networks in Gene Youngblood's influential *Expanded Cinema* in 1970:

'World communications ... diffuse and interpenetrate local cultural tradition, providing commonly shared cultural experience in a manner unparalleled in human history. Within this global network the related media share and transmit man's symbolic needs and their expression on a world scale. Besides the enlargement of the physical world, these media virtually extend our psychical environment, providing a constant stream of moving, fleeting images of the world for our daily appraisal. They provide psychic mobility for the greater mass of our citizens. Through these devices we can telescope time, move through history, and span the world in a great variety of unprecedented ways.'

From 'The Plastic Parthenon', quoted in Expanded Cinema

In 1968, Joseph Licklider published 'The computer as a communications device' with co-author and ARPANET pioneer Bob Taylor. This paper reinforced and inspired the work on ARPANET, and Licklider didn't mince his words: 'In a few years men will be able to communicate more effectively through a machine than face to face.'

The first world-around television satellite network link-up had been celebrated in 1967 in the UK by a live broadcast of The Beatles singing 'All You Need is Love'. The Whole Earth Catalogue and similar publications were fostering ecological ideas. At the same time that cybernetic theory was being constructed by great minds like Pask, Stafford Beer, Gregory Bateson and John McHale, ARPANET was linking American universities in the prototype internet, and the American architect Richard Buckminster Fuller was constructing vast geodesic domes (lattice networks of aluminium for Expo 67) another eccentric – American this time – was developing his notions of an intricate network of words linking *all* our textual culture. His name was Ted Nelson. He was a computer scientist with a masters degree in sociology, and he was talking about a global hypertext system he called Xanadu.

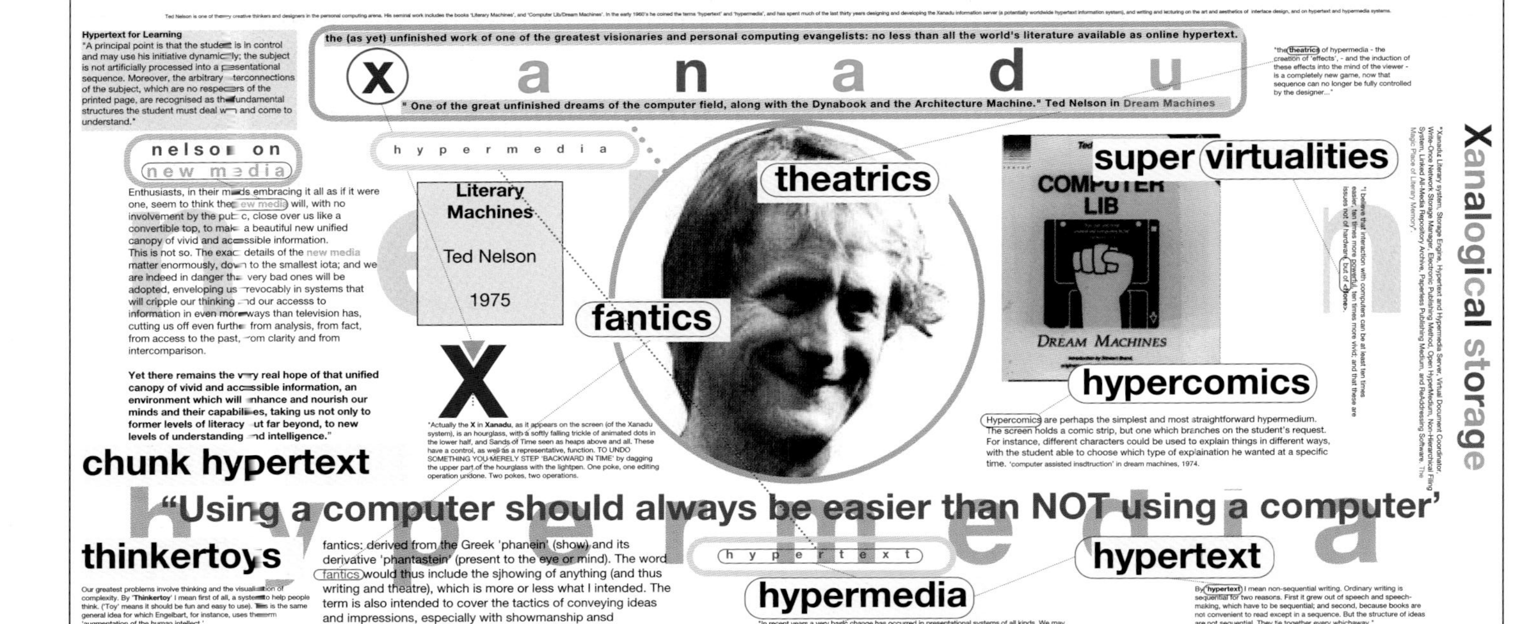

Ted Nelson is one of the creative thinkers and designers in the personal computing arena. His seminal work includes the books 'Literary Machines', and 'Computer Lib/Dream Machines'. In the early 1960's he coined the terms 'hypertext' and 'hypermedia', and has spent much of the last thirty years designing and developing the Xanadu information server (a potentially worldwide hypertext information system), and writing and lecturing on the art and aesthetics of interface design, and on hypertext and hypermedia systems.
Hypertext for Learning
"A principal point is that the stude is in control and may use his initiative dynamic ly; the subject is not artificially processed into a p esentational sequence. Moreover, the arbitrary terconnections of the subject, which are no respe rs of the printed page, are recognised as th fundamental structures the student must deal w and come to understand."
the (as yet) unfinished work of one of the greatest visionaries and personal computing evangelists: no less than all the world's literature available as online hypertext.
x a n a d u
" One of the great unfinished dreams of the computer field, along with the Dynabook and the Architecture Machine." Ted Nelson in Dream Machines
"the theatrics of hypermedia - the creation of 'effects', - and the induction of these effects into the mind of the viewer - is a completely new game, now that sequence can no longer be fully controlled by the designer..."
Xanalogical storage
"Xanadu Literary system, Storage Engine, Hypertext and Hypermedia Server, Virtual Document Coordinator, Write-Once Network Storage Manager, Electronic Publishing Method, Open HyperMedium, Non-Hierarchical Filing System, Linked All-Media Repository Archive, Paperless Publishing Medium, and ReAddressing Software. The Magic Place of Literary Memory".
nelso on
new m dia
Enthusiasts, in their m ds embracing it all as if it were one, seem to think the ew media will, with no involvement by the pub c, close over us like a convertible top, to mak a beautiful new unified canopy of vivid and ac ssible information.
This is not so. The exac details of the new media matter enormously, dow to the smallest iota; and we are indeed in danger th very bad ones will be adopted, enveloping us revocably in systems that will cripple our thinking d our accesss to information in even mor ways than television has, cutting us off even furthe from analysis, from fact, from access to the past, om clarity and from intercomparison.
Yet there remains the v ry real hope of that unified canopy of vivid and acc ssible information, an environment which will nhance and nourish our minds and their capabil es, taking us not only to former levels of literacy ut far beyond, to new levels of understanding nd intelligence."
h y p e r m e d i a
Literary Machines
Ted Nelson
1975
theatrics
fantics
super virtualities
"I believe that interaction with computers can be at least ten times easier, ten times more powerful, ten times more vivid; and that these are issues not of hardware, but of <tone>.
Ted
COMPUTER LIB
DREAM MACHINES
hypercomics
Hypercomics are perhaps the simplest and most straightforward hypermedium. The screen holds a comic strip, but one which branches on the student's request. For instance, different characters could be used to explain things in different ways, with the student able to choose which type of explaination he wanted at a specific time. 'computer assisted insdtruction' in dream machines, 1974.
X
"Actually the X in Xanadu, as it appears on the screen (of the Xanadu system), is an hourglass, with a softly falling trickle of animated dots in the lower half, and Sands of Time seen as heaps above and all. These have a control, as well as a representative, function. TO UNDO SOMETHING YOU MERELY STEP 'BACKWARD IN TIME' by dagging the upper part of the hourglass with the lightpen. One poke, one editing operation undone. Two pokes, two operations.
chunk hypertext
"Using a computer should always be easier than NOT using a computer'
h y p e r m e d i a
thinkertoys
Our greatest problems involve thinking and the visuali tion of complexity. By 'Thinkertoy' I mean first of all, a syste o help people think. ('Toy' means it should be fun and easy to use). s is the same general idea for which Engelbart, for instance, uses th rm 'augmentation of the human intellect.'
An important choice faces us: let the co puter perpetuate archaic methods of publishi , or use it to vault our minds into a hyperspace o hought.
fantics: derived from the Greek 'phanein' (show) and its derivative 'phantastein' (present to the eye or mind). The word fantics would thus include the sjhowing of anything (and thus writing and theatre), which is more or less what I intended. The term is also intended to cover the tactics of conveying ideas and impressions, especially with showmanship ansd presentational techniques, organising constructs, and fundamental structures underlying presentational systems
h y p e r t e x t
hypermedia
"In recent years a very basic change has occurred in presentational systems of all kinds. We may summarise it under the name 'branching', although there are many variants. Essentially, today's systems for presenting pictures, texts and whatnot can bring you different things automatically depending on what you do. Selection of this type is generally called branching. (I have suggested the generic term hypermedia for presentational media which perform in this (and other) multidimensional ways).
hypertext
By 'hypertext' I mean non-sequential writing. Ordinary writing is sequential for two reasons. First it grew out of speech and speech-making, which have to be sequential; and second, because books are not convenient to read except in a sequence. But the structure of ideas are not sequential. They tie together every whichaway."
ted nelson: hypermedia visionary

"A LONG-TERM EVANGELIZER OF PERSONAL COMPUTERS, TED NELSON WAS THE ROCK STAR OF THE EMERGING 'CYBERPUNK' MOVEMENT"

hypertext as network Theodor Holm ('Ted') Nelson has been singing the song of 'hypermedia' since he invented the word (just after he coined 'hypertext') in the mid-1960s. A long-term evangelizer of personal computers, 'literary hypertext', and the importance of 'media design' in the creation of software, Ted Nelson was the rock star of the emerging 'cyberpunk' movement in the early 1980s. His 1974 facsimile sketchbook *Computer Lib – Dream Machines* is probably the most influential book on interactive software design ever published. Nelson's dream was essentially literary. Nelson had coined the word 'hypertext' in 1965, around the time he delivered his first paper to the Association of Computing Machinery (ACM). His vision of hypertext as the means of interlinking human knowledge followed the ideas embodied in Vannevar Bush's 'Memex' article (see page 77), and was a rich one – he imagined several different modes of hypertext, from simple 'chunk' hypertext (what we call nowadays 'hyperlinks'), linking references, footnotes and commentary to a main document, to the vast global 'literary machine' he called Xanadu.

Xanadu was a vision of a network – in Nelson's phrase, a 'deeply intertwingled' network of interconnections or hyperlinks between bits of information embodied in electronic versions of books, articles, papers, critiques, essays, poems, dissertations, bibliographies, citations, notations, articles, all the various forms of literature. Hypertext and Xanadu were the software counterpart to the network infrastructures being developed by ARPA, Xerox, Datapoint, IBM and AT&T. Hypertext and networking developed in parallel, and were different responses to the same vision:

'Creative, interactive communication requires a plastic or mouldable medium that can be modelled, a dynamic medium in which premises will flow into consequences, and above all a common medium that can be contributed to and experimented with by all. Such a medium is at hand – the programmed digital computer. Its presence can change the nature and value of communication even more profoundly than did the printing press and the picture tube, for, as we shall show, a well programmed computer can provide access both to informational sources and to the processes for making use of the resources.'

JCR Licklider with Bob Taylor, 'The Computer as Communication Device', April 1968

Nelson's two-books-in-one 'Computer Lib/Dream Machines' was an inspiration to the generation of artists, designers and programmers emerging in the 1980s, and is still a treasure-trove of ideas and insights. His ideas – of a global hypertext library – and of computer software that could be entertaining as well as informative, were to materialize in various forms in the mid-1990s.

In his book *Microman* (1982) Gordon Pask provides a succinct description of Xanadu:

'Xanadu is primarily a data bank, a massive computerized reference library that contains an extraordinary assortment of material both published and private. Authors pay to store published material in the database, and it is freely available; a royalty is paid when anyone accesses it. Access to private material is free, but access and use may be restricted.'

In *Dream Machines* however, Nelson stresses the *distributed* nature of his program: 'People think that if the Xanadu system is going to store and supply so much stuff, it has to be an enormous program. Not so. The same smallish program running in every computer on a network, makes the overall system.' Sounds familiar? But while Nelson's system has some similarities with Berners-Lee's world wide web (eg a global, distributed hypertext system), Nelson was thinking about Xanadu in terms of a global franchise. He imagined setting up a network of public workstations – Xanadu Stands, with giant Xs echoing the famous M of the burger giant.

He even writes a jingle for it:

> 'The Xanadu Singing Commercial'
> (strings) It's got everything to give.
> It'll get you where you live.
> (chimes) Realms of mind that you may roam:
> Grasp them all within your home.
> (brass flourish) The greatest things you've ever seen.
> Dance your wishes on the screen.
> (brass bautant) All the things that man has known
> Comin' on the telephone.
> (tubular bells) Poems, books and pictures too
> Comin' on the Xanadu –
> (kettle drums) Xan-a-du – oo, the world of You-oo!
>
> **©Ted Nelson, Dream Machines**

Nelson's vision was acute. *Dream Machines* and its companion book *Computer Lib* were and still are totally inspirational, and jam-packed full of ideas, especially in stressing the importance of software design, and what Nelson called 'fantics' – 'the tactics of conveying ideas and impressions, especially with showmanship and presentational techniques, organizing constructs, and fundamental structures underlying presentational systems'. Although Xanadu (like the poem by Coleridge after which it was named) was never completed, Nelson's vision – a network of hyperlinked information riding on the physical infrastructure of a global telecommunications network – inspired a generation of programmers and software designers.

Why did Xanadu fail? There are several reasons, but perhaps the two main ones were that Nelson was proposing Xanadu as a commercial venture in order to license a proprietary system (not an open standard), and secondly, before there were any concrete examples to point to, hypertext and hypermedia were difficult concepts to communicate to the general public – as Apple Computer was to discover in the late 1980s.

the Hypercard experience In 1987 I attended an Apple Computer trade show in London. Organized by *MacUser* magazine, the special event that year was the launch of a new product, one that was kind of difficult to define, called Hypercard. Several designers, programmers and salesmen were on hand to explain Hypercard, and the keynote presenter was the science-fiction author Douglas Adams. It was a transforming experience. Adams was brilliant. To illustrate the hypertext concept (unfamiliar to most people at the time), he had designed a Hypercard program (called a stack – of cards) to store the details of his extensive record collection. He showed us how easy this was, and talked us through a search for his favourite album, The Beatles' *Sergeant Pepper's Lonely Hearts Club Band*, and his favourite track, *Day in the Life*. Clicking on a button, he called up the lyrics, and then played a digital audio clip of the 'ten thousand holes in Blackburn Lancashire' stanza. Explaining how this lyric had always fascinated him, Adams then displayed a card with a road map of Blackburn on it, and proceeded to dot it with 10,000 'holes' in the roads. For the next lyric line, 'Nobody knows how many holes it takes to fill the Albert Hall', he used Hypercard to calculate an average road-repair hole size, then multiplied this by 10,000 to reach a cubic footage total. To finesse his Hypercard demo, he then called up a three-dimensional wire-frame model of the Albert Hall, calculated the internal cubic space, and determined the actual number of holes it could contain.

This delightful and hilarious *reductio ad absurdum* perfectly cemented the central idea of Hypercard in the minds of Adams' appreciative audience: it was a hypermedia authoring program, could be scripted to perform calculations, could display many different data types, and could be interlinked in ways that echoed the 'associative links' of how we think. And it could be real fun too.

I had already worked on the design of several interactive video disks and knew exactly how clumsy most existing design or 'authoring' tools were.

Most of the early authoring tools required the services of a skilled programmer. They weren't 'what you see is what you get' (WYSIWYG) – the designer couldn't see what the finished design was actually going to look like until the laser disk video image and his graphic overlays were composited on the television monitor. So news of this authoring program that used simple, natural language 'scripting' (as opposed to esoteric coding), that was highly graphic, multimedia *and* non-linear was extremely exciting.

Hypercard turned out to be (almost) everything a designer like myself could want. The 'almost' was for two reasons: firstly, that Hypercard was 'platform specific' – it worked only on Apple Macintosh computers; and secondly, that it was then only a 1-bit program. The first Macs had 1-bit

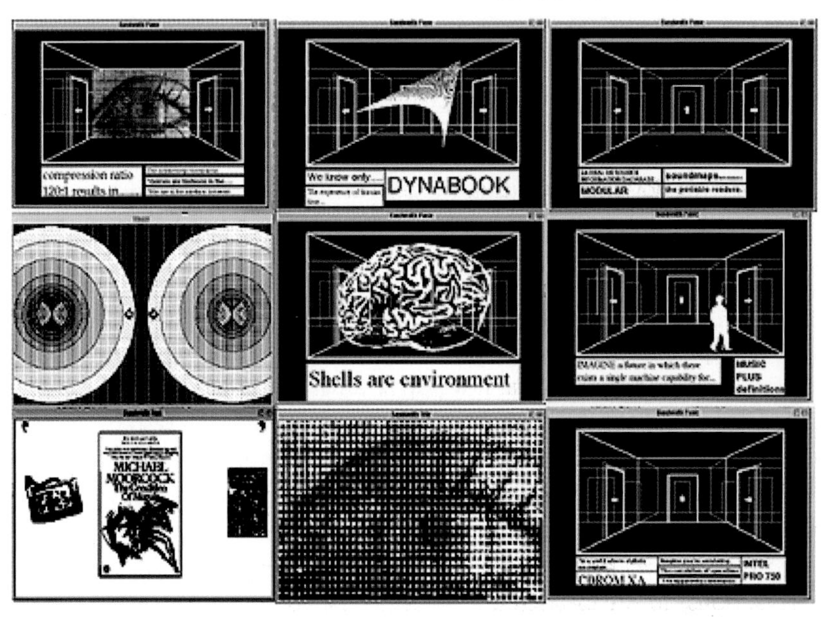

Bill Atkinson's Hypercard was bundled free with every Apple Macintosh computer in the late 1980s. It was based on the idea of a card-index, but various digital media (animation, pictures, text, programming, sound, video etc could be 'written' on each card, and cards could be electronically 'hyperlinked' too. This was my first attempt at a 'hyper-magazine' – designed and produced by Richard Oliver, Asif Choudhary and myself at the Computer Graphics Workshop in 1988–1989.

screens – they could display only black or white pixels, no colours, no grey scales. Hypercard was designed to work specifically on these machines, so it was limited to the screen size of those early Macs – the 7×5 inch built-in screens. And Hypercard, while allowing extensive internal networking of cards in a stack, and between stacks stored locally, did not talk to the net.

The Mac was revolutionary when it appeared in 1984, and was the first computer to really popularize the idea of the graphical user interface that had been developed and prototyped at Xerox PARC in the 1970s. It was designed to be extremely user-friendly and mouse-driven. At the time IBM PCs and most other personal computers had 'command-line' interfaces – the computer would prompt the user, who was then expected to type in the command he wanted the computer to perform. Now this was OK for many, but it wasn't a consumer solution. So the Mac was a revolution – the graphical user interface was an 'intuitive' way of illustrating the file structure of computer memory, and it came pre-configured, with an integrated screen and bundled software applications, ready to use immediately. It was a computer designed as a consumer electronic device.

THE MAC WAS
A REVOLUTION

However, the downside was that for designers and developers, the Mac was really hard to program. You needed to be an expert programmer *and* have spent a couple of months reading up on the Macintosh operating system.

This was where Hypercard really scored. After 1987, it was possible for a subject expert, with no computer programming experience, to create working, even elegant, multimedia interactive programs that would run on any Mac. Hypercard consisted of a 7×5 inch blank 'card', onto which could be placed text, bit-mapped images, programmable buttons, sounds and other media objects (animations, video, etc). Hypercard had an extensive set of tools for creating and editing media objects. Any number of cards could be created and linked by means of buttons or by writing scripts (programming instructions) in the card itself, for example, card animations could be created by scripting cards to display in rapid succession. Collections of cards, known as Hypercard 'stacks', could be distributed by floppy disk and played on any other Mac. Teachers, archivists and other professional information and communication professionals loved it. Games were written in it. Hypercard was the first widely popular hypertext system, pre-dating the

WWW by five years. Interestingly, the basic start card in Hypercard was called 'home', a convention that carried through into the WWW browser's familiar homepage. Hypercard was used by designers to create CD-ROM programs, point-of-information systems, non-linear presentations, stories, indices and encyclopedias. I created a 'hyper magazine' in 1988, as well as an A-Z reference tool for desktop publishing design.

Hypercard was the invention of Bill Atkinson, a visionary programmer who had been central to the development of Macintosh software. He had written the operating system Quickdraw procedures, and had co-written (with Andy Herzfield) the easy-to-use word processor MacWrite. His real triumph before Hypercard however was MacPaint, a brilliantly simple bitmap editor or 'painting' program. These two applications were bundled free on every new Macintosh, and were central to the success of the Mac. People could buy a Mac, plug it in, and straightaway they could be writing or painting – no configuration problems, no OS (operating system) tweaking, no software installations, just pure 'plug and play'!

Atkinson himself expresses the sense of empowerment this gave to previously technophobic users:

'The art of creating software that is usable by individuals is a communication skill. It is not a programming skill. Programming and what a software artist does is analogous to a pianist who needs to know how to move the keys and have that down cold so that he can concentrate on the feeling and message that he is portraying in his rendition of this music. So slinging the bits is an enabling technology for me to express and communicate and teach. The most exciting thing for me is when I see people amazed and pleased at the new-found power they got from a program, when they say, "Wow, I can do this!" That's the feeling people got back in 1984 when they saw MacPaint and started using it. It's the same kind of feeling that is going to happen here with Hypercard. But that feeling will be magnified, because the amount of power you get out of Hypercard is really so much greater. Hypercard is going to open up the whole meaning of what personal computers can be.'

Interview in 1987

While Hypercard, like hypertext, was a means of building a network of ideas and multiple-media forms, and embodying these in a transportable program (a stack), Apple didn't make Hypercard 'internet-ready'. It would be another five years before Tim Berners-Lee did for the internet what Apple had done for personal computing – make it user friendly.

the vision (partially) realized: the WWW Such are the quirks of history: that individuals can arrive at the same conclusions from entirely different directions, often without knowing what others have done. In 1980, Tim Berners-Lee, a young computer scientist, arrived at CERN (the international particle physics research centre in Switzerland) on a software consultancy. While he was there, he wrote a program called Enquire, his 'first web-like program':

'I wrote it in my spare time and for my own personal use, and for no loftier reason than to help me remember the connections among the various people, computers and projects at the lab (CERN). Still, the larger vision had taken firm root in my consciousness. **Suppose all the information stored on computers everywhere were linked**, I thought. Suppose **I could program my computer to create a space in which anything could be linked to anything**. All the bits of information in every computer at CERN, and on the planet, would be available to me and to anyone else. There would be a single, global information space.'

Weaving the Web

At that time, Berners-Lee was unaware that 'several people had hit upon similar concepts' (he didn't read Ted Nelson's *Literary Machines* until 1988) and in the first chapter of his important book, *Weaving the Web*, he refers to Vannevar Bush and his Memex machine, Nelson's Xanadu, and the seminal work of Douglas Engelbart, and how he discovered their 'hypertext' work later in his development of the web. He ends the first chapter with characteristic modesty:

'I happened to come along with time, and the right interest and inclination, after hypertext and the internet had come of age. The task left to me was to marry them together.'

Berners-Lee was to visit CERN several times during that decade, and made a number of proposals for 'official' funding to support the creation of a 'universal' hypertext system. By late 1990, unable to sell the idea to CERN, he had decided to go ahead and write the program himself. He called it the WorldWideWeb, and by December 1990 he had a client program up and running with the Hypertext Mark-up Language that he had written during the previous few weeks. This program, 'a point and click browser/editor', enabled the user to 'browse' HTML space – to decode and display HTML documents – and also, importantly, *to write and edit web pages* in HTML. During this time Berners-Lee also wrote the first web server – 'the software that holds web pages on a portion of a computer and allows others to access them'.

> “BY CHRISTMAS 1990 HE WAS ABLE TO DEMONSTRATE ALL THE COMPONENTS OF WWW”

Berners-Lee had written his WWW browser on a sophisticated workstation – one of Steve Job's stylish Next computers – and consequently, it ran only on Next machines. To demonstrate the universality of WWW, he asked Nicola Pellow, a student intern at CERN, to write a browser that would work on any computer. They decided that the best way of doing this would be to write a 'lowest common denominator' program, a text-only or 'line-mode' browser (Berners-Lee's Next browser was a user-friendly, point-and-click interface that could display images and graphics too).

To further demonstrate the universality of his program, Berners-Lee programmed his browser so that as well as files on HTTP servers (HyperText Transfer Protocol, another component in his system), it would also follow links to news articles and newsgroups on the internet that were transmitted in the FTP standard. By Christmas 1990 he was able to demonstrate all the components of WWW – the browser/editor, URIs (universal resource identifiers, the addressing system for HTML documents*), HTML documents themselves, and HTTP – all working with an extant and extensive body of internet information. He posted this work and his documentation for it – written (of course!) in HTML – on the first web server, info.cern.ch. This first 'website' also included information on WWW for newcomers to the web, with specifications and addresses for available software.

*In 1992, the Internet Engineering Task Force (IETF) changed this to URL – Uniform Resource Locator.

Importantly, the WWW was a truly distributed system:

> 'What was often difficult for people to understand about the design was that there was nothing else beyond URIs, HTTP and HTML. There was no central computer "controlling" the web, no single network on which these protocols worked, not even an organization anywhere that "ran" the web. The web was

not a physical "thing" that existed in a certain place. It was a "space" in which information could exist.'

Tim Berners-Lee, Weaving the Web

Through the first half of 1991, after months of frustrating attempts to get CERN to adopt WWW, Berners-Lee distributed the program, first to the limited number of people at CERN who had Next computers, then to some interested colleagues at Stanford Linear Accelerator Lab in Palo Alto, California. Eventually, in August 1991, he released the WWW for Next, the line-mode browser, and the basic server for any machine, and made it freely available on the internet. Berners-Lee actively evangelized the WWW program to both the hypertext and networking communities during 1991–1992, and due to lack of support at CERN, posted a request on the web for someone to write a 'point-and-click' browser for the three main types of computer (that is, other than the relatively rare Next machine): PCs, Macs and Unix machines. By April 1992, some students at Helsinki had programmed a browser for Unix machines running a GUI called X-Windows. A month later, Pei Wei, a student at UC Berkeley, also wrote a Unix browser, 'ViolaWWW'. 'Samba', a Mac web browser, was 'kludged together' at CERN, and with the wider availability of browsers, more and more people began to use the web, and many – mostly scientists or academics – began to create web servers of text and graphical information.

But progress in establishing the web as a 'universal' system was still slow. During 1992–1993 more browsers appeared, notably 'Arena' from Hewlett-Packard's Dave Raggett, Tom Bruce's 'Cello', and 'Lynx' from the University of Kansas, but it was the arrival of 'Mosaic' in February 1993 that finally catalyzed the web and thrust it upon the world stage. Mosaic was programmed by a student, Marc Andreeson, and a staff member, Eric Bina, at the National Centre for Supercomputing Applications (NCSA) at Illinois University.

It is important to remember that the WWW at this time wasn't the only information-sharing networking program in circulation on the internet. Other systems included the Wide-Area Information Server (WAIS), designed by Brewster Kahle and later sold to AOL, and Gopher, a menu-based system developed at the University of Minnesota.

The fate of Gopher is instructive. In the early 1990s it had quickly become popular in the internet fraternity as a way of navigating information and data stored on computers linked via the net. It did not involve hypertext, instead offering the user a series of nested menus in order to locate information they wanted. Cleverly, it used the internet protocols of FTP and Telnet (allowing users to log on to a remote computer), but disguised the complexity of the syntax of these protocols under a simple point-and-click menu. But as a commercial system, Gopher was doomed. In March 1993, as the Gopher software was proving so popular, the University of Minnesota decided to start charging a licence fee to commercial users. Tim Berners-Lee describes the result:

'This was an act of treason in the academic community and the internet community. Even if the university never charged anyone a dime, the fact that the school had announced it was reserving the right to charge people for the use of Gopher protocols meant it had crossed the line. To use the technology was too risky.'

Weaving the Web (1999)

Wary of potential litigation issues if they developed products based on Gopher protocols, commercial organizations simply stopped using it. Berners-Lee, anxious to see the worldwide adoption of the web, was acutely aware of the implications, and as early as April 1993 had obtained permission from CERN to put WWW in the public domain. The broader implication – that 'freeware' would come to dominate the web – was reinforced when Marc Andreeson left NCSA, met Jim Clarke (previously CEO of Silicon Graphics Corp, a leading work-station manufacturer), and set up a new company they called Mosaic Communications. (Later, they paid NCSA $3 million in settlement of litigation over the name and basic code for Mosaic and changed their name to Netscape.)

Netscape hired the core of the Mosaic development team and developed a browser, then called Mozilla, which they released onto the web for beta testing in October 1994. This became a common practice. Publishing free software in beta (nearly finished) stage meant that you not only benefited from many hundreds, even thousands, of users testing and commenting on your software but at the same time you were building a market for it, and getting press interest and publicity for your product.

But Netscape went a revolutionary stage further. In December 1994 it released the complete commercial version of its browser – now called Navigator – absolutely free on the web. Of course, all previous web software had been freely published this way, but Netscape was a commercial company, supposedly in business to make money. Where was the business model?

The truth was that the company was faced with the likelihood of massive competition, principally from Microsoft but also from other software developers (many of whom had subsequently licensed Mosaic code from NCSA). So Netscape rightly judged that it would make more money providing network services and developer software than selling consumer browsers. And it stole a march on its competition – Microsoft was completely wrong-footed, belatedly realized its mistake, and licensed some ready-made browser code from Spyglass Inc in order to incorporate this in its upcoming Windows95. So Netscape adopted the only winning strategy, gave away its browser for free, garnered huge publicity doing so, and captured about 75 per cent of the browser market within a few months.

Actually, at first, Navigator was free only for a period of three months, after which users were supposed to pay the licence fee. Instead, however, after three months, users just downloaded the next version of Navigator, which was also free. But Netscape stopped worrying too much about browser software fees when it went public in August 1995. A phenomenal IPO (initial public offering) at the time, the initial share price of $28 – considered too high for a company yet to turn a profit – went to $71 by close of trading, valuing Netscape at $4.4 billion.

As far as the commercial world was concerned, it was the Netscape IPO that marked the moment the web *got real* and became a serious marketplace and an all-important strategic consideration.

realizing the vision But the WWW as constituted in 1995 was still only a partially realized vision. The following are some of the developments we can expect as the World Wide Web Consortium and other designers and programmers try to create a fully realized, 'perfect' networked software system.

symmetrical media When Tim Berners-Lee designed the first WWW software on his Next Cube, it was both a browser *and* an editor. His web was conceived as a two-way or 'symmetrical' medium, and just as Hypercard was both an authoring/design and publishing/presentational medium, the WWW was not intended to be just an alternative publishing medium for established publishers and broadcasters. While there are a few applications that combine both browsing and authoring/editing functions (such as Netscape Communicator, and the W3C's own Amaya), few are as 'consumer-friendly' as dedicated browsers like Navigator and Explorer. OK, so maybe lots of people won't ever want 'symmetrical' media, won't ever want to create as well as to consume, but before the web, who would have said that anybody (apart from Tim and Ted that is) wanted a global interactive hypermedia system? And anyway, there happens to be lots of evidence that people *do* want symmetry.

" THERE HAPPENS TO BE LOTS OF EVIDENCE THAT PEOPLE **DO** WANT SYMMETRY. "

The most widely used services available on the web/net are precisely those that allow person-to-person communications. According to an October 1998 Intelliquest survey of what people are doing online, sending or receiving e-mail accounted for 89 per cent, followed by the gathering of information about a hobby or personal interest. E-mail and instant messaging, chat, consumer opinion sites, knowledge-sharing 'expert' sites, 'affinity' and counselling sites, genealogical sites, and personal homepage publishing are just a few expressions of the desire for two-way tools and 'symmetrical bandwidth'. E-mail is growing exponentially: MessagingOnline reported some 570 million e-mail boxes by the end of 1999 (up 84 per cent on the previous year), and this report predicts that on these growth rates, there will be around 1 billion mail boxes by the end of 2001. This indicates that we are only a couple of years away from the time when there are more e-mail accounts in the world than TV sets. And we haven't really started with multimedia e-mail, family album networks and social video conferencing yet.

How important is this as a development vector? There is already a polarization between the two modes of use, with the big multinational media companies promoting one-way (one-to-many) communication channels based on 20th-century notions of publishing and broadcasting. On the other hand, there is growing evidence (the success of peer-to-peer networking popularized by Napster.com, the growth of e-mail, the rising popularity of open-source software, etc) of the desire for the web/net to remain the 'people's medium'. My own estimate (entirely coloured, I confess, by my own ideological stance) is that 'peopleware' and 'socialware' will be really important growth areas this decade, especially as permanent online connection becomes more widely available, and the most successful networks will be those that provide symmetrical broadband.

ubiquity It is the destiny of WWW to be truly worldwide, a universal medium that offers universal access, regardless of culture, creed, nationality, ethnicity or gender. There are plenty of indicators that all the technical obstacles to universal global access will be overcome within the next few years. The number of global phone/data services offered by cellular and satellite networks alone should see most of the inhabitable world only an access device away.

And that's the rub – it's *technically* not difficult to build a 'people's access device', a solar-, clockwork- or wind-powered portable communications device, with a microprocessor and LCD screen, waterproof keypad, wireless modem or satellite-phone 'dish on a chip', and some EPROM or flashcard solid-state memory. AI experts such as Ray Kurzweil even predict that we will have voice-user interfaces and automatic language translation software during the first half of this decade. By combining all these components in silicon, then mass-producing them as simple 'player' devices without frills, unit costs could be squeezed really low – but someone's got to pay, and it's a substantial investment. This is a worthwhile project for the G7 group of industrialized nations, WTO (World Trade Organization) and World Bank to consider. The benefits? You Bailey-bridge the digital divide, provide Medicare, public health and education services, agriculture, forestry, fisheries and trade information co-operatives, and access to other information, entertainment and expertise, to micro-credit systems, and other alternative trading schemes, and above all, to community communications and the democratic empowerment that it brings.

permanent instant access The web/net is full of contradictions at the moment, and the most bizarre is that we have built a system capable of sending electronic messages and data all around the world in a fraction of a second or so, but most of us have to wait several tens of seconds every time we want to use the web/net while our computer uses a modem to dial into the network. Fortunately, many of the latest developments in internet access: including the proposed 3G mobile networks, and DSL, promise 24/7 access: permanent connection. No waiting. While ideas are fresh in our minds we scribble that note and mail it, or find that statistic or reference we need, videophone the girlfriend, or have the latest football score flash on our screen without delay.

Permanent instant access will radically affect how we use the web/net. It is like the difference between having a casual conversation with a friend, and writing a letter. It will be real time, any time, and it will become a 'natural' thing to do. And don't worry, you will only be paying for the time you're actually transmitting or receiving data, not for every one of the 24 hours a day that you're connected.

the knowledge web At the moment the web/net is a dumb collection of information. Sure, we can use search tools – engines and agents – to find information and services for us, but in the end we, the humans who populate the web/net, are the *only* arbiters of this information. We are the only ones who can interpret all this data, process all this information, and hopefully turn it into knowledge. Unfortunately, all those search engines, web-spiders and crawlers, search agents and the like, really aren't much good at *understanding* what they're searching for. They're getting better, of course, as companies like Autonomy and Broadvision (with their personalization and knowledge-retrieval software) have proved. But in the meantime, the amount of information is growing exponentially. The technology of search engines and agents, no matter how sophisticated, can't really hope to catch up and deal with this information explosion. What's needed is a way of describing and perhaps classifying the information on the web so that machines can read and 'understand' which computers and servers hold which information. And this is the idea behind Tim Berners-Lee's proposal for a 'semantic web'.

'I have a dream for the web, and it has two parts.

'In the first part, the web becomes a much more powerful means for collaboration between people. I have always imagined the information space as something to which everyone has immediate and intuitive access, and not just to browse, but to create ...

'... In the second part of the dream, collaborations extend to computers. Machines become capable of analyzing all the data on the web – the content, links and transactions between people and computers.'

Weaving the Web (1999)

So, not surprisingly, the World Wide Web Consortium* – the organization that Tim Berners-Lee inspired and represents and the closest the web/net has to a governing body – has been working on the file specifications, protocols and mark-up languages necessary to start building this kind of machine intelligence into the web. According to Berners-Lee, the semantic web 'is a plan for achieving a set of connected applications for data on the web in such a way as to form a consistent logical web of data'. Rather than relying on the AI community to develop software that will enable machines to 'think like humans', Berners-Lee proposes that we develop languages for 'expressing information in a machine-processable form'. The general model suggested for the semantic web is the resource description framework (RDF), which is a proposed standard syntax for the use of metadata (data that describes data) in every document (or 'resource') that is posted on the web – ie every uniform resource identifier and uniform resource locator (URL). This use of a standard syntax will mean that searches can be much more efficient, software agents will have much more precise data to work with, and the web will become a massive 'database' rather than just a huge collection of unclassified resources. Just as Peter Senge in *The Fifth Discipline* described the 'learning organization' as one that capitalized on its knowledge resources (human expertise, stored and structured knowledge), so the semantic web might be considered a necessary step in our progress towards a 'learning world'.

*The World Wide Web Consortium is open to any organization or business prepared to commit to a three-year membership at $50,000 a year. Charities and other not-for-profit organizations and smaller businesses pay $5000. This gives them membership of any of the W3C working groups, developing proposals for new WWW standards.

And private enterprise is having a go, too. Napster.com, while in contentious territory trading in information about copyright-protected materials (album and CD tracks), has nevertheless exploited the peer-to-peer structure of the network and created a way through which users can find and copy data files – not from a centralized server, but from any other participating computer user on the network. By signing up with Napster, the user lists the audio tracks he or she has stored on their computer, and from these Napster can create searchable indices for all other subscribers so that vast collections of digitally formatted music tracks – mostly MP3 – can be searched, located somewhere on the web/net, and copied to the user's hard disk or MP3 player. Whether or not Napster is finally closed down by the Recording Industry Association of America (RIAA) is largely beside the point. Napster didn't invent file sharing – the technology for this (FTP) has been around since 1974, and Napster's popularity (more than 2.5 million users) indicates that people really like sharing records in this way. Even if Napster and similar companies are shut down, Gnutella, the open-source file-sharing project, will continue – and because this involves no central database server, there is no 'company' to sue. Apart from the current litigation, the RIAA is proposing an encrypted music file format for the distribution of copyright music called SDMI (Secure Digital Music Initiative), but like other forms of data encryption, there is nearly always a sharp hacker somewhere who can break it – and publish and replicate the crack through the web. Napster, Scour, I-Mesh and similar file-sharing, peer-to-peer systems indicate a direction, not just for the commercial and legal distribution of popular music but for the 'semantic' web itself.

“THE PRINCIPAL IDEA BEHIND THE NETWORK COMPUTER IS THAT **ALL** THE SOFTWARE APPLICATIONS YOU NEED ARE DOWNLOADED WHEN REQUIRED FROM THE WEB/NET”

Increasingly we will find new peer-to-peer relationships, new virtual communities, new affiliate networks and special interest groups building on the kind of standards W3C is proposing for the semantic web.

the network is the computer The other main direction in which the web could evolve is that it may become the primary interface that we experience whenever we use a computer. In this scenario, instead of the web (the whole world of data) being addressable by us through a small window in a graphical user interface dominated by a desktop devoted to internal and local hard disks, the desktop would become the web and the local hard disk just a small part of that network. Several companies, notably Sun Microsystems (whose advertising strapline was 'the network is the computer') and Oracle, have been actively promoting the idea of network computing, and much of the anti-trust case against Microsoft was based on the proposal to integrate its Explorer browser into the Windows 2000 operating system. The principal idea behind the network computer is that *all* the software applications you need are downloaded when required from the web/net. The advantage of this? You always get the latest version, you pay only a rental fee, you don't need vast hard-disk space devoted to applications – indeed you rent server space for any permanent storage you need. My take is that the network computer (in the form of portable access devices or 'media players'/e-books etc) will *really* take off when we have 24/7 connectivity and broadband wireless (3G or beyond).

The implications of businesses operating in a real-time, constantly connected, broadband networked environment are many, and that's want I want to discuss next.

the e-commerce visionaries

The latest generation of network visionaries are those fired by the idea of the net as a marketplace. These visionaries recognized early on that the web/net-as-marketplace may be the logical triumph of consumerism. The fact that productivity growth rates in the US between 1995 and 1999 exceeded that of previous 'golden ages' of the US economy led e-commerce visionaries to believe that the new networked economy was an industrial revolution equal to, or more important than, the second Industrial Revolution of 1860–1900. They argue that in this emerging network economy, many of the old rules of business no longer apply, and that we must learn the new rules that are necessary to understand and to operate within this new economy. Drawing from many computer-based sciences, and from the study of complex systems and ecology, they have constructed elaborate metaphors and theories in order to help us understand what's going on.

The mainstream of this e-commerce vision of the future of the web/net is heavily weighted by the American experience of the success of free markets, and is also infused with West Coast utopian and libertarian ideology. Technological innovation, spurred by information technology and networking, is an increasingly powerful driver of the US economy, and is soon to be further amplified as the new technologies of bio-engineering and nano-engineering reach the stage of productivization. Partly because of the evident success of the American economy, this mainstream vision has been adopted lock, stock and barrel in many other parts of the world, and has become the dominant rationale driving global investment in the web/net.

In many ways it is a grand vision – the web/net encourages the development of 'people power' and 'consumer power'. And by opening up a global market, the web/net encourages global competition, speeding R&D, and ultimately resulting in extended choice and lower prices for all. Heavily promoted by global multinationals, by the World Bank, and by donor nation states, the 'network economy' is posited as a universal panacea and corrective to protectionist and interventionist economic systems, as well as being an antidote to centrist, undemocratic forms of government.

That not everyone subscribes to this e-commerce vision of the future will come as no surprise. It does not further the debate on the future of the web/net to characterize the current discourse as a black and white issue, as 'free markets versus protectionism', but increasingly the network economy is being promoted by evangelists who simply assume that the new global economy will inevitably unfold along American-style free-trade lines, despite the fact that many of the rest of the world's nations practise forms of capitalism that differ significantly from this approach. The debate on the future of the web/net will come to characterize this decade, and more especially since in 2000 the amount of web traffic outside the US for the first time exceeded the internal US traffic. The web is becoming truly global, and will come to reflect global opinion, not just the opinions of advocates of the kind of 'globalization' understood in the US.

This section of the book provides an overview of the e-commerce vision, describes some of the 'network effects' that are affecting business operations, and summarizes some of the objections to this mainstream view.

the network economy as business ecosystem

Business ecosystem. An economic community supported by a foundation of interacting organizations and individuals – the organisms of the business world. This economic community produces goods and services of value to customers, who are themselves members of the ecosystem. The member organisms also include suppliers, lead producers, competitors and other stakeholders. Over time, they co-evolve their capabilities and roles, and tend to align themselves with the directions set by one or more central companies. Those companies holding leadership roles may change over time, but the function of ecosystem leader is valued by the community because it enables members to move toward shared visions to align their investments, and to find mutually supportive roles.

James F. Moore, The Death of Competition

What does visualizing e-business as an 'ecosystem' mean? First of all, it's an interesting metaphor, and helps picture the e-economy as a deeply intertwined and interlinked network, with its mix of competing and co-operating species, each with individual, shared or overlapping food chains, but all together co-habiting and even perhaps co-evolving in the networked economy. From the perspective of an individual organization ('organism') in an ecosystem, the first and most important relationships are kin – in institutional terms, shareholders, workforce, management. Then we spread our concerns to include neighbours and partners – in business to suppliers, distributors, retailers, customers – and other stakeholders in our enterprise. But the 'business ecosystem' vision doesn't stop here – *all* the 'organisms' sharing our ecosystem are important to us in various ways, and this includes our competitors and other individual entrepreneurs and organizations which might *become* competitors in some aspect of our business, and of course all the *potential* customers for new products and services that *we* may be ideally positioned to create. Then there's the 'environment' itself, this collection of technologies that we are calling new media or e-media.

'... a business ecosystem is made up of customers, market intermediaries (including agents and channels, and those who sell complementary products and services), suppliers, and, of course, oneself. These might be thought of as the primary species of the ecosystem. But a business ecosystem also includes the owners and other stakeholders of these primary species, as well as powerful species who may be relevant in a given situation, including government agencies and regulators, and associations and standards bodies representing customers or suppliers. To one extent or another, an ecosystem includes your direct competitors, along with companies that might be able to compete with you or with any other important members of the community.'

James F. Moore, The Death of Competition

And how are we studying this new business ecosystem? The network economy is a phenomenon that has attracted attention from a wide variety of scientific disciplines, many of them not much older than the web/net itself. Social scientists, philosophers, economists, futurists, management consultants, and other observers of the networked economy have been borrowing from the arenas of complexity theory, game theory, artificial intelligence, artificial life, and economics, as well as the social sciences, and even the sadly diminished field of cybernetics to help understand and explain the complexities of the network economy; and even to derive new rules for networked businesses and entrepreneurs, and new manifestos for the rest of us.

The first of these was Kevin Kelly's *New Rules for the New Economy*. Based largely on the analyses in his earlier *Out of Control*, Kelly's 'rules' are his collection of heuristics for operating in the networked economy. These are derived from what Kelly calls 'The Nine Laws of God governing the incubation of something from nothing' – the ultimate chapter in *Out of Control*. Because Kelly builds his ecosystem analogy over 500 pages, his rules are hard to summarize briefly. Check out the originals. Here are a couple of heavily paraphrased examples:

Distribute being: complex systems such as economies are composed of millions of smaller units, whose collective behaviour gives rise to synergies and to 'emergent properties'. In the web/net these synergies and properties emerge from the interaction of the millions of human beings, millions of machines, millions of microprocessors, scanners, sensors, cash registers and other devices that are networked together. Kelly points out that these interactions can have the characteristics of a 'swarm' – temporary agglomerations of small 'units' (individuals, machines, processors) displaying similar behaviour. His advice? 'Find the overlooked small and figure out the best way to have them *embrace the swarm.'*

Control from the bottom up: networks, whether the web/net or an ecosystem, are governed from the bottom. There is no 'top', no centre, no seat of governance. In the internet, it is the routers, switches and data packets themselves that determine the flow of communications, not some central telephone exchange. The strategic advice? In this non-linear, non-hierarchical world, the organizations that are the most nimble, most able to spot potential change and react to it are the most successful, and the earliest warnings of such changes come from the 'edges', from the 'bottom up', from your customers, your workforce, your shareholders. The strategy? *'Let go at the top'* – manage devolution, listen to the edges, encourage distributed decision making, stay flexible, and hedge your bets with alliances, building affiliate networks to grow your business in partnership with others.

Cultivate increasing returns: Bob Metcalfe gave his name to the law that says the value of networks increases as the square of the number of nodes. Actually, the value of the network economy expands in value much more than this. Metcalfe's calculation was based on the number of one-to-one interactions possible as a network grew. But the web/net also allows multi-party 'conversations', narrowcasting (one to a few), and broadcasting (one to many). The lesson here is that the bigger you are, the bigger you'll get, and that the network economy is a 'hits' game for everyone where, like the record and book businesses, you don't try to predict the 'hits' but you manage your business by launching lots of new things.

“THE LESSON HERE IS THAT THE BIGGER YOU ARE, THE BIGGER YOU'LL GET”

Kelly's new rules are derived from basic network principles – the results of the study of complex systems, artificial life, and other new sciences. A more 'human-centric' approach to understanding the network economy is the great collection of 95 theses called the *Cluetrain Manifesto*. The idea of four writers and software designers – Rick Levine, Doc Searle, Chris Locke and David Weinburger – this is a clarion call to business corporations – listen to what's happening! The cluetrain is here right now – make sure you check out the clues! Read the writing on the wall!

'We are not seats or eyeballs or end users or consumers. We are human beings – and our reach exceeds your grasp. Deal with it.'

'Networked markets are beginning to self-organize faster than the companies that have traditionally served them. Thanks to the web, markets are becoming better informed, smarter, and more demanding of qualities missing from most business organizations.'

From the preamble to the online Cluetrain Manifesto at www.cluetrain.com

The *Cluetrain Manifesto* is Kelly's 'edges' talking up. It's the identification of the many qualities that are lacking in 20th-century-style businesses entering the 21st century. As a taster, here are the first ten in their non-Lutherian manifesto of 95 theses.

- Markets are conversations.
- Markets consist of human beings, not demographic sectors.
- Conversations among human beings **sound** human. They are conducted in a human voice.
- Whether delivering information, opinions, perspectives, dissenting arguments or humorous asides, the human voice is typically open, natural, uncontrived.
- People recognize each other as such from the sound of this voice.
- The internet is enabling conversations among human beings that were simply not possible in the era of mass media.
- Hyperlinks subvert hierarchy.
- In both **inter**networked markets and among **intra**networked employees, people are speaking to each other in a powerful new way.
- These networked conversations are enabling powerful new forms of social organization and knowledge exchange to emerge.
- As a result, markets are getting smarter, more informed, more organized. Participation in a networked market changes people fundamentally.

From the online Cluetrain Manifesto at www.cluetrain.com

some big and interesting issues There are several important issues that have emerged as a result of the insights of the Cluetrain team, and Moore, Kelly and others, into networks and business ecosystems. These include those of the property of self-organization, and the phenomena of the 'Mexican wave' or swarming behaviour that emerges as a result of the network-co-ordinated interactions of many individuals. But the issue that is most fundamental, I think, is that of *co-operation*. Networks imply and naturally foster co-operation, and as I have mentioned earlier, the internet was built on the spirit of academic and scientific openness and co-operation. The new entrepreneurial networked economy rests slightly uneasily on the 'peer-to-peer', 'open' foundations laid by the pioneers of this inter-

markets are conversations.
talk is cheap.
silence is fatal
the
cluetrain
manifesto
the end of business as usual
christopher locke rick levine
doc searles david weinberger

Cluetrain is a manifesto addressed to e-business practitioners from 'us' the users and consumers of the new media systems.

network. At its grass roots in the developer community, the 'open source' network thrives, co-operation thrives (user groups, consumer opinion networks, affiliation networks, etc). And there is even talk of a more co-operative strategy for business: 'co-opetition'.

co-operation: the rise and rise of open-source software

In a direct line from the original open standards of IP, TCP, HTTP and the other standardized protocols, operating systems and programming and scripting languages that determined the evolution of the web/net, the open-source software (OSS) movement has in the past few years become a quiet revolution, affecting the entire software industry. According to writer Esther Dyson: 'Open-source is basically software developed by unco-ordinated but collaborating programmers, using freely distributed source code and the communications facilities of the internet.'* (This doesn't mean that open-source products are free. Developers can productivize open-source creations and provide commercial support for them.)

*Esther Dyson 'Release 1.0' 1998 **www.edventure.com / release/1198.html**

Open systems are aggressively non-proprietary. They pose a direct threat to the business models of the big commercial software producers. In a famously leaked 1998 internal memo dubbed 'Halloween' by OSS evangelist Eric S. Raymond* (because the first version was written on October 31 1998), Microsoft engineers and executives discuss the implications of the open-source threat to Microsoft. Here are a few keynote quotes, courtesy of the author, Microsoft's Vinod Valloppillil, and Eric S. Raymond (my emphasised notes):

*Author of the key OSS text 'Musings on Linux and Open Source by an Accidental Revolutionary'.

'OSS (open-source software) presents a direct, short-term revenue and platform threat to Microsoft, particularly in server space. Additionally, the intrinsic parallelism and free idea exchange in OSS has benefits not replicable with our current licensing model and therefore presents a long-term developer mind-share threat.'
In other words, Apache and Linux are a major threat to Microsoft's server software market, and in the longer term, developers are bound to be seduced by the attractions of open-source development.

'Recent case studies (the internet) provide very dramatic evidence ... that commercial quality can be achieved/exceeded by OSS projects.'
Microsoft didn't see the web/net coming and was taken by surprise by the emergence and high quality of free browsers and open-source software and shareware.

'Linux and other OSS advocates are making a progressively more credible argument that OSS software is as least as robust – if not more – than commercial alternatives. The internet provides an ideal, high-visibility showcase for the OSS world ... The ability of the OSS process to collect and harness the collective IQ of thousands of individuals across the internet is simply amazing. More importantly, OSS evangelization scales with the size of the internet much faster than our own evangelization efforts appear to scale.'

Software that has 100,000 developers working on it simultaneously will inevitably be better and more robust than anything a commercial organization could offer. The internet also provides the distribution channels, the medium for user groups, e-mail lists, access to code libraries, mediating bodies as well as the 'showcase' for OSS 'propaganda'. And of course there's the 'viral marketing' idea here too – the web/net is a matrix of people, and people freely exchange opinion and comment with other people. Hyperlinked together, these people can spread good news and bad news really quickly around the planet.

'OSS projects have been able to gain a foothold in many server applications because of the wide utility of highly commoditized, simple protocols. By extending these protocols and developing new protocols, we can deny OSS entry into the market.'

Now comes the tactical response. 'Extending the protocol' was what Microsoft tried to do with Java – adding Windows-specific extensions that would, if adopted, have fragmented the Java developer community. In line with the recommendations in this memo, Microsoft is now developing its own 'standard' to combat Java – C#. But as Eric Raymond points out in his annotations to 'Halloween,' Microsoft seems to miss the point that OSS is not just a 'new' means to produce bug-free, reliable software, it's a much more fundamental threat. Esther Dyson describes it thus: 'It's about competing innovations which live or die in a market of other people deciding to adopt and enhance them, or ignore them. Interestingly this is an information market, unencumbered by prices on the one hand, or by bundling deals and marketing on the other.' (Esther Dyson 'Release 1.0 at www.edventure.com/release1/1198.htm). But it's actually even more fundamental than this – some have observed that it's an alternative to capitalism, a Kropotkin-like communalism or anarcho-syndicalism that is producing better goods than 'traditional' capitalism! Now there's an interesting idea.

Courtesy Eric S. Raymond and Vinod Valloppillil, quoted from 'Halloween-1 Open-source software – a new development methodology' at www.opensources.com/documents/halloween-1/

In open-source software, the source code is freely available. In open-standards architecture, hardware such as the personal computer is assembled to a common specification from a variety of ready-made components available from different suppliers (your PC may have a chip from Intel, from IBM, Cyrix, AMD or other microprocessor fabricators, a hard disk from Seagate, Micropolis, IBM, etc). They utilize widely recognized global standards. *And open standards are what the web/net itself is built upon*. Largely funded by the US government (through the Department of Defense Advanced Research Projects Agency), open-source software was the creative force behind the net. It still is – but now it's created by the largely unfunded efforts of tens of thousands of individuals.

“WITH 7 MILLION USERS, LINUX HAS ALREADY BECOME ONE OF THE TOP THREE OPERATING SYSTEMS FOR SERVERS”

The two most famous open-source contenders at the moment are Linux and Apache, and the prospect is bullish for these open standards, as the quotes from the Microsoft ‘Halloween’ document illustrate. With 7 million users, Linux has already become one of the top three operating systems for servers (with WindowsNT and Solaris) and is ‘portable’ – it is readily ported to new processors (for example, Transmeta's Crusoe processor is cheaper than Intel's chips, and more power-efficient). This freedom to run on alternatives to the ubiquitous Intel processor will mean that new chips will emerge to threaten Intel's virtual monopoly, prices will drop, and developers will be able to readily port their software through the range of access and computing devices. The open-source Apache server software has more than 60 per cent of the web-server software market.

If the essence of open standards thinking is co-operation, then the most appropriate business strategy for all players may be defined as ‘co-opetition’ – companies and organizations co-operate to create new standards, a new market is created, then these companies and organizations compete for market share. All stand to gain from initial co-operation, and indeed should not assume that continuing co-operative endeavours would be less profitable than cut-throat competition.

co-opetition Appropriately enough, the word was coined by the founder of Novell Networks, Ray Noorda (in *Electronic Business Buyer*, December 1993), to describe the mutual benefits of organizations co-operating (on standards, etc) in a competitive, highly networked environment. The theory of co-opetitive business strategy was examined in some detail by Adam Brandenburger of the Harvard Business School and Barry Nalebuff of the Yale School of Management in their 1996 book and is another of those potential benefits of networking that is changing the way we think about corporate strategy.

'Business is co-operation when it comes to creating a pie and competition when it comes to dividing it up. In other words, business is war **and** peace. But it's not Tolstoy – endless cycles of war followed by peace followed by war. It's simultaneously war and peace. As Ray Noorda, founder of the networking software company Novell, explains: "You have to compete and co-operate at the same time." The combination makes for a more dynamic relationship than the words 'competition' and 'co-operation' suggest individually. This is why we've adopted Noorda's word **co-opetition** and made it the title of our book.

'What's the manual for co-opetition? It's not Leadership Secrets of Attila the Hun. Nor is it Leadership Secrets of St. Francis of Assisi. You can compete without having to kill the opposition. If fighting to the death destroys the pie, there'll be nothing left to capture – that's lose-lose. By the same token, you can co-operate without having to ignore your self-interest. After all, it isn't smart to create a pie you can't capture – that's lose-win.

'The goal is to do well for yourself. Sometimes that comes at the expense of others, sometimes not.'

Adam M. Brandenburger and Barry J. Nalebuff, Coopetition

game theories and win-win strategies

Any rationale justifying a more co-operative approach to business cannot avoid the lessons learned by the game theorists during the post-World War Two period. The use of computers and mathematical analysis to study co-operation in populations of self-interested egoists arose from the study of games, and the subsequent game theories*, that were a product of our Cold War fears of nuclear holocaust. The issue then was extremely serious: how to find the political and diplomatic strategy that would best promote co-operation and reduce the risk of conflict.

*Game Theory was first formalized by John von Neumann and Oskar Morgenstern (**Theory of Games and Economic Behaviour**, 1944).

One method of studying how to promote co-operative behaviour is the game known as Prisoner's Dilemma, formulated by mathematician Albert Tucker, which illustrates perfectly the tension between self-interest (what is good for the individual) and co-operation (what is good for everyone). Prisoner's Dilemma is a classic example of a 'non zero-sum' game (in game theory a zero-sum game is simply one whose outcome is that there is a winner and a loser). Non zero-sum games allow for co-operation, for the possibility of a 'win-win' outcome, where no one loses, everyone gains.

The classic prisoner's dilemma (there are many variations, but they address the same kind of dilemma) is as follows. You and Harry Lyme have been arrested by the police and interrogated in separate cells. You can't communicate with each other. You are both told the same thing: If you both confess, you will both get four years in prison. If neither of you confesses, other police evidence will mean you both get two years' imprisonment. If one of you confesses but the other doesn't, the confessor will go free and the other will go to jail for five years.

What's the best strategy for resolving this dilemma? At first glance, the winning strategy appears to be obvious – you should confess and go free, stitching up Harry completely. But of course Harry realizes this and confesses too, so you both end up in jail for four years. However, if you had both co-operated and not confessed, you would each have only two years to serve.

This game is played repeatedly, often against a computer, and the object is for you to figure out Harry's (or the computer's) strategy and use that to minimize your total sentences. Over the years, games theorists have proposed many 'win-win' strategies. Robert Axelrod in his book *The Evolution of Co-operation* describes how he held a competition for the best Prisoner's Dilemma strategy – the strategy that, in repeated iterations of the game, would result in minimum jail sentences for both you and Harry. The winner was a simple strategy called 'tit for tat' – you co-operate on the first move (ie refuse to confess), then on subsequent moves you confess or not (in game theory lingo: co-operate or defect) exactly as Harry did on the previous move. Axelrod went on to develop a mathematical analysis to show how co-operation based on reciprocity (tit for tat) could emerge in a population of egoists (with only a small proportion of natural reciprocators) and furthermore resist the invasion of other strategies.

The results of Axelrod's analysis, co-authored with biologist William Hamilton and applied to biological evolution, were published in the journal *Science* in 1981, and received a prize from the National Association for the Advancement of Science. The tit-for-tat strategy – 'reciprocal altruism' – was hailed by many as a key to our social evolution. Tit for tat seemed to be the best strategy for mutual success in Prisoner's Dilemma – any better strategy has more complicated rules. Tit for tat is the only evolutionarily stable strategy for co-operation within species. Christians would recognize this strategy as the root of the moral guidelines 'Turn the other cheek' and 'Do unto others as you would have them do to you'.

co-operation and competition Tit for tat and other strategies of co-operation that emerge from game theory would seem to be especially relevant in the high-speed networked world where instant communications amplify our every action, and where everything is 'deeply intertwingled'.

But there are many competing strategies in the business ecosystem, just as there are in natural ecosystems. The first rule of playing games is 'watch the other players', because your best game strategy will often depend on the strategies adopted by your competitors (if you're thinking zero-sum) or your co-opetitors (if you're thinking win-win). Co-operation thrives in the network, but competition is amplified too. The fact is that in 1981, 46 companies controlled most of American media. Five years later, this had shrunk by competitive takeover and by merger to only 29 companies, by 1989 to 25, and during the 1990s the process accelerated. By 1997, just seven companies controlled most of what Americans read, watch and listen to. Inevitably, competition is alive and well as the basis of business strategy. There are three generic competitive strategies: 'cost leadership' (aggressive competition on price), 'differentiation' (competing on innovation and value), and 'focus' or 'niche' strategy (focusing on niche markets). But now there's co-opetition too (co-operating to build markets, competing to share them).

“IN 1981, 46 COMPANIES CONTROLLED MOST OF AMERICAN MEDIA. FIVE YEARS LATER, THIS HAD SHRUNK TO ONLY 29 COMPANIES. BY 1997, JUST SEVEN COMPANIES CONTROLLED MOST OF WHAT AMERICANS READ”

The best tactic in a co-opetition strategy is the insight, summarized by Brandenburger and Nalebuff, as 'the importance of focusing on others – of putting yourself in the shoes of other players and trying to play out all the reactions to their actions as far ahead as possible. By adopting this perspective, a company may, for example, discover that its chances for success are greater if it creates a win-win, rather than a win-lose, situation with other players. In other words, companies should consider both co-operative and competitive ways to change the game.'

game theory and co-opetition There are five main elements in game theory: players, added value, rules, tactics and scope.

Players include you, your competitors, your suppliers and your customers, and also 'complementors' – those who create markets, or add value to your product, but don't directly compete with you. Applying only competitive strategies – focusing only on how to eliminate competition – misses the 'network benefit' of increasing your overall benefit to your customer by developing and nurturing complementors.

Sometimes it can be difficult classifying complementors. For example as far as a record label is concerned, is Napster a complementor or a competitor? Sure, Napster is taking business away from you, but isn't it also pioneering ways to reach your customers? Just how could peer-to-peer exchanges be leveraged into your current business model? And in a much more personal sense, do fanzines illicitly using your copyright materials threaten or enhance the business of selling records?

By broadening your vision and strategy formulation to encompass the other players – besides competitors and customers – you are already ahead of the game, thinking win-win and not win-lose.

In *New Rules*, Kevin Kelly describes this understanding of the overall 'value net' in the chapter 'Feed the web first':

'Maximize the value of the network. Feed the web first. Networks are nurtured by making it as easy as possible to participate. The more diverse the players in your network – competitors, customers, associations and critics – the better. Becoming a member should be a breeze. You want to know who your customers are, but you don't want to make it hard for them to get to you (IDs, yes, passwords, no). You want to make it easy for your competitors to join too (all their customers could potentially be yours as well). Be open to the power of network effects: relationships are more powerful than technical quality. Especially beware of the "not invented here" syndrome. The surest sign of a great network player is its willingness to let go of its own standard (especially if it is "superior") and adopt someone else's to leverage the network effect.'

For example, one of the factors in Netscape's early success on the browser market was the number of interorganizational relationships that it fostered in the crucial early years. And this wasn't just in an attempt to gain industrial profile. Yes, the early partners – Sun, Hewlett-Packard, Apple, IBM, Oracle – were the 'everyone but Microsoft' usual suspects (indeed Netscape became a kind of magnet for those organizations worried by Microsoft's dominance in the marketplace), but Netscape signed up co-development, marketing or standards arrangements with many more organizations than did Microsoft in the development of its Explorer counter-attack. Between 1995 and 1997, Netscape announced 139 external agreements, as against Microsoft's 38. The agreements covered technology co-developments (agreements with Netscape plug-in developers, deals with, and acquisitions of, component software developers), marketing and distribution relationships (bundling arrangements, exclusive or optimized content deals, co-branding, etc), and also the participation in standards committees and standards development coalitions. Netscape's 'netcentric' approach – what Kelly calls the 'feed the web' strategy – was developed alongside a radically different approach to marketing commercial software – another netcentric gambit – giving away your software for free. And, by using its network of customers as 'co-developers' – beta-testing new versions 'in public' as it were – Netscape was able to add new features and bring new versions to market very rapidly. During the period 1995–1997, for example, Netscape released 25 beta and finished versions of Navigator – a release of some sort every 3.7 weeks!* This frenzied assault on the market indicated the new network economy paradigms – continual product development and instant distribution. In this and other aspects of its integrated approach to product development, marketing and standards development, Netscape elegantly exploited its understanding of 'network effects', but Microsoft wasn't slow to learn from this.

*These statistics are from the excellent analysis of the 'browser wars' in 'A Tale of Two Browsers' by Raghu Garud, Sanjay Jain and Corey Phelps at **www.stern.nyu.edu/~~regarud/browserchat/strat.html**

Added value is what each player brings to the game, and in the record label example could include all kinds of ways of enhancing network effects, such as free online music samplers, tour guides, 'authorized' fanzines or fanzine networks, merchandise networks, concert and chat web casts as well as special editions and other digitally enhanced products. Or it may mean creating, or catering for, the kind of new personalized music-buying services possible with 'mass-customization' manufacturing processes, and personal profiling matched to catalogue databases.

In game theory, 'rules' are the laws and regulations pertaining to the organization's operation, and the contracts that determine our freedom to manoeuvre in the day-to-day intercourse with suppliers, distributors, developers and other 'friendly' components in our value network. Contractual arrangements we can directly do something about. 'Rules' also include the international standards to which products and services conform. And many of the new standards are created by ad hoc affiliations and cross-industry working parties – they reflect the influence of their creators. In the business ecosystem, standards-creation and regulation bodies are complementors. And if you try to buck the standard, remember what happens to naughty boys. Microsoft is still being sued over its non-standard implementation of Sun's Java in Windows98. As a result, litigation has effectively stopped Microsoft updating its Java Visual J++ developers tools – it has effectively given up on the prospect of competing in the Java development tools market (IBM has now filled this niche). From having a leading product to a non-product in a couple of years is the result of zero-sum thinking in what might have been a 'win-win' situation. Microsoft tried to bend the standards 'rules' in its favour, but wasn't playing the co-opetition game, and in the middle of 2000 it resorted to plan B: rolling out an alternative 'standard' in the shape of its C# (Csharp) development language, which experts say mirrors Java in many respects (though it will only work with Microsoft platforms and it will be easy to convert Java code to C# code, though not the other way around). C# probably means the end of Microsoft developers' support for Java, but there are plenty of Java developers out there, happy to use a (nearly) 'write-once, run anywhere' tool, that already has vast libraries of available support.

In the real-time flux of networked economies, uncertainty is a major factor in strategy formulation. Tactics can be created to influence how other players perceive this uncertainty. For example, there is a marketing technique called FUD, which involves sowing the seeds of 'fear, uncertainty and doubt' about competitive products or services in an uncertain or confused market. FUD is used when a competitor comes up with a better and cheaper product than yours, and the only defence you have is to resort to spoiling tactics such as scare-mongering and malicious-rumour spreading. The web/net is provided with many unofficial and virtually untraceable channels for spreading misinformation, as the 'insider trading' scams and misinformation market hoaxes of mid-2000 demonstrated. Microsoft has famously used FUD tactics to fend off competition in the past, notably in defending its MS-DOS5 operating system against Digital Research's DR-DOS (the rumour was spread that DR-DOS had a problem running Windows). Another tactic alluded to in the 'Halloween' memo quoted from above is that of 'shifting standards' (in the sense of 'shifting units') – that is, actively encouraging the creation of new 'open' standards in order to deliberately confuse the marketplace. As open-source commentator Roger Irwin notes:

'Another aspect of the software industry is that there are many standards-making bodies. Many standards are set by ad hoc industry groups and very often their scope overlaps and they compete for a while before either one group gives up or they merge their common interests. The presence of a "Goliath" (large software corporation) on a standards group gives it instant credibility, and "Goliath" is able to supply many resources, sponsor the group and push it to forge ahead in the face of competition. They can do the same with the competing groups, either directly or via subsidiaries and associates. The net result is a plethora of highly detailed conflicting standards. "Goliath" has the resources to comply with all standards, and make them ever more complicated ("embrace and expand" is the buzzword), whereas "David" must try to select the eventual winner, and even so will struggle to comply with the frequently unnecessary sophistication which also serves to clamp sudden innovation. When the dust settles, only one standard will become "de facto", and many "Davids" will fold because they had not backed this option. The "Davids" who got lucky by being behind the right group will, nonetheless, have their hands tied by the serious constraints of the specification.'

Roger Irwin, 'Management Guide to SS Tactics' at www.geocities.com/SiliconValley/Hills/9267/sstactics.html

Scope covers the boundaries of the game. Of course, in this ever-changing new media ecosystem the 'boundaries' are a lot more flexible and indeterminate than the monopoly board of traditional business. The boundaries need constant evaluation by planners and managers, not only to detect competitive threats from previously unlikely directions, but also to detect or anticipate and create possible co-operative action that could be beneficial for all players. And not only direct competitive threats but competitive opportunities too. Your competitors may be (almost certainly are) prototyping products and services, devising new routes to market, inventing marketing and promotion techniques, in other words performing a net-wide research and development exercise (with built-in user trials to boot) from which you can benefit. Watch the other players! Microsoft quickly 'learned' from observing Netscape's strategems during the nine-month period when it enjoyed market supremacy with its Navigator browser. For example, it decided to give away Explorer to *all* users (Netscape had charged commercial customers between $39 and $79) and it considerably speeded up the production of new versions of Explorer.

“WATCH THE OTHER PLAYERS! MICROSOFT QUICKLY 'LEARNED' FROM OBSERVING NETSCAPE'S STRATEGEMS”

The lessons we can learn from business ecosystems thinking, then, are how to benefit from the 'properties' of networks – the network effects that Kelly, Moore, Cluetrain and others have culled from their observations, and from the cyberneticists, systems thinkers and ecologists who have been developing the 'systemic approach' over the past 50 years.

The lessons are:

Being in touch

- Network, network, network: exploit all the links you can. Live the network: team up for success.
- Watch the other players: and not just the competition, all players.
- Watch the environment: aggregate the forecasters.
- Watch the fringes – the 'edges'; watch the artists and 'far-out' designers; watch the 'taste space' – the fashion and style indicators; watch the prosumers and early adopters.
- Listen to the edges and talk to the edges in your own network.
- Build networks of relationships: technological co-development, and joint ventures, affiliations or partnerships in the creation of common standards, in marketing and distribution, etc.

- Distribute knowledge and access to knowledge throughout your business and stakeholders.
- Maximize the search space in your monitoring of strengths, weaknesses, opportunities and threats.

Customers

- The mass market becomes a market of one – your customer.
- Become one with your customer: talk the same 'language of equals', make a partner of your customer.
- 'Community precedes commerce' – watch the (online) communities, watch the peer-to-peer networks.
- Let the customer help determine your strategy: they know more about their needs than you do.
- In the network economy, listening is a real-time, 24/7 job. How responsive is your organization? Where can you build auto-responsiveness into your operations? How rapidly do you fold customer feedback back into your operations? How 'personal' is your service?

Products

- Watch the waves – prepare for the 'hit product'.
- In a network of equals, what value can you add? Where and how can you add your unique assets, intelligence or knowledge?
- In an instantaneous commercial environment, there is a premium on continuous product development and marketing.
- Use open standards where possible, avoid proprietary systems.
- Scarcity is no longer the only criterion of value.
- The web/net will continue to spread. Everything and everybody will be connected, and 'all nodes in a network are intermediators'.
- Fixed prices will give way to responsive, market-conditioned, real-time pricing of products and services.
- Co-operation with customers and other players opens the possibility of creating bundled services and hybrid product solutions in real time.

Operations

- In an environment of instant price/value comparison, what are you competing on?

- The web/net fosters horizontal integration rather than vertical integration.
- Services will become more important than mere products.
- 'Maximize the opportunities for others' – build openness into your products and services.
- Networks encourage the full integration of the value chain, and the opening of each node in the value chain to other players – suppliers, retailers, distributors ... creating the possibility of new ways to collaborate with partners and customers.
- Share the wealth – reward and retain key employees.
- In a global web/net, just how parochial are you?
- Think 'relentless innovation, brilliant service, genuine helpfulness'.
- Integrate all aspects of your value chain into a 'value web'.
- Plan for the big: we're only five years away from a web/net of 1 billion people.
- All companies are retail companies.
- Nourish core values, subject everything else to continual reappraisal.
- Prepare for the 'free' – a characteristic of the two main drivers of the web/net: microchip production (Moore's Law) and bandwidth provision (Gilder's Law) is that prices per unit are dropping on an asymptotic curve – approaching the free.
- Connect all aspects of your business: incorporate all stakeholders in the monitoring, research and planning operations.
- Investigate every potential action for win-win opportunities.

However, some observers doubt whether these network effects are real or simply metaphorical. For example, David Bennahum, a writer and contributing editor of **Wired**, argues that the idea of Kelly's 'Law of Plenitude' (based on Metcalfe's Law, and the opposite of the traditional supply and demand economics that 'scarcity confers value'), which is the foundation of much of the network effect rationale, spells big trouble for e-businesses:

'In these and other cases, new economy theorists assume that what's good for consumers is good for business. That is a subtle, potentially fatal, error. Free products are indeed good for consumers – but they are rarely good for business. Yet, in effect, freebies (a personal computer, personal finance software, streaming-media client applications) are the premise behind many of today's internet companies. In most cases, scrutiny of the business model reveals the give-away service to be a loss leader, designed to aggregate a large number of people, with the entrepreneur gambling that this audience's value to marketers will offset the financial loss from providing a product below cost.'

David S. Bennahum, 'The Biggest Myth of the New Economy' at www.strategy-business.com/opinion/00102/page1.html

In an article for *www.strategy-business.com* entitled 'The biggest myth of the new economy', Bennahum points out that this business model is nothing new, it is the model which has been used for years by television networks – you give away your products (TV programmes) to viewers for free, then sell your audience to advertisers and marketers. Inferring that Kelly's 'new rules' are good only for the very early stages of the network economy, he points up the logical problem of the 'Law of Generosity' or 'Embrace the Free' argument:

'If everyone is giving away goods at or below cost to gather networks of people, then networks of people may themselves become commodities. Indeed, as such networks proliferate, the value of providing a new network diminishes, while the difficulty of attracting members' attention increases.'

And he argues that as the other 'new rules' are based largely on Metcalfe's network effect, they are all logically suspect:

'Most of the other tenets of the new economy derive from the network effect, and each, in its way, exhibits a similar loopiness, grounded in the use of metaphor, rather than arithmetic, to justify its accuracy. Consider the "Law of Generosity", a.k.a. "follow the free". According to new economy logic, if the value of a network increases in proportion to the number of people using it, then the most valuable things of all will be those that are given away. Plenty of successful high-tech companies give away goods: Microsoft's Internet Explorer web browser, Qualcomm's Eudora e-mail program, Sun's Java language. Their presumption is that only by giving away products can companies build loyalty, and thereafter capture revenue for a premium product or ancillary service.

'But in most cases, the Law of Generosity might better be called the "Rule of Power". Microsoft gave its browser away because its primary goal was to overcome the upstart Netscape Communications Corporation (now part of AOL). Sun Microsystems Inc. created Java and dispensed it gratis to overcome the threat that Microsoft might edge its way from the personal computer market into the workstation market. In both cases, the companies used their existing dominant market position, and their ability to finance loss-making operations, to lock competitors out of their businesses. Rather than resembling new economy thinking, the axiom "follow the free" calls to mind efforts by 19th-century robber barons to dominate the steel, coal, oil and railroad industries. In fact, as US District Court Judge Thomas Penfield Jackson ruled late last year in the Justice Department's case against Microsoft, the Law of Generosity actually goes under another name: antitrust.'

Bennahum is just one of the critics of what Bruce Sterling has described as the 'technophilic-utopian' perspective, which sees the web as the natural evolution of capitalism and the next logical development in democracy. Sterling sees the future of 'cyberspace' being determined by the dynamic between the technophilic-utopians and the capitalist-pragmatarians:

'The future of cyberspace today is in the hands of two rival camps, which might be roughly described as technophilic/utopian and capitalist/pragmatarian. Their philosophies can be summarized as "fast, cheap and out of control" and "planned development of hyper-real estate". To continue the frontier metaphor, the utopians might be compared to squatters, mountain men and trappers – or perhaps hapless tribes of Aborigines. The rival camp, which conceives of itself as "civilization", is in basic control of formal land grants, the legislatures, the army and the rail-roads.

'The fast, cheap and out of control crowd has three advantages: speed, reckless courage, and the ability to scrape by on low budgets, ie to live off the land. Their ability to govern cyberspace over the longer term is almost non-existent; like other technical pioneers, most will be starved-out, bought-out, overpowered by the consequences of their own success, or simply put out to pasture. At the moment, however, they can strongly influence the emergent shape of cyberspace – and therefore the shape of its future bureaucracies – by confronting society with a series of faits accomplis. They therefore resemble the American "filibusters", or the French explorers of Africa, who dragged imperial authority into the wilderness by aggressive, bold, and sometimes illegal explorations. The techno-utopians can jam Adam Smith's "invisible hand" into the cyberspace data glove, and force the market to come to grips with the formerly unthinkable.

'However, the advantages of the capitalist pragmatarians are manifold and vast. They control the purse strings, and the levers of power that confer social legitimacy on business, governmental and scientific enterprises. "Cyberspace" offers a window of opportunity for radical technical change, but the window will not remain open indefinitely. It will be carefully shuttered, lest chill winds disturb the paying customers.'

The Future of Cyberspace: Wild Frontier v. Hyper-real estate'

But some Europeans (and Americans!), from both left and right, take a different view, and consider both of Sterling's 'camps' to be part and parcel of a single hybrid ideology emerging from the West Coast of the US. Andy Cameron and Richard Barbrook, in a famous critique of Kelly published in 1996, dubbed this 'the California Ideology'.

'With McLuhan as its patron saint, the Californian Ideology has emerged from an unexpected collision of right-wing neo-liberalism, counter-culture radicalism and technological determinism – a hybrid ideology with all its ambiguities and contradictions intact. These contradictions are most pronounced in the opposing visions of the future which it holds simultaneously. On the one side, the anti-corporate purity of the New Left has been preserved by the advocates of the "virtual community". According to their guru, Howard Rheingold, the values of the counter-culture baby boomers will continue to shape the development of new information technologies. Community activists will increasingly use hypermedia to replace corporate capitalism and big government with a hi-tech "gift economy" in which information is freely exchanged between participants. In Rheingold's view, the "virtual class" is still in the forefront of the battle for social change. Despite the frenzied commercial and political involvement in building the"information superhighway", direct democracy within the electronic agora will inevitably triumph over its corporate and bureaucratic enemies.

'On the other hand, other West Coast ideologues have embraced the laissez-faire ideology of their erstwhile conservative enemy. For example, **Wired** – the monthly bible of the virtual class – has uncritically reproduced the views of Newt Gingrich, the extreme-right Republican leader of the House of Representatives and the Tofflers, who are his close advisers. Ignoring their policies for welfare cutbacks, the magazine is instead mesmerized by their enthusiasm for the libertarian possibilities offered by the new information technologies. Gingrich and the Tofflers claim that the convergence of media, computing and telecommunications will not create an electronic agora, but will instead lead to the apotheosis of the market – an electronic exchange within which everybody can become a free trader.'

Richard Barbrook and Andy Cameron, 'The California Ideology' from Very Cyber, May 1996, available online at the Hypermedia Research Centre website www.wmin.ac.uk/media/HRC/ci/calif6.html

Other critics of Kelly and the California Ideology include Steve Best and Douglas Kellner*. But David S. Bennahum is the most ascerbic. In 'The Myth of Digital Nirvana', he disparages it so:

*Steve Best and Douglas Kellner, 'Kevin Kelly's Complexity Theory: The Politics and Ideology of Self-Organizing Systems' at **www.uta.edu/huma/illuminations/best7.htm** (Best and Kellner are authors of **Postmodern Theory: Critical Interrogations,** Guilford Press, 1991).

'The fusion of psychedelic '60s philosophy with information theory – where once peyote was a catalyst to insight, now the computer held that title – laid the foundation for today's vision of the net as nirvana.'

Kelly's critics take him to task for the use of inappropriate and misleading analogies between biological systems and economic systems, for technological determinism, and for the misappropriation of the facts of computer history. Unfortunately, all Cameron and Barbrook could come up with as an alternative to the (mainstream) California Ideology was a return to the kind of mixed-economy, state interventionism typified by the French 'Minitel' experiment. But not suggesting an alternative doesn't mean that their criticisms are in any way invalid.

So, you should be aware that considerable debate surrounds the idea of the business ecosystem. It is grounded in the contentious California Ideology which itself is driving many of the developments in new media, but it is not gospel. *Caveat emptor!*

'We are now engaged in a grand scheme to augment, amplify, enhance, embrace and extend the relationships and communications between all beings and all objects. That is why the network economy is a big deal.'

Kevin Kelly

So, despite the starry-eyed fundamentalism of the California Ideology, and the commercial and ideological scepticism of its detractors, there is the startling *fact* of the web/net. This great network wasn't ever intended to become a giant e-commerce machine that carries the values of the laissez-faire free market and democracy around the globe, bringing wealth and freedom in its wake. Sure, if you believe the California ideologists, it may do just that. But this was never an explicit or implicit goal of *any* of the pioneers of the net. Indeed, commercial activities on the internet were prohibited under the National Science Foundation's 'Acceptable Use Policy' until 1992, and NSF still restricts commercial users from their NSFNET-backbone infrastructure. The NSF policy states that the purpose of the NSFNET backbone is 'to support open research and education in and among US research and instructional institutions, plus research arms for non-profit firms when engaged in open scholarly communication and research'.

The analysis of network effects and the subsequent creation of new rules and manifestos as guides to e-commerce business operations has created many important insights into the nature of transactions in a high-speed, global communications network. In the application of these 'rules', however, managers should apply a healthy dose of scepticism and common sense – the 'new rules' don't amount to a new theory of economics, and 'follow the free' doesn't suddenly mean that profit-making activities are any less important than they are in 'traditional' business.

“IN THE APPLICATION OF THESE RULES, MANAGERS SHOULD APPLY A HEALTHY DOSE OF SCEPTICISM”

a marketplace of ideas In the broader perspective, it may be that e-commerce is just *part* of the growth cycle of the web/net. The true potential of the web/net may be closer to the ideals of the early network pioneers than the dot com entrepreneurs.

The web/net can be considered a rather belated constituent of Roosevelt's 'New Deal' – a largely federally funded enterprise intended for the good of all, leveraging tax-payers' dollars to create a shared educational and scientific resource that is currently the focus of an attempted hijack by those who want to see it solely developed as a giant marketplace – a global shop window for global media and consumer-goods retailers. Or it can be considered as a stage in the 'natural' evolution of capitalism – in an age of consumerism, devolving power into the hands of the consumer, much as

Western democracies gradually extended the franchise. Or it could be considered a logical evolution of evolution itself – in humankind's evolution into a planetary animal. In the 1930s, H.G. Wells described the potential of mankind globally pooling its intellectual capital as indicating the possibility of a 'world brain'.

the vision of the value web But wanna-be world brain or not, the web/net is in a phase of extremely rapid expansion, fuelled by the vision of a seamless cybernetic matrix of production, distribution, marketing and consumption – a new 'value web' in which entertainment, information, goods and services are intermingled with increasingly better-defined niche markets, increasingly detailed knowledge of individual consumers, and increasingly better ways of correlating and catering for the experiences and desires of disparate individuals. Such a web would also encompass the opinions of other users, the perspectives of user groups and consumer-protection organizations, the informal chat space of online communities, and increasingly, the means of staying in touch audio-visually with our friends, family and colleagues, wherever they are. This new value web blurs entertainment, information, education and advertising into seamless edutainments, infotainments and advertainments, where in one online experience the user may be interactor, researcher, bill-payer, browser, reader, conversationalist, player, viewer, listener, shopper and buyer at different stages of the session. In this techno-optimistic view of the future, we are gradually aggregating *all* of the following in the web/net:

- **all** the information we have acquired over the millennia;
- **all** the wisdom and knowledge that has been distilled and stored in museums, galleries, books, encyclopedias;
- **all** the expertise and knowledge of all the humans on the planet;
- **all** the courses at **all** schools, colleges and universities;
- the means for **all** people to communicate with each other – **all** the telecommunications services, from newsgroups and bulletin boards to voice, fax, e-mail, videophone, multi-user video conference, virtual worlds and chat zones;

- the means for **all** people to access information, of virtually whatever kind they want;
- **all** the services we need to conduct our lives: banking, trading, auctions, financial services, real estate and travel agencies, booking agencies;
- access to **all** the products created by **all** the people **all** over the world;
- **all** the varieties of digital entertainment: movies, television, video games, books, magazines;
- the tools for the creation and distribution of **all** digital media, available to **all** people;
- **all** the news, by means of radio, television, newspapers, web casts, e-mail, messaging, etc, in the form of 24-hour newscasts, daily news, weeklies, digests, documentaries and current affairs commentary;
- the tools for the creation and distribution of news and comment, available to **all** people, everywhere;
- virtual social spaces in which **all** people can gather, chat, discuss and debate the issues that affect them;
- the machinery for electronic referenda to allow **all** people to make their voice heard in increasingly efficient digital democracies.

This is an amazing package. But it's very important to remember that *we are only just beginning* to explore this vision of the web/net.

We have begun to develop our big picture of what's going on with a look at the visions and inspirations of the web/net and computing pioneers, but next I want to explore another view of new media: the result of the convergence of television, computing and telecommunications.

6 the big picture: convergence

SO, STARTING FROM THE TOP – THE BIRD'S-EYE VIEW – let's begin with 'convergence', that over-used word that helps describe what is happening right now. Just as now, the idea of 'convergence' was the central theme driving many of the developments in telecommunications in the late 1970s and 1980s, and during that period several writers analyzed the various routes towards the broadband network.* But those otherwise excellent overviews often used very technical diagrams to describe convergence.

*For example, see **World Communications: new horizons, new power, new hope,** edited and published by Gaston Lionel Franco, 1983; **The Wired Society** by James Martin, Prentice Hall, 1978; and **The Micro Revolution** by Peter Laurie, Futura, 1980.

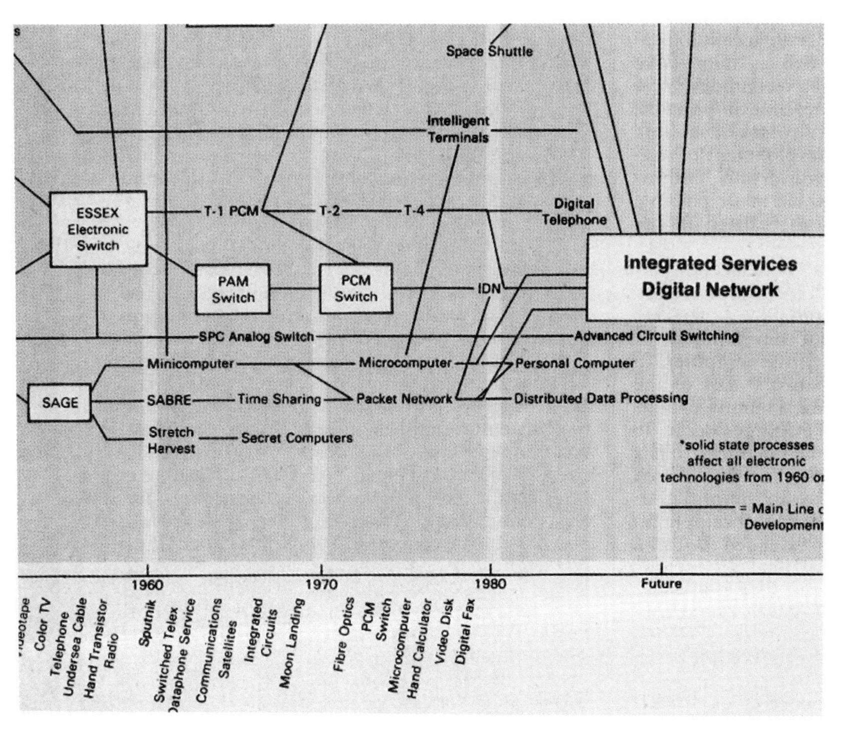

This is the map of the future as perceived in the early 1980s. It is the 'vision' that most of the large telecoms companies subscribed to, and describes the various

routes towards the convergence of media, computing and telecommunications, here represented as the 'integrated services digital network' or ISDN route. Towards the end of the 1980s and early 1990s we started to use the term 'information superhighway' to describe a similar route to convergence. Then the web happened. Detail from diagram by F.H.K. Henion from World Communications: New Horizons, New Power, New Hope, edited and published by Gaston Lionel Franco (1983).

So, let us start with a much simpler picture: the diagram designed in the late 1970s by Nicholas Negroponte, Director of the MIT Media Lab.

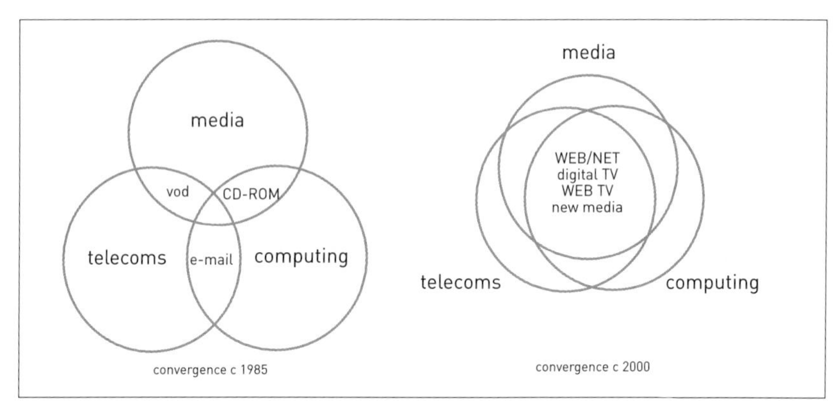

This is my version of a diagram that was designed by Nicholas Negroponte to illustrate the kind of territory in which the Media Lab would operate in the 1980s. Stewart Brand reproduced this in 'The Media Lab: Inventing the Future at MIT' (1987). It shows Negroponte's very early understanding that the new media world is created by the convergence of three main industries: the media industry (publishing in all its aspects, broadcasting, advertising); the computer industry, and the telecommunications industry (you could roll consumers electronics into this diagram too, but it is more or less an offshoot of 'computing' nowadays, and anyway, it spoils the neatness of the Venn overlaps).

convergence in the digital domain So why are all these major infrastructural sectors converging? The answer is simple: digitalization. From the early 1970s, the microprocessor became not only the central component in computers but the basis of telecommunications switching mechanisms too. The microprocessor also became the central driver of the burgeoning consumer electronics industry. And remember that by the early

1980s we had already gone through the first boom in computer 'video' games – games that ran on cheap computers, consoles and arcade slot machines. The computer was spawning brand-new 'media' almost as soon as it was invented (first microprocessor: Intel 4004, 1971, first video game: Pong, 1972, first PC flight simulator: 1980, virtual reality, 1981).

> BY THE EARLY 1980S WE HAD ALREADY GONE THROUGH THE FIRST BOOM IN COMPUTER 'VIDEO' GAMES

The digitalization of the telephone network started about the same time (first digital switch, 1976); and in the banking sector, money was already largely a digital commodity (first ATMs (automated teller machines) introduced in the 1960s).

The effect of the computer on the media business wasn't really obvious until the 1980s. Its impact came in two overlapping waves: the digitalization of production (c.1980–1992), and the digitalization of delivery (c.1985–now). And with the concomitant gradual redesign and retooling of the traditional media-production technologies, by the mid-1980s it was obvious that eventually all media would be subsumed into the digital world. The first medium to succumb was the first mass medium: print.

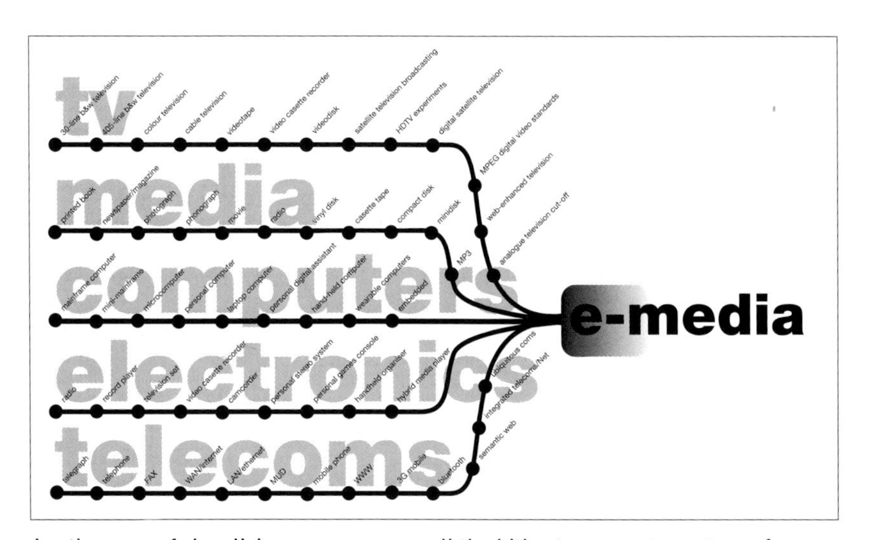

Another way of visualizing convergence: all the hitherto separate vectors of development in television and other media, computers, consumer electronics and telecommunications crunched together as all these sectors entered the digital domain over the last 20 years.

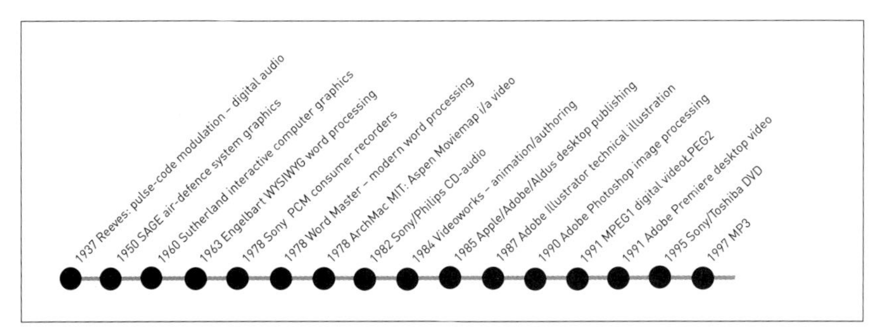

During the past 30 years, all the media we are most familiar with were subsumed into the digital domain of the computer. All 'content' became 'software', and therefore 'interactive'. And not only the dominant 20th-century media, television – but all other 'mass' media too. 'Convergence' applies to everything touched by the microprocessor.

digitalization of print Starting with the basic units of print production – the type fonts that had previously been cast in metal – computer scientists, engineers and typographic designers worked together to design and build much better tools for designing and setting type, building typesetting tools that were keyboard operated and directly produced camera-ready artwork. By the early 1980s, these typesetting tools had been integrated into 'page composition' software, and by 1985, these tools had been made available to ordinary consumers as desktop publishing (DTP) systems. The first of these was Apple Computer's system, a Mac computer with high-resolution screen, Aldus Pagemaker page composition software, Postscript – the code that translated bitmapped screen images into high resolution printed output – and the laser printer that could output to a (then phenomenal) resolution of 300 dots per inch.

During the 1980s I was teaching graphic design at a London college, and DTP made an enormous impact. Using software and the user-friendly Apple Macintosh computer, for the first time designers (at a reasonable price) could see what their design would look like without having to resort to reprographic photography or printing page proofs with a conventional press. With the magic of Postscript (developed by John Warnock at Xerox PARC, and brought to market by his company Adobe), designers could develop their design interactively on screen, then click the mouse and get a laser-printed page proof. This methodology accelerated the traditional design process literally by days, liberating the designer from the tyranny of the conventional design and visualization process.

Despite the early technical and expressive restrictions of DTP, it was obvious from day one that this new digital technology was going to transform the design and reprographic business. There were several reasons for this: by putting powerful typesetting and layout tools directly in the hands of the designer, at one stroke savings were made on expensive services such as typesetting, reprographic processes and image scanning; by collapsing the design process, DTP systems allowed designers to speed up the concept-to-print lead-time, or alternatively use the time saved to explore other design solutions, and at last the 'uncertainty' was taken out of the design process – designers took direct control of the means of production.

It wasn't just the print process that was accelerated by computers. One of the earliest commercial applications of computer imaging and graphic design software was in the production of artwork for 35mm slides, the

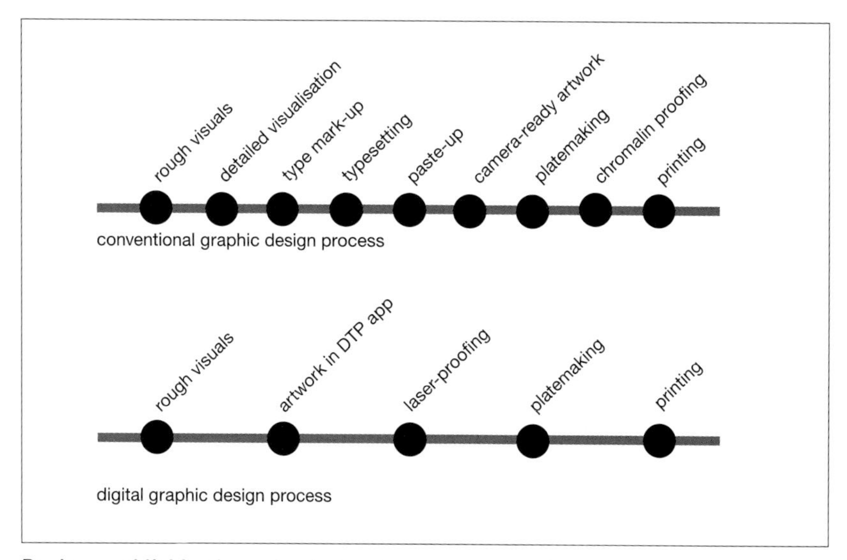

Desktop publishing brought electronic typesetting and page composition tools within the budget of most graphic designers. DTP provided the designer with two main benefits: intimate control over the design process, and much shorter production times. Within a decade, digital graphic design had become the norm.

primary components of audio-visual displays. Artwork could be prepared on screen, then output to 35mm film through a specially adapted camera, or by photographing the monitor screen directly.

from 2D to 3D Printing (design for print) was just the first in a stream of media that was sucked into the digital domain during the 1980s. By the end of the decade, technical drawing (drafting and engineering drawing) was digital, and from 2D drawn elevations, software such as AutoCAD could construct three-dimensional visualizations of the object you were designing. Architects, product designers, interior designers, exhibition designers and others were quick to realize that, using just one set of tools, you could provide both technical plans *and* superb computer-modelled visualizations – you could see what your new chair, building or car would look like before it was made. You could simulate its use, view it from every angle, and finely tune your material requirements and construction methods, all from your digital drawing board. The advantages were obvious: the design process was faster; plans and drawings could be output directly to laser-cutting jigs; the CAD (computer-aided design) software was like a spreadsheet that could calculate materials requirements for the object being planned. The idea of 'rapid prototyping', combined with 3D simulation, enabled architects and other designers to build elaborate, highly realistic, three-dimensional models of their projected designs in the virtual space of the computer, and then let their clients 'walk through' these models, literally 'feeling' the space, well before the physical building took shape in the real world.

from 3D to animation Of course, the new art of computer graphics animation used the same kind of software, but here, instead of concerning themselves with the engineering principles necessary in CAD, computer scientists and artists concentrated on achieving visual sequences that closely simulated reality. Computer graphics imaging (CGI) was a global effort – key algorithms (bits of code that could produce different visual effects, such as smooth-shading of contours, or textural effects for different materials, or aerial perspective) were developed in the US, Japan and

Europe, and these algorithms would gradually be programmed together to create integrated tools for the creation of hyper-realistic, three-dimensional, moving imagery. By the mid-1980s, companies such as Evans & Sutherland and Rediffusion Simulation were manufacturing sophisticated flight simulators for the training of military and commercial pilots – simulators with computer graphic visualizations so real that they easily suspended the disbelief of trainee pilots.

CGI was a great tool (and toy!) for film-makers and animators, providing them with total control over the entire *mise en scène* – the sets, locations, atmospherics and lighting that are features of an animated film – and with control over virtual cameras that could provide previously unheard of flexibility: in lensing (for example a seamless zoom from ultra-wide angle 18mm lens to extreme telephoto 5000mm lens); in camera movement; indeed in every aspect of the film, which was now controllable right down to each one of the million or so individual pixels (picture elements) that comprised the digital image. From the earliest use of computers in feature film animation (Disney's *Tron*, 1982), to the fabulous computer-generated effects of *Terminator2* (1991) and the almost wholly digital production of *Star Wars Episode 1 – the Phantom Menace* (1999), film-makers kept all of us abreast with the latest developments in digital film production in the most entertaining way imaginable.

“DIGITAL AUDIO SIGNALS COULD BE COPIED AND EDITED ENDLESSLY WITH NONE OF THE LOSS OF QUALITY EXPERIENCED IN ANALOGUE COPYING”

On the consumer desktop, as each new generation of microprocessor provided more power to deliver the millions of calculations necessary for 3D animation, and as 3D computer graphic imaging software applications gradually made previously high-end animation tools available at prices even students could afford, these tools permeated down to the 'ordinary' consumer.

sound and video The audio compact disk was launched in 1983, utilizing a digital sound technique called Pulse-Code Modulation (PCM), and together they created a demand for a range of audio recording and processing tools that output in this digital format (copying and re-copying are an essential part of the sound-mixing and editing process, and digital audio signals could be copied and edited endlessly with none of the loss of quality experienced in analogue copying). At the top end of these tools were the expensive, dedicated machines (computers dedicated to a specific function) such as the

Fairlight Composer, while a little later these tools arrived at the desktop with applications like SoundEdit, a program for digitizing and manipulating and editing sound on the Mac, available for less than $100.

Later in the decade, desktop software tools for digitizing and editing video became available, competing with expensive dedicated hardware and software systems such as the Quantel Paintbox.

By the early 1990s, designers and producers had access to a complete suite of media-creation and processing tools and, using one general-purpose com-

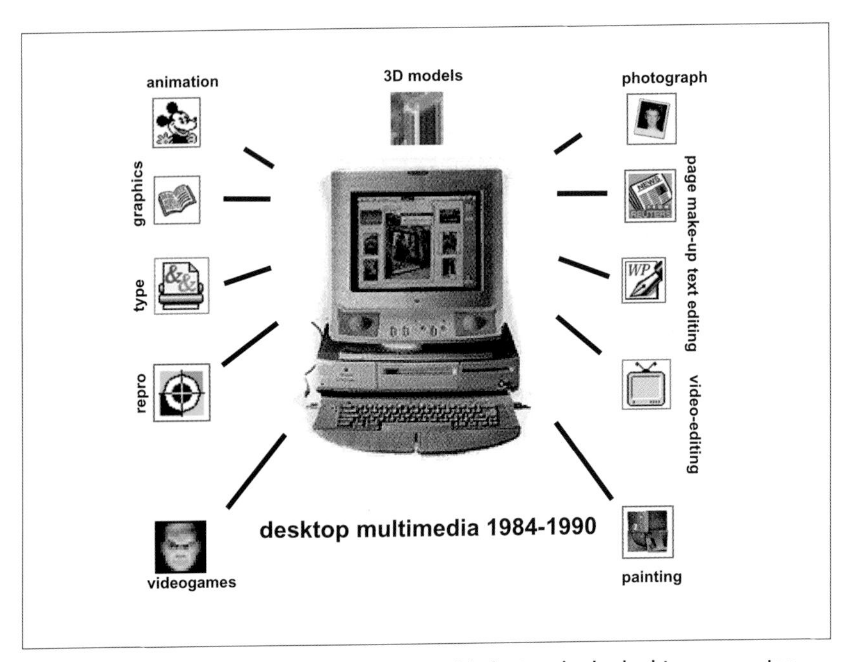

By the early 1990s, an artist or designer could sit at a single desktop computer and manipulate the entire spectrum of media. Different software applications made the PC into a dark-room, a drawing board, a painter's studio, a video-editing suite, a sound-mixing desk, an animation rostrum, a three-dimensional construction kit, an engineer's drafting table, a typewriter and graphic design studio, instantly. Designers began to explore the multiple use of these media, choosing the most effective means of communicating ideas for particular audiences, and creating works that gave the user a choice of how information should be presented.

puter (a PC or a Mac) could create really 'multimedia' programs: programs that integrated video, computer animation, digital audio and digital graphics. Also at this time, the first compression formats for broadcast-quality digital television appeared (the MPEG codecs – compression-decompression algorithms). The digital media spectrum was complete – sound, television and video, animation, graphics, audio-visuals.

What did this mean? It meant that on a single computer, all these different media could be edited, processed, mixed together and output to videotape, CD-ROM, or to digital data projectors. These media had 'converged' in the digital domain of the computer. And designers were quick to appreciate the power of such convergence: books that talk, illustrations that move, comics that animate, diagrams and maps that show pictures and video, photographs with sound effects. For the first time ever, the designer's palette included all the familiar media of communication, and added the possibility of entirely new ways of telling 'stories' through the medium of the computer (see 'The big picture: the media matrix').

delivering convergence

first of all: disks

'All' that remained, then, was to develop consumer-friendly digital channels that could deliver these new multimedia products to mass audiences. And to some extent, this is where we still are. The history of the past 20 years has been punctuated by attempts to create a consumer-friendly mass-market multimedia device. The first was the CD-ROM (invented in 1985), a spin-off from the digital audio compact disk. This could store well over half a gigabyte of digital data but initially could deliver it fast enough only to support very small, cigarette card-size video frames. So it was very much a medium for computer users, not a mass market in the mid-1980s. Early CD-ROM publishers were constrained by the limited number of people who had CD-ROM drives in their computers.

In order to get round the data-delivery speed limit and make the CD-ROM a video carrier, several workarounds of the technology were tried during the

Voyager pioneered digitally 'enhanced' media – first on laserdisc, then on CD-ROM and floppy disk. The delightful Dazzeloids CD-ROM by Rodney Alan Greenblat extended the medium of children's illustrated books to include animation, sound effects, reading tutorials and interactivity. Other Voyager products included enhanced movies (such as Dick Lester's 'Hard Days Night'), non-fiction 'expanded books' by the likes of Marvin Minsky and Martin Gardner, fiction titles by William Gibson and others, and enhanced adult graphic novels like the brilliant The Complete Maus by Art Spiegelman. Image courtesy and copyright 1994 Rodney Alan Greenblat.

late 1980s, including Philips' CD-i and Intel's DV-i. These were technological cul-de-sacs, but consumer electronics manufacturers such as Philips and Sony learned a lot about how *not* to sell the new digital media. CD-ROM gradually became ubiquitous, but the irony was that publishers who had made large losses trying to sell CD-ROM multimedia programs before there was a critical-mass market now ignored it as a medium, and it became largely a way of distributing computer application software. An exception to this was the 'enhanced CD', the inclusion of a multimedia section on an otherwise standard music CD. Users could buy the latest Spice Girls CD and get the video, some stills, an interview and the song lyrics in the multimedia section by playing the CD in their computer CD-ROM drive.

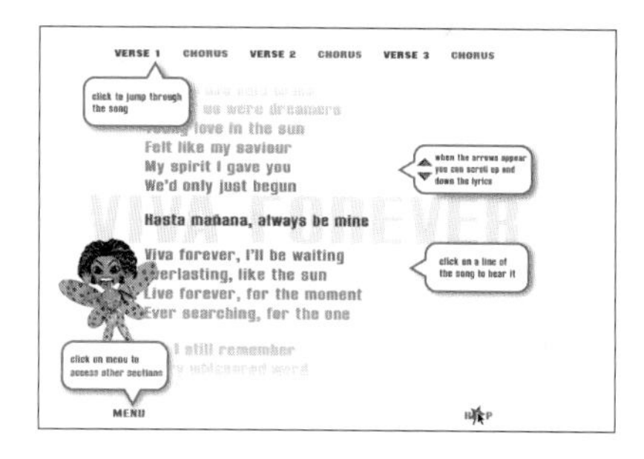

From the mid-1990s, AMX Studios pioneered the design and development of 'enhanced CDs' – ordinary audio CDs with an additional multimedia track that could be accessed in a CD-ROM drive. Typically, multimedia components included a promotional video, scrolling lyrics, a photo album, biographies and discographies, and interviews with the artists – all within a format that extended the idea of the 'album sleeve' into the digital domain. Screenshots courtesy of Malcom Garrett, AMX Studios.

But the first disk media to really work as a multimedia carrier was DVD (digital versatile/video disk), introduced through 1994–1998. DVD works because it is a familiar compact disk format, it is random access, twice the resolution of VHS (near broadcast quality, MPEG2), stores lots of data – enough for entire feature movies – has great CD-quality sound, and works in a variety of players, drives and portables. It is also available in DVD-ROM and DVD-R (data storage and recordable options), so it looks set to be possibly the last disk-based medium to reach a mass market (if networks don't become ubiquitous, the next disk-style media may be solid-state). By 2000, DVD drives were becoming a common feature in PCs and games consoles, much as CD-ROMs had become a standard feature of PCs and laptops in the mid-1990s.

solid-state In 1997, NEC (Nippon Electronics Corp) announced it was working on a 1-gigabyte RAM chip. It called it the 'solid-state disk' as it offered about 30 per cent more storage than a CD-ROM – an amazing 1000 megabytes of memory in a chip! Whether solid-state memory can ever compete on price with easily replicated disks is of course a moot point. The material and construction cost of a RAM* chip or an EPROM is currently much higher than the few pence for bulk disk replication, but solid-state technology removes the need for disk drives or moving parts, providing an ideal rewritable, judder-proof mobile storage device and wiping out the additional cost of disk drives at the same time. This kind of storage is proving really popular in laptops and handheld computers, as well all kinds of consumer electronic devices, especially digital cameras and MP3 players. And it will no doubt be the storage medium of choice for the coming downloadable e-books, e-magazines and e-newspapers.

*RAM is random-access memory – memory that can be written to and erased from repeatedly. ROM is read-only memory – it can be written to once only, after which it is 'read-only'. EPROM is eraseable, programmable ROM – it can be written to many times and read from many times.

Known generically as Flash Memory, and marketed in several different formats such as CompactFlash, DataFlash, SmartMedia and Sony's Memory Stick, such solid-state devices in 2000 could store up to a significant 160Mb of data and are becoming the principal means of storing digital photographs, MP3 files, e-books and other digital media in portable consumer electronics gadgets. The great advantage that Flash Memory has over mechanical devices such as floppy disks and miniature hard disks is that it uses much less power, is shock-proof, and it can also be 'hot-swapped' (memory cards can be changed without powering down the device) without loss of data. A disadvantage is that memory rewrite/erase cycles are limited to around 1 million operations (no problem, unless you plan to download more than 500 tracks a day for the next 50 years).

An ideal, easy-to-use, relatively low-cost and convenient personal memory medium, Flash Memory is the enabling technology behind the new generation of portable media players, such as the Rio player, Sanyo's Fisher and Philips' Rush MP3 players, which can be linked to PCs in order to download digital music MP3 files available from thousands of websites. And these MP3 player devices aren't just appearing in the Walkman-style personal stereo system boxes popularized by Sony, they are becoming 'wearables' too – like the Sharp Portable Memory Player, which integrates player and earphones in an innovative wearable device. Casio has introduced its 'Wrist Audio Player' too, storing up to 33 minutes of music in a 32Mb memory card, as well as being a fully functional wristwatch and stopwatch.

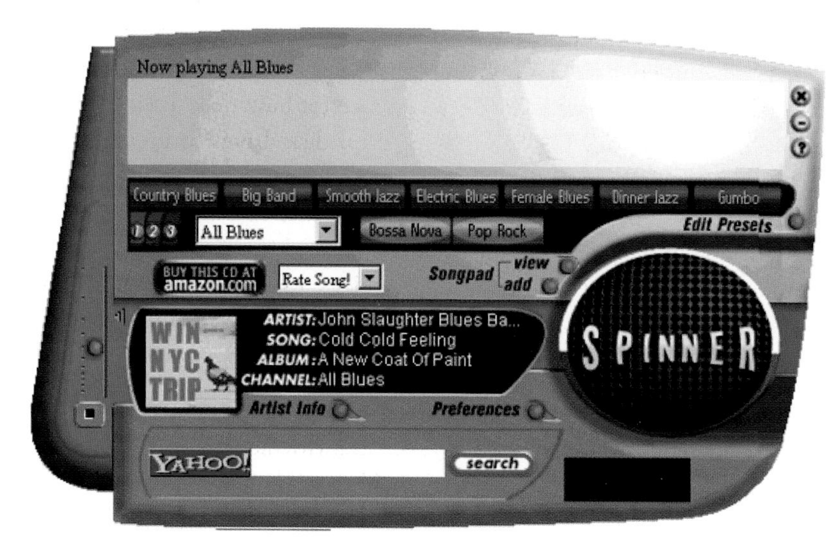

MP3 music files can be copied to solid-state portable players or played directly on the PC by means of 'jukebox' software such as that created by Spinner. Over 1400 music tracks are available to store and play on this 'net-radio' application, which also lets you tune in to BBC World Service, CNN Radio and many more internet radio stations. Download from www.spinner.com. Image courtesy of spinner.com

Samsung's Photo-Yepp is the first multimedia MP3 player I have seen, and points towards the future of such media players. Able to download and store images and text (lyrics) as well as MP3 tracks, and offering 120 minutes of voice recording too, Photo-Yepp is a harbinger of the kind of hybrid media players we can expect to emerge during this decade. With increasingly capacious Flash Memory storage, and larger LCD (liquid crystal display) screens, such devices could become really 'personal' multimedia players cum web/net access devices: downloading, storing and displaying videos, music and electronic books, as well as magazines, newspapers and other media.

wire But the big breakthrough in multimedia delivery systems came not from disk or solid-state media but from a completely unexpected source – let this stand as a warning to all futurologists! – the internet. Or more precisely the world wide web (referred to as the web/net in this book). What happened here is very instructive. All the experts (including Bill Gates – and me!) were listening to the big telcos with their predictions that eventually mass broadband delivery would materialize via their integrated services digital networks (ISDN), or through a combination of fibre and ISDN, or cable and satellite – the implication being that if we waited long enough, someday they might get round to constructing these networks.

Until the web appeared in the early 1990s, the internet was still pretty much the domain of the 'techie' – it was a command line-driven, text-only network. None of the big corporations, peering ahead to the 'superhighway', were looking at the internet. They were full of talk about 'fibre to the door' and 'fibre-coax hybrids' and other big infrastructural developments. Meanwhile, a young British scientist working at CERN in Switzerland created a program and protocol that would enable him and his scientist buddies to easily swap multiple-media documents with each other. He called it the world wide web, and distributed the source code freely on the internet. The important lesson here is that in new media, big things are often invented by someone who just wants to solve a local problem. Berners-Lee and the WWW. Pierre Omidyar and e.bay. David Filo and Jerry Yang and Yahoo!, Jeff Bezos and Amazon, Linus Torvalds and Linux, the list is extensive. All these are examples of how networks foster bottom-up creativity. The Melissa and

“NONE OF THE BIG CORPORATIONS, PEERING AHEAD TO THE 'SUPERHIGHWAY', WERE LOOKING AT THE INTERNET”

Love-bug self-replicating computer viruses are examples of the same bottom-up approach – the dark side of the same network coin.

The web, and the HTML 'viewers' that were built for it – the graphical browsers such as Mosaic and Navigator – provided the means to carry all kinds of multimedia data – video, audio, graphics, photographs, animations, even radio!

One main vector into the future sees the web becoming a broadband medium, and there are several ways this might happen – see Chapter 7, 'Bandwidth'. Proponents of this possible future see the broadband web as the best of all possible worlds – the net as we know it but broadband, offering 24-hour continuous connection, a truly symmetrical 'publishing' system, as much data as you want, no wait times, the web subsuming all other media so it becomes the one ubiquitous interactive mass medium for the 21st century. In this scenario, the web would fold itself around all the broadcasting and publishing media. It would also become a gigantic street market (using digital 'cash' as well as credit-card transactions). It would become the largest teaching machine ever built, and would integrate information retrieval, learning and entertainment in a new soup of 'infotainment', possibly supplemented by 'advertainment'. In this increasingly likely scenario, the web/net would become the primary means by which most people would access *all* the entertainment (TV, films, music, books, games, simulations, etc), all the news (electronic papers and magazines, TV and radio news), all the information (research databases, libraries, museums, etc) *and* – the killer app – it would also provide *all* the means to communicate with each other around the world (e-mail, phone, fax, user groups, bulletin boards, virtual communities, video mail, video conferencing, etc).

The vision sounds very grand and holistic, but given the current developments in processing power and bandwidth (and all the other technologies that are covered in Chapter 7), this is an increasingly likely scenario.

DTV Another vector towards a possible mass multimedia delivery medium is digital television (DTV). There are several possible directions this might go (see Chapter 7, 'Bandwidth' and 'Access devices'), and indeed there are several parallel directions it is taking at the moment. Let's just consider some of the main issues here.

the promise of digital television The TV and electronics industry has been speculating on the development of 'high definition' TV (HDTV), since the early 1980s. That the old analogue TV broadcasting system needed radical upgrades there was no doubt, but the direction HDTV should take – even whether it would be analogue or digital – was (and to some extent still is) in contention. Different nation-states pursued their own national and regional agendas in proposing specifications for HDTV. The US, Japan and Europe proposed several non-compatible systems based on their commitment to established analogue television standards such as PAL, NTSC and SECAM, and the US alone had seven major HDTV proposals, in both analogue, hybrid analogue-digital, and digital formats. It wasn't until 1993, when Japan's analogue proposal was dropped and MPEG2 had begun to emerge as the digital compression format of choice, that digital became the only game in town.

The arguments for HDTV included: it's a logical, 'natural' development of a familiar technology (97 per cent of European households and 99.75 per cent of US households already have a TV); a very high definition picture (800–2000 scan lines, more than twice the resolution of analogue broadcasting systems); stereo sound (often Dolby format); better use of available broadcast spectrum (with digital broadcasting, because there is no crosstalk between channels broadcast in adjacent areas of the spectrum, more channels can be squeezed into the spectrum allocated by regulators); etc. In other words, HDTV was 'ordinary television', only more, and better.

What in fact was happening was that the TV industry was still locked in the 20th-century 'broadcasting' paradigm, and HDTV was considered as a means of merely increasing resolutions and multiplying the number of channels. It wasn't until 1994 that the voice of the future (our 'present') began to make itself heard. For example, at the 1994 Superhighway Summit (the title is revealing!) Steve Case, president of AOL – the only delegate representing the newly emerged internet/web community – delivered what would be the first body-blow to the broadcast industry, the first clue that the future of media was likely to be a very different one from the vision of HDTV as conceived over the previous 15 years:

'What's really happening here is the emergence of a new medium that will be interactive and participatory. I think those are the key components, sort of shifting the balance of power from the producers and packagers and distributors, and putting more of that power in the hands of consumers to select what they want, when they want it.

'But more importantly we think it's not just distributing old things in somewhat new ways – it's really creating new things. And we think the real soul of this new medium will be communications, creating electronic communities by bringing people together who currently aren't able to really get together to talk about issues they care about, whether they be political issues or hobbies, what have you.

'And certainly there will be movies on demand, and certainly there will be interactive shopping, and certainly there will be games and everything else you hear about. But what really will drive this, as I said, is some of the new things that will emerge, and we think that the real focus should be on this aspect of community.'

Steve Case, speaking to the Superhighway Summit, January 11 1994, as recorded by industry expert Craig Birkmaier (www.digitaltelevision.com/future14.shtml)

The audience for Case's prescient observations were the major luminaries of the US broadcasting, computer and media industries, including Reed Hundt (Chairman of the FCC), Al Gore (the future Vice-President, credited with the 'invention' of the superhighway), Barry Diller (QVC), Larry Ellison (Oracle), John Malone (TCI), Richard Notebaert (Ameritech), Brian Roberts (Comcast), Michael Eisner (Disney), Gerald Levin (Time Warner), Rupert Murdoch (News Corporation), Michael Schulhof (Sony) and Raymond Smith (Bell Atlantic).

And quite suddenly, from this point on, the entire future of digital television, as conceived by the 1980s generation of media moguls, was called into question. Six years later, Case's AOL actually acquired the media giant Time

Warner in one of the biggest takeovers in American corporate history (in a deal worth $165 billion, albeit described as a merger). Some body blow!

As mentioned earlier, by 2000, just six companies controlled most of what Americans read in books, magazines and newspapers (and on the net), and watched on television and at the movies (see Ben H. Bagdikian, *The Media Monopoly*). In 1983 the figure was 50 companies.

“BY 2000, JUST SIX COMPANIES CONTROLLED MOST OF WHAT AMERICANS READ IN BOOKS, MAGAZINES AND NEWSPAPERS (AND ON THE NET), AND WATCHED ON TELEVISION AND AT THE MOVIES”

Now, despite this possibly ultimate example of the convergence of power, and taking into account the fine things AOL/Time Warner is espousing about open access (ie about not monopolizing the new media), most of the mega-media conglomerates still don't get what is happening. For example, in the launch of digital television in the UK by Sky Digital, OnDigital and others, the new digital TV medium was described in promotional literature as 'what's all the fuss about digital television? – It's simply a new way of getting better TV'. There was little or no mention of the words 'interactive' or 'internet'. Now, according to PricewaterhouseCooper's 1999 survey of television viewers, 82 per cent of those surveyed said that 'the benefits of DTV had not been substantiated in their minds' and 45 per cent 'do not see a need for it'. I wonder why?

Sure, there's nothing wrong with better pictures and more channels, but in launching a new digital service that sidelines the two key factors of 'being digital' – that is, interactive control and networking – the digital broadcasters have demonstrated quite clearly that they still haven't got 'it'.

And – you've got it – the 'it' we're talking about is the 'big picture'.

The promise of digital television, as re-conceived by Steve Case and other internet entrepreneurs (and shared by the rest of the net generation), is still a promise.

what digital television could be So what could – or should – digital television deliver? Does it mean simply the convergence of more and more power in the hands of fewer and fewer media brokers? Or should it be a step towards the seamless integration of the communications, media and computing industries as conceived by Negroponte, George Gilder and others?

As an illustrative snapshot, consider the following. DTV is not simply another means of broadcasting. It is potentially an extension of the networking system, a means of providing high-bandwidth access to lots of serial content (TV) inside an interactive infrastructure, an infrastructure that also supports person-to-person communications, two-way 'publishing', home video networks, virtual community building, games networks, computer applications, simulations, virtual realities and all kinds of other interactive activities.

Now this is an exciting prospect, and I believe the DTV broadcasters will eventually come (ie be dragged kicking and screaming) to realize that this is the future of media. I think the DTV broadcasters really missed their chance in the late 1990s. Perhaps if they had developed a set-top box that offered internet access *and* digital TV at the same time, and offered this from day one of their launch, they could have been real contenders in the new media marketplace. Of course, these are early days, and the competition will certainly heat up as the 'big idea' becomes more focused ...

'The writing on the wall is writ large, and it says "the future of media is digital and interactive".'

Bob Cotton, presentation to Channel 4 Television, 1992

In a sense, it doesn't really matter (to anyone other than the DTV companies themselves) that the DTV broadcasters don't yet share this vision. Thankfully, they aren't the only players in this great game of inventing the future of media. In fact, the big surprises in this respect are from two previously unlikely contenders.

mobiles! In 1998, five of the world's telecommunications standards organizations launched the 3G project, a global partnership to develop the specifications for a 'third generation' (3G) of mobile phone technology (first generation: analogue, second generation: digital, third generation: broadband). When it is implemented during 2001–2003, the 3G standard will transform the ubiquitous mobile into a high-bandwidth internet access device. Already mobile phones are 'WAP-enabled', meaning that they can access the web through the ether by means of special wireless application protocol web servers. The industry is forecasting growth rates for these new services based on the exponential success of both mobile telephones and the internet. For example, by January 2000 more than 24 million people in the UK owned a mobile phone. Put the mobile and the internet together, so the argument goes, and how can you go wrong?*

*The answer is 'easily'. The average 2000 AD WAP-enabled mobile phone is not a natural web browser, nor an e-book-style 'reader', nor a TV or MP3 player, nor a personal digital assistant (though companies such as Nokia, Ericsson and others are making great strides in developing hybrid products in this area). And the kind of services that would begin to provide mobile users with relevant time- and geography-based information are still in development.

Licences to operate 3G networks were put out for tender or for auction throughout Europe. For many countries this represented the final deregulation from national 'telecomonopolies'. By May 6 2000 the UK 3G spectrum auction (started on March 2) closed with the five winners bidding more than £22 billion for licences. Why so much? Because not only do the licensees see themselves offering mobile access to high-bandwidth services mediated by the internet, but importantly (unlike PC access to the internet) they will have a built-in billing system with which to meter it. Of course, the portable electronic devices used to access media, news and communications services from the 3G network will be very different from the current mobile access devices (which are mostly based on the 2G mobile phone) and may include some of the possibilities I review in Chapter 7, 'Access devices', including hybrid handheld computers and media readers or media players of different kinds.

games consoles! Another of the new contenders in this race to provide access to the multimedia network was, until recently, equally unlikely – it is the games console. The latest generation of games consoles by companies such as Nintendo, Sega and Sony are extremely powerful computing machines. They are able to generate very high-resolution computer graphics in real time – that is, from computer code embodied on a CD-ROM, DVD or other distribution media (such as a solid-state memory embedded in a cartridge, or code downloaded from the web), these machines can recreate 3D visuals and sounds in response to the game player's control of the joystick or mouse, instantaneously. Games such as Doom, Quake and RidgeRacer are examples of real-time CGI. Flight simulators are another example. They hold the promise of 3D virtual environment interfaces *and* high-resolution media access, combining digital television, video games, and broadband web/net access in a number of exciting hybrids of television and computer graphics, although these have yet to be designed.

The generation of consoles launched between 1999 and 2001 went even further. For example the Playstation 2, Sony's latest console, not only generates graphics in real time but also has a built-in DVD drive, 'firewire', a high-bandwidth digital video input device, and a high-speed ethernet connection for internet access too. So what, you say? Well, Sony is planning to deliver this 'access device' for around £300!

The lynch-pin of Sony's broadband media strategy, the PS2 is a games console-cum-DVD player-cum-broadband internet access device. Powerful enough to provide the terrain-mapping guidance for a Cruise missile, the PS2 promises a revolution in home entertainment – easing the switch from TV to PC – to many, the PS2 will also introduce broadband networked entertainment, via Sony's vertical rack of entertainment services and multimedia content provision. Sony will face competition from Sega's Dreamcast, Nintendo's GameCube and Microsoft's 'X-box' console – as well as special games/graphics chips (like the Nuon) installed in DVD players and set-top boxes.

Sony is clearly positioning the Playstation 2 in the same territory as the other digital delivery contenders we have surveyed in this book – as a multimedia access device with future-proof technologies that are capable of handling video, television and music narrowcasts from a broadband web. Indeed, although the PS2 launched in Europe in 2000, Sony was not planning to implement its secure-transaction media distribution network until 2001 – it is definitely in it for the long haul. And then there's the Playstation 3 ...

" THE 'GREAT GAME' OF THE EARLY 21ST CENTURY IS DEVELOPING THE MEDIA ACCESS GATEWAYS OR PORTALS "

convergence – big technology for big audiences The convergence stakes are big. The £22 billion UK 3G licence auction, and the $165 billion AOL-Time Warner 'merger' are all the indicators we need as to just how big. The 'great game' of the early 21st century is developing the media access gateways or portals, the means by which most people will turn on, tune in, channel hop and surf in this media-driven century.

As we have seen, there are several technologies – and several industries – competing to provide the dominant media gateway. But what of the audience they are trying to capture? How do people (consumers, viewers and readers) fit into our big picture?

the new media audience By January 2000 there were 250–400 million people in the world regularly using the web/net. Of these, 30–40 per cent were aged 35–49 (according to Neilson); 40 per cent were women (in the US the gender-usage figures are close to parity).

This is a sizable constituency (and a big market – note the weighting towards the large disposable-income group) by any standards.

But there's more to this than statistics. There are several other factors to consider in building a picture of the people who will be using and viewing the new media, and these include not only the size, make-up and aspirations of the audience (in marketing terminology, the demographics and psychographics), but importantly it means examining the changing nature of how people in a multi-million-website and multi-channel media network use this new medium.

redefining audience The old notion of audience is another factor that is going through a radical shift, as radical a shift as the changes in media technology themselves. This stems from the different ways we engage with media technology. For instance, consider the difference between conventional television viewing and typical computer usage. As TV users, the more channels we have access to, the more we channel hop, but apart from locating the programme or channel you want to watch, TV is a 'passive' experience – you just sit back and watch (actually, all perception is highly interactive, but we'll come back to that later). TV sets are dedicated machines and watching television is an essentially linear experience.

There are two, maybe three, ways of looking at the likely changes in this scenario. The first is that the computer will absorb the TV. The second is that the computer will be integrated with the TV, initially through a set-top box or plug-in games console, eventually in what George Gilder called a 'teleputer' (an integrated PC/TV). The third is that neither TVs nor PCs will be involved (it's the mobile route described above). But at the moment, the television set is still a dedicated machine, whereas the computer – a general-purpose machine – is quite capable of being re-programmed instantaneously to deliver a movie, live TV, a word-processing program, a video game or a web browser. Computers are a non-linear medium and using computers is an interactive experience. Of course, watching a movie (through a DVD drive or CD-ROM) on a computer monitor is similar to watching a movie on a TV set, but the difference is (a) you're probably watching the PC movie on your own, and (b) you're probably much closer than the 6–10 feet (2–3 metres) viewing distance of the typical TV viewer.

With the PC/digital movie, you are also more in control – you can instantly hop from one movie sequence to another, instantly replay that good bit, and generally change aspect ratios and explore the movie enhancements. In all these respects, you are still a PC user even while watching a movie on a computer monitor.

As television converges with the computer (actually, as the computer eats the TV), so old-fashioned passive 'viewers' become proactive and reactive (interactive) 'users'.

Another take – as we learn more and more things we can do on the computer – edit our digital snaps; transfer and digitize video, then edit and title it; send e-mails with image and video attachments; download, store and play MP3 audio tracks; run all kinds of applications; design our own newspaper; publish and maintain our own website; surf a million or so websites; navigate our avatar through virtual worlds; join user groups on our favourite subjects – so we become much more than members of an audience. We become active participators, becoming both broadcaster and publisher, and reader and viewer, at the same time. In the interactive new media networks, 'people are content' – they create communities, affinity groups, user groups, bulletin boards, auctions, swap and share markets, new non-fiscal currencies, homepages, and a plethora of other activities in which in turn other people engage, both as spectators and participators. So content is not just something created by professional publishers working from the 'top-down', but something that is also created by 'ordinary' people working from the bottom-up.

In fact, the networked computer encourages individual creativity – 'ordinary' people are discovering that they can take control and really *use* the new media. For example, people-generated content – e-mail – is by far the most popular media on the web and, as bandwidth increases, multimedia e-mail (video, slide shows, MP3 clips and digital-photo attachments) will become a massive growth area. According to a Messaging Online report at NUA (*www.nua.ie*), by the end of 1999 there were 569 million e-mail accounts worldwide. And with the number of accounts doubling every year, the same report predicts 1 billion accounts by the end of 2002. The issues of e-mail, virtual worlds, user groups and other people-generated content are surveyed in more detail in 'people are content' in Chapter 7 'Content and software'.

Of course this personal empowerment is a two-edged sword, and sometimes creativity can be channelled in a negative direction – the solitary hacker writing and disseminating powerful, world-encompassing viruses, for example.

consumer to prosumer Another way in which audiences are changing is also technology-driven. It is the easily discernible trend, going back to DTP, of software to 'migrate downwards'. What happens is that, as soon as hardware developments (processor power, memory, input/output devices, RAM, etc) are capable of supporting it, new software for computation-intensive media processing and editing is developed. At first this is for high-end workstations and dedicated processor-based machines (for example, in the desktop publishing arena, machines like the Crosfield and Scitex electronic page composition machines). A few years, or even months, later, when this processing power (obeying Moore's Law) becomes available at consumer or 'desktop' level, the high-end software migrates (ie is rewritten or independently developed) for consumers. Consumers therefore, after a certain lag time, have access to 'professional' software (and hardware). Consumer-level digital video camcorders now have many of the features previously found only in professional ENG (electronic news gathering) cameras. Conversely, consumer-level cameras are widely used by the new generation of video-journalists – the one-man reporter/cameraman/sound recordist roles that emerged as the television industry fragmented and deunionized in the 1980s. Professionals use prosumer technology, and ordinary consumers use prosumer technology, ergo people become 'prosumers' – 'professional consumers' – aka media producers.

people are creative: people are media Now you might say, this is all very well, but it doesn't mean that 'ordinary' people are creative enough to use these new prosumer tools, does it? The surprise here is that many experts do believe just that. The new media designer and writer Bob Hughes brilliantly surveys the arguments in *Dust or Magic*, pointing to the findings in Robert Weisberg's book *Creativity – beyond the myth of genius*. The main points are 'creativity is universal, but you're most creative at what you do most'; 'everybody's creativity is different'; and 'it takes special skill to be "creative in a medium"' (that is, media have their own characteristics, and it takes time to learn how to use a new medium to communicate effectively with other people at a distance).

The observation that we *all* have at least the *capability* to become creative in using e-media is a factor largely unrecognized in the current mega-corporation (top-down) world of new media. In the coming networked 'edutainment' world of desktop and set-top supercomputers, this becomes another interesting (potential) growth vector. People become publishers.

There is another very important way that people will impact on e-media: people won't only generate new content, as described above, they will actually *become* the new content. What I mean by this is explored in more depth in Media Matrix: Content & Software but essentially refers to the fact that e-media *aren't* just the digital reiteration of old media, they are the space, the cyberspace, in which all kinds of new communities and affinity groups are emerging, new peer-to-peer media, and even hybrids of old and new media – the reality TV 'surveillance soaps' such as Channel 4's *Smart-Hearts* and its version of Dutch TV's *Big Brother*. People are content too.

7 the big picture: the media matrix

what we have created During the past 30 years we have witnessed the creation of a unique artefact: the largest machine ever invented, a hybrid artefact of software and hardware that wasn't planned or designed in the formal sense (of having a single 'master' designer, or even a co-ordinating central design team), and that now spans the world and operates very successfully with virtually no imposed regulations, with but a minimum of centralized planning.

'The (WWW) system had to have one other fundamental property: it had to be completely decentralized. That would be the only way a new person somewhere could start to use it without asking for access from anyone else. And that would be the only way the system would scale, so that as more people used it, it wouldn't get bogged down. This was good, internet-style engineering, but most systems still depended on some central node to which everything had to be connected – and whose capacity eventually limited the growth of the system as a whole. I wanted the act of adding a new link to be trivial; if it was, then a web of links could spread evenly across the globe.'

Tim Berners-Lee, Weaving the Web

As we have said, this global machine, created by the internetworking of computers and computer networks, and the interconnecting of information through hypertext, illustrates Metcalfe's Law – that networks increase in functionality by the square of the number of nodes they encompass. In other words, one telephone is useless, two telephones are better, hundreds of telephones become useful, thousands of telephones become an essential service, millions of telephones constitute a critical mass – the point at which the telephone becomes a ubiquitous and essential part of our environment.

critical mass media The number of computers and local networks interconnected in the internet reached this kind of critical mass sometime in the mid-1990s. Now it is as hard to envision life without the internet as it is to imagine life without the phone. The internet is still doubling in size every year, and shows no signs of having reached anything like a natural limit (though what this limit is and when it might be reached is difficult to figure: is it equivalent to the number of people with television sets? radios? phones?). By the end of 2001, if the current 100 per cent per annum growth rate continues, there could be 1 billion users.

Indeed, all the immediate signs are that the internet will grow ever more rapidly in response to several new technological developments that are due to come on stream through the early noughties, notably digital television (which will provide internet access through the television set), broadband mobiles, and low earth orbit satellites (these will provide internet access to previously unwired static and mobile internet access devices anywhere in the world). Many other developments, in bandwidth provision, processing power, in 'smart' software, new interface technologies, and in the variety of consumer electronics appliances that will provide internet access (alongside a multiplicity of other functions), are also in train and promise quantum leaps in coverage, low-cost access, and in the variety of multimedia services they can offer. As we say, you really ain't seen nothing yet.

'The internet now is like the universe a few seconds after the Big Bang ...'

Robert X. Cringely, 'The Glory of the Geeks', TV series broadcast in the US, June 1998

mapping the new media landscape

As we have shown, it *is* possible to make sense of the 'solution space' of the new digital media. We can trace the 'path dependencies' of industrial momentum, we can understand the visions that filter these developments and that favour certain vectors of development over others, we can see why digital computers drive the process of convergence, and we can see the train of next big things and killer apps parading the undeniably sexy technologies liberated by the computer and by the human intellect.

In order to further clarify our conceptual model of what's happening, I have designed a schematic diagram (*see also* p. 52) that classifies developments as clusters of activities surrounding some key development vectors. These include bandwidth, memory, processing power, access devices, content and software.

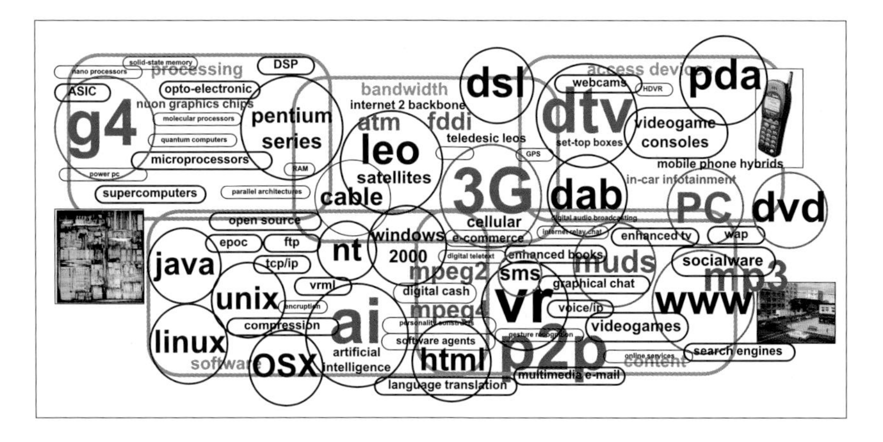

bandwidth

'Three years ago (1994), all the phone networks in the world combined carried an average of a terabit a second. Today, companies are sending 3 terabits* per second down a single fibre thread the width of a human hair. Put those numbers together and – in a direct line from the quantum discoveries at the beginning of the 20th century – you have the assurance of boundless bandwidth in the 21st.'

George Gilder, The Gilder Technology Report, 1997

*Terabit = a million million bits.

Bandwidth is the signal-carrying capacity of a communications channel, and in digital terms is measured in bits per second. The higher the bandwidth, the more complex the signals that can be transmitted. For example, to transmit your voice over the telephone requires only a few kilobits/sec (kbps), while transmitting MPEG1 digital video (equivalent to VHS-quality analogue video) needs 1.5 megabits per second. The next wave of development in new media networking will be a product of the race to provide ubiquitous broadband service across the entire network spectrum: for both static (home and office-based) and mobile access devices, in virtually every part of the world. Such is the momentum behind this race to broadband, with virtually every telecommunications company on the planet taking part, all the signs are that it will happen much, much more quickly than experts predicted back in the 1980s. Why? Because back then the technologies that we presumed would provide broadband networking were all physical – they were fibre optics, coaxial cable or hybrids of the two. The cost of laying these physical networks (and the physical disruption they augured) was enormous. Projections went into hundreds of billions of dollars. What is new is that the vision of the broadband future – while capitalizing on the immense investment in physical infrastructure over the past 20 years, all the fibre, cable and improvements in wire telephony – is now tinted with the rosy hues of wireless media: cellular networks, microwave, sub-millimetre radio, infra-red, and just about every other way of transporting information through the ether. It's not only much cheaper to build a wireless network infrastructure, it causes far less disruption too. With wireless, countries like China will be able to leapfrog 30 years of infrastructural investment, and come up to speed with the West, and indeed China is already doing so, with more than 300 cellular networks spanning the country's 33 million subscribers (1999 figures). (See *www. teletechnics.com* and *www.cellular.co.za* for lists of cellular developments in countries all around the world.)

Most wired users currently access the internet on a low bandwidth connection, via modems capable of up to 56 kbps, but there are several technologies that promise a rapid escalation of bandwidth over the next few years, and these include both physical and ethereal media. The current physical hot favourite is DSL, the Digital Subscriber Line technology that offers data rates of up to 8 Mbps through ordinary (analogue) telephone lines. It does this by taking advantage of unused frequencies on the phone line (that is, it uses a different part of the frequency spectrum than analogue voice signals), so you can still make ordinary 'voice' calls at the same time as sending or receiving data. Apart from its bandwidth, the other attractive feature of DSL is that it is always on – there's no dial-up wait to go online.

“THE OTHER ATTRACTIVE FEATURE OF DSL IS THAT IT IS ALWAYS ON – THERE'S NO DIAL-UP WAIT TO GO ONLINE”

Forrester Research predicts that more than 16 million US households – a quarter of all online homes – will enjoy broadband connections by 2002. It predicts that about 20 per cent of these will be through DSL, with most of the remainder through cable or satellite connection. Telechoice Inc forecasts that by the end of 2000, more than 1 million DSL lines will be installed in the US.

In the UK, BT is offering its BT OpenWorld DSL consumer service at about £40 per month. DSL works optimally only when you are less than 3.5 km (as the wire goes) from the exchange, so while this is a brilliant broadband technology, some 15 per cent of the UK population won't be able to access it. BT OpenWorld is also an ISP, but BT is having to offer DSL services to other ISPs too. The service that most home users will purchase from their local or national telco will be ADSL (asymmetrical DSL) which provides more bandwidth down stream than up, but with upstream rates from 128 kbits/sec to

1.5 Mbps, it is still vastly superior in cost and speed to alternative methods (unless you are already a cable subscriber). SDSL (symmetrical DSL) on the other hand provides equal data rates in both directions. But there are a whole slew of DSL standards – VDSL, HDSL, CDSL, etc – so sometimes the technology is described generically as xDSL. Currently the high end of DSL is VDSL (very-high-bit-rate DSL), offering 52 Mbps downstream and 13 Mbps upstream.

wire, cable, fibre and wireless There are a variety of high-bandwidth delivery systems apart from DSL, including the older broadband(-ish) technology, ISDN, but this offers only a maximum 128 kbps bandwidth and is more expensive to install and use because it requires a digital phone line and a special terminal adaptor or PC expansion board. Other broadband media include cable, with cable TV network operators offering broadband data connections of up to 10 Mbps downstream, through coaxial cables and 'cable modems' that can also deliver MPEG1 video streams. But the problem with cable is that because you share bandwidth with other local subscribers, actual downstream speeds can fall to around 1.5 Mbps (300 kbps upstream), depending upon the number of simultaneous users. More than 63 million Americans subscribe to a cable TV service, and many cable companies offer internet access via cable modem as an extra. Like DSL, cable is an 'always on' access solution, offers very high bandwidth, and it's cheap – about $40 per month.

Fibre-optic networks promise enormous bandwidth, but currently (optical) fibre is still too expensive to lay right up to the door of subscribers. It is mostly used for network infrastructure, but new techniques such as Wave Division Multiplex (WDM) promise low-cost, high bandwidth provision via fibre in the near future. Indeed some visionaries are convinced of the medium- to long-term future of fibre.

'Just as the market share of centralized computers dropped from nearly 100 per cent in 1977 to less than 1 per cent in 1987, our research at The Gilder Technology Report suggests that the share of analogue voice in the global telecom market will drop from more than 80 per cent in 1994 to less than 1 per cent in 2004. Thousands of ISPs, with WorldCom at the helm, will prevail, with ever-spreading networks of fibre, optimized for data. And the imperatives of 186,000 miles per second are spawning a whole new generation of low-orbit satellites, from Iridium and Globalstar to Teledesic and now Celestri.'

Gilder Technology Report, 1998

satellites and cellular But aside from all these physical, 'wired' connections, it seems likely that the next big breakthroughs in broadband will come through the ether: beamed down to us from satellites or accessible through our ubiquitous mobile cellular networks.

Satellite broadband requires a mini-dish antenna to receive internet data via satellite at about 400 kbps, only a fraction of the bandwidth of DSL or cable. But satellite is available everywhere, and may be the only broadband choice for rural users, or those outside DSL range. Another advantage is that you can get digital satellite TV as well. The disadvantages? This system still uses an ordinary modem for upstream communications, limiting you to around 56 kbps. It's an asymmetrical 'broadcast' solution, and as this is how many people use the web/net, this assymmetry is fine. Another disadvantage of satellite is that of lag times between interactions as the signal is travelling a long distance to and from the satellite. In the US in 2000, the main contender in the satellite market was Hughes Network System's DirecPC, which requires a 21 inch antenna or mini-dish, a satellite modem card, and a modem connection to an ISP. Browsing the web via satellite broadband is exactly the same as browsing via ordinary dial-up modem – except that it's much, much faster. Downloads are made at speeds of 400 kbps – around eight times the speed of current modems. While your input is sent at 56 kbps through your modem and phone line, the downstream channel is via satellite (GEOS at 22,200 miles up), picked up by your dish and decoded by the satellite modem card in your PC. DirecPC can cost $20–$110 a month, depending on usage, to which you have to add your ISP bill, or pay DirecPC another $10–$20 a month.

“BROWSING THE WEB VIA SATELLITE BROADBAND IS EXACTLY THE SAME AS BROWSING VIA ORDINARY DIAL-UP MODEM – EXCEPT THAT IT'S MUCH, MUCH FASTER”

The mobile (cellular) broadband world is still developing, but it's riding on the back of bullish projected sales figures that are based on the extraordinary growth of mobile phone ownership and internet usage, so most service providers plan to implement broadband (3G) services in two main stages over 2000–2006. The first stage is '2.5G', a kind of halfway house. By as early as the end of 2001, GSM (currently capable of only 10 kbps) will upgrade to GPRS (General Packet Radio Service) standards (up to about 80 kbps), and by 2002 to full 3G standards, which offer up to 2 Mbps to static mobile users, 384 kbps to pedestrians, and 144 kbps to car travellers. Some of the core technologies for 3G, such as EDGE (enhanced data-rates for GSM evolution), are still in R&D. But as an indication of the industrial momentum behind broadband mobile, consider the announcement in April 2000 that Sony, Texas Instruments and Symbian would be combining their technologies to produce a range of 2.5G and 3G mobiles and portable access devices, bringing together Texas Instrument's low-power digital signal processor (DSP) chip, Symbian's EPOC operating system (developed by Psion for its handhelds), and Sony's Memory-Stick (flash technology storing 64 Mb of data on a card the size of a stick of gum). Such a product range from Sony promises a hybridization of communications, handheld computing and broadband media access (music and video) in a single portable machine, no doubt styled to be as desirable as its other portable products, such as the Vaiao sub-notebooks.

The idea of a broadband *wireless* world wide web, through which all the standard web/net services (e-mail, messaging, e-commerce, searching and browsing, etc) are accessed, and by means of which high-quality, high-speed MP3 and MPEG audio and video can be downloaded, is obviously attractive to big 'super-verticals' like Sony Corporation, which see mobile access fitting neatly alongside Playstation 2 in their panoply of broadband products. Sony CEO Nobuyuki Idei says: 'Sony can be the number one company in the broadband network society. That will be a much bigger role than Sony has ever had. But we can't just wait until broadband arrives. And we can't merely follow the dot com companies or Microsoft or anybody else. We have to take advantage of everything the technology and the new economy provide. We have to prepare while we still have time.' Sony announced its 'bit-drive' broadband business (B2B) service in May 2000. Due for launch in Japan during July 2000, bit-drive will initially provide corporate customers with a range of services through a broadband cellular infrastructure operating at 1.5 Mbps.

Sony isn't alone in its awareness that broadband wireless networks will be central to telecommunications – and to media distribution – in the first decade of this century. All the major players in telecommunications, computing, consumer electronics and media are developing strategies that they hope will position them at the forefront of these developments.

The consensus is so international that it seems likely that this emerging broadband wireless world wide web may also be the truly *global* WWW, especially as an increasing number of satellite launches are planned to fill the gaps in coverage, providing both voice and data services wirelessly around the planet, to mobile and static users alike. For example, in May 2000, Inmarsat announced a $1.4 billion investment in its Broadband Global

Area Network, based on three geostationary satellites (GEOs), and providing 432 kbps bandwidth 'virtually anywhere in the world' – and it is compatible with 3G cellular networks too. From 2002, the Microsoft/McCaw cellular 'Teledesic' network will use a constellation of 840 LEO (low earth orbit) satellites to provide global broadband services.

But despite this drive to broadband, no matter how much bandwidth you've got, you'll always want more. Why? Because applications and media seem to naturally expand to exceed the bandwidth available. That's just another aspect of the inescapable Parkinson's Law. So, alongside the development of broadband systems, we will see the development of increasingly more effective data compression and decompression algorithms and hardware.

The compression of digital signals to squeeze more performance from transmission systems means that such signals have to be decompressed at the receiver's end. This brings us to the second major factor in the future of mass media: the microprocessor.

processing To crunch and compress digital signals, and to decompress them and convert them back into high-quality video or audio or stills or multimedia information, and to do this in real time (ie with no apparent delay), means heavyweight signal processing power. For the receiver (or 'client' end), this power has to be available in low-power-consumption chips that are cheap enough to fuel the affordable consumer electronics appliances (the set-top boxes and mobile personal communications systems) and computers that people want.

There is a convenient law that can be applied to developments in microprocessor power: Moore's Law, after Gordon Moore, the co-founder of Intel. Back in the mid-1960s, Moore noted that integrated circuits doubled in power every 18 months, while costs remained static (this is why computers always seem to be about the same price, but get increasingly more powerful). Moore's Law has held true for the past 30 years, and experts reckon it's good for at least another 20 using current silicon-chip technology. After that, there are several alternative processor fabrication technologies (including gallium arsenide and germanium), several computer-architecture alternatives, such as opto-electronic computing, molecular computing and nano-computing, and then there is the potential of parallel processing architectures, where entire networks of processors are integrated into silicon and can process millions or even billions of instructions simultaneously. What this means is that microprocessors will go on doubling in power every 18 months for the foreseeable future. By 2010, according to Andy Grove, CEO of Intel, we will have supercomputer-powered processors – chips capable of 1000 MIPS (million instructions per second), and running at speeds of over 1 gHz (1 billion vibrations/sec). Apple Computer was staking a claim on this territory in 1999, hailing its new G4 computer as 'the first desktop supercomputer'.

'Already, scientists are making critical breakthroughs in new processor technologies involving everything from quantum switches to growing human neurones on silicon sheets to computers made entirely of DNA strands. These last are, metaphysically at least, the most compelling of all.'

Michael S. Malone, Intel

Not only does this mean that decompressing (and decrypting) better-than-broadcast-quality video and multimedia streams in real time is no problem, but our set-top boxes and handheld internet access devices, our computers and other consumer electronics equipment will have enough power to generate and visualize complex simulations of real-world events and processes. These may be anything from stock-market simulators to artificially intelligent teachers, online auto-paramedics, highly realistic pet simulations, to travel simulations, even the kind of 'mirror-world' real-time scenarios envisaged by David Gelernter of Harvard University, and described in Neal Stephenson's excellent sci-fi novel *Snow Crash*. Then there's the possibility of really interactive movies – real-time computer-generated scenarios in which we can wander freely, interacting with pirates, cowboys, Indians, gangsters, stars and starlets at will.

'It (parallel processing) allows the computer itself to operate like a modern corporate information system, with various operations all occurring simultaneously throughout the firm, rather than like an old corporate data-processing hierarchy, which forced people to waste time in queues while waiting for access to the company mainframe. Promising huge increases in the cost-effectiveness of computing, parallel processing will bring supercomputer performance to individuals.'

George Gilder, 'The Technology of Liberation' in Ray Kurzweil, The Age of Intelligent Machines, 1990

"SOME ESTIMATES INDICATE THAT THERE MAY BE AROUND 50 BILLION MICROPROCESSORS ALREADY IN USE THROUGHOUT THE WORLD – TEN TIMES MORE MICROPROCESSORS THAN HUMANS!"

an internet of supercomputing power When commercial computers were first developed in the early 1950s, experts predicted that we would need no more than five or six of these room-sized boxes of thermionic valves to service all the computing requirements of the UK. We now have an estimated UK computer population of at least 20 million. In addition, and in the UK alone, there are literally tens of millions of microprocessors in other equipment and products (for example, a new car may contain more than 100 microprocessors), and we also have around a score or so (26 in 2000) supercomputers in the UK. Some estimates indicate that there may be around 50 billion microprocessors already in use throughout the world – ten times more microprocessors than humans! (Microprocessor sales have been doubling every year since 1995, when 3.5 billion were sold.)

As the power of microprocessors escalates according to Moore's Law, and as their relative costs continue to decline, the inevitable result is that *within this decade* we will have a global network of supercomputer-power access devices. The possibility will be that each of us in the digitally empowered world will have a supercomputer-powered handheld, games console, PC or set-top box, and we will be interconnected to each other by the variety of means described above. There will also be a wealth of super-powered microprocessors that talk to each other outside the mediation of human beings – in machine-to-machine networks that weave their intricate wireless patterns of intelligence through every aspect of our environment, in our roads, our cars, our buildings, our clothes, our food packaging, our fields, our rivers and even the air that we breathe.

What will happen when millions of supercomputers are available? The spreadsheet was the first killer app for the personal computer (alongside word processing and databases); what will the first supercomputer killer app be? One thing's for sure: this kind of supercomputing power will easily run the new kinds of 3D real-time media (such as 3D games, virtual environments and simulations), and will also be able to handle the virtual 'neural networks' (software machines that learn) needed to drive sophisticated 'smart' applications.

SMART DUST

Smart dust is one name for minature sensor devices that have built-in microprocessors, sensors and wireless communications technologies, all in a device about the size of a grain of sugar.

Smart Dust is the name of an initiative at a US university aiming to develop integrated devices or MEMs (micro-electromechemical devices) – extremely small machines that contain a sensor, a power supply ('thick-firm' battery and solar cell), analogue circuitry, bi-directional optical communication, and a programmable microprocessor. The aim is to squeeze these components into a 1 mm cube. By mid-2000, engineers had got a MEMs that was about 100 cubic millimetres in size.

Smart Dust is the brainchild of Kris Pister and Randy Katz at the University of California, Berkeley. They envision smart dust sensors being used for military and security surveillance, and for collecting meteorological, biological or environmental data. Smart dust could be scattered over an area of some square miles in size, and the micro-miniature devices would be able to talk to each other, while a central communications station (such as a laptop or special binoculars) would wirelessly (optically at present) build a detailed data map of the area.

With sensors for sound, vision, chemical sampling, temperature, etc, smart dust or similar MEMs products will, if engineers can deliver on their promise, provide some of the ubiquitous intelligence-gathering resources in our 'wired' or 'wireless' world, providing valuable monitoring tools for farmers, fishermen, conservationists, ecologists and scientists. They may, of course, also turn out to be yet another pernicious form of pollution (but then again, what about biodegradable MEMs?).

memory As one of the implications of Moore's Law is the decreasing cost of processors (relative to their power), we can also apply Moore's Law to the cost of memory. Not only is solid-state memory (RAM, ROM, flash memory and other chip-based memory) getting cheaper with each new generation, but disk- and tape-based memory media costs are declining too. Each generation of personal computer since the early 1980s has offered more hard-disk storage for roughly the same price. And compare the most common digital optical media, CD-ROM, with DVD. Both these storage devices share the same common platform, a 5 inch diameter disk, but whereas the 1981 technology of CD-ROM can store only 640 megabytes of data, the 1995 technology of DVD – on the same substrate, and at the same physical cost per disk – can store 4.6 gigabytes.

Howard Strauss of Princeton University has estimated that the cost of memory is declining about 25 per cent each year; that is, the cost of RAM (chip memory) in 2000 was about $1 a megabyte and by 2004 it will cost 25¢ a megabyte. Disk storage, at 5¢ a megabyte in 2000, was declining at a similar rate, so that by 2004 a megabyte of storage will cost 0.5¢.

Logically, then, if this trend continues, by the end of the decade the cost per megabyte of disk storage will be in the region of 0.0005¢, by which time the cost of a megabyte of RAM memory will also be negligible. As the analyst George Gilder has pointed out, this trend in memory costs echoes the asymptotic downward curve in the cost of transistors. Each generation is cheaper than the last (Gilder estimated the average cost of a transistor in 2000 to be 4000-millionths of a cent). It's an 'asymptotic' curve because it will never reach zero, just get so cheap that for all intents and purposes it will be free.

the trend towards the free Does all this sound a bit surreal? Howard Anderson, Managing Director of the Yankee Group, is famous for criticizing Gilder's predictions as being *too conservative*. He cites the decreasing cost of bandwidth: 'The cost of a T1 (1.54 Mbps) line coast to coast (across the US) in 1985 was $40,000 a month. Today (1995) – under $2000 a month, a drop of 95 per cent.'

So, in this abstraction, if processing power, memory and bandwidth are going to be virtually free by the end of this decade, what does this mean to all of us in the real world? Or as Howard Anderson puts it: 'Assume the following: by 2000, computing is free, and bandwidth is free. Now – design the future!'

Remember that, as Nicholas Negroponte points out, more bandwidth *dosen't* mean better communication: 'Yes, bandwidth will be free, but so will computing. The future will not be driven by either MIPS (processing power) or BPS (bandwidth), but information and entertainment content.'

This is true: most of us have to process too much information already, even at the low bandwidth through which we currently access the web/net. But surely communication quality and personal choice are what counts here. Some of us will prefer the high-band presentation of an idea through a well-structured video documentary; some will prefer it in electronic book (text) form; others might like a computer software simulation; others a live video phone-style conference with subject experts, or with expert popularizers. Others might like to stick with the text and images of HTML. The point is that in the forthcoming broadband web/net, everyone will have a choice, and those who prefer the video won't be penalized by extra costs or lengthy download times.

web/net access devices To return to our question: what will happen when millions of supercomputers are available? The first ways these super-chips will impact on our lifestyles will probably be in the variety of broadband web/net access devices. These super-chips will power a wide variety of internet access devices, in the home and on the road, and designers have envisaged access devices that range in scale from smart cufflinks to Dick Tracy-style wristwatch TVs, and from intelligent 'wearables' (all the components of a computer sewn into our clothes, and powered by our body movements) to smart rooms where each wall is a projection screen. From iconic tetrahedrons that magically obey your spoken commands and control your 'home edutainment system', to anonymous VCR-style set-top boxes, to smart fridges and other domestic appliances, and including network computers, mobile media players, personal digital assistants, personal communication systems, even personal computers – the range and diversity of access devices will visibly transform our cultural environment.

internet access devices in the home In the home, advanced (digital) television sets will gradually replace analogue sets as the deadline for phasing out analogue broadcasting (2006 in the US, around 2010 in the UK) approaches. In the meantime, the stop-gap technology for TV viewers will be the set-top box (STB), an anonymously styled pizza box containing some digital signal processors (for decrypting, decompressing and converting digital signals to analogue outputs for display on your old TV set), a hard disk, a modem, and perhaps a smart-card slot or card swipe (for digital cash and credit transactions). Attached to the STB will be a small satellite dish (currently about 12 inches but soon this may be miniaturized on a special chip).

Eventually, however, most people will have dedicated digital television sets. These DTV sets will marry some, if not all, the functionality of a personal computer (hopefully!) with the ease of use of a TV set, offering a suite of programming from multi-channel television to web-enhanced TV, to well over 1 million websites in a video-enhanced internet. Further to this, DTV will offer a variety of proprietary interactive services (from home banking to home shopping, including a new digital Teletext service). The average consumer will have an enormous range of choice, from passive TV watching through to interactive web browsing and home shopping, all through the same access device – more electronic entertainment and information choice in the home than ever before.

And this won't *all* be the kind of one-way, broadcaster-to-viewer entertainment that we became used to in the 20th century; the broadband, supercomputer-powered web/net will be the 'people's media'. Just as most of the packet traffic on today's web/net is down to e-mail, so too, I will bet, much of the demand for bandwidth during this coming decade will be driven by people-to-people (in network terms, peer-to-peer) applications, such as multi-party family video conferencing, virtual care, telecommuting, tele-medicine and other forms of socialware, groupware, distance learning, and similar interactive, multi-participant activities.

In an information-saturated world though, people will more than ever want to relax with the passive media of movies and television. The interactive bit will be the amazing array of choices they will have. But the very range of choice may dictate that even this level of interaction – hopping through 500 channels – will have to be automated. In the late 1990s, a radically new take on the idea of interactive television emerged. This wasn't based on any fancy multiplexed satellite or terrestrial TV broadcasting technology, nor yet on the developments in web TV or DVD, but on putting power and choice in new media firmly into the hands of the people who consume it. The idea was simple (all good ideas are simple in retrospect): combine a DTV tuner, low-cost hard disks and modem in a box. Add some personalization software and a website-based electronic programme guide (EPG) service, and you've got 'ReplayTV': a digital home recording system (or hard-disk video recorder, HDVR) that you can program with your preferences, then leave to automatically search the online EPGs for matching titles on all the channels you subscribe to and record the programmes as MPEG2 files on your hard disk – up to 28 hours worth! You've then got a fully interactive 'TV channel' of your very own, to browse, programme-hop, fast forward or watch at your leisure. By putting this level of (automated) choice directly into the hands of users, ReplayTV and similar HDVR systems (Tivo, for example) effectively subvert the plans of those digital broadcasters who think that interactive simply means the provision of more and more channels of more-of-the-same programming. The 'network effect' lesson here? Devolve the power of the network to the user.

Digital television, in integrated sets or through set-top boxes, implies that this range of choice will be browsed and navigated by means of remote-control pads communicating to the TV from the viewing couch. Of course, no one has yet designed a successful integrated multi-function system based on the television (the only precedents being the tortuous nightmare of VCR programming, and the 'too little – too late' technology of Philips' CD-i), but a variety of remote-control devices are beginning to emerge. These range from remote QWERTY keyboard and keypads, to video game-style consoles and magic wands. Eventually, voice-recognition technology will play a major role here, especially when the internet has a simpler addressing system. Nor has anyone yet designed a really easy-to-use computer (though the i-Mac comes close), so there's a lot of work in store for aspirant 'human factors' students in designing and engineering the ideal hardware and software interface for the new 'teleputers'.

“THE 'NETWORK EFFECT' LESSON HERE? DEVOLVE THE POWER OF THE NETWORK TO THE USER”

Another of the principal access devices, in the home and in the office, is the personal computer. This will be the typical Pentium or Mac PC, with a video adapter and satellite access so that you can downlink and watch large windows of video embedded in websites. Some service providers are already offering digital TV and broadband web access as a package, both running on a PC. A subset of the PC is the NC (network computer), a reiteration of an older model of computing where dumb terminals were attached by a network to a mini or mainframe computer and shared processing time on that. The NC, with its onboard processing power, can be simpler and cheaper than a standard PC. All the programs, files and applications you need are stored on a number of devices on the network, and you just access the stuff you need much like you'd use a web browser. The advantage of the NC comes in lower unit costs, software that is always up to date, seamless integration of internet information and communication tools with your local area (office/studio) network, and your 'desktop network' (of scanners, printers, CD-ROM, etc).

But as I said in Chapter 6, I think the really big surprise for most people will be the emergence of the games console as one of the main domestic web/net access devices. Why the games console? There are a number of reasons, including the fact that these machines will contain a phenomenal array of computing power, they will have built-in modems or broadband network connections such as Firewire and Ethernet, they will be DVD-based, and last but not least, they will also play brilliant 128-bit quality games! But above all, they will be cheap – around the £300/$400 mark.

In fact, apart from their raw graphics rendering power and adventurous cabinet styling (page 171), there may be very little difference in actual functionality between the PC and the games console. For example, the US version of the Playstation 2 will probably contain a hard disk (maybe as well as an 8 Mb memory card) and modem (either built-in or as a peripheral unit, neither of these was available in the Japanese launch PS2). The PS2 will also include a virtual Java machine, allowing it to run millions of Java 'applets', just like a 'normal' PC.

But the underlying difference between the two platforms is that the central processing unit chip (the Pentium3 or whatever) in the PC is designed to run a wide variety of applications (ie it's a general-purpose machine), whereas the PS2 CPU – what Sony calls the 'emotion engine' – is designed to do one thing superbly: run real-time 3D games. Of course, it will process other applications too – run web browsers, e-mail clients and other applications – but its *raison d'être* is *gaming*. What difference will this make? Well, it means that the PS2 will be extremely good at delivering some of the main strands of multiple-participant entertainment, including 3D real-time games, virtual real-time environments, and real-time simulations, that I expect to flourish in the broadband environment.

But Sony won't have it all its own way with the PS2. Both Nintendo and Microsoft have similar plans to grab broadband-access market share through games consoles with the Microsoft X-box and Nintendo Dolphin. The competition is on two levels, ostensibly for the roughly 40 million Americans who play games on consoles (29 million) or PCs (11 million), but really for the 90 million US homes with TV sets.

Microsoft's X-box has a very competitive (currently only vapourware) specification, but Microsoft is entering what is for the company a brand new market, and it is up against a formidably successful market leader, with established developer networks, promotion and distribution chains. In the meantime, Nintendo and Sega, even after losing market share to Sony in the 1990s, are still feisty, have a large fan base, and still produce brilliant games.

What's the potential here? With their 3D graphics-rendering and superior sound and image quality, and the ability to link to a broadband web/net *and* built-in or peripheral hard-drives and memory cards, there's the possibility of unique blends of broadcast, narrowcast or disk-based MPEG2-quality video with high-resolution, real-time 3D graphics overlays or mattes. More conventionally, these machines will download and play movies, television programmes and other video content, and of course MP3 or similar audio files from the net. No doubt Sony and other hardware console manufacturers will provide attractive proprietary portals to lever maximum advantage from their vertical offerings.

on the street Mobile users will be spoilt for choice, with a range of internet access devices that hybridize a variety of previously quite separate technologies. For example, expect to see digital cameras combining personal organizer, stylus handwriting recognition, audio voice recording, and internet access (e-mail and messaging, and JPEG image transfer), and perhaps even more hybridization with a basic PDA (personal digital assistant) that becomes a stills camera, a digital radio, a web browser, a fax machine, mobile phone, TV set, video camcorder, voice memo recorder (etc) on demand whenever the user plugs in the appropriate smartcard or (eventually) presses the appropriate button. Digital radios with CD-quality sound, wireless modem, cell phone and datacast reception, even TV reception, will also become a popular access device on the street.

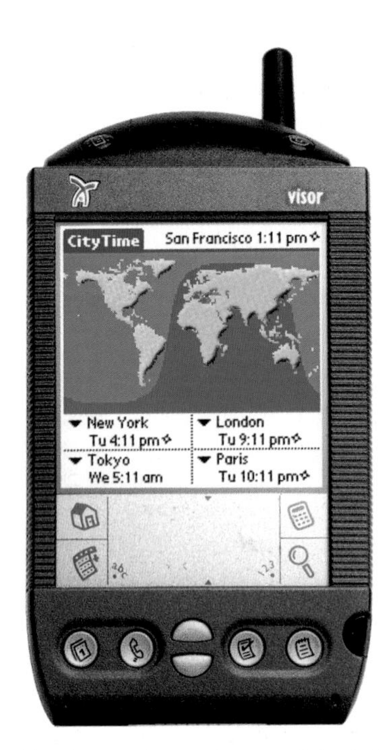

Handspring have pioneered the hybrid portable digital device – the handheld that can become different media machines simply by inserting a new extension module. Based on the highly successful Palm handheld and running the Palm operating system – and designed by Palm founder and designer Jeff Hawkins the Handspring Visor can become a digital camera, a remote-controller, a mobile phone – and soon an MP3 player, e-book reader – and so on.

> IN THEORY, AUTOMATIC LANGUAGE TRANSLATION COULD ALSO BE AN INTEGRAL PART OF SUCH A WORLDWIDE SYSTEM

for everyone I believe that it is the destiny of a world wide web to be ubiquitous, as equally available in Namibia as in New York, and now the possible route to such a future is at least moderately clear: a combination of low earth orbit satellite communications, cellular radio, geostationary digital radio/TV broadcasting, fibre, cable and wire landlines, and some really low-cost hybrid internet access device, powered by solar cells or clockwork generators. In theory, automatic language translation, coupled with digital radio broadcasting technology, could also be an integral part of such a worldwide system. The value such an interactive, primarily wireless communications channel would have in providing access to healthcare and education, medicare, agriculture, permaculture information, weather forecasting, remote-sensing data, training and communications in places previously excluded from the net, is enormous, but what is needed is global effort (orchestrated by the G8 countries, or by the UN, perhaps), to design and mass-produce really cheap, solid-state people's access devices – integrated single-chip/LCD screen or TV-feed devices that can be manufactured in sufficiently large numbers to make them effectively free.

Automatic language translation is just one of the products of more than 50 years of global research into artificial intelligence, and it is AI that is driving many of the really radical developments in content and software.

smart media Since World War Two, and following the seminal work by Alan Turing and others on cryptanalysis during that war, universities and research foundations all over the world have been funding research into artificial intelligence. At first this research was regarded by many as rather peripheral and even frivolous, the grail quest for machine intelligence, and the development of chess-playing machines. However, in the 1980s, spin-offs from AI research, including robotics and expert systems, created major changes in industrial production throughout the world, and recently real, industrial-strength products such as speech recognition, practically unbreakable encryption, and automatic language translation have at last emerged, and further iterations of AI will reverberate through the next few years of new media developments.

Not least among these are trainable software agents – software entities that can be trained for specific tasks – and profiling engines – software that automatically filters information according to the personal tastes and requirements of the user (these engines form the basis of all kinds of personal newspapers, customized informsation channels and other personalized services). Other important applications of AI include the development of dynamic reasoning engines (the essence of a good software agent), personality constructs (building simulations of particular humans), e-cash encryption (secure digital cash), copyright encryption (digitally labelled copyright information invisibly embedded in digital artefacts), artificial life, and IPR (intellectual property rights) audit-trail software (this enables IPR holders to trace the republication and re-use of copyright materials throughout the networked environment). In sum, these developments, hand in hand with W3C's semantic web proposals, will transform the internetworked environment into a 'smart' environment, combining the virtues of a universal vade-mecum and a full-time personal assistant.

'Many futurists predict that seven (chip) generations from now, the descendants of these chips (PentiumII) – for the same price – will construct software agent "avatars" with human characteristics that will act as our personal assistants, helping us shop, planning our days and organizing our lives. These chips will also bring speech recognition to word processors and order-entry systems. They will generate 3D wall-sized graphics for television, teleconferencing, even custom-made movies. They will direct our vehicles for maximum safety and create virtual worlds we will walk through. They will instruct our children, monitor our health, replace lost body parts and, through a grid of billions of sensors, connect us to the world in ways that we can only dimly imagine.'

Michael S. Malone, 'Intel: One Digital Day' at www.intel.com

the emergence of the personality-user-interface 'Personality constructs' illustrate just how radical these AI technologies can be. For example, we will describe a PerCon designed by Hollis Research, a small, highly innovative, UK software team. The PerCon is a way of storing a profile of a person in a kind of expert system, embodied as a set of video sequences of a real person's head and shoulders. Conversations with the PerCon are conducted by means of a text panel that the human interlocutor uses to type in his or her side of the conversation (soon normal speech will be used). The PerCon program stores a wide range of pre-recorded responses. When the human types a question or a comment into the text panel, the PerCon parses the input, computes its 'meaning', deducts, then searches for and displays the most appropriate response. This happens in real time (ie within half a second or so), even on today's standard PCs. It's a most eerie feeling, conversing with

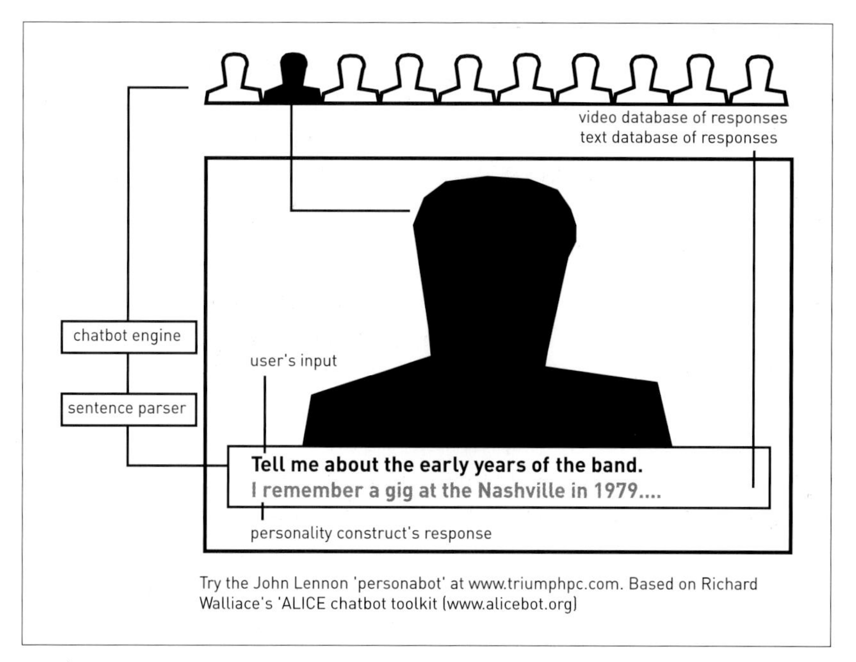

Try the John Lennon 'personabot' at www.triumphpc.com. Based on Richard Walliace's 'ALICE chatbot toolkit (www.alicebot.org)

The 'personality construct' encapsulates video interview responses from a pre-recorded database, a parsing and inference 'engine' that 'reads' your text input (question or conversational line), determines the most appropriate response, finds and displays it in real time. You can embody responses from real people – or enact famous characters from history. Shakespeare for dinner anyone?

a machine that has such a human face, and the PerCon, which is essentially an expert system based on a real person, really does embody the character and personality of the subject. This is just the beginning. Dynamic reasoning (aka 'thinking') will dramatically increase the efficiencies and 'common sense' of such software agents. Think of the possibilities – a construct of Shakespeare, Einstein, Mozart, indeed anyone, alive or dead, fictional or actual, about whom we have sufficient information, enacted maybe, but reflecting the aggregated totality of information on the subject. This is a people-friendly expert system if anything is. It could be a psychotherapist, a language teacher, a mentor, a guru, a financial adviser – a simulation, and visualization, of expertise in any subject.

Ananova is the first news-reading synthespian. Developed by Press Association and Edinburgh's Digital Animation Group, and recently changing hands (to Orange) for a reported £95 million, Ananova is pure software. Geared to read 'lip-synch' from a phonemically marked-up text, Ananova is also able to physiologically interpret her newscasts. Her mark-up language also includes 'visemes' – markers telling her when it's appropriate to smile, smirk, roll her lustrous peepers, sigh or groan – and when to wink, blink, twitch, shrug and look away. Check her out in real time at www.ananova.com.

Another example of 'synthetic person' or 'synthespian' front ends is the delightful Ananova (*www.ananova.com*), the 'virtual newscaster' developed by the Scottish Digital Animation Group (DAG) for the Press Association, and bought by Orange Telecom in July 2000 for $144 million (£95 million). Ananova is the front end to an advanced search and news-retrieval mechanism. 'She' is a computer animation and she speaks through speech-synthesis technology resident in your own PC. Effectively, she is a lifelike text-reading machine. The texts that she reads to you are modified to improve the phonetic delivery through synthesizers, and marked up with a special language that enables authors to determine her facial expression (DAG calls it her 'visemes'), providing the right expression to go with the story or news item she is reading, and also those little human ticks and twitches, blinks and winks, smiles and guiles that add visual expression to our conversation.

In my view, Ananova, and other synthespians currently vying for eyeball time (such as Channel 5's Vandrea, DAG's Tmmy, and others), are the first examples of what will be a major trend in human-computer interface design: the 'personality user interface'. Talking to a person, even a synthetic person, is infinitely better than typing and clicking into a standard graphical user interface (GUI).

Invented at Xerox PARC in the 1970s, the GUI was popularized as an 'easy' way of controlling computers in the 1980s, first by Apple with its MAC OS, and then by Microsoft with its Windows software. GUI was a breakthrough for personal computing at that time, as anyone who remembers the sterility of the command-line interface will testify. But GUIs don't really work very well on the small screen sizes of handheld web/net access devices. All that typing and scrolling is too fiddly on a mobile, so Ananova, and synthespians like her, offer another, more natural interface metaphor. With speech recognition and speech synthesis, an 'intelligent' engine to parse spoken input and infer what is required, and a 'thin client' approach (where Ananova or her ancestors are stored on the access device itself, and draw only the low-band text and data they need from the web/net), you will be able to talk to your 'friend' in your mobile, and he or she will act as your personal assistant or agent in much the same way that John Sculley envisaged in the late 1980s with the virtual 'Phil' on the virtual Knowledge Navigator. You will be able to customize the looks and personality of your synthetic friend, as well as his or her voice characteristics, to your personal taste, and he or she will be the mediator that searches and retrieves information, news and sportscasts for you, and that listens and obeys your commands.

With smart media like this, for the internet or the web read global library, online university, personal assistant, electronic office, personal tutor, translation machine, electronic newsroom, personal mentor, and so on. In other words, the web/net will become the extended embodiment of

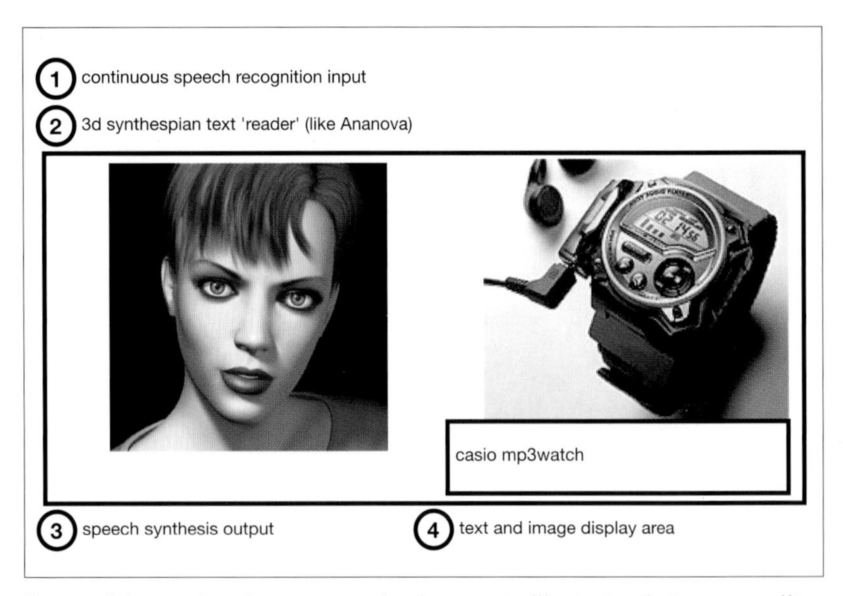

I've used the synthespian news-reader Ananova to illustrate what a personality user interface could look like. Just a talking head, you say? But that's the point – most input and output is as though you were talking to another human being. Sure there's a graphic panel for when the Ana PUI needs to show you something (a picture, map, diagram, chart or video, for example), but in most handheld devices, the PUI will be the main interface. When we will have PUIs like this? Well, we're 'nearly' there – we have most of the tools and technologies to do this. But the AI itself is the stumbling block – we have good continuous speech recognition, good search agents, good speech synthesis – but the 'clever' bit is still in development. Five years?

Turing's 'universal machine', able to act for us in all kinds of highly customized and personalized ways. When we start adding networked microprocessors, digital signal processors, and sensors of all kinds (optical, aural, physical, olfactory, chemical, electromagnetic) to this mix, then the 'internet' (will it still be called that?) will become something much more than all these things. It will become an extension of our eyes and ears and other senses right around the world. We will be able to check out the street life in Montmartre, Sloane Square, or in Tribeca (or anywhere else that's interesting) at the click of a mouse, get expert online help in every discipline under the sun, monitor the rainforests in Brazil, tune into a harbour web-cam in Phuket, view geothermal submarine vents, monitor the chemical output of a factory in Detroit – in other words, reach out into the real world as well as the cyberspace of our culture. We will be connected to millions of other users, to a great searchable archive of information and data (a real 'Encyclopedia Galactica'), and to a network of smart sensors and real-world interface devices. And as a huge bonus, we will have all the ingredients of a people-friendly planetary management tool in our hands at precisely the time we need it most.

content and software: new content for new media

This brings us to content and software, two extensive and rapidly converging areas in a network that will gradually subsume *all* the mass media we are now familiar with. The idea of new media content has been misconstrued by many publishers and broadcasters, who persist in viewing the new media as just another means of delivering more of the same content, recycled from their archives or marginally re-purposed from their current output. Not, I hasten to add, that there's anything wrong with this approach, it's just that it's not the only way of thinking about content – just the most obvious. As Herbert Marshall McLuhan pointed out, we tend to look at the future as if through a rear-view mirror, in this case perceiving new digital interactive media in terms of old-style broadcast or published media, much as we once described the automobile as a horse-less carriage.

There are three issues* that I want to deal with here: one is that what we are dealing with here is primarily a *telecommunications* network, not merely another broadcasting network, and given this, that people-to-people media will be as important as one-to-many media (traditional content); secondly, that the new media have to add considerable value to compete with the well-matured established media (otherwise why change?); and finally, to survey some of the indicators that will help determine the brand new network media that will emerge this decade. These 'really new' media are the technologies and 'content' that have emerged only in the past few decades: the

*Some of the issues that affect content and software, such as the intermediary software and hardware for browsing, finding and retrieving the content and software we want from an increasingly large search space, are addressed in 'The vision thing' and 'The next big thing'.

video game, virtual reality systems, computer modelling and animation, artificial intelligence, simulation software, multi-user domains, graphical chat spaces, and of course the hypermedia web itself. Increasingly, these software systems combine and synergize the four unique characteristics of new media: digital multimedia, artificial intelligence interactivity and networking.

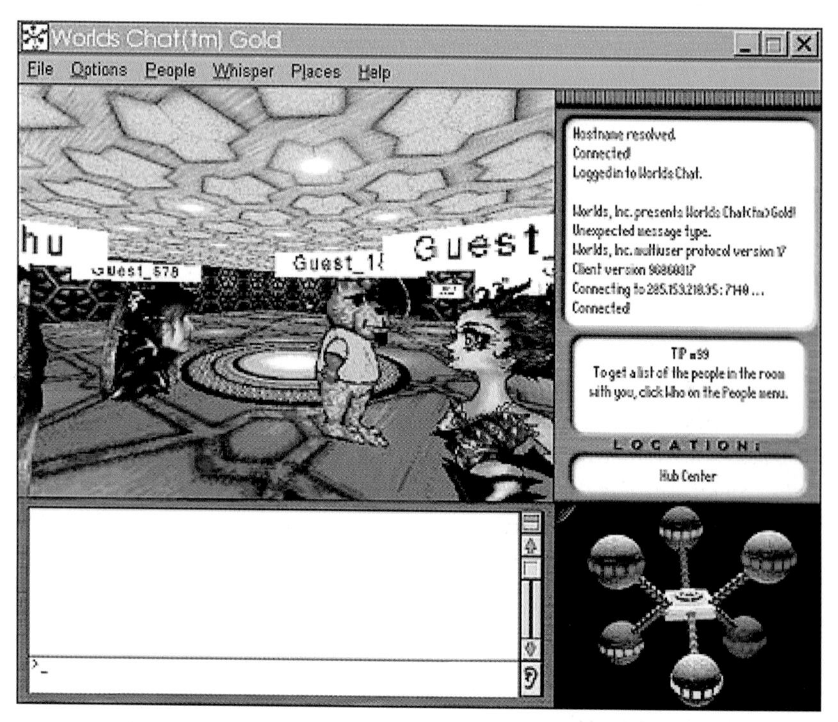

MUDs and MOOs predated the world wide web by about a decade, but then they were 'only' text-based experiences. Nowadays multi-user 'worlds' are rich 2D and 2D experiences, with 3D avatars, fractal landscapes, artificial life 'natives', embedded media and much more besides. When we see the integration of internet telephony (when we can actually chat to each other rather than text each other), and when we've got broadband networks, artificially intelligent synthespians, brilliant personalization, smart search agents to find 'personality matches', and fluid motion-control avatars, (etc) then virtual worlds will become the mainstay of P2P communications, just as e-mail and messaging are now.

content is people Almost everything that we are developing in the new media business is trending towards establishing ever-more pervasive and intricate means by which we communicate with each other. New media is much more about the media of human-to-human communication than it is about the one-to-many media associated with 20th-century broadcasting. One-to-one and many-to-many will be the dominant traffic of the network of communications systems we are building.

The fact that we are dealing with a 21st-century telecommunications network, not a broadcast network as perceived by TV and radio broadcasters in the 20th century, requires a radical shift in thinking, from thinking of content as 'media' – as electronic versions of books, magazines, newspapers, records, TV, radio and film, for example – to thinking of content as people and the interaction between people. The fact that sending and receiving e-mail consumes the bulk of online user time (according to Intelliquest, 89 per cent of average online time is spent this way), and that 7 *trillion* e-mails were sent in 2000, puts *'content is communication'** into perspective, and as we pointed out above, multimedia e-mail (of video and digital still photos, for example) will further blur the line between content providers and consumers. In the more conventional sense of content, GeoCities (*www.geocities.com*), the fourth most popular internet venue with 650,000 subscribers providing their own hobby and special-interest websites, is one example of how electronic communities generate their own content; online auctions (eg *www.ebay.com*) are another, and there are many other examples.

*Investor information sites such as Motley Fool rely on user contributions for their rich coverage of the market; e.pinions.com trades in peer-to-peer product reviews and critiques; Napster in peer-to-peer music copying; and in the more 'conventional' internet there are more than 14,000 newsgroups on USENET, used by millions of people every day.

The web/net is *not* just another one-to-many broadcast medium. Its destiny is to remain symmetrical, providing equal two-way bandwidth for both sending and receiving*, allowing the user to be both content consumer and content provider.

*Or at least sufficient up-stream bandwidth in asynchronous systems, such as cable, satellite, and ADSL.

The net will certainly subsume all of the 20th-century traditional one-way media forms, so we will be able to access news, books, television and records and the rest from it. But people – the 350 million-plus interacting individuals that make up the cyberspace population, a population that is doubling every year – are what makes the web/net so different from 20th-century media. As I have mentioned, most people cite e-mail – currently the most widely used person-to-person application – as the major attraction of

There's a delightful heterogeneity in the avatar scene right now – mixtures of 3D and 2D, photo and illustration, representational and fantastic – as users can easily define their own avatar, or customize them from a wide range provided by the world vendor. As bandwidth increases, worlds will become more and more realistic, deploying real-time, first-person rendering engines like those developed by ID software (Doom, Quake, etc), and avatars will become more 'natural' and more 'expressive' too – after all, they are the 'body language' of cyberspace.

the net. E-mail will evolve rapidly as broadband, 24/7 constant access becomes the norm. We can expect a surge in multimedia mail facilities, maybe using the kind of peer-to-peer (proprietary, or HTTP-based) exchange technology popularized by Napster. Among the changes we should look for are video and audio e-mail or instant messaging, personal webcasts and web-cam virtual private networks, multi-party home video conferencing, and an increased use of 'voice-over-IP' (internet telephony) as well as hybrid combinations of internet telephony, e-mail and messaging.

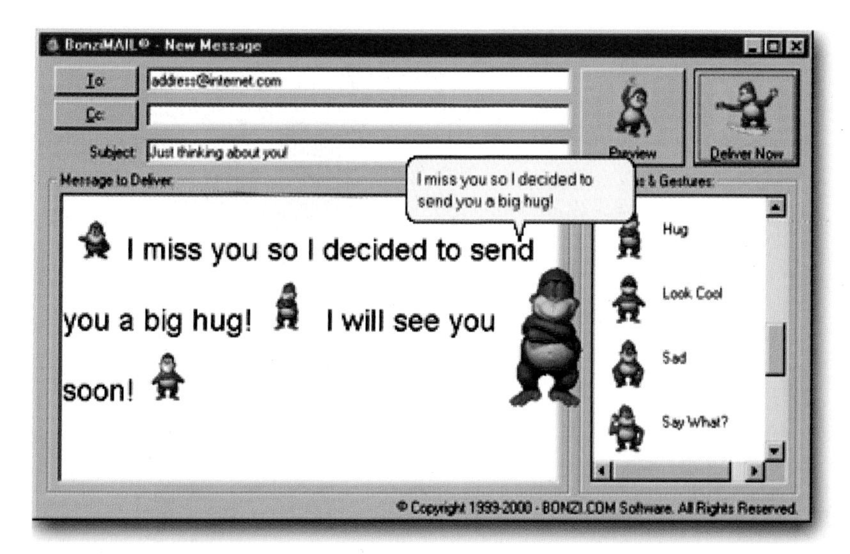

E-mail and messaging are the most popular P2P software. Trillions of these electronic messages are sent each year. As network bandwidth increases, expect to see various multimedia enhancements: integrated voice-mail, video-mail, multimedia presentations, and the like. BBmail by Bonzi.com provides animated avatars to illustrate and punctuate e-mail messages. (image courtesy www.bonzi.com)

But these 'P2P' (peer-to-peer, but also people-to-people) services, or socialware, are just the beginning. In my opinion, this genre will be the mainspring that drives much of new media content development through this decade. It's worth tracing a brief history of P2P in order to further round out our big picture. Then we can extrapolate from this, and speculate on the future of multimedia telecommunications, virtual communities and other forms of P2P socialware.

a brief history of P2P

However, socialware encompasses a wide range of applications and an even wider set of acronyms, including MUD (multi-user domain), MOO (object-oriented MUD), MUSE (multi-user simulated environment), MUVE (multi-user virtual environment), MUA (multi-user adventures), and MUSH (multi-user shared hallucination), but these terms all relate to P2P socialware. They are means of extending social interaction through the network, and the underlying trend is that these socialware apps are increasingly creating the means to communicate in a wide variety of natural language means (through voice, gesture, expression, appearance, etc), in increasingly rich multimedia environments. It is logical, and probable, that these shared social cyberspaces will eventually integrate all the means of communicating through the web/net in a seamless environment that increasingly mimics or simulates (or parodies!) real-world, real-time social interaction. The application of these technologies in business communications is generically called 'groupware' (see Chapter 8), but here I want to focus on software that is designed to involve users in casual, social interactions.

The first imaginative exploration of how people should share the virtual space of the networked computer was the MUD (originally multi-user dungeon later multi-user domain or dimension). These were shared virtual spaces or domains which provided users with textual descriptions of each part of the domain. They were, and are, a kind of imaginary, literary space, much like reading the description of Gormenghast in Mervyn Peake's trilogy. Previously, one of the first computer games, Adventure (co-designed by Will Crowther at BBN and Don Woods at the Stanford Artificial Intelligence Lab in the late 1960s), had used similar text instructions and descriptions to let the user navigate through an imaginary environment. In MUDs, the user was able to move around in a virtual, imaginary space and importantly, chat with other users who happened to be in the same 'location'. The first MUDs were text-based, literally written descriptions of the shared cyberspace.

“THEY WERE A KIND OF IMAGINARY, LITERARY SPACE, MUCH LIKE READING THE DESCRIPTION OF GORMENGHAST IN MERVYN PEAKE'S TRILOGY”

The idea of virtual communities – online communities of people with common interests – has been around since the early 1980s, and inspired what was probably the first cyberspace sci-fi novella, Vernor Vinge's *True Names**, which appeared in *Dell Binary Star #5* in 1981. The first MUD was created a couple of years earlier by two students at Essex University in the UK, Roy Trubshaw and Richard Bartle. In spring 1979, Trubshaw wrote the code for the first proto-MUD in MACRO-10 (the machine code for the university's DEC-PDP 10 mini-mainframes) as a game that, according to Richard Bartle, 'consisted of little more than a series of interconnected locations where you

*'LucasFilm's famous online community 'Habitat' (now run by Fujitzu) was directly inspired by **True Names**. In hypermedia, fact and fiction catalyze each other.

Microsoft chat (formerly comic chat) is a freely downloadable IRC (Internet Relay Chat) chat client, initially released as part of Explorer v3.0 in 1996. Using this program, your online chat sessions unfold with your chosen comic strip character (avatar) 'speaker' by means of a speech bubble. The program uses semantic analysis of the sentences you type in order to control the gestures of your avatar. Developed by David Kurlander and the Virtual Worlds Group at Microsoft, and illustrated with characters and settings drawn by Jim Woodring, Microsoft Chat is another indication of the rich multimedia future of P2P software.

Vernor Vinge's 1981 novella 'True Names' illustrated the potential of the MUD (multi-user domain) and the use of avatars, only a year or so after the invention of the first MUD by Richard Bartle and Roy Trubshaw, at the University of Essex, UK, at the end of the 1970s. 'True Names' in turn inspired Lucasfilm's 1985 'Habitat' virtual world. (image courtesy Vernor Vinge/Gary Ruddell/Baen Books)

could move and chat'. Rewritten by Trubshaw almost immediately (and this time described as a MUD), the second version was more sophisticated, and was supported by a database stored as a separate file, to which users could add during play. Trubshaw invented a special MUD definition language (MDDL) for this database, which stored the rooms, objects and commands that defined the MUD. The database was, however, too easy to add to and resulted in the creation of rooms and commands that were inappropriate, confusing, and detracted from the MUDs 'game play'.

A third version was created during late 1979 and early 1980, again by Trubshaw, but this time in the BCPL (Basic Combined Programming Language) code, which was easier to manage and required less memory (the code had to be smaller than 50 kb to run on the PDP 10). This MUD was later extended and improved by Bartle, who added many of the features now commonly associated with MUDs, such as mobiles (objects that you acquire and carry with you from room to room), containers (cupboards, caves and boxes, etc), and some infrastructural components (for example, relationships between different players and their mobile tools in the same rooms), and importantly, he 'added all the stuff about getting to be a wizard' (ie reaching the level of being able to create new aspects of the game).

But while purely text-based imaginary environments are (like pure hypertext fiction) engaging and fascinating, and demand some rewarding cognitive effort from the user, the future of P2P is in rich, visual environments that use both 2D and 3D graphics to illustrate the shared environment. One of the first of these 'graphical worlds' was Habitat, developed at Lucasfilm Games by Chip Morningstar and F. Randall Farmer in 1984–1986. This was a comic-strip-like world in which users were represented by cartoon characters (avatars) that could be controlled by keyboard commands and made to move around in the 'world' – ie move from frame to frame within the regions of the 'comic' (of which there were many; at one stage the early version of Habitat had around 20,000 different 'regions'). Users talked to the avatars of other users by creating a speech bubble and typing their message into it. Avatars could move around, pick up, put down and manipulate objects, and make gestures as well as conversation. Habitat was versioned as Club Caribe, and now owned by Fujitzu survives as Worldsaway on Compuserve (soon to be available on the web/net).

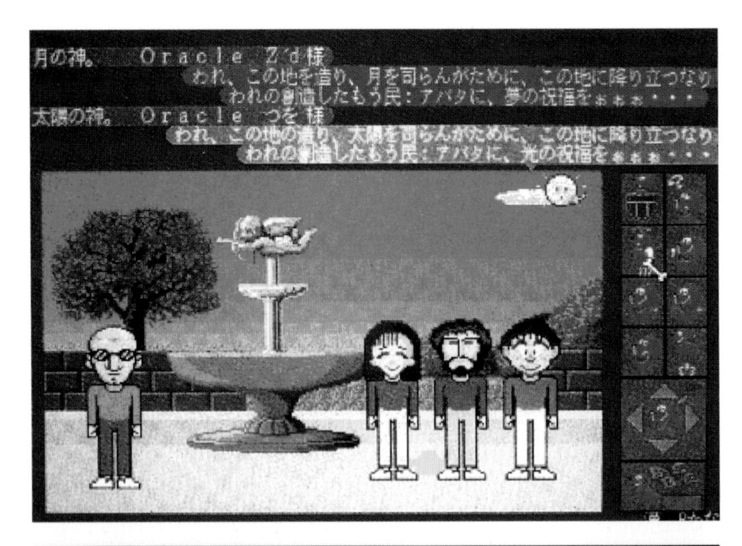

Designed and implemented in the mid-1980s, Habitat was the first highly sophisticated 'commercial' virtual world. Designed for a commercial low-band online service, Habitat was designed to run on low-cost Commodore 64 computers, and at its most popular, it reached a group of over 15,000 regular users. Constrained by bandwidth and processing power, Habitat exploited a low-definition popular medium – the comic strip – in order to provide world views and avatars. Avatars spoke to other avatars by means of comic-strip-like speech bubbles. For more on Habitat see 'The Lessons of Lucasfilm's Habitat' in Michael Benedikt, 'Cyberspace: Next Steps', MIT Press, 1991. (images courtesy Lucasfilm/Fujitsu)

The next step in the evolution of P2P was in 1988, when the Finn Jarkko Oikarinen created Internet Relay Chat (IRC). A program and protocol designed to allow real-time, synchronous, multi-party text conversations to take place via the internet within a scrolling window on each user's screen, Internet Relay Chat is based on a network of hundreds of IRC servers (that is, servers running IRC software), supporting IRC networks in various parts of the world, and communicating with each other using the common language of IRC protocol. You connect to an IRC network by using an IRC client, an application that sits on your PC and lets you log on to an IRC server. Available from the server are hundreds of 'channels' of different discussions and conversations, and the user can choose which he or she wants to 'listen in' to (read the dialogue) or join. Contributions from users are relayed from IRC server to IRC server and appear in a common window as a string of dialogue made up of contributions from many people in many parts of the world. IRC also allows users to establish private chat rooms for more focused or discreet conversations.

Then in 1990, Pavel Curtis of Xerox PARC created the MOO. MOOs differ from MUDs in that they are not a static environment presided over by a group of controlling programmers. MOOs offer all users the opportunity to construct spaces and objects, or to write additional code, that enhances or expands the virtual environment. MOOs are open-source software, and the source code is freely available from PARC. So unlike MUDs, MOOs are continuously being created and modified by their users. But MOOs are still primarily text-based, imaginary environments, still part of the web/net incunabula, not indicators of the future.

However, by the mid-1990s, and as a result of continuously increasing processing power (Pentium, PowerPC) and faster connections (56 kbps modems), multi-user domains were beginning to assume the multimedia forms that will characterize them through this coming decade. A sophisticated example of the new multi-user domains (part chat room, part games site, part animated puppet show, part adventure game, part simulation), The Palace was created in 1995. Initially conceived as a virtual casino – the GamePalace – where users could play electronic versions of traditional card, table and board games, as well as chat and gamble, The Palace was the brainchild of Jim Bumgardner, a multimedia designer and expert programmer, then at Time Warner Interactive. Bumgardner envisioned The Palace as a complex networking

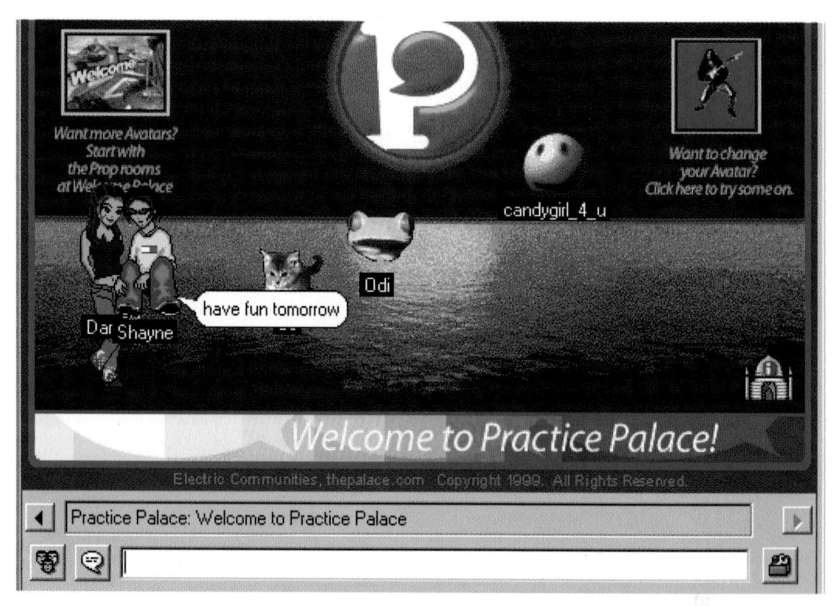

It's still early days for graphical chat-zones or 'Worlds'. With few personalization and filtering tools available to identify strangers with similar interests and tastes, conversation can be disappointingly trivial. Expect to see major breakthroughs in these areas, and in the development of more sophisticated and expressive avatars. (image courtesy www.thepalace.com)

system that would allow users to wander freely, engaging in games, chat and other activities as they wanted, not limited by a gaming objective (like Adventure, Zork, Myst or other previous 'virtual world' fantasy games).

'I had always enjoyed chat programs, and thought it would be fun to do one that provided some of the immersive qualities of 3D virtual reality, yet at the same time wouldn't excessively tax your CPU. I also wanted to provide a goodly amount of creative freedom both in the ability to build worlds and in how you could modify your appearance. My solution was to make things as simple as possible. For example, although a background picture might look like a room or like a landscape, I was careful not to program the software to explicitly act like either one. By using 2D graphics, I made it the role of the user to determine what the world meant, not the software.'

Jim Bumgardner at www.jbum.com/history

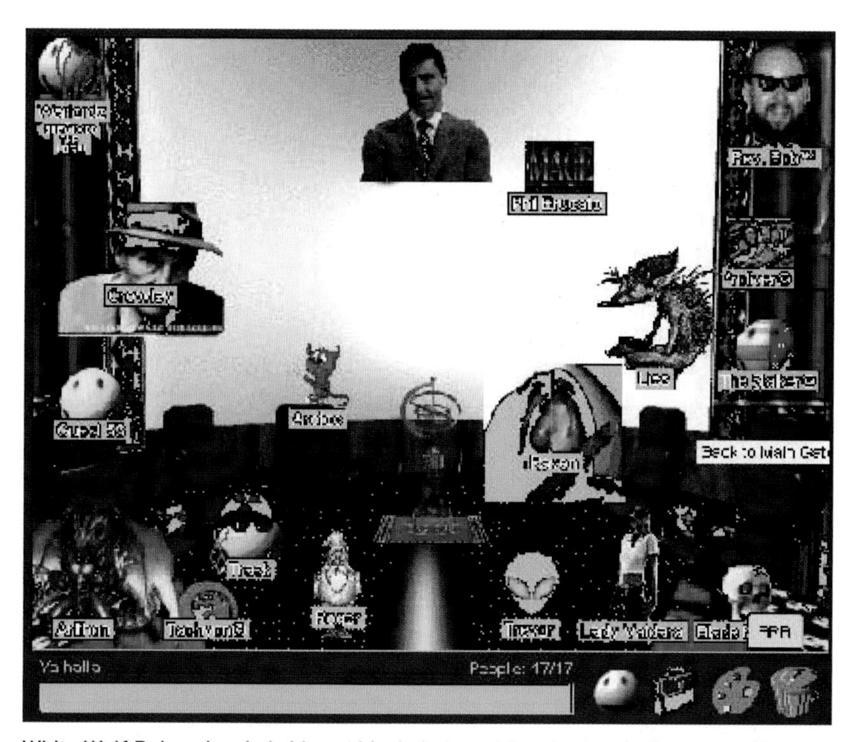

White Wolf Palace is a hybrid graphical chat world and role-playing game. Users can adopt various characters from the pantheon of 'World of Darkness' inhabitants, or can simply indulge in 'in-character' casual chat with other users. (image courtesy www.white-wolf.com)

The essence of the human-computer interface of graphical worlds like the Palace, Worldsaway and Alphaworld is that the user creates or chooses an animated image to represent them in the virtual world. Then, using keyboard or mouse commands, the user can move this avatar through the virtual world, make gestures of welcome, shake hands, shrug shoulders, dance, skip and frolic, and 'talk' to other avatars that are in turn being manipulated by their human owners. The advantage of graphical over purely text-based worlds is the wider range of interpersonal, non-verbal communication modes available – from movement and gesture to facial expression, to clothes and apparel, make-up and tonsure. Graphical worlds have 'body language'.

Stephenson wasn't the first to describe virtual multi-user worlds in science fiction, but he is very good, and the 'Metaverse' described in Snow Crash has been very influential in indicating the future direction of MUD developments. (image courtesy Neal Stephenson/Bantam Books)

As early as 1992, three years before The Palace appeared, the science-fiction writer Neal Stephenson had visualized where these graphical worlds might be heading, and how avatars might look and interact. His hero is called Hiro, and the graphical world is a 'metaverse' called simply 'the Street':

'As Hiro approaches the Street, he sees two young couples, probably using their parents' computers for a double date in the Metaverse, climbing out of Port Zero, which is the local port of entry and monorail stop.

'He is not seeing real people, of course. This is all part of the moving illustration drawn by his computer according to specifications coming down the fibre-optic cable. The people are pieces of software called avatars. They are the audio-visual bodies that people use to communicate with each other in the Metaverse.'

Neal Stephenson, Snow Crash

Avatar kits on current graphical worlds are really basic. You choose from a selection of pre-designed symbols and images or alternatively up-load a photo or drawing to modify as your avatar. Of course, using avatars to represent the user in digital space had already been explored quite thoroughly in 'role-playing' video games and in virtual reality, and in fiction by Vernor Vinge, William Gibson and others, but graphical worlds brought these techniques of P2P-computer interaction to a much wider, web/net user group.

> “THE FIRST FISH SYNTHESPIAN WAS OPERATED BY A PUPPETEER WEARING A DATA GLOVE”

And the technology for creating avatars is rapidly becoming more sophisticated. Indeed, at the extreme of these developments, full-body 3D scanners and 'data suits' can create accurate three-dimensional data sets describing your body, and use motion capture techniques to enable you to move your virtual body in entirely natural ways, either replaying a set of pre-rendered animations, or ultimately, manipulating the data set in real time (like a flight simulator). Now widely used in digital motion-picture effects, video games and video special effects, real-time motion-capture was pioneered by Brad de Graf in 1988, and later commercialized and productivized by several companies, including Jim Henson Animatronics, SimGraphics, deGraf/Wahrman, and Canal Plus MediaLab, which created the Bert the Fish digital animatronic for Nickelodeon children's TV in the early 1990s. Bert was blue-screened and appeared beside a human presenter, seeming to talk to him or her. The first fish synthespian was operated by a puppeteer wearing

The BT/BBC/Sony/Illuminations joint venture created the prototype broadband 3D world exploring the Inhabited TV theme. 'Inhabited TV' is a vision of future television services in which multi-user virtual environments deliver unprecedented levels of audience participation. Social chat and interaction are mixed with professional content and programming to create online communities.' The Mirror explored many possible features of broadband 3D worlds – including embedded media, avatar boutiques, e-commerce and multimedia chat-spaces.

a data glove, who controlled Bert's body movements, and an actor who spoke Bert's lines and controlled his facial expressions.

'Performance animation' is the manipulation and animation of 3D computer models in real time. Controlled by a puppeteer wearing a data glove (providing live motion capture), Bert the Fish is generated by a powerful Silicon Graphics Onyx RealityEngine2 workstation, and is blue-screen matted into the live Nickelodeon TV studio, where he 'floats' in studio space, 'chatting' to anchorman and guests alike. Will future avatars be controlled in real time by their users? (image courtesy Canal Plus MEDIALAB)

As I have pointed out elsewhere, there is a general trend in digital technology in which the tools that last year were the province of the professional (and cost a lot of money), this year become accessible to the prosumer, and next year become cheap enough for the ordinary man in the street. As vir-

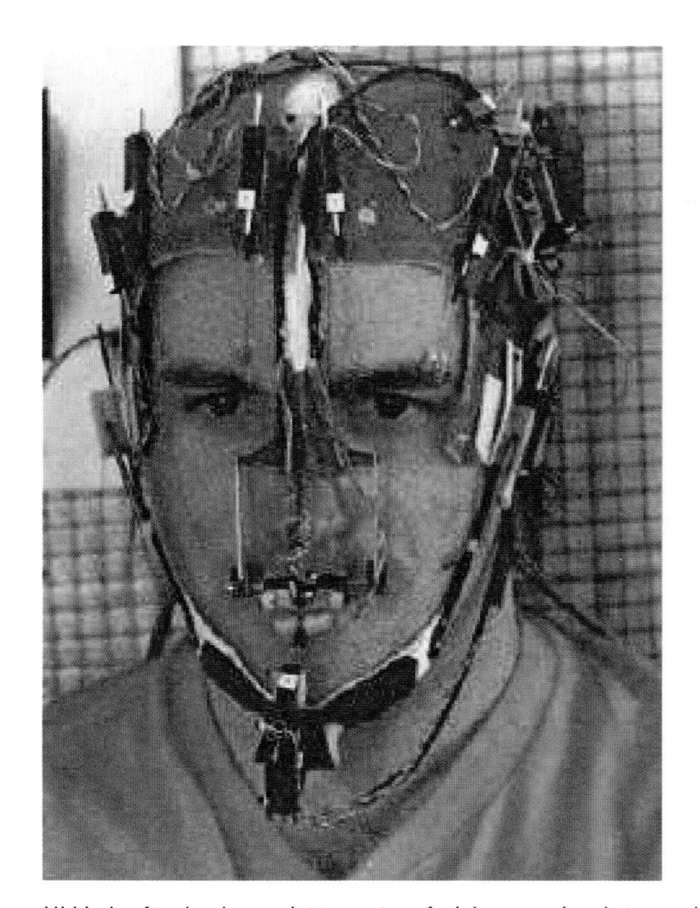

All kinds of technology exist to capture facial expression data – and then to apply this data to a computer-generated 'synthespian'. Character-Shop's 'Waldo' series of face, body and hand motion-capture rigs use position-sensors to capture the subtleties of physical expression and movement. (image courtesy The Character-Shop at www.character-shop.com)

tual worlds like The Palace and Worldsaway become ever more realistic as a result of increased processing power and bandwidth, we are likely to see more sophisticated tools for avatar creation, editing and control becoming available to all. And the same is true of the world creation tools, the 2D and 3D computer modelling applications used to create or to personalize our own virtual real estate.

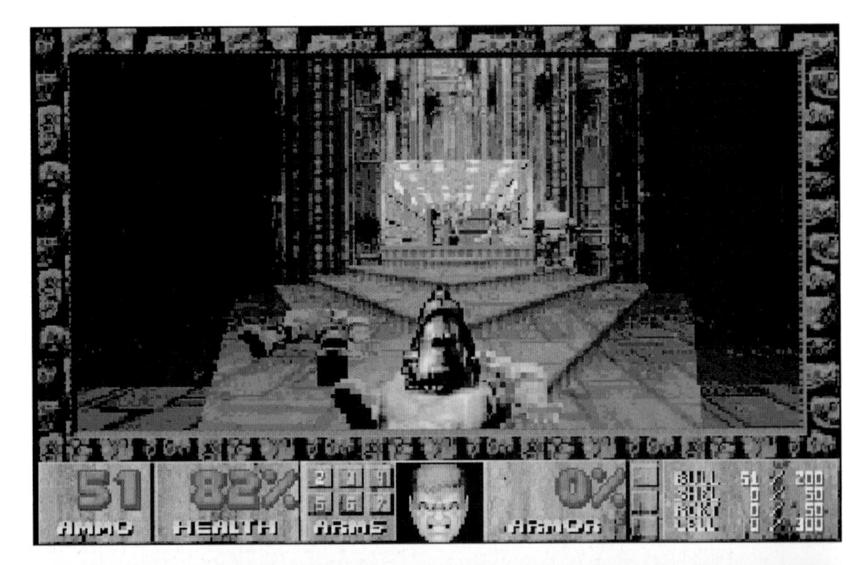

Two famous videogames illustrate the potential of 3D world environments – combine the high resolution detail of Myst with the multi-user networking and real-time freedom to explore offered by Doom, and you begin to define the future of networked virtual worlds. 'Doom' courtesy of ID software (www.idsoftware.com) and 'Myst' courtesy of cyan (www.cyan.com).

The end product might be a three-dimensional, photographically rendered, highly realistic virtual world that we navigate in real time (like Doom), with our avatar moving under our real-time control through virtual spaces that we have also helped to create or to capture from the real world. This is a likely scenario, as the dominant trend in computer graphics has been towards the creation of ever-more realistic, photo-quality 3D spaces; and several multi-user real-time 3D engines have been created over the past decade. Furthermore, the expectations that have been nurtured by fictional representations like those of Stephenson and Gibson will continue to drive the development of tools and techniques to make this happen ('technology apes art').

But whether these high-resolution worlds will provide a better user experience than the cartoon-like Habitat is a moot point. As McLuhan pointed out, low-resolution images require more cognitive effort from the viewer – we use the minimal clues from such images to round out our perception of the space depicted in the comic – and so we actively participate, with the artist, in the creation of a consensual reality (or a 'shared hallucination' as William Gibson describes it). Many people find this experience more satisfying than photo-reality, just as many prefer the low-band radio to the high-band television, because 'the pictures are better'. Of course, there is no reason why users could not choose the cognitive level they are most happy with, whether this is text, cartoons or stereo VR.

Strangely, the idea of creating a virtual world that brings together people from many different parts of the real world – and acts as a free-form, drop-in-when-you-want-a-chat, venue; that is robust enough for thousands of simultaneous visitors; that is responsive enough to accommodate constant or intermittent user updates, and that can carry many different forms of media and software (movies, music, games, applications, etc) as well as e-commerce, advertising and sponsorship branding – hasn't taken hold with many of the big publishing and broadcasting companies, perhaps because of the threat that peer-to-peer networking (such as Napster's file-sharing P2P technology) poses to their precious film and music and book copyrights.

Or maybe it's because they still don't understand that the future of media is going to be much more about P2P, not just about the one-to-many content delivery of the past century.

adding value to content: 'enhanced media' The second content and software issue concerns the shift from passive to dynamic media – the variety of added-value that digital, interactive networks can confer on content when it is transformed into software. And perhaps the main issue here is: why download a book or record, or a television programme, when there are already well established, convenient ways of reading, listening and viewing?

In terms of television, the answer is that during the first decade of the new century, analogue TV broadcasting will be totally replaced by digital – after some time around the middle of the decade (2006 in the US), we won't have a choice. But generally, the answer is obvious to new media designers – and to economists. It lies in what Nicholas Negroponte calls the shift from atoms to bits. Why ship weighty books and cumbersome video tapes in their physical embodiment at great expense when you can just ship the real 'content' – the ASCII or PDF code, the MP3 music file or the MPEG2 encoded video signal – for no cost, directly over the web/net? Why pay for delivery when the consumer will come and collect what they want?

Of course we all know it's not as simple as this – we know that people love books and records, they like collecting objects, and like the simplicity of the telly. People are collectors, they like the physical evidence of their culture, they like the beauty and the diversity of printed books, the convenience and style of magazines, and they take pride and pleasure in their record collections.

But as we have seen, the technology for collecting, storing and accessing digital media is changing rapidly, indeed has really only just begun to hint at the kind of easy-to-use, high-resolution interactive devices that will come to characterize 21st-century media. Print-quality, paper-like screens, solid-state memory, powerful processors, searchable books, customized TV; the electronic book with its 'personal library' capacity; the solid state Walkman – ultra-low battery consumption and no moving parts; and the HDVR – no tapes to buy, and smart software agents to collect and record your favourite programmes for you – there's no doubt that these technologies will appeal, and it's only a matter of time before these new media will become overwhelmingly attractive, not least because they will be cheaper. If the text of a book, the 'pure' content, can be downloaded for a tenth of the cost of a

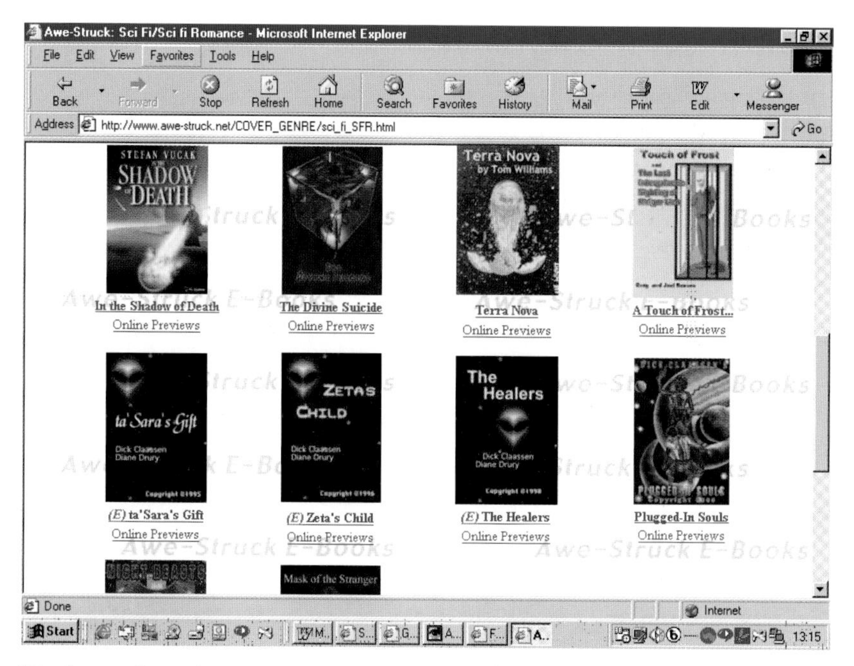

The future through a rear-view mirror: the web 'shop-window' display looks awfully familiar, but awe-struck.net stock a range of innovative electronic texts, and several e-comics, including be-radical's 'Latex'. E-publishers offer the same range of literature genres as print publishers, but Awe-struck.net's science fiction collection includes titles only available as e-books. Awe-struck titles can be dowloaded in various formats – HTML, floppy-disk, Palm, etc – from around $4. (image courtesy www.awe-struck.net)

printed book and it's just as high resolution, plus it's random access, searchable, never forgets your place, stores your notes and comments, holds 30 or 40 of your favourite books, and connects to the vast web library machine too, won't the attraction of such a tool be decisive?

At some point in the near future our conception of a book collection will change from that of just a collection of paperbacks and hardbacks on our bookshelves to the personal web space and portable memory space that holds our collection of digital texts*. This won't need to be a large collection. In fact it will probably contain only the books we are reading at the moment. There will be no point in collecting books when we have instant access to

*In 2000, the internet bookstore Amazon.com held information on about 2.5 million paper books in its catalogue, but these were **paper** books. Project Gutenberg, created by Michael Hart in 1971, aims to digitize and make available all public – domain literature on the web/net as 'e-texts' (ASCII text files, which 99 per cent of computers can display. Hart aims to have the first stage of Project Gutenberg – a 10,000-volume electronic public library – available before the end of 2001.

Project Gutenberg has the grand aim of making all public-domain literature available on the web as downloadable text files. Such endeavours will encourage commercial e-book publishers to consider adding value to their e-publications, perhaps in some of the ways prototyped by the Voyager Company in the early 1990s.

every book in the biggest library on the planet, of being able to download *any book we want*, from the canon of classics to the latest novel, technical manual or scientific treatise. I know it's not the same as the physical presence of your favourite and personal collection of books, but these new e-books won't replace these collections, just provide a 21st-century, functionally superior equivalent. As McLuhan said, no new media ever replace older media, they just subsume them. Post e-books, our book collecting will likely be far more concerned with the aesthetic and tactile qualities of the book itself, the book as artefact rather than as repository of text.

P2P: problems and opportunities For publishers, broadcasters, artists, film-makers and writers, the implications of high-bandwidth networking, cheap hard-disk and solid-state memory, new access devices, and peer-to-peer network technology are awesome. They rightly fear that these technologies, along with MP3 and future data compression standards such as MPEG4, are threatening the very basis of their business. Peer-to-peer networks, such as those pioneered by Napster (*www.napster.com*)*, mean that individuals can 'share' copyright material by copying it directly from one user's hard disk to their own without paying any copyright fee at all. What's

*Napster only allows users of its network to swap MP3 files, but a third-party product called 'wrapster' lets you disguise any file as an MP3 file, and so allows you to share any files over the Napster network.

worse for IPR holders, some of the variants of Napster, such as Gnutella and FreeNet for MP3 (and other) file swapping, are decentralized (no central server is involved) and therefore really hard to take legal action against. Most of the software that users need to enable P2P networking is available as freeware or open-source software, and some of this file-sharing software provides high levels of anonymity for their users. Of course, the record business and Hollywood are fighting back and trying, rather belatedly, to establish their own encryption formats, like the CSS (Content Scrambler System) for encrypting digital movie files on DVD, and the SDMI (secure digital music initiative) for digital music files. But the stable is empty, the cat is out of the bag and the bird has flown. It's going to be very hard to undo this kind of file sharing. More than 20 million people were using Napster during the summer of 2000, and like car-boot or garage sales, transactions on

“MORE THAN 20 MILLION PEOPLE WERE USING NAPSTER DURING THE SUMMER OF 2000”

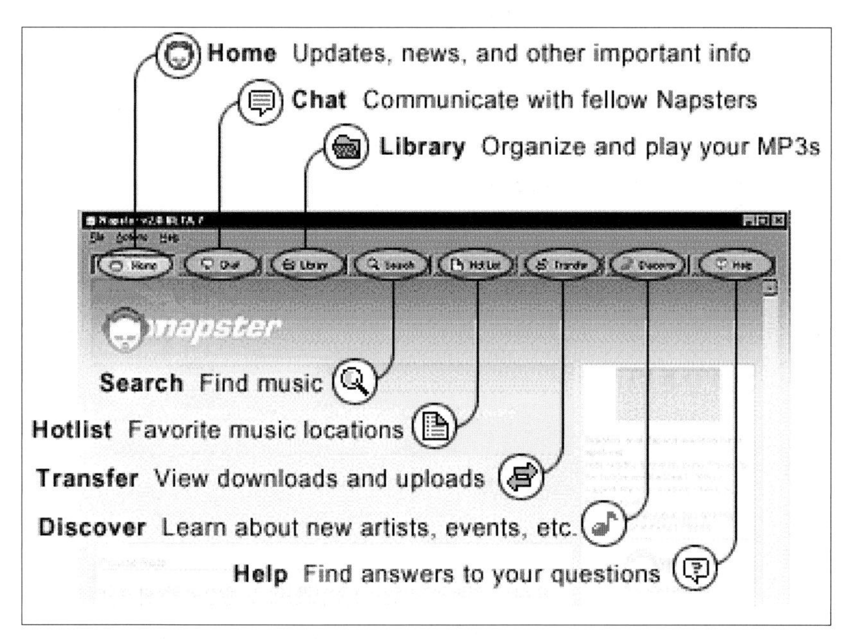

Globally networked electronic people-to-people exchanges threaten to subvert traditional media distribution channels. What Napster made possible for MP3 files, so we will see a variety of P2P exchanges spring up for all other digital media. As network bandwidth increases, this distribution model will also begin to impact on broadband media – on television, video and movies.

this scale are virtually impossible to track, let alone police (although the British Phonographic Industry was doing its best, tracing thousands of Napster users to their IP address). Add to this the fact that many Napster users trade directly with each other outside the Napster network, and it's the *reductio ad absurdum* of the free market.

But the central idea behind peer-to-peer networking – that of *immensely simplifying* the previously complex process of swapping files directly from machine to machine around the internet – is promising and could transform many publishing operations. P2P also promises new search strategies, allowing new kinds of engines to search *all* the contents of every machine on the network, not just the content of web pages. The browser pioneer Marc Andreeson has already invested in InfraSearch, a search technology that proposes to do just this. Alternatively, P2P could be used to set up online auctions, or possibly to sell stocks and shares, without any middleman or auction site involved (see also Chapter 8).

The challenge for publishers and broadcasters (and other rights owners) is to work out how this peer-to-peer technology might be used as a distribution medium for legitimate content acquisition. Their strategy has to be 'If you can't beat 'em, join 'em'. If they don't, there is a great danger of them being disintermediated in three ways – by P2P file sharing of course, but also by their own artists or writers using P2P to establish direct access to fans and to readers, and furthermore, by entrepreneurs or new 'remediators' inventing or discovering other ways to generate income from this rather anarchic situation.

digital enhancement: content becomes software 'The content of new media is old media.' So saith McLuhan. And that is particularly true for this first phase of digital media development, as broadcasters and publishers leverage as much advantage and profit as they can from their copyright holdings in linear media.

Although the history of enhanced digital media is relatively short, stemming mostly from the work of various digital designers, researchers and publishers since 1980 – specifically from the Advanced Technology Group at

Ten years ago, Bob and Aileen Stein's Voyager Company pioneered electronic books. On CD-ROM and floppy-disk, Voyager's 'expanded books' explored all the advantages that electronic book formats offered the reader. Searchable, hyperlinked text, electronic 'bookmarks', pop-up notations, animated illustrations, working drafts, author interviews, and even Quicktime VR panoramic virtual tours of the authors' work-place – the 'enhanced book' format introduced all these ideas. The expanded book format worked particularly well on 'The Complete Maus' – Art Spiegelman's Pullitzer-award winning, dark graphic novel on the Holocaust. Expanded with interviews, diaries, preliminary sketches, full-page spreads and detailed comic frames, Maus is the classic example of digitally enhanced content. (images courtesy Bob Stein, Voyager)

Apple Computer (The Guides project for Grolier Electronic Publishing), and from the remarkable Voyager Company, which produced hundreds of seminal 'expanded books' and movies between 1985 and 1997 – it was during this period that the principal devices of enhanced media were conceived, designed, prototyped and productivized.

What is digital enhancement? It covers all the many ways that extant linear content – books, movies, documentaries, television programmes, music albums, etc – and iconic content – photographs, maps, paintings and graphic art – can be digitally extended and expanded, mainly by the provision of hyperlinked additional information.

For example, the expanded books published by Voyager often featured a range of digital enhancements, including a searchable index and table of contents 'menu', hyperlinked footnotes and annotations, electronic bookmarks and Post-it Notes, extended bibliography and web links, author's biography, interview with the author, background and contextual information, quiz on the book's contents or subject matter, working roughs or preliminary sketches, and often video or audio interviews or features. The first Voyager products were on laser disk and CD-ROM, but with the launch of Apple's laptop Powerbook in 1992, they started producing delightful expanded books on floppy disk. Although a far from perfect electronic book device, the Powerbook was portable, sexy, and ran Apple's hypermedia application Hypercard, the principal authoring tool at Voyager*. It was a ready-made market, and Voyager catered for it with a range of more than 250 titles, including William Gibson's cyberpunk novel *Idoru*, Rodney Alan Greenblat's delicious *Dazzleoids*, an illustrated 'talking book' for children, Martin Gardner's *Annotated Alice*, Marvin Minsky's *Society of Mind*, and many other key texts.

*For an in-depth discussion of the early enhanced book publishers, authors and designers, see Bob Hughes' excellent **Dust or Magic: Secrets of Successful Multimedia Design.**

While the next generation of electronic books won't be based on Hypercard (which unfortunately runs only on Apple computers), they will almost certainly be prepared in the variety of existing formats for text delivery: as HTML (or XML) and PDF texts (worldwide, there are more than 100 million copies of Adobe's Acrobat Reader for its page-description format (PDF) files), as well as in proprietary formats such as Rocket Reader and PRCDOC for Palm. Microsoft is also including its Microsoft Reader e-text client in Windows.

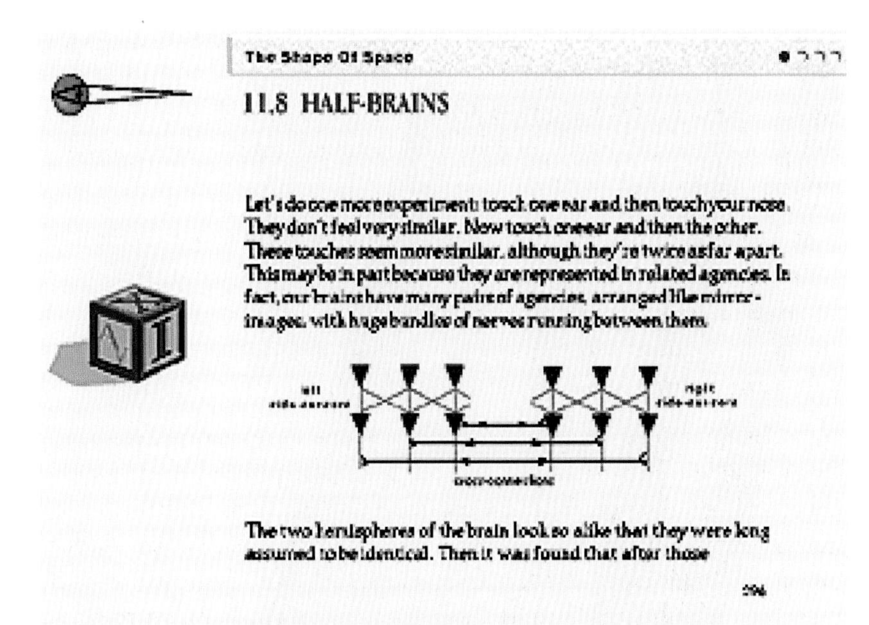

The Shape Of Space

11.8 HALF-BRAINS

Let's do one more experiment: touch one ear and then touch your nose. They don't feel very similar. Now touch one ear and then the other. These touches seem more similar, although they're twice as far apart. This may be in part because they are represented in related agencies. In fact, our brains have many pairs of agencies, arranged like mirror-images, with huge bundles of nerves running between them.

The two hemispheres of the brain look so alike that they were long assumed to be identical. Then it was found that after those

This digitally enhanced version of AI guru Marvin Minsky's book describing his theory of consciousness reinforced Voyagers claim to the high-ground of electronic publishing. Society of Mind included a hyperlinked QTVR panorama of Minsky's study, archive footage from the MIT AI lab, an interactive timeline of Minsky's life, a selection of his articles and papers, a bibliography, video interview – as well as the complete, searchable and annotated text of the printed book. (images courtesy Bob Stein, Voyager)

This new generation of e-books* will emerge over the next few years, as solid-state display and web/net access devices converge to create powerful, pocket-size e-books that can display web-based content as well as download, store and display e-texts. An e-book that can search the web both conventionally and on a peer-to-peer basis, locate the e-text you want, download it and store it alongside several dozen such 'books' will be a killer app that we can expect to see very soon. These new devices, signalled by products such as the Rocket e-book, will be the literary equivalent of MP3 players. Product design is all-important here, and my guess is that the successful e-books will provide both web access and e-book storage and display, and importantly have good 'heft' – be really easy and

*During 2001, expect to see the final proposals for a new e-book format, first proposed in 1999, the 'Open ebook' (OEB) standard, created by a consortium of e-book and traditional publishers and Microsoft. The difference between PDF and OEB is that PDF carries fixed, pre-formatted book texts that are not interactive and cannot be reformatted on the fly. PDF will be suitable for some texts (novels, etc) where interactivity is either unnecessary or irrelevant, but OEB and XML will be able to provide the full range of enhancements for non-fiction texts. Security and copyright protection is an unresolved issue here. In spring 2000, Simon & Schuster published Steven King's **Riding the Bullet** – the first novel by a major writer to be published exclusively as an e-text – selling 400,000 copies. The PC-based encryption of this text was cracked within two days of publication! New software from Adobe, called PDF Merchant, ascribes rights to PDF publications to a particular computer, but despite this, the security issue for e-books remains as contentious an issue as encryption for music or movie files.

The Rocket e-book is one of several contenders for the e-book 'reader' market. Readers are available in both hardware and software modes – for PCs, and Palm and other handhelds – but the paperback-size, lightweight, multi-book storage and display capabilities of a hardware reader will be a very competitive marketplace. Perhaps it's inevitable that such devices will become general purpose 'e-pads' – wireless network access devices, with a web browser, and the ability to download, store and display several different media formats (JPEG images, Quicktime or AVI video clips, MP3 audio files, in other words 'enhanced books' – as well as e-texts. This is how your newspaper and magazines will arrive in 5 years' time. (Image courtesy of Nuromedia at www.nuvomedia.com)

ergonomic in use. They may indeed be general-purpose networked PDAs such as the Palm (for which e-texts are already available), or they may be dedicated e-book readers, or even hybrid multimedia readers that can download, store and display e-books, video, MP3, newspapers and magazines, etc, but the crucial balance must be struck between flat-screen display size, pocketability and useability. This new iteration of e-books is unlikely to follow the example of Voyager's unique publications, with their experimentally wide range of multimedia 'enhancements'. Instead, we are likely to see the new e-text publishers take a much more pragmatic and cost-effective approach, providing a basic set of enhancements which might include interactive TOC (table of contents) menu, search engine, hypertext-linked features, illustrations, bookmarks, and web links to other authorial and contextual material.

The opportunities for publishers in this transition period from atoms to bits are enormous, but so are the threats. New business models – or revamped older ones, such as subscription periodical publishing (the model favoured by Dickens and Conan Doyle) – must emerge to accommodate the problem of the illegitimate replication of e-texts. Currently, mainstream e-publishers are not doing themselves any favours here, pricing proprietary e-texts just the same as they price hardback printed publications. This is the same mistake the music business made with the high pricing of CDs and their unwillingness to face the issues presented by the new networked routes to market.

Other net-centric business models, such as publishing free or low-priced sampler e-texts in order to build a market and promote the sales of traditional hardbacks or paperbacks, will probably have only a transitional effect. Soon e-books will boast the same 'readability' as paper books, and they will be even lighter in weight, as well as storing dozens of texts and their digital enhancements (so there will be little premium in paper editions). But recently, Baen, the established science fiction publisher based in New York, successfully piloted this e-text promotional strategy. From September 1999, Baen started its 'eWebScriptions' service, offering quarter-of-a-book size pre-publication instalments of books for a subscription of $10 a month. One of its first titles, *Ashes of Victory*, by David Weber, was boosted into the hardback best-seller lists, partly as a result of this strategy. Feedback from readers showed that even those who had downloaded the complete book in HTML were still buying the printed version. People like collecting and displaying atoms! As Anthony Powell says, 'books do furnish a room' – and e-books just won't, will they?

Alternative net-centric business models, such as periodical publication, advertisement-supported publishing and direct vanity publishing, have been shown to work successfully. Fatbrain.com exploited an interesting niche when it noticed that the market for short works – novella, white papers, manuals, short stories and essays of 10–100 pages (the length that users would conceivably print on their personal computer inkjet or laser printer) – just wasn't being catered for in traditional publishing. The 'E.Matter' PDF format publications at its spin-off business www.mightywords.com – at around $4 a pop – are priced by authors, with Mightywords taking a 50 per cent retailer's commission. Mightywords uses a form of public key encryption (allowing machine-specific copies only) to protect authors' copyright. Random House has invested in Xlibris.com, which provides a 'no fee, no frills' e-publishing package for authors tired of reading rejection notices from paper publishers; and Barnes & Noble has backed iUniverse.com, which offers a $99 package for authors (free if the work is out of print). But there is more, as yet relatively unexplored potential in subject-specialist e-publishing, especially as personal profiling technology reveals readers' tastes and recommendations, enabling this information to provide recommendations for other readers with similar interests.

“THERE IS MORE, AS YET RELATIVELY UNEXPLORED POTENTIAL IN SUBJECT-SPECIALIST E-PUBLISHING”

enhanced digital music The current standard for enhanced music on disk is 'enhanced CD' (e-CD, also called CDPlus), a standard that allows a multimedia track to be included on a standard audio CD so that it can also be played in interactive mode in any CD-ROM drive. Such multimedia tracks feature additional content for the record buyer and, like album packaging and sleeve notes in the old vinyl days, proffer considerable added value. E-CDs surfaced in the mid-1990s, and were perceived by some music industry futurists as a means of bringing music publishing into the multimedia age while retaining the conventional disk retailing model. Typically, such e-CDs featured enhancements such as a promotional video, scrolling synchronized lyrics, discographies, timelines and biographical notes on the artists, stills galleries, web links to fanzines,

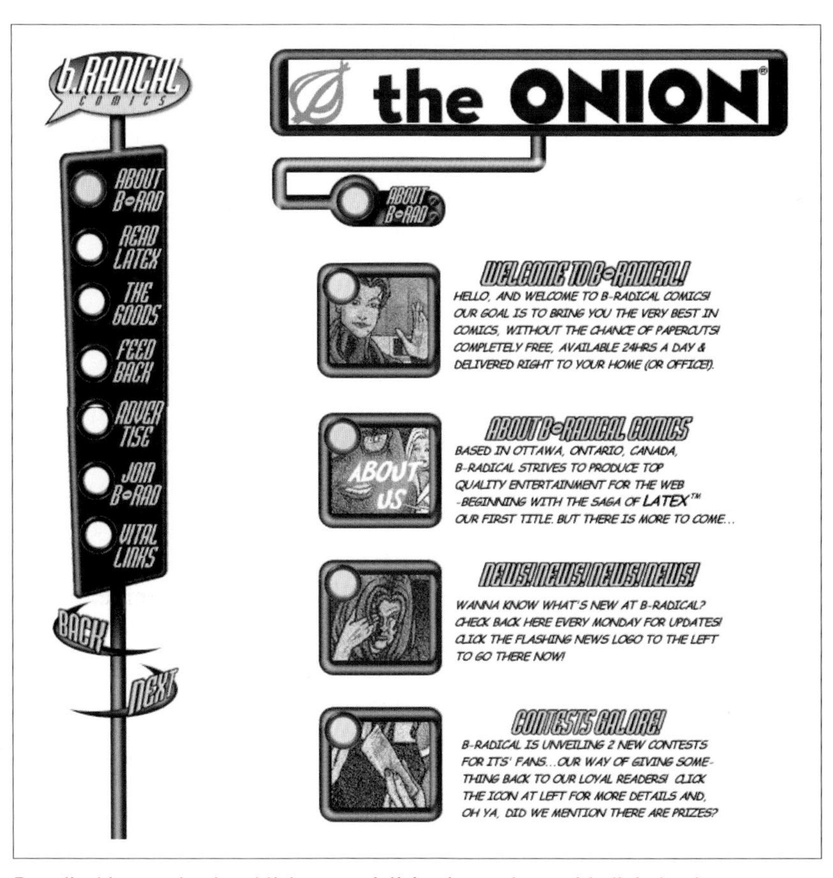

B-radical is an e-book publisher specializing in comics – with digital enhancements such as animation, and sound. But these are early days for e-publishers, suitable portable e-book readers that can download, store and display a variety of 'enhanced book' formats – including animation, video and audio files – are still just around the corner. (Image courtesy of b-radical at www.b-radical.com)

record company or band site, screen savers and desktop wallpaper, as well as promotions for tours and other related products.

When we started producing e-CDs at AMXStudios in the mid-1990s, these were considered attractive assignments for multimedia designers, although they were fairly proscribed as to content (to satisfy recording industry conditions determining multimedia content on disks that were eligible for chart entry) – the restriction of a limited 'palette' is often a useful discipline for naturally adventurous designers. But at the same time the requirement was for e-CD material that closely matched the style and personality of the artist and the record. They also had to be turned round quite quickly and economically. Often for these reasons, at AMX, a single multimedia designer would tackle the e-CD, producing everything from video digitization and formatting to Flash and other animations, stills and graphics and additional audio, all wrapped in cool and appropriate interface design, and finished within a few days.

But even the best commercial e-CDs tended to look formulaic compared with the much more extravagant non-commercial projects and products produced by individual artists and by experimental studios such as Audio-ROM, whose *Shift Control* won BAFTA and Milia d'Or awards (*www.audiorom.com*). Artworks like this transcend the enhanced CD genre by offering more holistic interactive experiences, often combining sound and video sequencing and manipulation tools and 'toys', games, and a much closer integration of interactive art and music than the industry-regulated e-CD allowed.

Experimental projects, such as those produced by Audio-ROM and other indies, indicate one of the possible futures of enhanced music. As bandwidth and access-device processing power increase in tandem, we can expect to see many more such seamless mixes of computer graphics, digital music formats, and other multimedia components, including real-time virtual reality – this time not just on disk but within the web/net itself. These tracks may utilize MPEG4 and other compression techniques to add interactivity and to integrate various enhancements.

There seem to be two main directions for networked digital music: the peer-to-peer distribution of music tracks both inside the music business and tangential to it (independent musicians publishing their work directly) to a range of PCs and set-top boxes, portable, solid-state players, networked games consoles and third-generation cellular mobile devices; and secondly, the development of increasingly rich and 'synaesthetic' music-based artworks that bring together mixed media, networked communities and individuals, live performance, and web casts, to create experiences that would virtually revisit the territory explored in Andy Warhol's Exploding Plastic Inevitable nightclub, and satisfy even the wildest dreams of Marinetti and his 'Art of Noise' futurists.

enhanced television content In the 1980s the Media Lab at MIT had produced prototypes of digital television news delivery, showcasing the interactivity and richness of enhanced news. In the 'Tell Me More TV' project, viewers were given a 'tell me more' button they could press to drill out and down from newscasts into background briefings at various levels. At that time, MIT imagined that digital television and its multimedia enhancements (the extra video, the maps, animated graphs, text and graphics, etc) would be simulcast in parallel channels or multiplexed and separated out by the 'TV' receiver, that would then store the enhancements locally for interactive browsing if and when the viewer/user pressed the button, and indeed this is the general model of interactive television today. But although Tell Me More TV was a prescient prototype, even the Media Lab whizz-kids didn't envisage the phenomenon of the web. Yet even on the cusp of the web age, when the debate over the future of television still focused on high-definition television, Media Lab chief Nicholas Negroponte was aware that it wasn't picture quality or aspect ratio that would be selling digital TV, it was content.

'Absolutely nobody in the HDTV or digital television world is really thinking of programming and how it impacts content. The closest we get is how will it impact delivery, so that you get movies on demand or 150 channels. I think what will happen – which is really important – is the content.'

'An Interview with Nicholas Negroponte' at the Media Lab, March 25 1993, from Frank Beacham's 'Questioning Technology' at www.beacham.com

The web changed things fundamentally. It was rather unsettling for the old media masters – who had taken on board the 1980s consensus vision of the media future as dominated by the fibre-optic superhighway providing the distribution channel, with HDTV as the access device – to find that actually, it was neither of these. Instead it was a low bandwidth, ramshackle agglomeration of networks, connecting PCs (not TVs), designed by geeks, run by hackers, and populated by a new breed of entrepreneurs, none of whom had much to do with the 'big media' industry.

First of all, WebTV arrived with the claim that it was 'the future of television, today'. WebTV is a set-top box and a range of services, some available through the internet via modem, and some through satellite via a dish. Sony and Philips manufactured the first WebTV set-top boxes. The original service, introduced in 1995 (now called the 'classic' service), connects to the internet and offers 'e-mail on TV'. A year later WebTV Plus was introduced, and offers the classic service, plus 'enhanced interactive TV', on-screen TV listings (electronic programme guide) and automatic VCR programming. At the premium end, from 1999, Personal TV, which was beamed down from

HOME | PRODUCTS | COMPANY | SEARCH

Interactive Television has ARRIVED!

What is Interactive TV?

Interactive TV merges the Internet and television so you can participate in new ways with your favorite shows. You can play along and match wits with contestants on Wheel of Fortune® and JEOPARDY!®. Vote in a live poll while watching Judge Judy. Access entertainment headlines on E! Receive up-to-the-minute news coverage with NBC Nightly News. Get sports stats. Voice your opinions. Chat live with other fans. **All from the comfort of your couch. All while watching TV. And all you need is WebTV® Plus.**

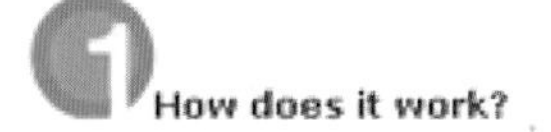

1
How does it work?

2
What shows?

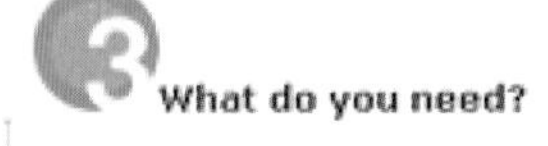

3
What do you need?

WebTV was among the first to deliver 'convergence' in the home – perceiving that the combination of television and the internet would be a 'killer platform'. Of course 'interactive television' encompasses a range of different technologies and different features – there are DSL, cable and satellite versions of interactive TV, which offer various levels of interaction from downloading any programme you like whenever you want it (video-on-demand), to selecting a convenient start time from several channels all showing the same movie (near-VOD), or offering different camera-angles on a sports event, to various enhanced TV formats offering linked websites and e-commerce services, and a wide range of proprietary online interactive services.

an Echostar satellite to the WebTV dish and satellite receiver, 'let's you watch what you want, when you want' and offers 'advanced TV features such as the ability to pause programmes in progress for up to 30 minutes and then resume watching'.

Microsoft bought WebTV in August 1997, upgraded the services on offer, opened up the satellite option, and improved the readability of the proprietary browser, designing special software to minimize screen flicker and optimize the readability of text displayed on a television set. The enhanced TV from WebTV depends on the genre of programme, but typically includes sports statistics, additional information, trivia games, interactive polls, simulations and 'info-graphics', purchase of show-related products,

The BBC were quick to realize the potential of 'web-enhanced' TV, first with BBC.co.uk, then the commercial site www.beeb.com. No direct links existed between the TV signal and the website, but the online programme enhancements provided an extremely useful service for viewers, proving detailed information, such as recipes, or consumer-guidance for used-car buyers as on the Top Gear pages. (Image courtesy of the BBC at www.topgear.beeb.com)

the ability to join in on some game and quiz shows, and chat with other viewers. The television programming featured on WebTV, however, seems to be much the same as other digital TV packages, typically including NBC, HBO, Discovery Channel, MSNBC, PBS, The Learning Channel and The Weather Channel – in other words, standard 'linear' programming. The two basic WebTV services add web-based enhancements to these channels, providing more than 350 hours of interactive programming per week.

In the UK, BBC Online has been providing similar web-based broadcast media enhancements to its radio and television shows, though the link between the broadcast programme and the enhancement is not direct but usually only in the form of a URL featured at the end of the programme. However, the web-based enhancements are of a very high quality, and set an example of the kind of hyperlinked enhancements that add depth and breadth to television and radio broadcast programmes. And demand for this kind of 'convergent viewing' (watching TV and accessing the internet at the same time) appears to be growing. According to a January 2000 survey by Showtime Networks, nearly one in five US households exhibits this kind of 'convergent behaviour' – that's nearly 18 million people, some 80 per cent more than a similar poll revealed at the end of 1997.

“DEMAND FOR THIS KIND OF CONVERGENT VIEWING APPEARS TO BE GROWING”

The root of these kinds of enhancements are the protocols for HTML-based television enhancements, and specifications for signal transport and reception devices, defined by the Advanced Television Enhancement Forum (ATVEF), which is a cross-industry alliance of companies representing broadcasters, cable TV networks, and the personal computer and consumer electronics manufacturers. Founder members include Microsoft WebTV, CNN Interactive, DirecTV, Intel, NBC Multimedia, Sony, Warner Bros, the Walt Disney Company, and more than 100 other major 'adopters' of the ATVEF protocols. The essential mission of ATVEF (*www.atvef.com*) is 'to specify a single public standard for delivering interactive television experiences that can be authored once using a variety of tools and deployed to a variety of television, set-top, and PC-based receivers'. The production advantages of such a global standard are obvious, and the fact that the ATVEF specifications are based as much as possible on networking standards like IP and HTML means they have a wide general application. In situations where the content provider knows the specific capabilities of the receiving device, other forms of data can also be sent over the ATVEF transport, including popular multimedia content written in Java and VRML (Virtual Reality Mark-up Language).

But HTML-based enhancements certainly aren't the end of the interactive television story. As broadband access becomes ubiquitous and new interactive technology and access devices are collapsed down to chip level and integrated within the TV set itself – or one of the many access devices described above – the horizons of interactive TV will expand far beyond the limited enhancements on offer today. For example, Telecruz Technologies produces chip sets and related software for manufacturers to add interactive features to television sets. And Telecruz is just one of the many contenders in the race for a slice of the projected multi-billion-dollar interactive television market.

There are many other companies touting patents and proprietary hardware and software, including ACTV Inc with its HyperTV 'individualized television' and SpotON news products. These incorporate a patented 'pull' service, called the Wolzein Process, which allows users to 'pull' relevant content from the web/net to enhance TV programmes (equivalent to a constantly running search engine providing relevant links), while HyperTV lets content producers and advertisers 'push' internet content to consumers, all synchronized to a TV or video – or audio – programme. But VM Labs' Nuon chip set is already in production, and is built into the Samsung Extiva DVD player which went to market in July 2000. This is the first of several Nuon-powered DVD players and signals a pathway into 21st-century digital media that converges the games console and the high-resolution video player to marry three powerful media – the movie, the video game and computer graphics. As an illustration of the potential of the Nuon-powered players, consider the range of built-in media tools that offer the user interactive control: 20x digital zoom on any part of the current image, seamless panning, multi-picture strobe, fast forward and reverse with ultra-smooth motion, and an easy-to-use graphic interface that gives users control over all the parameters of the movie projection. There's also a virtual light machine that provides user-selected, computer-generated *son et lumière* effects to accompany any CD track.

However, this interesting list only hints at the real capability of Nuon-powered devices. Nuon evangelists anticipate that clever programming and program design will gradually merge the movie and the virtual environment *and* the game in a seamless digital art form. But a word of warning. Almost every hardware launch in this convergent arena has made similar claims for its technology. When Philips launched its Compact Disk Interactive product in the late 1980s, it paraded a then very interesting compact disk-based system, painting a picture of CD-I as the medium of the future, 'interactive television today', and the like. 3DO made a similar play in 1993 with its 32-bit games console. No doubt Microsoft will be presenting its games console, the prototype X-Box, in a similar light. But it won't be long before we can test the Nuon claims for ourselves. Apart from Samsung, several other manufacturers have licensed Nuon technology. Toshiba launched Nuon/DVD players in May 2000.

But why stop at the convergence of games, movies and VR? Why not finesse the technology with broadband network capability too? Indeed, this is what the latest generation of 128-bit games consoles aims at. The objective is convergence. Not just the convergence of the television and the web (although this is the most common meaning of convergence nowadays), but Convergence with a capital C. It is the logical extension of many of the developments described in this book. What will these soon-to-be-with-us devices be like? It's useful to imagine such a 'super-convergent' machine and guess at the kind of software and functionality it will have. This is a simple scenario-building exercise that you could plot using the kind of concept maps described earlier. Some of the technologies and programming to factor into your diagram include DVD disk drive (soon with DVD-R recordable functionality); flash memory for personal profiling and preferences storage, broadband web/net connectivity (through any of the means described above); powerful 128-bit and up processors with special video, graphic processing and sound processing chips (ie like Nuon); local hard-disk storage; and remote control via a variety of devices (keyboard, joystick, dataglove, remote keypad, voice-user-interface, etc). What kind of entertainment/information applications would best exploit this potential?

But in the short term, what these convergent systems offer is the means to transport and decode extra enhancement data (video, 3D and 2D graphics, and web) alongside or embedded within a television signal. Some of them offer personalization software too, giving users the option of automating the channel selection process, and of limiting the enhancement catchment area to subjects of their choice.

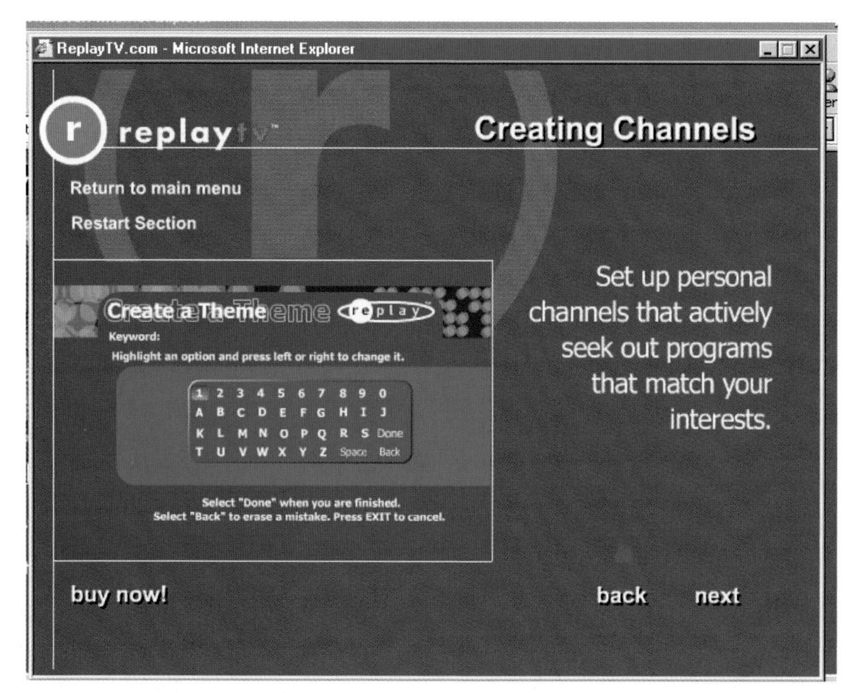

ReplayTV brought digital technology to the video recorder. With a hard disk instead of a video cassette drive, ReplayTV stores up to 40 hours of MPEG2 digital video. A modem connection gives access to online electronic programme guides, and personalization software lets you programme the machine to search and record your favourite programmes. Suddenly channel schedules become irrelevant – you have your own interactive TV channel to play with.

personal television In a world of several hundred channels, pay-TV, and movies on demand, personalization software in the TV access device is going to be an important growth area. Some of the commercially successful personalized TV solutions threaten the conventional broadcast business model, based as it is on viewer retention, co-ordinated sequential programming, and sponsorship and commercial breaks. Take for example the new generation of digital home video recorders such as ReplayTV and Tivo. These clever devices combine the recording functions of a VCR, modem access to the internet, and personalization software, allowing viewers to pre-select the kind of television programmes they want to see. Once personalized, these machines will connect to the web/net, access a central database of electronic programme guides (or search a range of EPGs) published by the different digital TV broadcasting channels that the viewer subscribes to, find the programmes that match the viewers requirements, and automatically programme these for recording. Not much new here, you say. But the other clever bit about these video recorders is that they use high-capacity computer hard disks instead of video tape, and record movies and television in MPEG2 digital formats, over *four times* the resolution of VHS. With no tape drives, there is no spooling back and forth to find the programme you recorded. Instead the hard disk video recorder (or personal video recorder) can store up to 420 hours of programming, and automatically builds a menu of these stored programmes, offering users a really interactive TV experience – instant replay and random access to programming through screen menus of recorded programmes.

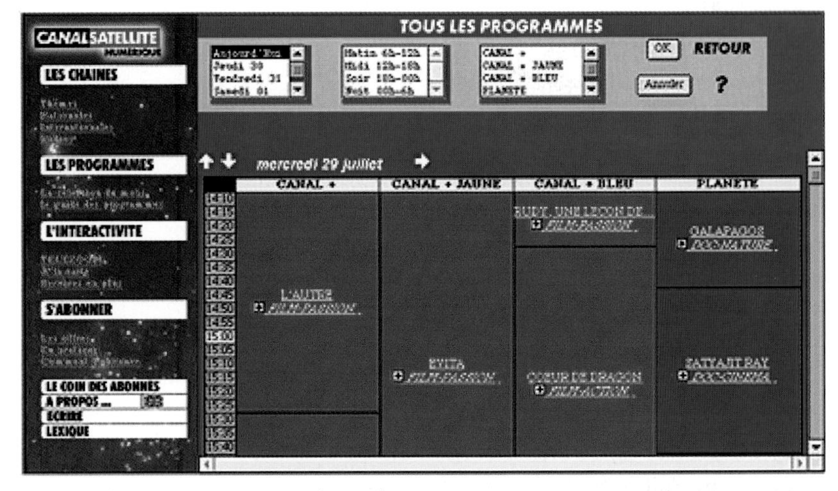

Electronic Programme Guides (EPGs) are the online TV programme listing guides, and may become important portal sites, just as search-engines did in the 1990s. EPG sites will become much more sophisticated, with programmable video recording, personalization, filtering and VOD programme purchasing agents – designed to negotiate-for and purchase one-off broadcasts that conform to your requirements and are within your pre-set price limits. Such EPGs could also be the means by which you filter – or customize – the commercials you receive.

These hard-disk video recorders or 'personal video recorders' are revolutionizing digital television both as stand-alone recorders and as components of set-top boxes. Combining time-shift viewing with personalization software HDVRs automate all that tedious programming you had to perform on the humble analogue VCR.

The personalization technology developed by Tivo has been adopted by Sony for its next-generation digital video recorder, the Digital Network Recorder, by Philips for its Personal TV Recorder, and by AOL for its AOLTV set-top box, for introduction in 2001. In mid-2000, Tivo, a Linux-based HDVR, licensed Spyglass Inc's Device Mosaic browser software, which allows synchronized broadcast and internet content over both digital and analogue video systems, using cable, terrestrial, satellite and internet services. It is also one of the first embedded browsers (stored in a ROM chip in the device) to be fully compliant with the ATVEF standards. In the UK, Tivo boxes manufactured by Thomson Multimedia were introduced during autumn 2000 in conjunction with British Sky Broadcasting.

Such HDVRs put real power into the hands of the viewer, devolving editorial and sequential presentation from the broadcasters to the user/viewer. The implications of personal video recording for broadcasters includes the end of channel loyalty, indeed even of temporary periods of sequential viewing. As far as HDVR users are concerned, the TV broadcasters can forget about balanced daytime or evening-long programming, they become mere providers of content units – an anonymous, irrelevant source of programmes, not of *programming*.

“THEY BECOME MERE PROVIDERS OF CONTENT UNITS – AN ANONYMOUS, IRRELEVANT SOURCE OF PROGRAMMES, NOT OF **PROGRAMMING**”

And broadcasters are looking for new business models to accommodate HDVR viewing. Some have threatened to restrict access to their EPGs, but some are being more realistic, even positive in their approach. For example, during 2000, TimeWarner Cable trialled a free ReplayTV service as part of its cable TV provision in Southern California, with expectations of increased pay-per-view revenues and premium content purchases, ‘as viewers would have more control of what and when they watch’.

software becomes content: pointers to the future of content

Devolving editorial and vee-jay or ‘master of ceremonies’ power to the viewer through personalization software is one way of thinking about the future of content, and as we have seen, peer-to-peer (or people-to-people) content is another. While there is some small amount of research and development of content *specifically* designed for the new media coming from the television industry itself, there are many independent artists and creative teams exploring the potential of the new networked media, pushing the envelope of the digital domain, mixing video, software and networking with artificial life, bio-feedback, implant prosthetics and performance art, and surveillance cameras with webcasts and television broadcasts. It is here we must look for clues to the future of content.

Artists play an important role in indicating possible directions of developments in content creation for new media. Why is this so, and why should new media differ from conventional content creation? The reason is simple: these are very new media technologies. The central driver in digital media development, the microprocessor, is only 30 years old. The internet only 31. The web is a fledgling eight-year-old. Virtual reality is sweet 16 (though Jaron Lanier didn't coin the phrase until 1989), video games quite mature at 29, mobile phones* about to mature into a third generation at 21, AI the oldest at 55 – mostly really young technologies. And they are developing so rapidly that there really hasn't ever been a stable platform to experiment with. So there hasn't been a lot of time for designers, directors, writers and other traditional content creators to really come to terms with this new medium.* And it does take time. For example, it took about 50 years after the invention of the moveable typeface and the modern method of printing books for someone (Antonio Blado and Aldus Manutius in Italy) to come up with the idea of page numbering, indices, tables of contents and other user-friendly devices such as the Roman typeface and small, 'portable' bound books. The movies took some time to mature too. Although early films by Georges Méliès showcased many filmic effects, it wasn't until Edwin Porter's movies of 1902–1903 that modern editing techniques were introduced, and not until D.W. Griffiths (*Birth of a Nation*, 1915) and Sergei Eisenstein (*Battleship Potemkin*, 1925) that the first feature movie classics appeared.

*Cellular radio technology was developed in 1947, but modern mobiles appeared around 1980, with services in Tokyo and trials in Chicago.

*In many aspects of new media content creation, it is **only** artists who have explored the potential of this rich mix of media, technology and networking. The best survey of this exploration over the past 20 years is in **Ars Electronica: Facing the Future**, edited by Timothy Druckrey.

The new media combine three concepts never before encountered in mass media – they are digital (mediated by a microprocessor, and able to carry multimedia content); and as they are computer-mediated they are also programmable, non-linear and interactive; and nowadays they are networked too, and therefore global. So artists and media creators face a quadruple whammy – exploring the nature of narrative and content creation in a multimedia, non-linear, programmable, networked environment. Now, there aren't any direct precedents for this kind of creative endeavour. Although there are some pointers in multimedia performance from early modernism, such as Marinetti's *Art of Noise*, the Dada *Cabaret Voltaire*, the Russian Revolutionaries' *AgitProp* processions and performances, and the work of Kurt Schwitters and others at the Bauhaus, these were all pre-computer, pre-network pre-AI, and pre-video, one-off events, not modern media.

The three more or less unique qualities of our current new media – digital multimedia, computer-mediated interactivity and networking – emerged separately as a result of experiments in content creation in three distinct arenas: interactivity in computer or video games; multimedia and interactivity in disk-based media (mainly video disk and CD-ROM); and artificial intelligence software in games and other applications, finally merging to combine multimedia, interactivity and networking, mainly as a result of the world wide web. The history of content creation in these new media is nevertheless too long and too interesting to do justice to here. I will highlight what I think are the really significant contributions to our new media, those that had a seminal impact, had considerable commercial success, and pointed the likely directions of future development, but refer interested readers to the classified bibliography of books and links.

software becomes content: interactive and 'intelligent' content While there are a few examples of pre-digital interactive media, such as Morton Heilig's 1957 Sensorama simulator, the breakthroughs in digital media provide the most relevant examples of interactive entertainment. The first computer game was created in the US as early as 1962 (Spacewar, programmed by Steve Russell at MIT, running on a PDP-1 mainframe), but the first mass-produced commercial video games didn't arrive until after 1971, following the success of Nolan Bushnell's Pong arcade game. Highlights of the first decade or so of computer games must include Space Invaders (Midway, 1978), Lunar Lander (the first vector-graphic game, 1979) and Asteroids (both from Atari, 1979), Sega's Monaco Grand Prix (a 2D, bird's-eye view racing sim, 1979), and Namco's Pacman (1980, reputedly the most popular arcade game of all time).

But while some of these were games in the parlour-game idiom, simply transposed to the computer, the real core of interactive media content – issues that we still grapple with today – revolve around the problem of how to create movie-like experiences with compelling narratives while still giving the user the freedom to interact with the programme. At least this is how many interactive media creatives perceive the problem. These issues obviously haven't stopped the past two (or three?) generations of kids spending upwards of $30 billion on video games over the past 30 years.

One of the earliest experiments in multimedia simulation was Morton Heilig's personal sensory cinema 'Sensorama'. Sensorama simulated a motorcycle ride through Manhattan, complete with rushing air, exhaust fumes, vibrating seat and stereo sound – as well as fast flowing wide-angle movie images.

Attempts to combine narrative and interaction were pioneered in the early text-based role-playing games*, such as Adventure and Zork, and these used the limited computer memory required by text to provide multi-forking paths of narrative, rather like a story by Borges, and provided many interactive puzzles and tests along the way.

*Designers of interactive adventures of this kind quickly become aware of the 'combinatorial explosion' of options created by allowing the user freedom to explore the branching options at every stage of the adventure. Text descriptions require very little memory, and the hypertext-like linking of story elements that seem to offer an unlimited sense of freedom for the user are only really possible in this text-only universe.

Early video games, like Nolan Bushnell's seminal Pong simply – but brilliantly – simulated familiar real-world games. Within a decade of Pong, kids were spending over $1 billion a year on video games, and game designers were incorporating simulation, real-time computer graphics, role-playing, artificial intelligence – and many other potential components of the 'interactive movie'.

Despite the brilliance of the early video games, and the way games like Space Invaders brought a taste of cybermedia to the traditional 'olde world' pubs of London in the late 1970s, the first games that really gave me a vision of the future were an idiosyncratic collection, including Dragon's Lair, the first video disk-based arcade game (Cinematronics, 1983). When I discovered Dragon's Lair in late 1983, just when I was planning my first laser disk production, I spent a couple of hours in Leicester Square's games arcade watching the entire game contents flip through on the screen. The game was malfunctioning, and although not able to 'play' it this first time, the faulty machine played every sequence of animation as it was laid down on the disk, providing a fascinating insight into the game's construction.

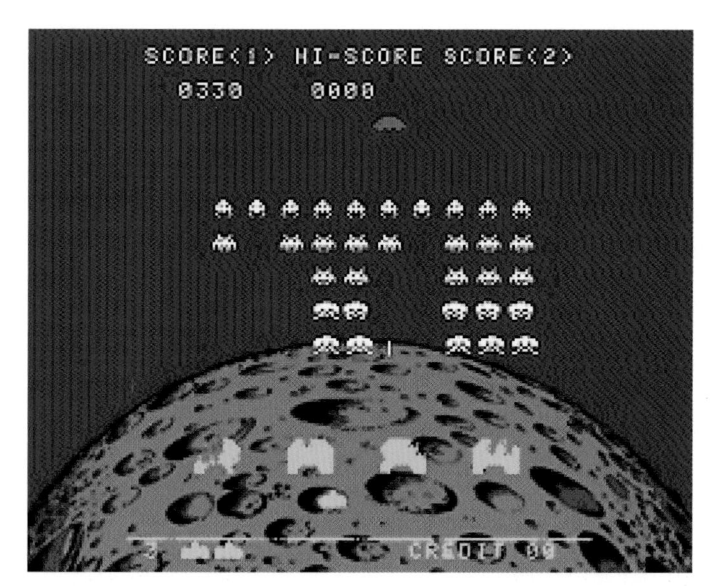

In the late 1970s, the flickering pixels of the Space Invaders console screens provided a taste of digital entertainments to come. Designed by Toshihiro Nishikado and manufactured by Taito in 1978, Space Invaders was one of the most successful arcade games ever made, and influenced many subsequent arcade games. It was licensed by Atari and versioned for the Atari 2600 home video game console – the first game to be ported from arcade to console.

Then there was Will Wright's brilliant SimCity. Released by Maxis in 1987, this was the first 'god game' I played. It was a pictorially brilliant simulation in isometric projection, that invited the user to build and manage an entire city populated by mini-synthespians called Sims. Actually, SimCity didn't start off as a simulation game, as designer Will Wright explains:

'SimCity evolved from Raid on Bungling Bay, where the basic premise was that you flew around and bombed islands. The game included an island generator, and I noticed after a while that I was having more fun building islands than blowing them up. About the same time, I also came across the work of Jay Forrester, one of the first people ever to model a city on a computer for social-sciences purposes. Using his theories, I adapted and expanded the Bungling Bay island generator, and SimCity evolved from there.'

Quoted from S. Reeder (1992) in 'Making Sense of Software: Computer Games and Interactive Textuality' by Ted Friedman at www.duke.edu/~tlove/simcity.htm

In 1983, Dragon's Lair brought laser disc resolution to the games arcades. Designed by Don Bluth, a former Disney animator, and manufactured by Cinematronics. Directing the actions of the central hero 'Dirk the Daring', you accessed different pre-rendered video sequences on the laser disc – brilliantly designed by Bluth to create a seamless gaming experience.

SimCity and its spin-offs (SimEarth, SimAnt, SimLife, SimFarm, SimHealth, SimGolf, SimTown, SimTune, SimIsle, and SimCity 2000), and the 1999 SimCity 3000 (which sold more than 657,000 in that year alone) and The Sims (where Sim characters are no longer little pixellated pixies but come to life with personalities and life objectives of their own), are a set of powerful indicators as to the likely future of interactive entertainment.

The significance of SimCity was that it really didn't need the gaming element additions insisted upon by the publishers, Maxis, in 1987 (these included ready-made scenarios such as earthquakes, reactor melt-downs and other disasters, even an invasion of the city by Godzilla) – the business of building and developing the simulated city with a limited budget, and keeping its population of Sims content, was absorbing enough. More like an open-ended toy rather than a game, these kinds of simulations, inspired directly by Jay Forrester's pioneering work on system dynamics (as described earlier, Chapter 2) will be major components of the original computer-mediated content produced during this decade, perhaps especially The Sims, which moves the action from city management to people management. Users are able to choose from predefined virtual people (Sims) or create their own from scratch, in which case they can determine how they look and what personalities they have. Users are given $20,000 for each Sim household, and most of this goes on renting or buying somewhere to live (sound familiar?), so the game is about how well you can develop your Sims into successful, happy, fulfilled virtual beings on a limited budget. The genius of The Sims is the way it appears to mirror the real world, while still offering a compelling entertainment experience.

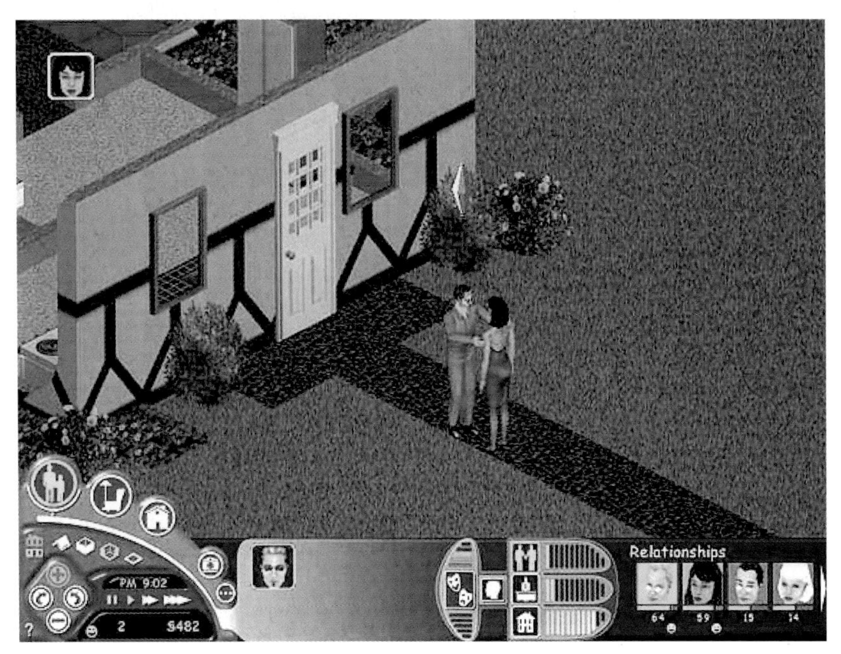

Synthesizing the soap opera and the tamagotchi, Will Wright followed his successful SimCity and other simulations with The Sims – a 'people simulator', where players have to raise an entire family of simulated human beings on a limited budget. The game provides an astonishingly detailed variety of perspectives on The Sims as they grow, learn, graduate and pursue their careers.

I haven't space here to cover all the exciting vectors of development that indicate the possible future of interactive entertainment of this kind, but I just want to explore this particular vector another couple of stages.

The next program that really fascinated me was the remarkable CD-ROM Myst, created by Robyn and Rand Miller and published by Cyan in 1994. This was the first CD-ROM that really impacted on the world of computer games, which at the time was dominated by Nintendo and Sega (Nintendo's Donkey Kong Country was climbing the charts, and Sony launched its Playstation console that year). Myst became the top-selling computer game of all time (Myst and its sequel 'Riven' have sold over 10 million units), despite having no characterizations, no heroes, no villains, and no shoot-em-ups. In fact, Myst broke most of the rules of computer game design (as perceived at that time), mainly because Robyn and Rand, who shared a background of designing educational games in Apple's Hypercard (The Manhole, 1988), invented an entirely new kind of game, one where the user never dies, where the user is the only inhabitant of a deserted fantasy island and is left to decode and deconstruct the game much as users were left to explore the virtual Aspen in the ArchMac laser disk prototype (see below). Myst brilliantly exploited the relatively high capacity (640 Mb) and relatively low bandwidth (the single-speed CD-ROMs of the time could deliver only about 150 kbps) of the CD-ROM to deliver a set of pre-rendered, high-resolution (for the time), computer-generated images of the mysterious island, into which were embedded many hundreds of clues, puzzles and messages from the island's previous inhabitants. I remember watching a young designer – an experienced computer games player – as he reached the 'end' of Myst. It had taken him nearly 20 hours in total to work through the game play of the disk and explore the various levels. And this is the real value of interactive software – a movie you usually watch only for a couple of hour; the same number of frames in an interactive adventure yield ten times more entertainment.

But outside the game or toy genres, the first attempt to create content that specifically exploited the interactive, multimedia nature of the new media was probably the Aspen Movie Map created by Andy Lippman, Michael Naimark and other members of the Architecture Machine Group (later to become the Media Lab) at MIT in 1978–1979. Lippman photographed every street of the

Robyn and Rand Miller's Myst became the most successful game ever, and was probably the first 'adult' game – no shoot-em-ups, no being killed and having to start all over again – full of intellectual and logical puzzles, cryptic clues and sumptuously rendered 3D computer graphics, Myst broke completely new ground. (Image courtesy of Cyan at www.cyan.com)

city of Aspen, Colorado, at intervals of about 3 metres, and arranged these images on a set of the newly invented Philips video disks so that under computer control, viewers could interactively 'travel' through the city images, turning right or left at road junctions, and even stopping to virtually explore buildings en route. This was a 'proof of concept' project, designed to showcase the potential of the new interactive media, but as the first example of surrogate travel, it became a seminal influence for many young designers exploring the potential of hypermedia during the following decade.

In many ways John Carmack's famous real-time shoot-em-up Doom is on the direct conceptual line from Movie Map and Myst to future interactive movies. Like Myst, it was a first-person perspective, 3D game, but there the similarity ends. Doom was exciting, visceral, and more than a little scary, whereas Myst was peaceful, contemplative, intellectual and fascinating. Actually released a year before Myst, ID Software's Doom was a major milestone in the history of interactive entertainment. Built around a 3D

Doom introduced first-person, real-time gaming to a mass public in 1996, taking the video game industry by storm. Designed by John Carmack and produced by ID Software, Doom was a first-person shooting game with an innovative real-time graphics engine that gave users apparent freedom to explore the Doom environment and to try to avoid being shot by the homicidal inhabitants. This was scarily visceral gaming – the other side of the gaming coin from Myst. (Image courtesy of ID software at www.idsoftware.com)

engine designed by John Carmack, Doom was a brilliant real-time shoot-em-up. But what is important here is that it was also a networkable game. Several people could play Doom and simultaneously inhabit the same game space. It was marketed through the web/net too – more than 15 million copies of the shareware version were downloaded from the web between 1993 and 1995. ID made 150,000 sales directly, setting up its own 800 call service, and Doom was licensed to other publishers and other platforms too, including Sega. Nearly 2.6 million full-price copies of the game and its sequel DoomsdayII: Hell on Earth, were sold up to 1999.

Related to Doom in the real-time nature of its interaction and visualization, the next interactive entertainment indicator I want to mention is the personal computer flight simulator, epitomized by Microsoft's renowned Flight Simulator, first published in 1980. More than 3 million copies of this program have been sold worldwide, and the Pro version is so realistic that pilots can use time spent in simulated flight to qualify for some portion of their annual logged air-time hours. You can take flying lessons on the latest version, Flight Simulator 2000, which has accurate flight modelling for most popular aeroplanes, and even downloadable real-time weather. Extending the participatory nature of digital media, another simulator, Electronic Arts' Flight Unlimited III, features a scenery editor with a vast collection of buildings, cars, trucks, animals, trees, people and landscape features that can be selected from pull-down menus, or dragged and dropped onto the landscape primitives.

The program engineering that goes into flight simulations, and into games such as Doom and Quake – the 'be there, go anywhere' illusion of real-time environments – has been explored in purely web-based technologies such as Virtual Reality Mark-up Language (VRML), which utilize special software clients or 'viewers' to enable users to move through 3D environments downloaded from the web. Apple Computer and other companies have also developed facsimile 3D virtual realities using specially stitched-together panoramic or fish-eye images that the user can 'inhabit' as though they were really immersive environments (Apple's Quick-time VR, Live Picture Corp's Java-based Live Picture, and others).

towards the interactive movie Many of these best-selling games and tools have their web/net enhancements too, sites devoted to VR techniques, game play, cheats, special editions (even The Seven Deadly Sims!), fanzines, chat forums and newsgroups. Games and virtualities like these become the focus of contemporary mythologizing, spawning endless commentary, debate and downloadable plug-ins and extras.

But my suspicion is that Hollywood wants more – they want 'interactive movies' where the user can step into the film and engage in the digital-celluloid adventures first-hand, becoming a 'star' of the movie in the way visualized in the Arnold Schwarzenegger movie *The Last Action Hero* (John McTierman, 1993).

The future of interactive movies becomes slightly more focused when we imagine hybrids of previous forms of interactive entertainment with the networking potential of new media: for example, by combining elements of the role-playing game; the 'god game' simulation; the surrogate travel programme; the real-time visceral interaction of the flight simulator and the Doom-like shoot-em-up; and the multi-player potential of high-band and mobile networks, with the kind of faux 'artificial intelligences' represented by chatterbots and 'personality constructs', and their representation on screen as life-like – or otherwise realistic – synthespians, then we are beginning to define the territory of future interactive entertainment. Combine these elements in a high-band version of the kind of virtual worlds (graphical chat rooms) that began appearing on the web/net a few years ago, and one can see that a lot of the spade work for the interactive movie has already been done.

There is one other strand of new media content creation that I will explore here briefly: the new genre of surveillance soaps launched in the UK by Channel 4's *Big Brother* and *Smart Hearts*, and the BBC *Survivor* series. Surveillance soaps are inspired by webcam sites and older candid-camera programme formats, and fuelled by the availability of cheap, wireless video cameras (many wireless 'spy' cameras and webcams are available now for less than $100). Surveillance soaps are classic examples of enhanced television and can be supported by sophisticated websites that archive much of the show's footage, feature live webcams, as well as detailed biographies, and diaries, of the participants. The TV show becomes the broadband 'front end' for the interactive website, and income is derived from both streams, as well as brand-related merchandising, such as theme music. *Big Brother* and other formats thrive on audience participation, as viewers vote on who gets to stay in the show to win the big prizes on offer to the ultimate survivor.

> “SURVEILLANCE SOAPS ARE CLASSIC EXAMPLES OF ENHANCED TELEVISION”

The Dutch company Endemol invented the *Big Brother* format back in 1994 (originally a 365-episode series, but 100 shows or less in its abbreviated format) and it has gone on to pull in record audiences in Holland, Spain, Germany and the UK. In the Netherlands it captured about 30 per cent of the television audience during its 100-day run, and the associated website took 52 million page views during this period. Interestingly, *Big Brother* was the first show that US television has ever bought from non-English-speaking European countries for prime-time viewing.

With over 300 million page views and 25 million video downloads, Victoria Real's Big Brother site vividly illustrated the power of Internet/TV. In 2000 'Reality TV' became the flavour of the summer as a dozen individuals competed in a knock-out competition for a £70,000 cash prize. The companion Big Brother website became one of the most popular UK sites as the TV series achieved record viewing figures.

when software becomes content Somewhere in this melting pot of software, hardware technologies, networking and programme and series format creation, the ghostly future shape of digital media content is emerging. Now in this short summary of the range of enabling technologies, formats and ideas that are indicators of the possible future of interactive entertainment, I want to talk briefly about artificial intelligence in video games, then go on to describe progress in simulation.

Why do I pay so much attention here to video games? Because games, as Philip Meggs pointed out in a *Print* magazine article some years ago, are the harbingers, the forerunners or 'early warning systems' of technology changes:

'In general, games often function as society's early warning system: they cushion culture shock by allowing people to prepare for future upheavals. Playing cards printed from wood-cuts in late Medieval Europe enabled illiterate citizens to learn counting, symbol recognition, and cognitive skills on the eve of the typographic revolution. In the same sense, the video game phenomenon acclimatized citizens to the impending computer revolution.'

Philip R. Meggs, 'Will Videogames Devour the World?', Print, Vol XLVL:VI

As such, games point to the future of interactive entertainment and software design generally, as Ted Nelson realized in 1990.

'To see tomorrow's computer systems, go to the video game parlours! Go to the military flight simulators! Look there to see true responsiveness, true interaction.'

Ted Nelson 'The Right Way to Think about Software Design'

We have already seen that software can become content – video games and simulations are 'just' software, but they can create landscapes and other real and fantasy environments in which to embody games, quests, adventures, narratives, puzzles and much, much more. And as we pointed out above, the algorithms used to create flight simulation, virtual reality, real-time 3D games (and other games) create content that is non-linear – that is not just a one-off linear experience like watching a movie – but content that can be enjoyed, explored and experimented with again and again.

In the early 1980s, the video game pioneer Trip Hawkins, in an influential article in *Byte* magazine, proposed a definition of successful entertainment software. According to Hawkins, software should be 'simple, hot and deep'. 'Simple' means easy to get into, with no manuals or guidebooks to read before you start; 'hot' means that it makes optimum use of the hardware – the graphics, sound and processing power of the platform; and 'deep' means that there should be a lot to explore, with several levels of depth in terms of information, characterization, strategy and so forth. These principles of good software design are just as relevant today, and the world wide web itself is a classic example of 'good' software in this respect – it's easy to use, exploits the client computer's multimedia capabilities and server search technologies, and is as 'deep' as you want.

But in the past few years, entertainment software designers have injected another level of depth into video games. Exploiting the pay-off of more than 50 years of research in artificial intelligence, games designers began to use AI techniques in games in the 1980s, exploiting a range of programming techniques to make their games 'smart'.

AI in interactive entertainment So with 'width' coming from the kind of simulations that offer the user apparently complete freedom of movement through a virtual computer-generated world, and with 'depth' coming from the sense that you are involved in a 'living' world, populated by 'thinking' beings and evolving life forms, a world made up of hundreds or thousands of plots, sub-plots and individual aims and objectives, how close are we now to the interactive movie? Well, the task of building intelligence into machines (AI) has some way to go, but we're getting there. Computers are essentially 'dumb' machines, all they can do is 'compute' – perform mathematical operations and calculations – but they can do this extremely quickly and unerringly. The trick with AI (or 'machine intelligence') is to model the subtleties of human thought in an algorithm, or other real-world behaviours rapidly compute and present the result, in such a way that the computer can do what it's designed for and extremely good at.

There are many types of AI used in entertainment programmes like games. The three most common types are, firstly, 'roaming AI' – which models the movement of game objects and the decisions they make that determine the way they roam around in the game world. A typical implementation of this type of AI is in shoot-em-up space games, where aliens can often track the movements of the player and go after them. Roaming AI is used whenever a computer-controlled object must make a decision to change its current path, either to progress the game play, or simply to conform to a particular logical development, such as responding to the gamer's attack by firing back, or evading the gamer's fire. Roaming AI can also determine the pattern of the object's behaviour, either along predetermined paths (for instance, always chasing the gamer, subject to obstacles and other parameters) or by using random-number generation to modify the pattern of behaviour.

Secondly, 'behavioural AI' describes the process of creating 'behaviours' for objects in the game, usually by determining a ranked set of responses that the object will make under different conditions, and determining which of these behaviours is appropriate to a particular condition, or 'state' of the game. In the space game example, this type of AI would determine the behaviour of aliens by ascribing different percentages of response behaviour to different aliens in order to imbue them with individual personalities. So for example, an aggressive alien might chase the gamer 50 per cent of the time, evade 10 per cent of the time, fly in a pattern 30 per cent of the time, and fly randomly for the remaining 10 per cent. A more passive alien would have different percentages of these behaviours.

Lastly, 'strategic AI' is any AI that is designed to play a game with a fixed set of rules. So strategic AI is the program that governs which of the moves in a computer chess game is the most appropriate in terms of improving the chances of winning the game. These can be very powerful programs, as Gary Kasparov discovered to his dismay in May 1997 when IBM's Deep Blue became the first opponent (machine *or* human) to beat him over a six-match game. Strategic AI combines the techniques of 'weighting' and 'look-ahead', first to calculate the score for each play at any state of the game, then to use a table of possible predetermined moves to identify the most advantageous play. The smarter the AI is intended to be, the more computing power, or time, is needed to calculate the best strategy from the escalating range of options available.

“AI HAS COME A LONG WAY IN THE PAST 50 YEARS”

So, 'artificial' maybe, but not quite really 'intelligence' yet, is it? This is true, but then we are considering only *some* of the implementations of AI in only one small genre: video game design. And we are not describing the future of interactive entertainment so much as the *indicators* of these possible futures. AI has come a long way in the past 50 years, and not just in strategic AI, as Deep Blue has proved. Another AI spin-off, Robotics, has transformed our industrial culture, and is beginning to impact on our domestic culture, with the clever implementation of smart software recently in Tamagotchi, and in Aibo, the robotic dog, the first of Sony's cyber-pets. At the launch of Aibo (Japanese for 'partner'), Sony Vice-President Toshitada Doi predicted that cyber-pets would be the 'next big thing':

'The last ten years of the 20th century were dominated by personal computers and the internet. For the next ten years, until 2010, we are certain that robots with independent movement will be the big thing.'

And the public really like Aibo. All 3000 of Sony's $2000 robotic dogs were sold out within 20 minutes of their launch in Japan. Armed with a Sony Memory Stick memory, and a 64-bit RISC processor with 16 Mb of RAM, running Sony's Aperios real-time operating system, Aibo has 18 joints producing 250 different movements, and AI software that enables it to simulate emotions such as happiness and anger, and to 'instinctively' crave companionship. More than this, each Aibo has the capacity to 'learn' and develop its personality, according to how its owner treats it.

Aibo has been described as 'the first new product of the 21st century', and the first two letters of its name indicate the importance of AI in this developing entertainment sector.

By the way, AI is going to impact on very many more aspects of our lives than just entertainment. In education and distance learning, in medical diagnosis expert systems, in voice recognition and voice user-interface systems, in domestic 'slave' robots for household chores, and as babysitters and nursing helpmates; in the form of web-based agents and 'bots' providing smart search engines, online help and subject-expertise, from current search-bots and

What with chat-bots, search agents, shop-bots, personal digital assistants, and hundreds of other 'bot' and 'agent' applications, Artificial Intelligence software is blossoming, and will characterize content and software developments throughout this decade. (Image courtesy of the Sony Corp.)

shop-bots, to possible lawyer-bots, trader-bots, and consumer-bots – the possibilities are endless. Perhaps the most important AI application will be the kind of automatic language translation systems described by eminent AI practitioner Ray Kurzweil in *The Age of Spiritual Machines*:

'(By 2009), translating telephone technology (where you speak in English and your Japanese friend hears you in Japanese and vice versa) is commonly used for many language pairs. It is a routine capability of an individual's computer, which also serves as her phone.'

Ray Kurzweil, The Age of Spiritual Machines

But to return to interactive entertainment. AI will continue to play an important role here in the development of game characters and personalities, in the development of responsive and adaptable (learning) game and world environments, in artificial life ecosystems and virtual pets, and in creative computer applications such as painting, story and poem generators.

So finally I will summarize the state of the art in the simulation of these main components of interactive movies: the simulation of place, or people and of story.

simulating place and people Place simulation was, as we have seen elsewhere in this book (see Chapter 4, 'Towards man-computer symbiosis'), invented by Ivan Sutherland in the early 1960s in his 3D real-time, computer-generated environments. The techniques he developed at the University of Utah and elsewhere were later developed by his company, Evans and Sutherland, into military and commercial flight simulators. Sutherland's work was to inspire the massive effort to replicate reality that has driven computer graphics pioneers over the past 40 years. What we see now in the special effects of movies such as *Gladiator* and *The Perfect Storm* are the sum of all the inventions and discoveries in computer graphics over these decades, from simply learning how to remove the wire-frame lines that delineate the non-visible side of an object, how to model light by tracing individual rays of photons, to creating realistic shading and reflections, to simulating the appearance of thousands of different textures and surfaces, to model explosions, fire, and atmospheric conditions, to model animal and humans – their skin texture, hair and fur – and most recently to model their movement through the world. There have been many brilliant insights and discoveries by many brilliant 'art/scientists' such as James Blinn, Alvy Ray Smith, Andy van Dam, Ken Knowlton, Benoit Mandelbrot Michael Noll, Ed Catmull and many others, including *Toy Story* director John Lasseter, and the guy who modelled birds flocking and bees swarming, Craig Reynolds. Slowly but surely we have learned how to simulate the macro and the micro of reality, from fractal landscapes to insect movement.

In the past 15 years or so we have also developed elaborate technology for capturing natural body movement and fleeting facial expressions, and have invented ways of embodying this data in our computer-generated people, in video game kick-boxers, and in the synthespians, avatars and virtual actors, in virtual animals, even in the recreation of long-extinct species. In other words, we have all the visual tools we need to create the ultimate interactive movie, and as we have seen, during this same period we have also developed several interesting interactive technologies, such as the MUD, the video game and the flight simulator. But there is one other, related, technology that I must mention.

interactive technology Ivan Sutherland's influence was not limited to computer graphics. He also pioneered virtual reality, and inspired later generations of VR innovators, such as Jaron Lanier and Jon Waldern. In the 1980s, VR technology was developed in the US and UK, and the first commercial products appeared in the early 1990s (W Industries' Virtuality stand-up podiums in the UK in 1990, and the Battletech Centres in the US). VR has several physically disturbing effects, including disorientation and nausea, which have limited its commercial development, but as a means of interacting with computer-generated media, it's hard to beat. VR completely breaks down the old user-screen-computer idea of interface, and in doing so blurs the role of the spectator and author. The viewer/user/participant is placed right inside the computer-generated environment, and like a member of the audience in a Living Theatre production, becomes an active participator in the play rather than a passive onlooker. VR is in many ways an example of the kind of shared conceptual model that Joseph Licklider suggested would

The Virtuality stand-up VR podium provided a safe venue for the first commercial VR experiences. W Industries, founded by VR pioneer Jonathon Waldern. With software like Battlesphere and VTOL providing virtual reality experiences in space battles and Harrier Jump jets, Virtuality introduced a generation to real-time, immersive virtual experiences.

be the really important aspect of computer-mediated communications between groups of people.

And VR is getting better, with point-source audio, force feedback, 'texture sensors', digital 'smell' and other extensions of the visual-haptic world. However, cumbersome helmets and visors aren't the answer – they're just not user-friendly enough. But what if we could make our real environment, our living room, a virtual reality? Then we would need no embarrassingly geek-like wearable viewers and visors. The kind of technology being developed at the MIT spin-off E-Ink might provide the answer. E-Ink is developing some pigments – inks and paints – that contain many millions of micro-capsule particles. These micro-capsules have two sides, black and white, and can be flipped by an electrical charge. E-Ink's aim is to provide pigments for e-book readers, but e-book readers made of paper, just like a conventional book. Paper books could be printed with e-ink, then as e-texts were loaded into them each page would electronically flip into the typeface chosen by the user and display the e-text just like a 'printed' text.

Colour versions of this technology will enable entire rooms to be painted with E-Ink pigments, and become giant flat screens for the display of moving 360-degree VR imagery. How our fragile sense of stability and balance would be affected by such wrap-around VR we can only guess, but bio-feedback should enable each user to keep the VR at comfortable levels of motion and frame rates.

story technology Finally, what about the stories or games or other scenarios that will drive such interactive movies? We've already mentioned the first, text-based interactive adventures: the first interactive story simulator was probably the early 1970s Colossal Cave Adventure role-playing game (RPG) written by Donald Woods and Will Crowther. A text-based interactive fiction, Adventure started life as a simulation of a real cave, and became the first example of a story generator that depended on user interaction. Interactive fiction involves the user in exploring the range of story options decided by the author, and creating a unique story line by clicking through text scenes and discovering new scenarios.

“ADVENTURE BECAME THE FIRST EXAMPLE OF A STORY GENERATOR THAT DEPENDED ON USER INTERACTION”

Willie Crowther worked at Bolt, Beranek and Newman (BBN, the ARPANET innovators) in 1972. A speleologist in his spare time, he had mapped the Colossal Caves in Kentucky for the Cave Research Foundation. Inspired by the first board-based role-playing game Dungeons and Dragons (by Gary Gigax), Crowther used these real maps as a guide, and working in Fortran on the BBN PDP-10 mini-mainframe developed a prototype interactive fiction for his children.

Don Woods later went on to work at PARC, Sun and General Magic, but in 1976 he was working at SAIL (Stanford AI labs) when he found a copy of Adventure on one of the minis there and contacted Crowther by sending an e-mail to *crowther@sitename*, where *sitename* was every computer then on the internet. He proceeded to work with him on developing the program to accommodate the then current wave of interest in J.R.R. Tolkien's *Lord of the Rings*, a huge cult classic (which had inspired Dungeons and Dragons) especially popular among hackers and computer students. Indeed, parts of the SAIL lab were given Tolkien names.

Zork was written by the Dynamic Modelling Group at MIT in June 1977, installed on a DEC PDP-10 mini-mainframe computer, and networked through ARPANET. Within six weeks (without any form of 'advertising', and while still in development) it already had a nationwide gamer community. By 1979 the Dynamic Modelling Group had founded 'Infocom' and determined to re-write Zork 'so it would run on something cheaper than a $400,000 PDP-10'. The Apple 1 (personal computer) version came out in 1980 and sold 6000 copies in the first eight months. Since then, Zork has become a legend in role-playing interactive gaming and interactive fiction, and a landmark in the ongoing quest to create a true 'interactive movie'.

The narrative in text-based adventure is created by the user choosing from a number of options at each node in the adventure. All these options have been pre-scripted by the game's author. However, there are other ways of generating or simulating word-based content. In the 1960s, the first dialogue generators (now called 'chat-bots') were developed by AI pioneers Joseph Weisenbaum and Terry Winograd. Weisenbaum's Eliza was a dialogue generator whose performance was modelled on that of a Rogerian psychotherapist. Winograd's Racter 'could talk about anything you wanted, as long as it was about the coloured blocks that made up Racter's entire world'. At the time, AI experts were trying to develop programs that would appear to be clever enough to pass the 'Turing Test', proposed by Alan Turing as a test to decide whether a computer conducting a text-based dialogue with a human (without the human knowing if he or she was talking

'More intelligent than some people I know' is one rather sad comment on the Alice chat-bot. Alice stands for Artificial Linguistic Internet Computer Entity. General chat-bots have to have a wide vocabulary and a clever parser to provide 'realistic' conversation. Alice is an open-source project freely available under the terms of the GNU Public licence (same as Linux). Chat-bot technology will play a major role in 'personality user interfaces', interactive movies, and distance learning software. Created by Richard S. Wallis, Alice utilizes his 'artificial intelligence mark-up language' or AIML – an easy-to-use language that enables non-specialists to write chat-bots. One goal for AIML is that if lots of expert individuals create smart chat-bots, then these can be merged into a 'super-bot' with a wide range of subject expertise.

to a machine or a human) could fool the human into thinking that they were talking to another person.

A contemporary version of Eliza is available online at *http://users.surfree.net/juventus*. These clever chat-bots were programmed to respond in a human-like way in dialogue with human beings – as long as the subject of conversation didn't stray much from the program's arena of expertise. Although Eliza's conversation is pretty limited, it nevertheless proved satisfying enough for several people to continue 'chatting' to it *even when they knew it was a machine they were talking to*.

As I mentioned before a different take on the issue of developing 'realistic' chat-bots for interactive fictions (and for other purposes, too) was taken by Hollis Research in the early 1990s. These AI experts built a prototype of an artificial character they called a personality construct. This construct was in fact the front end to an extensive database of responses and conversational gambits pre-recorded from a human subject. A wide range of typical questions were put to the human subject, whose responses were recorded and stored in a database. When the user typed a question for the personality construct, the question would be parsed and its probable meaning inferred, then the most appropriate response found in the database and played back to the user. This process was extremely fast – near real time, so the impression the user had was of an extremely realistic conversation with the PC-based 'personality'.

Another more recent virtual character is the newscaster Ananova, created by the Edinburgh-based Digital Animation Group for the Press Association. This delightful synthespienne basically 'reads' text files of news stories to you by means of the voice-synthesizer program in your computer. A computer-generated model, based on a composite of some real female newscasters, Ananova reads text that has been scripted with an embedded mark-up language. This not only carries a phonetic version of the text story – the 'phonemes' – but also contains information on the visual facial expression – the 'viseme' – that Ananova is to assume to make her delivery more realistic. Visemes govern the smiles, winks, blinks, nods and arched eyebrows (and all the other ideosyncratic expressions, tics, twitches, etc) that make up the facial 'body language' of a real human speaker. (Ananova proved so successful she was sold to Orange Telecommunications in 2000 for £95 million.)

Ananova is a text-reading machine – a look-alike virtual newscaster whose specially marked-up news scripts include instructions for phonemic pronunciation ('phonemes' – delivered through the host-computer's voice synthesizer), and for the appropriate facial expressions to assume for different news stories (these are called 'visemes', and control the computer-generated model that is Ana.) Image courtesy of Digital Animation Group, Edinburgh (www.ananova.com)

But clever chat-bots notwithstanding what of the 'stories' themselves, the scripts of the interactive movie? Could these ever be automated or created by a machine?

The answer is not yet. But we can imagine an expert system much like those designed to embody the expertise of lawyers or doctors, but this time storing the expertise of writers, authors, story tellers and movie screen-play writers. Such a system might also store information and examples of narrative theory and story types from the great analysts of myths and story telling like Joseph Campbell and Vladimir Propp. Such a system could theoretically generate endless varieties of stories.

Then there's the interesting work of Selmer Bringsjord, at the Minds and Machines Lab at the Rensselaer Institute in New York. Starting in 1991, Bringsjord began to develop story machines – programs that would generate short stories*. Bringsjord's literary algorithms are the sophisticated product of a long line of AI research into machine creativity. Artists, choreographers,

*For the best books on machine creativity see Jascia Reichardt, Gene Youngblood, Donald Michie and Pamela McCorduck, in the bibliography.

composers, poets, writers and others have been working with computers since the 1950s, and some of the earliest machine-generated poetry that I have come across was programmed by Margaret Masterman and Robin McKinnon Wood at Cambridge Language Research Lab in the late 1960s.

Here's a sample of their haiku algorithm reproduced from the *Cybernetic Serendipity* ICA exhibition catalogue of 1968:

1
eons deep in the ice
I paint all time in a whorl
Bang the sludge has cracked

2
eons deep in the ice
I see gelled time in a whorl
Pffftt the sludge has cracked

3
all green in the leaves
I smell dark pools in the trees
Crash the moon has fled

During the 1990s, Bringsjord created a machine intelligence called Brutus which 'could tell any stories you like, as long as they were about betrayal'. Bringsjord sees his work as an essential step towards the interactive movie:

'Brutus.1 represents the first step in engineering an artificial agent that "appears" to be genuinely creative. We have attempted to do that by, among other things, mathematizing the concept of betrayal through a series of algorithms and data structures, and then vesting Brutus.1 with these concepts. The result, Brutus.1, is the world's most advanced story generator. We use Brutus.1 in support of our philosophy of **weak** artificial intelligence – basically, the view that computers will never be genuinely conscious, but computers **can** be cleverly programmed to 'appear' to be, in this case, literarily creative. Put another way – as explained in my book **What Robots Can & Can't Be** – we both agree that AI is moving us toward a real-life version of the movie **Blade Runner**, in which, behaviourally speaking, humans and androids are pretty much indistinguishable.'

Selmer Bringsjord, from his website www.rpi.edu/~brings/, 1999

I think Brutus is a clever example of 'weak AI'. Judge for yourself:

'Simple Betrayal'

'Dave Striver loved the university. He loved its ivy-covered clock towers, its ancient and sturdy brick, and its sun-splashed verdant greens and eager youth. He also loved the fact that the university is free of the stark, unforgiving trials of the business world – only this **isn't** a fact: academia has its own tests, and some are as merciless as any in the marketplace. A prime example is the dissertation defence: to earn the PhD, to become a doctor, one must pass an oral examination on one's dissertation.

'Dave wanted desperately to be a doctor. But he needed the signatures of three people on the first page of his dissertation, the priceless inscriptions which, together, would certify that he had passed his defence. One of the signatures had to come from Professor Hart.

'Well before the defence, Striver gave Hart a penultimate copy of his thesis. Hart read it and told Striver that it was absolutely first-rate, and that he would gladly sign it at the defence. They even shook hands in Hart's book-lined office. Dave noticed that Hart's eyes were bright and trustful, and his bearing paternal.

'At the defence, Dave thought that he eloquently summarized Chapter 3 of his dissertation. There were two questions, one from Professor Rodman and one from Dr Teer; Dave answered both, apparently to everyone's satisfaction. There were no further objections.

'Professor Rodman signed. He slid the tome to Teer; she too signed, and then slid it in front of Hart. Hart didn't move.

'"Ed?" Rodman said.

'Hart still sat motionless. Dave felt slightly dizzy.

'"Edward, are you going to sign?"

'Later, Hart sat alone in his office, in his big leather chair, underneath his framed PhD diploma.'

From the program by Selmer Bringsjord at www.rpi.edu/dept/ppcs/BRUTUS/brutus.html

"WE HAVE WAYS OF DEVELOPING REALISTIC, COMPUTER-GENERATED VIRTUAL ACTORS OR SYNTHESPIANS"

In summary, we seem to have most of the components of the kind of interactive movies that people like to dream about. We have ways of developing realistic computer-generated virtual actors or synthespians, even in the low bandwidth web (take a look at *www.ananova.com*); we can produce photo-realistic and realistically fantastic fractal environments and atmospherics as the *mise en scène* for these virtual actors; we are developing the AI to give them personality, learning abilities, and 'character' too; and variants of 'strategic AI' may soon give us the games engine that would drive narrative plots through such a virtual environment. We already have multi-user graphical worlds and multi-player versions of real-time 3D games like Doom, and prototype chat-bots we can natter to.

So is this the future of interactive content? Well, it's going to be a mix of the three main areas we have described here – P2P people-ware (including 'surveillance' genres); enhanced media; and for want of a more succinct phrase, interactive movies (albeit of the networked, multi-user variety) – and the main technologies alluded to here – simulation, video game design, artificial intelligence and computer graphics imaging. Though if you want my guess, somewhere in this rich mix of art and technology we will be taken by surprise in the next few years as some contemporary Eisenstein, skilled in communication, media design and programming, comes up with something that emerges 'bottom-up' from the web/net and astonishes everyone.

8 the next big thing

a history of the next big thing

fashion, capital and technology

In the rapidly developing world of new media, I guess it's not surprising that each technological innovation – or the invention of a new way of using an existing technology – should be heralded as 'the Next Big Thing' (NBT). Remember that up to 1995* there was widespread scepticism about the whole new media sector. As far as most people were concerned, the web sprang up from nowhere. The internet was a small, non-commercial world inhabited by academics, hackers and other social misfits. The web wasn't taken seriously at first, even by the look-ahead companies that had been rapturously evangelizing the superhighway*, such as the big telecoms companies (AT&T, BT, the Baby Bells) and even the big software companies (Microsoft, Oracle, Lotus). This scepticism seemed perfectly natural at the time. How could *this* be the superhighway? We had been led to believe that the superhighway would come through glamorous fibre optics, not the old POTs (plain old telephone system) network, that it would mix television and software, offering movies on demand, interactive television, and personal video conferencing. We had been told that it would be *broadband*. And the web/net in the early 1990s was hardly that. So it's not surprising that the business world looked askance at these developments and really didn't sit up and take notice until 1995.

Given this scepticism – that this was simply an amateur network, and couldn't possibly compare with what the 'real' professionals were planning for the real superhighway – it wasn't surprising that, with the obvious popularity of the web/net with ordinary people, attention should focus on each new technology that promised to make this amateur network a real commercial proposition. Hence the search for the Next Big Thing.

*This was the year that the web/net 'got real' in commercial terms. Netscape, a minuscule, 16-month-old software house formed by Marc Andreeson (who had invented the first graphical web browser) went public. For more than a year before, Netscape's main product – the Navigator browser, had been given away free on the internet, and the company was losing $4 million, yet when it went to market in August 1995, it was massively over-subscribed and capitalized at $2.6 billion. It was the turning point – the web/net suddenly got real. Browsers were the next big thing.

*'An information superhighway was defined as being ubiquitous (having millions of people connected), digital, switched (interactive), and broadband.' From BT presentation for Agenda for Action in the UK, House of Lords, 1996.

The next big thing is a product of market forces – it gives investors in the new media a temporary focus and develops a cosy community of belief, a bandwagon, that because lots of people are investing, this new technology must be a winner. NBTs are indications that the apparently pragmatic and scientific technology sector is just as susceptible to the nuances of the zeitgeist that we call 'fashion' as anything else. The next big things are generally really interesting technologies or business models that have had some initial, indicative commercial or critical success, and have successfully evolved beyond the 'vapourware' stage – the kind of hype and spin surrounding a technology that is still on the drawing-board – and become the focus of media and investment interest for a period of time.

The siren-song of the next big thing resonates through new media history. It's as though everyone knows there 'must' be a single technology that will define the potential of the new media market – a killer app – and this becomes the object of a grail quest. Actually, what I think is happening here is that the high-tech world of new media has so much fascinating stuff happening that next big things are simply the way of parading these technologies, one at a time, to strut their stuff on the worldwide web stage (ie test them in the real-time marketplace), and check their killer app status. And really what is happening is that during this periodic cycle of next big things, we are gradually absorbing the idea that new media is really a fantastic montage of *all* the next big things, and more, that this super collation of technologies is going to go on producing unlooked-for synergies, symbioses and other hybrids. And that this process is not just a continuation of, or natural product of, capitalism, it is the natural product of communism too, and according to some, may just be the way that Gaia and homo sapiens were 'meant' to evolve.

The trouble with the life cycle of next big things is that it is often too short for the technology, or service, or business model to be fully developed and exploited. The typical life cycle of an NBT goes like this. A new technology is developed, looks promising, is heralded with considerable vapourware, is launched to fanfares of media spin, produces at least one potentially viable and/or popular commercial application, spreads around the net by a kind of viral marketing process, then it either succeeds and goes on to become a ubiquitous component of the new media scene, or interest wanes, another NBT comes along, and investment and critical attention are directed along this new vector. Often the lifespan of a viable and sustainable NBT is cut short in this process, in which case the ex-NBT becomes submerged in the clutter of real-time events, and if it's really good (or some new technological development makes it relevant again), it emerges sometime later as a born-again NBT.

The NBT of server push and its expression in the profiled push news service Pointcast is highly instructive in this regard. After the initial surge of enthusiasm that greeted its launch in 1996, during which 8–10 million people downloaded the Pointcast client software (see below), the regular user base settled down to a respectable 1.5 million. By the year 2000, this user base had declined to a still viable 400,000, and new owners decided to replace Pointcast with a new, refined 'push' service called Entrypoint.

As far as users go, there's nothing wrong with push or with Pointcast (I was one of the 400,000 disappointed by the Pointcast shutdown); in fact, in the current information explosion (over a billion web pages in 2000, with perhaps another million or so being added daily), profiled server push services – where only the news and information you want are sent to you automatically each time you log on – really make sense. You don't have to search for news every day, you get *only* the news you want, and it's there on your screen automatically (Pointcast was an animated screen-saver too). Certainly, network operators didn't like Push (it hogged bandwidth and clogged the network), but as far as users were concerned, in many ways it was the bee's knees. The lessons here are that NBTs often don't have time to reveal their true potential; that the idea of the NBT is sometimes better than its expression in a particular product; and that NBTs can't be considered in isolation from the media matrix of the web/net – as the web/net shifts in new technological directions, so the NBT may find a new expression. For example, look for a renaissance of push as the wireless application protocols (WAP) are implemented for cellular telephony (during 2000). WAP-Push could become the central means of 'narrowcasting' in the m-world.

“YOU DON'T HAVE TO SEARCH FOR NEWS EVERY DAY, YOU GET **ONLY** THE NEWS YOU WANT”

This brief survey of next big things is offered for two reasons – as instructive examples of how and why new technologies become the focus of investment interest; and as a briefing on these interesting technologies which, despite many of them being currently out of fashion and 'yesterday's big thing', often have the potential to resurface as the next big thing in the future.

Of course, the NBT may not be just a new technology – it may be a new business model, or a radical marketing concept – but in the new media, it is most likely to be a product of technology, a newly perceived synergy, or symbioses, or simply an optimization of existing technology, or the expression of an opportunity created by the introduction of a brand new technology. Examples of the former include the e-commerce revolution personified by Amazon.com, the auction craze initiated by OnSale and e.bay, and the viral marketing techniques (giving away software on the web/net) deployed by Tim Berners-Lee and CERN to distribute the WWW code itself, and by Marc Andreeson and Jim Clarke at Netscape to market their Navigator web browser and to grab market share in the face of the imminent Microsoft Explorer launch. NBTs are instructive guides to the ways ideas and technologies develop in the real-time, converging world of networked media. They illustrate how a new idea (a new business, marketing concept, route to market, etc) can emerge from the perception of some novel relationship betwixt and between the various old and new techno-social components of the web/net.

Because the web/net obviously is not just technology, it is techno-social. It is people too. It is made up of individuals, affinity groups, user groups, fraternities, families, parties, adhocist tribes, pressure groups, peer groups, special interest groups, fan clubs, etc, and people find their expression in the multiplicity of communications media that have already been (or are soon to be) subsumed by the web/net: telephone, e-mail, voice-mail, fax, attachments, webcam narrowcasts, conferencing, real-time messaging, chat, groupware, virtual worlds (MUDs), radio, concerts/webcasts, social video conferencing, user groups, bulletin boards, etc. And, as we discuss later, this vast mesh of people and machines is creating its own social, cultural, political and commercial momentum.

The possibilities for new synergistic or symbiotic relationships between technology and people in the web/net are manifest. Here are a few that reached the status of next big thing over the lifespan of web/net so far, ie the past six years or so.

new media: old content – 'content is king' Take a look at the programming roster of any of the newly launched UK digital satellite channels and you'll see why the old media moguls are so fond of old content solutions

– no wonder that 'content is king'! To the global super-vertical media owners, the new digital media offers a golden chance to dust off those box-office treasures from the dim and distant past, top and tail them as golden oldies, digitize them and set them off on a future-proofed career circulating the multiple channels and territories of the 21st century. In other words, 'content' in new media terms generally means old media content (movies, music, books, magazines, etc), re-purposed by the process of digitization and interactive enhancements to become 'new content'. Even though ideas of content are changing, as the new technologies give birth to brand new media (like the flight simulator, video game, MUDs and virtual reality), good content is an essential ingredient of new media product development. (The issues of content are covered in more detail in Chapter 7, 'Content and software'.)

Why content? Because in the click-driven networked media, it's even easier to channel-hop or surf-on. 'Your competitor is only a click away.' Good content is desirable because it's 'sticky' – it attracts and captures audiences rather like flypaper, and if it's episodic or regularly updated, users will come back again and again.

The realization that the availability of content in new media channels would be the determining factor in their success stems partly from the experience of the consumer electronics companies – Sony, Philips and JVC – in the famous video-standards 'war' of the 1970s. Three competing home video-recording standards were launched in the period 1970–1976, Sony's Betamax (1975), Philips' V9000 (1970) and JVC's VHS (1976). Despite the video professionals' endorsement of Betamax as the 'best' system, VHS went on to win over more consumers, and eventually became the world standard for home video-recording. The explanation for this? There were several, including the fact that VHS was an open standard, but decisively, the VHS system was launched with many more pre-taped movies than its competitors – it had content from day one.

After this experience, galled by losing out to a technically inferior product, Sony went on a 'content-acquisition' binge, developing its joint venture with CBS Records (formed in 1967), acquiring the movie production facility and valuable archive of Columbia Tristar in 1991, developing Sony Electronic Publishing and Sony Computer Entertainment to create brand new digital product, partnering with CableVision in 1999, and generally tooling up for broadband. The same motive drove the AOL network to acquire the publishing and broadcasting giant Time Warner in 2000. Because, this NBT would have it, 'content is king' – all else being equal, the availability of content will be the decisive factor determining success in the broadband era. For the user, a downside of this is that poor-quality, old content gets recycled along with premium titles, and because it's cheaper and easier to show repurposed archive materials, less money gets spent on developing or encouraging new, made-for-digital content and we get lost in 'yesterday land', a retrospective, closed circle of nostalgia for mid-20th-century television and movie and music golden oldies.

search engines

The web is really only about seven years old. Although the WWW program was launched as early as 1991, for most people it was text-only for its two-year gestation period. The first widely used graphical browser, Mosaic, wasn't available until 1993. So the web search engines that we know and love are real newcomers, even compared with arcane search devices such as Archie and Jughead that searched the internet up to the mid-1990s. During this period of transition (1990–1995) the internet/web (net/web) expanded rapidly (from 100 websites in 1993 to about 100,000 websites by 1995), spurred by the easy-to-use web and the graphical browsers developed for it – and in fact almost the entire history of search engines pre-web is condensed into this half-decade. Archie, a tool that searched for FTP (downloadable files), appeared in 1990, the Wide-Area Information Server and Gopher in 1991.

Perhaps the first *web* search engine was Matthew Gray's World Wide Web Wanderer (1993), which was also the first 'know-bot' or search 'agent'. Gray had written his Wanderer program in June 1993 to determine how many websites there were on the web/net. At that time his Wanderer found 100 unique sites (representing about 20,000 pages). Nine months later Wanderer found 1200 sites. The web/net reached 1 million sites (320 million pages) in 1998, and (probably) hit 2 million sites late in 1999. Since 1994, when Jerry Yang and David Filo started their classified index of websites with its integrated search engine (Yahoo!), dozens of search engines have been invented

Image and multimedia search engines are now providing the means to search the web for non-text materials. Although they still mostly rely on text-captions and picture-label searches, considerable development is taking place in 'image recognition' engines that use a variety of pattern-recognition techniques to find images similar to an example picture. (Image courtesy of Altavista at www.altavista.com)

to help people cope with the exponentially increasing number of websites and HTML documents (an estimated 1 billion pages on the web by 2000, growing at the rate of 1 million a day). Search engines are an essential tool in managing this flow of information.

Most search engines work by deploying software that automatically wanders or 'crawls' around the web/net, creating an index of URLs and associated contents. These indices are what you search when you type a query into a search engine. The problem with search engines is that even the best of them can't keep up with the phenomenal rate of growth in the number of web pages. In a 1998 study, two researchers at Princeton NEC Research Centre found that the top search engines were only searching

“THE PROBLEM WITH SEARCH ENGINES IS THAT EVEN THE BEST OF THEM CAN'T KEEP UP WITH THE PHENOMENAL RATE OF GROWTH IN THE NUMBER OF WEB PAGES” about 50 per cent of the total number of web pages (Hotbot was best with 57.5 per cent of the web indexed). NEC repeated the study in 1999 and found that the situation was deteriorating – then the search engine with the widest coverage of the web was Northern Light, but even it had indexed only one-sixth (16 per cent) of the estimated total number of websites.

According to the web research organization NUA (*www.nua.ie*), there may be another reason why search engines don't index large parts of the web/net – simply because it's not commercially viable for them to do so. NUA points out that the sites most likely to be found on a typical search engine are US-based, commercial and 'highly trafficked', ie used by many hundreds of thousands of people (potential 'eyeballs' for the banner advertisers).

The solution? For users, there are currently only two solutions to this search engine shortfall. Either use a meta-search engine – software that combines results from *all* the search engines (the first meta-search engine, MetaCrawler, was released in 1995; it is now called Go2Net.com) – or alternatively find a search engine that specializes in the subject within which you are searching.

search engine portals Search engines became the next big thing in the mid-1990s when it became apparent that many people were using their favourite search engine sites as gateways or 'portals' onto the web/net. They are obviously logical places to start surfing. Indeed, in early 2000, in Go2Net's top 100 most popular websites (see *www.100hot.com*) the major search engines (Yahoo!, Lycos, Excite, Magellan, Webcrawler and AltaVista) all featured in the top ten, alongside the established network portals such as MSN, AOL and Netscape. And by 2000 many of the most popular search engine sites were rapidly turning into general portals, offering free e-mail, e-commerce links, and news and other information content.

search engine development vectors Essentially, there's a lot of room for development in the search engine sector. The principal vectors of development include natural language interfaces (such as that offered by AskJeeves, where parsing techniques are used to derive text-string search

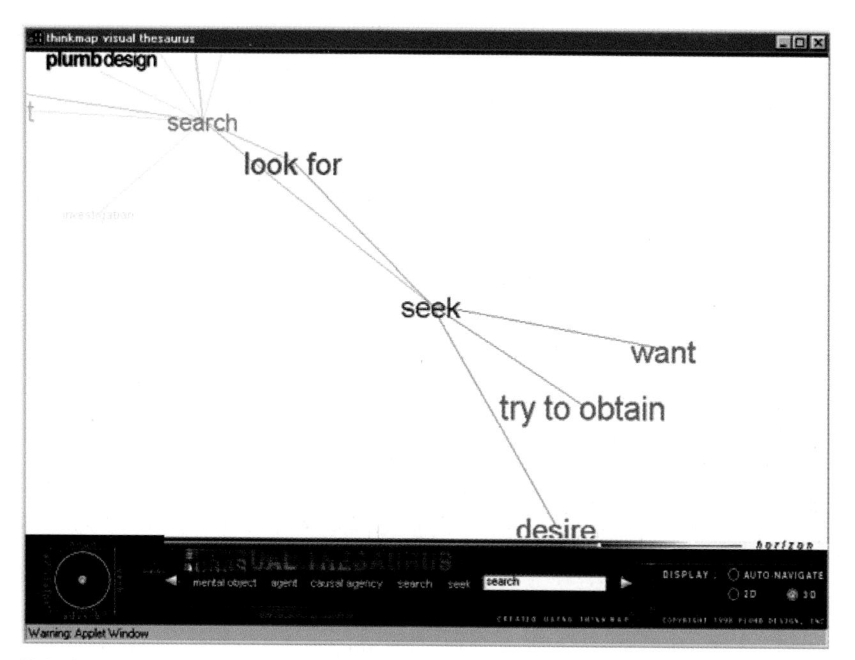

This dynamic, functional, and easy to use and to understand thesaurus interface from Plumb Design, points the way to future dynamically visualizing browsers, where the user follows schematic 'trails' of connections and is able to drill down into the diagram to access the connected web page or reference.

items from ordinary questions); the use of 'smart' software to provide searches that aren't just based on matching text strings, but use pattern-recognition techniques and statistical analysis to 'mine' information (such as Autonomy); translation services, such as those offered by AltaVista; specialist 'subject-specific' search engines and directories (such as the Internet Movie Database (*www.imdb.com*), and the Virtual Library Museums Pages (*www.icom.org/vlmp*); the filtering and weighting of search engine results using various methods (Google, IBM's Clever project); search utilities that embed their functionality into every computer-displayed document (such as flyswat and ThirdVoice); visual concept-mapping (such as Kmap, Infospiders and WebSOM self-organizing maps); and intelligent search agents (Autonomy, Agentware, Firefly, etc).*

*Search technology has developed within the R&D area of artificial intelligence and now uses pattern recognition and sophisticated probability theory to mine text and other data. Michael Lynch is the scientist behind Neurodynamics and Autonomy, leaders in a field that includes Inktomi, Oracle, Inxight, Plumdesign and HNC.

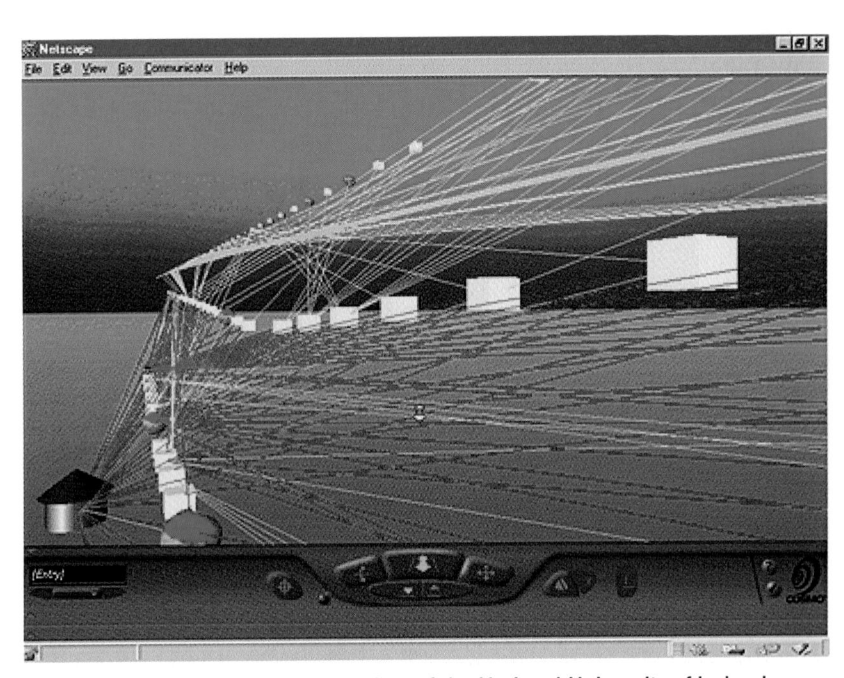

David Cleary and Diarmuid O'Donoghue of the National University of Ireland developed 'Visual Expresso', combining meta-search engineering and 3D data visualization using VRML (Virtual Reality Modelling Language) techniques to represent data structures on the web/net. In this screenshot, generated by Visual Expresso, the objects are web pages, and the lines represent the hyperlinks between pages. Many researchers are trying to perfect 3D information browsers and either consciously or unconsiously they acheive visualizations of cyberspace akin to William Gibson's original vision: 'Unthinkable complexity, lines of light ranged in the non-space of the mind, clusters and constellations of data. Like city lights, receding.' (Gibson, Neuromancer 1983). The search engines of the future will represent information and data in all kinds of visual, spatial and dynamic relationships – with over one billion pages (in 2001), the process of searching the web/net must be fun as well as functional and fast.

future search tools Of course, when you start to think about the *ideal* search utility, you envision possible hybrids and intersections of *all* these vectors; for example, a search portal with a personality-user-interface (a search engine with a human face – one you can talk to) combining voice recognition, speech synthesis, search engines and search agents, and user-profiling ability, together with highly visual, dynamic concept mapping. Such a utility (yet to be designed of course) would have a virtual person interface, a 'talking head', that recognized your voice, knew your personal tastes and preferences, parsed your verbal query, sent out search requests (or customized intelligent search agents for you), then presented its findings verbally, alongside illustrated concept maps of the search space for you to explore. Most of the ingredients for such a utility already exist – take a look at the Press Association's text-reading synthespian Ananova (*www. ananova.com*) and imagine 'her' with a search engine, agents and concept mapping software at her disposal. In this scenario, the virtual person or personality-user-interface becomes a digital companion, a virtual private secretary, ready to do your bidding on a 24/7 basis. In the late 1980s, Apple Computer explored many of these possibilities in its video of the Knowledge Navigator that illustrated many of these ideas.

Other strong indicators point in the direction of the embedded search engine, a ubiquitous utility that, like flyswat (*www.flyswat.com*), automatically scans and analyzes every text document window on your screen – web page, e-mail or word processing document – and creates on-the-fly hyperlinks (underlined in a delicate and unobtrusive yellow/green) for words that it recognizes (ie that it has access to from its server-side web index). The integration of search utilities into the whole desktop environment is another step towards the kind of seamless hyperlinked information space envisioned by Ted Nelson and other Hypertext pioneers. Put these desktop tools together with information management tools such as SpotOn and iHarvest – utilities that help you organize the notations (the URLs, quotes, notes and images) you collect on your search trawls – and a cooler, embedded, search utility development vector emerges.

web browsers

The technology of graphical web browsers was incorporated in Tim Berners-Lee's original WWW proposal in 1989, and it provided for a consistent user interface for displaying HTML documents no matter what the client computer hardware was. The WWW program was written on the then state-of-the-art Next Cube computer, running Unix, and most of the other first-generation browsers were also Unix-based (they included Viola by Pei Wei, and Midas by Tony Johnson). Unix was, and still is, the internet professional's operating system, powering servers like those from Sun,

Hewlett-Packard, IBM and Silicon Graphics. And because of this, it was the second WWW line mode browser, written by Nicola Pellow, that most other people came to when they accessed the CERN site for information about the web. Because only a few users enjoyed the Next computer graphical user interface version of WWW, the web was initially thought of as a text-only service.

The command-line browser was OK for scientists, academics and experienced computer users, but it definitely wasn't a consumer-friendly tool. To many non-professionals, it looked like just another text editor. Only the small number of Next users saw the real potential of the graphical web browser, and it took another three years before the general public realized this.

Mosaic, the first popular, easy-to-use, graphical web browser, was designed by Marc Andreeson and his team at the National Centre for Supercomputing Applications at the University of Illinois in 1993. Its success was immediate. For the first time ordinary people with ordinary PCs were able to browse the WWW and display HTML documents and associated graphics in a single browser window that used the familiar point-and-click interface first popularized in the Apple Macintosh interface, and later by Microsoft Windows. Importantly, Mosaic displayed graphics 'in line' – that is, embedded in a text document. The earlier Unix and Next browsers had displayed graphics in separate screen windows. This innovation opened up the web as a giant desktop-publishing tool.

Mosaic wasn't the only graphical browser developed at this time (others included Cello, Viola and Midas), but Mosaic was easy to install and use, it was marketed well, and importantly, it came with 24-hour user support.

Andreeson left NCSA in March 1994 and formed Mosiac Communications (later renamed Netscape Communication Corporation) with Jim Clark, the founder of Silicon Graphics. In October 1994 they launched the beta version of their Navigator browser, and made it available as a free download on the web. This first version of Navigator amplified browser performance by introducing continuous document streaming (enabling users to interact with HTML documents while they were still downloading, rather than wait for the entire document to be downloaded), multiple simultaneous network accesses (several documents could be downloaded at the same time), and support for high-resolution JPEG images. The finished Navigator browser (version 1.0) was launched in December of that year, and millions

“NETSCAPE GRABBED 75 PER CENT OF THE BROWSER MARKET WITH THIS FREEWARE STRATEGY” of individuals downloaded the free software. Netscape grabbed 75 per cent of the browser market with this freeware strategy, which continued the tradition of mutual co-operation in the creation and distribution of tools and information that had been a hallmark of the internet and its academic and scientific community. Netscape's income was derived from sales of server software, and sales of browser software to commercial clients.

By June 1995, Netscape Communications Corp had gone public and raised a then phenomenal $2.6 billion, despite the fact that it was making losses of $4 million on the previous year's trading. Sound familiar?

server-push Most of us use web browsers to surf the net. We do this by clicking on hyperlinks. These hyperlinks send a request to the relevant server and the server then sends the requested information back to us for display in our browser window. This is called 'client pull' as we (the 'clients') are directly initiating a request, 'pulling' the information we want from the server. Another way of getting information from the web/net is by having the server automatically send or 'push' the information to us. 'Server push' is the generic description of information that is sent from the server to the client without a *direct* request from us. Server push includes news services and e-mail services that send us information as the result of a programmed request, that is, of us filling in a form that both registers us with the push service, and specifies the subject matter we want. Some server push services require that we have a special client program (other than a browser) running on our computer – this is usually downloaded when we register with a push news service. Then, every time we log on to the web/net, information and updates on the previously specified subjects is automatically sent (or 'pushed') to us and stored for display in our push client application.

The first really popular server-push news service was Pointcast, launched in 1996. Back then, when I saw Pointcast running for the first time, I realized what a powerful tool this was. Pointcast was a really clever software development. When you registered, you downloaded the Pointcast client application onto your PC (after a few months a Mac version was available too), while at the same time you filled in a simple electronic form that specified which channels you wanted (the choice included some of the major international and national US newspapers and news agencies, as well as many local US news sources – yes, it was very US-centric. Each channel could then be personalized by a selection from a content sub-menu, so that you could choose from general news, sports, fashion, business and other categories. This registration and personalization process took just a couple of minutes.

From then on, every time you went online, Pointcast would invisibly download its latest news, complete with hyperlinks, onto your hard disk. A narrow Pointcast control strip appeared above the taskbar, and your personal news service was up and running. You could click on any of the headlines that began to stream across the control strip and then read full articles on the Pointcast website. Furthermore, by setting Pointcast as your default screen saver, after a few minutes of computer inactivity the entire screen would become an animated, personalized, electronic newspaper. Pictures, animated headlines, text summaries, and occasional advertising banners would fill the screen, so that even when you weren't working you could keep up with the latest news. This was Pointcast's killer feature – it demonstrated clearly that server push could act as a very effective narrowcasting or 'netcasting' service. Remember that this was at least a couple of years before Shockwave and Flash animated-content changed the web into a multimedia medium – the Pointcast screen savers were the first intimation for many of us that the web could be more than just a static graphics and text medium.

As mentioned earlier, Pointcast went through the typical life cycle of an NBT. Launched with considerable fanfare, it was an early example of how the then narrowband web/net could look: animated, full-screen, and sexy. It was free (the concept of freeware had reached general public attention when Netscape gave away Navigator). The business model was 'advertising-supported freeware', with the potential of targeted advertising based on the user's channel profile. Pointcast spread like wildfire, purportedly achieving more than 8 million downloads in the first year of operation. In screen-saver mode it advertised itself on millions of screens in countless offices and studios worldwide. Pointcast settled to a regular user base of around 1.5 million, but for several reasons (bandwidth-clogging on intranets, large file sizes on client hard disks, and lack of continuous product development), dropped to around 400,000 users before the plug was pulled in early 2000.

Pointcast combined a server-push personalized news and information delivery program with an animated news-presentation screen saver. This dynamic combination pointed up the usefulness of personalized server-push in a world with a rapidly growing number of information sources.

The new owner of Pointcast, Entrypoint Inc (a fusion of Pointcast Inc and Launchpad Technologies Inc, creator of e-wallet – software that enabled single-click secure purchases anywhere on the web), has re-invented and relaunched its push service as EntryPoint, a service that combines the personalized news capabilities of Pointcast with a number of other services – e-wallet, an MP3 player, real-time stock quotes, and special travel and sports channels.

Since January 2000, there has been some interesting competition in the form of another toolbar-based push service, NetSanity's virtual personal digital assistant (VDA), which neatly flips the push idea into what they call 'XML-pull' (XML is extensible markup language, a kind of super HTML). NetSanity's VDA is toolbar-based and allows users to aggregate information on their favourite websites and news services into one desktop resource, the

NetSanity's 'virtual digital assistant' – a free desktop toolbar that allows personally customized 'instant' connections to around 20 different content, commerce and community providers. With a 'no-advertising' business model relying on co-branded sponsorship and per-click transactions (e-commerce commissions), NetSanity's VDA, is also relying on viral marketing to establish an intended user base of 5 million by 2001 (users can e-mail the VDA – with their selection of content providers – to friends).

VDA toolbar. The pull technology NetSanity has developed is much lighter on bandwidth than push. What the VDA does is allow users to customize the content of their VDA, to methodically and automatically retrieve tiny bits of updated information from websites selected by the user, and display these in the toolbar, so users can see the latest changes in their chosen websites without launching their browser; and receive updates on stock prices, breaking news, e-mail, auction bids and other time-specific information. The VDA also has yellow pages, maps and a search engine utility.

By mid-2000, when NetSanity's VDA was up and running and Pointcast became Entrypoint, the server-push publishing paradigm was already looking forward to rebirth as a means of narrowcasting information to mobile access devices – to the Palms and Psion handhelds, the other PDAs, and WAP-enabled mobiles. The future for this kind of cellular broadcasting, especially in the sector of providing location-specific services to mobile users, looks extremely promising.

portals In a real sense, portals are always the next big thing. As early as the mid-1980s, when America Online (AOL) led the gold-rush to sign up as many internet users as possible, there was an industry-wide realization that owning the portal – the gateway through which people access the network – was the key to success in the multi-channel, mega-information environment that was then called cyberspace. From around 1985 up to the end of the century, the portal competition was for the PC-web/net market, and the main contenders by the turn of the millennium were AOL (yes, AOL had 22 million members, and also 'owned' Compuserve's 2.7 million, had access, by acquisition, to Netscape's 25 million registrants, and had vertically integrated its portal with a network offering that included the content giant Time Warner), Microsoft Network (MSN) and Yahoo! (not a network but a search engine/content directory).

These three industry leaders grew to dominance in the PC-oriented web/net market of the 1990s, but it is clear now that the PC will be only one of the ways through which people access the web/net in the 21st century. And, of course, portals will change as the web/net and its access technologies change and evolve.

“THREE INDUSTRY LEADERS GREW TO DOMINANCE IN THE PC-ORIENTED WEB/NET MARKET OF THE 1990S”

The three companies that dominated the portal market in early 2000 were 'general' portals, rather like the old television networks, attempting to provide something for everyone, and inevitably achieving a kind of corporate blandness as a result. AOL and MSN succeeded largely because they were aggressively marketed as 'safe' solutions to the growth market of web/net newbies* – the implicit message here was that the net was a dangerous place, full of pornography, paedophile rings, viruses and other undesirable content, and that membership of the commercial networks offered protection from these excesses.

*Consider the fact that as the web/net doubles in size every year, every year 50 per cent of web/net users are 'newbies' – newcomers to the new media networks. This is the sector where the established portals come into their own.

Despite their success so far, there are indicators that the web/net is ready for a switch from the general portal idea. Software that allows sophisticated personalization (customizing portal and content to reflect your tastes and interests) points the way. Personalization in this context generally means that you choose from a selection of content offered by the portal. In this way you can indicate your taste for sports news, current affairs, business and so on – a fairly basic level of customization, but nevertheless a valuable service. Of course, the general portals were quick to offer personalization features, with a spate of new product launches during 1999, including MyExcite, MyNetscape, MyYahoo! and MyLycos, but these remained fairly bland and 'newbie' oriented.

Now that the technology exists for personalized content portals, and for highly personalized hardware access devices (eg PDAs, mobile phones, palm-tops, handhelds, soon wearables), and given the fact that the number of choices is proliferating exponentially, it is likely that portals will evolve into much more responsive entities during the next decade.

As an indication of just how portals might evolve, consider these possible development vectors – from personal to group to corporate/institutional, these are likely to be the shape of portals for this decade.

the personal, public/private portal What do you want when you go online? Well, everyone is different. They want different things, different news, specific local information, and this is precisely the point of the personal, public/private portal (PP/PP). The PP/PP offers a range of tools for users, allowing them to customize their homepage according to their requirements and their tastes and preferences. These tools would include web e-mail, web calendar/diary, integrated messaging service, customizable tickers to keep you informed of news headlines, specialist site updates, a range of electronic programme guides relevant to the media channels you subscribe to, local weather and traffic information, home banking, portfolio management, personal development and education services, etc. And it's not just about choosing the tools you need. The PP/PP enables you to customize the form and the content of your portal too. Profiling software from a variety of suppliers (including Broadvision, Autonomy and Firefly) lets you build a personal profile that resides in software, and defines the parameters of a variety of search devices – agents, crawlers, search engines, syndication networks, push channels, user groups and other mediators – that go out into the web/net and find, collect, collate and re-present content relevant to your personal profile.

Other levels of customization would include the look and feel of your PP/PP – the browser style and operation, the content layout and hierarchy, and for example the way your PP/PP is customized for the particular access device(s) you use. In fact, soon you'll be able to choose and customize, if necessary, your personal synthespian portal host or hostess, the style of presentation you prefer (sound and tone of voice, emotional and expressive quality, etc). Personal synthespian hosts and hostesses, personal 'masters of ceremonies', are yet another next big thing reviewed later in this section. Why public/private? Because another likely development is that with the realization of just how valuable your personal profile data could be, you might want to exchange this data, to sell it or swap it for access to some free or discounted service. This is the 'public' personal data you want to trade, while there may be a range of data (perhaps including your medical records) that you wish to remain private.

personal professional portal Another vector that is just as promising is the personal professional portal (PPP). This is the means by which you maintain contact with your peer group; with specific agents trawling the infosphere to find and filter the stuff you need to know about your sphere of professional interest; with access to your organization's intranet, to professional bodies; and to push services from relevant specialist news channels, academic and research reports. Groupware such as teleconferencing, project planning, SIGs, collaborative teleworking, messaging, shared diaries, chat and user groups, would also be integral parts of this kind of portal.

enterprise information portals On a corporate and institutional level, the EIP (enterprise information portal) extends the corporate portal into a kind of enterprise-wide portal-cum-intranet, combining knowledge management, company databases and groupware communications tools with content management and personalization, in a kind of networked management information system. Declared an interesting 'investment space' by Christopher Shilakes and Julie Tylman of Merrill Lynch's Enterprise Software team in November 1998, EIPs are an amalgamation of software and networking applications that enable companies to 'unlock internally and externally stored information' and that provide personalized gateways to the information needed to make informed business decisions. The main objectives of EIPs are to provide competitive advantage, a better return on investment than proprietary customized systems (and they may have revenue-generating potential too), access for everyone concerned (as a well-planned and executed intranet should do), and, by providing a more efficient means to access relevant information without surfing and searching, they can increase productivity as well.

Using both push and automated pull technologies, EIPs can provide a 'one-stop shop' for corporate and industry-specific content and the means to interrogate and confer with colleagues and other experts upon such content. But perhaps the overall objective of such portals is to converge the human intellectual experience and knowledge embodied in the company together with its stored information base in a kind of corporate expert system that is accessible to, and can be queried and discussed by, all concerned in the enterprise. One of the early apostles of computer-mediated communications, Murray Turoff, writing in 1976, noted:

'I think the ultimate possibility of computer conferencing is to provide a way for human groups to exercise a "collective intelligence" capability. The computer as a device to allow a human group to exhibit collective intelligence is a rather new concept. In principle, a group, if successful, would exhibit an intelligence higher than any member. Over the next decades, attempts to design computerized conferencing structures that allow a group to treat a particular complex problem with a single collective brain may well promise more benefit for mankind than all the artificial intelligence work to date.'

Murray was right. But if you also integrate the fruits of AI research, in the form of advanced search agents, data mining, expert systems and personalization, into his 'collective intelligence', you have written the brief for future advanced EIPs.

family portal, affinity portal On a personal level, the portal can be more friendly, more like the village or suburban promenade, a place to go to meet friends, family and extended families, or to bump into strangers with similar interests to yourself. These affinity portals can be demographic too – they can be customized (personalized) to your selected age group and gender, your geographic area, even to a specific subject, such as a football team or rock band.

the e-commerce portal Perhaps one of the obvious growth areas in portals will be connected to the rapidly expanding e-commerce sector. Here, the various portal technologies we have mentioned so far – personalization, search engines, knowledge-management systems, software agents, personality-user-interfaces and the like – will almost certainly be combined in various ways to provide us with the essential tools for consumers (all of us!) involved in the biggest marketplace on the planet: the e-commerce web/net. These tools will include the means of filtering and finding information on products and services that we want or need, and the means of locating and negotiating the best deal on offer (not just the best price). I call these two consumer essentials 'really useful advertising' and 'my personal metashop', and they will both be components of an ideal e-commerce portal.

really useful advertising I described really useful advertising in my 1999 pamphlet *You Ain't Seen Nothing Yet* (ICA):

'Forget 500 channels. There's only going to be one channel: yours.' (Alan Kay)

'Alan Kay's perception of how very personal the experience of mediating the vast number of new channels of the information explosion could be is the essential key here. The same kind of smartware tools that advertisers and marketeers now regard as heaven-sent could be used by the consumer to completely subvert their manipulations. Profiling software can be used to filter all incoming material (the upcoming, third-generation web will use a mix of pull and push publishing) and exclude anything that the user does not want. This raises the attractive prospect of really useful advertising. There are many times when you welcome advertising – when you're thinking of buying a new car, suit or computer (or planning a holiday or whatever), you really want all that product-specific information, and at those times you welcome the prospect of selectively perusing the range of choices and the personal empowerment does not stop there: deal analysis, price comparison, financing deals, discounting, and other highly customized services will be widely available.'

“THIS RAISES THE ATTRACTIVE PROSPECT OF REALLY USEFUL ADVERTISING”

Really useful advertising uses the personal profile of the user embodied in the e-commerce portal to locate, classify and display advertising, product announcements, press releases, reviews and comparative analyses (etc) related to the type of product or service in which (through our profile) we have expressed interest. It would be like a really specialist magazine – it would contain adverts and all the other product information mentioned above – but just for the things we want to buy.

personal meta-shop A corollary to this focused advertising service would be the personal meta-shop, the electronic shop window that displayed actual products that our profile 'knew' we were interested in. Knowing our interest in these products or services, suppliers from all over the web/net could pitch to us directly through our personal meta-shop, displaying their products and their sales pitches at the same time. Of course, the perfect consumer portal would also have the means for us to access consumer organization reports, product endorsements, product user groups, trade reviews and the like to counterpoint these sales pitches. Our meta-shop, in other words, would provide us with all the means that the network offers to make our decision the right one. And not only on price – current shop-bots go for the lowest common denominator, price, to the exclusion of the 'best deal', the aggregate sum of best quality/price ratio, based on brand name and reputation, guarantees, delivery times and costs, upgrade paths, accessories, availability, reviews, financing (etc) – all the aspects that a simple shop-bot ignores.

With complex products such as pension plans, mortgages and personal equity plans, the e-commerce portal would assist with deal-analysis software, expert guides and access to user groups, or to expert human help via a call centre. The personalized e-commerce portal is an expert system for ordinary consumers and will of course be responsible, through its smart agents, for leveraging the most advantage out of our personal profile. If I choose to sell my profile to advertisers and retailers, I want access to free tools, free content and value-added services, or even some form of payment, in return.

new portals for new technologies As new access devices and new modes of accessing the web/net become commonplace through the next decade, so new kinds of portals will emerge to cater for the demands and possibilities created. The EPG portal, for example, could grow from the personalization technology embodied in HDVRs (set-top boxes and hard-disk video recorders such as the Tivo and ReplayTV). EPGs aggregated from all the channels you subscribe to and personalized to your viewing requirements and habits are already a feature of HDVRs. Companion web portals could provide all the enhancements you need to make these a really interactive experience. Merged with personalized content from TV magazines (features, reviews, interviews, webcasts, soap storylines, sports features), with portal-specific services (such as video on demand movie rentals and pay-per-view events coverage), and with your favourite synthespian expert system as a master or mistress of ceremonies, there's plenty of room for interesting developments in this area.

As mobiles begin to threaten the PC as the major access device for the web/net, and as new kinds of portable viewers and media players emerge in the wake of broadband 3G cellular networking, so new kinds of media-access portals will emerge, offering MPEG2 and MPEG4 movies and TV, MP3 music and RealAudio radio, digital audio broadcasts (digital radio) and even (with mobile video phones), mobile video conferencing. Combined with voice telephony, integrated messaging, real-time chat, and location-specific WAP services, these could well be the next big thing of this decade.

Another of the web/net access devices that will come to prominence in the early years of this decade is based on the games console. Sophisticated computing machines such as the Sega Dreamcast and the Sony Playstation 2 – with phenomenal processing power, special chips for video, graphics and audio processing, with built-in, high-speed modems, with ethernet ports for broadband networking, and built-in DVD drives, and with control devices specifically designed for high-speed interaction – are bound to become leading contenders in the broadband access-device market. Portals geared to these consoles will favour Sony's cross-media verticality, a portal that links seamlessly with games, movies on demand, cablevision television content and broadband web access for music and other entertainment, not forgetting games networks, multi-player gaming environments and global gaming competitions. Sony has plans to use the Playstation platforms to dominate new media access during this decade, and has formed an overarching division, Sony Broadband Entertainment, to explore initiatives in the broadband arena.

software agents The ideas behind software agents have been around since the early 1970s, so why on earth should they be in a list of next big things? The easy answer is that they *still are* a next big thing – they just haven't got big yet. But almost everyone agrees that they *will* be big. Alan Kay, the computer scientist genius who gave us the dynabook concept and masterminded the design of the first personal computer graphical user interface in the 1970s, was calling agents 'the next big thing in interface design' back in the mid-1980s. So why are they going to be big, and why have they taken so long?

Software agents are programs designed to assist people, and (sometimes) to act on their behalf. As such, a software agent will enjoy four main characteristics: autonomy – it will have control over its actions and be able to initiate actions without corresponding with its human user or other entities (other humans, other agents); it will be reactive – be able to 'sense' its environment and respond to changes; it will be able to communicate – with its human user, other humans, other agents; and it will be goal-driven – have a purpose, and be able to pursue that purpose until it has been achieved. Other attributes include mobility – the ability to move from computer to computer through a network; adaptability – the ability to learn and to change their behaviour based on their experiences; and continuity – functioning all the time. Agents can also be self-reproducing and co-operative, able to replicate themselves and work with communities of other agents in the solution of their given task.

Software agents are a logical development of several strands of research into artificial intelligence, networking and human-computer interaction. What the AI fraternity want to end up with is a computer that we don't necessarily see but that is present all the time, sensing our movements, our facial expressions, gestures, biometrics, eyeball direction, etc, and listening to our voice commands. Such a computer would be able to converse with us in natural language, translate languages for us, in real time, and always be connected to the web/net (its vast, global memory, and access point for communications with the rest of the world). It would be able to delegate tasks to thousands of intelligent software agents that it could create and customize on the fly to perform all kinds of search, retrieval, editing, comparison, deal analysis, even transactions, for us.

“SUCH A COMPUTER WOULD BE ABLE TO CONVERSE WITH US IN NATURAL LANGUAGE”

Now this is not just science fiction, *Star Trek* stuff. While admittedly we're some way away from this kind of really 'personal' computer, most of the bits we need for it have been developed already or, like natural language recognition and intelligent software agents, are in advanced stages of development. The prospect is that we will all become owners of many thousands of such digital slaves – as many software agents as we want, digital slaves that will perform all kinds of tasks for us, 24 hours a day, without complaining, without being paid for it. With the prospect of a guilt-free 'age of plenty' in store, who can argue that software agents are not the next big thing?

WHAT AGENTS COULD DO FOR US

– Search for information: statistics, quotations, results, features, news, correspondence, pictures, diagrams, animations, maps (etc), and to aggregate this, classify it and even summarize it according to our requirements (eg compile a personal magazine or newspaper, report or executive summary).

– Build networks of 'friends of friends'
– Extending our personal social network to potentially encompass a large and ever-expanding social space formed by interlocutions between a network of software agents ('friend of a friend finder', MIT).

– Find people and clusters of people with the same interests or profiles (Yenta, MIT).

– Explore the world by interacting with software agents that represent particular areas as expert guides (such as Wherehoo, MIT).

– Monitor road traffic through a network of agents in vehicles (Trafficopter, MIT).

– Sample or listen in to a range of thousands of real-time conversational groups and recommend those of interest to the user (Butterfly, MIT).

– Monitor websites, and inform us of changes in content.

– Customize and personalize sites and push channels and EPGs.

– Recommend books, movies, websites, records and other media according to the profile of the user, and to the profiles of similar users.

– Locate specific books, records, movies, television programmes, negotiate for and purchase them (using our digital signature), and download or record them to our hard-disk video recorder, e-book, MP3 player or other device.

– Match our requirements for holidays, houses, rental accommodation, and a wide variety of other goods and services.

– Perform best-price and best-deal searches and comparisons including the comparison of value-added propositions (such as widely available shop-bots, and Tete-a-Tete, MIT).

- Perform product comparisons.
- Filter e-mail, voice-mail, faxes and other in-tray communications, edit and classify by importance.
- Bid for us at online auction sites.
- Collect, collate and classify location-specific information that the agent assesses will be useful to the user as they move through the real world (Impulse, InShop, streetWise, Remembrance Agents, and Restaurant Recommendation WAP System, MIT).
- Automated knowledge sharing within an organization (MindShare, MIT).
- Provide intelligent 'look-ahead' guidance in browsing complex databases or the web/net itself, by comparing the user's profile to the range of possibilities revealed by their recent search queries (such as Letizia, MIT).
- Locate experts, guides, mentors and other human (or soon machine) intelligences within an organization or community, to assist us in a particular task (for example, guidance in making complex financial transactions vis: 'Apt Decision', MIT).
- Broker our 'consumer profile' in return for specific 'free' or micropayment services.
- Track and monitor usage of copyright material throughout the web/net.

(derived partly from **http://mevard.www.media.mit.edu/groups/agents/projects**)

games consoles as broadband web/net access devices

The idea that internet access is available only through a personal computer is very last century. As we pointed out earlier, the surprise players in the internet access market are the WAP mobile phone (becoming the 3G phone through 2000–2002) and the games console. During early 2000, Nintendo, Sony and Sega announced or leaked their strategic plans to develop their respective games consoles into broadband new media/internet access devices. These 128-bit* consoles will feature extremely fast processors, special graphics and sound co-processors, DVD drives, and fast internet access ports or built-in modems, variously deploying wire, cable or wireless networking.

*128-bit refers to the number of bits (0s and 1s) the machine can process simultaneously.

Microsoft is also playing this console game, although at first sight its X-box looks more like a PC than a console, featuring as it does a PC CPU, 8 Gb hard drive and an ethernet port, albeit with special graphics and sound processors and the ubiquitous DVD. Price will be a determining factor in the success of the X-box.

The X-box and Nintendo Dolphin will not appear until 2001, giving both Sega and Sony some breathing space to establish their competing broadband systems. With its 1.5 mbs cable modem, Sega has thrown a direct challenge to Sony which, while not offering a modem, is equipping the Playstation 2 with an ethernet and other ports for an all-digital broadband connection to a network.

consoles in broadband strategies In Sony's case, the Playstation 2 will be the central component in a broadband strategy that goes way beyond the games market, embracing the entire Sony new media business. The existing company divisions of Sony Online Entertainment, Sony Pictures Entertainment and Sony Music Entertainment are now overseen by an umbrella division, Sony Broadband Entertainment. This will manage a super-vertical entertainment market, integrating games, movies, music and the web/net with consumer electronics and computing. Sony is also developing online banking and other online services. Playstation 2 sold 1.4 million units during March 2000 – the first month of sales in Japan – and was expecting to ship around a further 10 million units to the European, US and Japanese markets in the year to March 2001.

Sega is building broadband partnerships with Japanese cable TV networks, and Nintendo has pre-released the specification of its Dolphin 128-bit console, again featuring DVD and modem access.

So what is the significance of these console access strategies? Well, consoles are easier to set up and to use than PCs. And video game interface design has set high standards in 'plug and play' ease of use. Games consoles are also familiar items to millions of people: up to 2000, Sony had sold 56 million Playstation 1 consoles, and Sony's games division contributed 40 per cent of the parent company's overall profits during 1999, more than movies, TV, music or consumer electronics. The video game business overall earned $6.3 billion worldwide in 1999. On top of this, games consoles are relatively cheap to buy, certainly compared with a PC, averaging around £300 (about the real cost of a set-top box). The realization that the low-cost games console was not only more powerful than many PCs, offered really interactive entertainment, played DVD movies *and* offered broadband internet access has made the industry radically redefine its attitude. Games consoles are pre-eminently entertainment media, they have a huge market footprint, and they look set to challenge the PC, and the set-top box, as major competitors in the non-mobile broadband future.

future broadband console developments and applications

How will the broadband-console develop? There are several directions for both hardware and software. The home entertainment system could be the counterpoint to the home business system – the 'play'-station as opposed to the workstation – and become integrated with high-definition digital television, hard-disk video recorders, DVD players, home media systems, and home-area networks. In this scenario, the console could become the central unit of a system combining music (disk and downloads) television and video (broadcast, disk and downloads), games (disk and downloads) and an increasingly broadband web/net. With the rich potential of combining high-resolution video – movies, television, camera, video conferencing, webcam, CCTV and other sources (both online and from DVD) – with powerful, high-resolution, real-time computer graphics (games, virtual reality, simulations, sports recreations, etc), *and* with broadband web/net access, the digital blue sky is the limit. The more dramatic applications of this console convergence include holistic sportscasts, where video and biometric coverage (from television cameras, embedded CCTV, wearable sensors and mini-videocams, smartdust sensors, etc) is under interactive user control (with parallel streams of professional and amateur commentary from any one of 100 or so video journalists and expert sports commentators, or from any one of the 100,000 audience who are equipped with broadband mobile videophones), is combined with 3D computer graphic real-time recreations (stored for replay and what-if? scenario visualization and deconstruction after the game), plus all the web-enhanced media (such as game strategies, player profiles, team profiles, statistics, trends and interactive interviews with players, coaches, managers, chairmen, etc) available through the web/net.

“THE DIGITAL BLUE SKY IS THE LIMIT”

Then there are the real-time virtual mediascapes – 3D virtual realities that provide walk-through explorations of media channels, people-to-people forums, multi-user gaming environments, MUDs and other socialware. There could be many 'flavours' of real-time mediascapes, including those devoted to advertainment and edutainment, to commerce and to education. These mediascapes marry ideas from the theme park, the multi-user game, the interactive advert or distance-learning courseware and present them integrated within real-time, walk-through virtual environments, creating educational environments (Legoland meets Exploratorium in Toy Storyville, with Pokémon learning mentors and curriculum agents as guides), 3D product theme parks (World Fair-style virtual theme parks or 'Adlands'). Other applications might marry live participation from many thousands of GenY and GenZ participants inputting video, still and audio (voice and MP3) commentary from thousands of locations around the world in a kind of rolling global street party, as world capitals, large and small, play host-of-the-day to the global village.

The grand project of recreating the city of Paris on the Internet as a 3D computer-modelled virtual reality was initiated by Canal Plus – Europe's leading digital TV provider – back in 1997. The idea is a good one – you create a geographically familiar environment, build e-stores and virtual cinemas, book-stores, museums, galleries – in other words, create a simulation of the real city experience. Mixing education with surrogate travel, e-commerce with entertainment, advertising with sight-seeing, chat-spaces with 3D worlds, Deuxieme Monde has the potential of providing the hybrid experiences typical of e-media. (Image courtesy of Canal Plus at www.canalplus.fr)

No, this is not 'just' blue-sky speculation (although I would strongly defend this kind of 'guesstimation' as a valuable (and cheap!) component of new product development). Big, hard-nosed multinationals, such as Sony, BT, Viacom, AOL/Time Warner, Canal Plus, the Symbian Group and others are working on just such speculative explorations of the future e-media sphere – the BT/Sony/BBC collaboration on 'The Mirror' (inhabited TV) project is just one example. And there are many other similar projects, or R&D in the enabling technologies for such developments, under way in the techno-academic world – at MIT, Stanford, Carnegie-Mellon, University of Utah and many other centres of excellence around the world. Many of these explorations are rooted in the science fiction and cyberpunk visions that we examined in Chapter 4.

online auctions The success of e-bay, QXL and other auction sites not only demonstrates the actuality of the web/net as a global marketplace but also signifies the fact that the new media are equally as much about people as they are about media. In other words, online auctions are a classical example of the techno-social web, an exploitation of the convergence of a critical mass market of many millions of individuals, a networked medium – the web/net, and software for the databasing and auctioning of many millions of items.

Since 1995, when OnSale was launched by Alan Fisher and Jerry Kaplan, the online auction market has expanded rapidly. By 2000, estimates of total annual online auction sales hovered between $2.3 billion and $4.5 billion, from an actual figure of $1 billion in 1998. The front-runners in 2000 included e.Bay, Ubid, Amazon, Bid.com and QXL.

To me, the significance of online auctions is that although they seem to be an entirely logical adaptation of the web/net to serve an ancient market function, they have actually turned out to be a commercial surprise. The flea market style, the auction process, the garage-sale connotations, and the hobbyist, often manic collectors who initially used these sites, tended to disguise their commercial potential. 'Real' business did not see that what e.bay, OnSale and other auction sites were doing was no less than what the telecoms companies had done for more than a century – broker the intercourse between many millions of users, and make a small charge on each transaction. The first sign that this was a business sector to take seriously was the initial public offering of e.bay in September 1998. This valued the company at a staggering $1.9 billion, a figure that was later dwarfed by its end-of-year $9.9 billion market value.

Interestingly, the (over?) valuation of e.bay left other online auction businesses standing. The original site OnSale finished 1998 worth a relatively paltry $779 million, while Ubid was valued at $1 billion. Yes, this was the start of the dot com IPO silly season.

That there will be other surprise commercial successes emerging from the web/net I have no doubt. e.bay, by combining the ideas of the flea market

One of the most successful of the auction sites that emerged in the mid-1990s, E-bay describes itself as 'the world's first, biggest and best person-to-person online trading community'. With an average of 1.7 million users, more than 7 million registered users and a 24/7 operation that handles over 375,000 new items daily, e-bay indicates the importance of P2P 'content'.

and the garage sale with the attraction of the auction, raised the profile of the online auction as a tool for consumer-to-consumer transactions. And as we enter the 21st century, this model is starting to be deployed for business-to-business transactions too and is already becoming a next big thing.

Other vectors that will be worth watching are the adoption of micro-payment schemes in online auctions (auctions become a cash marketplace); the introduction of alternative payment schemes, such as barter, LETS (Local Exchange Trading Systems) and Time Dollars; fragmented (specialist) auction sites; WAP auctions (auctions with mobile participants); and, of course, the increased use of video and multimedia (as bandwidth grows) to make the auction experience more 'real'.

REASONS TO BE ONLINE

For absolute beginners:

- web/net allows long-distance communications at local call rates;
- web/net allows free access to more than one billion pages of information, on all subjects;
- buy books, records, show tickets and other things at discount prices;
- get free newspapers, radio stations, magazines;
- information and news on sports, hobbies, movies, music, books, etc;
- publish your own website;
- free personal e-mail;
- send letters and pictures to relatives and friends around the world;
- get information from government agencies, charities, other organizations;
- get services such as weather, train times, maps, plane tickets, etc;
- browse and buy at the biggest flea market in the world;
- get free educational materials, research information, pictures and illustrations.

For IT experts:

- web/net technology provides cheap alternatives for business networking;
- use web/net tools and network to build secure, cheap virtual private networks;
- web/net provides free and low-cost IT solutions, software solutions and APIs;
- web/net uses international standards for communications;
- web/net allows easy publication of company databases;
- web/net provides free access to code libraries, user groups and IT SIGs.

For designers:

- web/net is a new publishing medium – electronic versions of newspapers, magazines, books, etc;

- new opportunities for designers in graphics, animation, video, audio, illustration, etc;
- new opportunities in interface (screen) design;
- learn how the web/net supports multimedia publishing;
- stay in touch with the latest news of design and designers around the world;
- access picture and image libraries for source and reference materials;
- get news on all the latest design tools, software and hardware;
- extend the market for your work around the world;
- publish your own web portfolio of work;
- work with other designers in different locations.

For activists:

- access alternative news sources from around the world;
- join newsgroups and debates on every subject;
- research facts and information on every subject;
- communicate with other activists in a totally secure environment;
- publicize events, activities, demonstrations, debates, meetings, etc;
- conduct opinion polls and online debates;
- canvas support and focus protest at global companies, governments and other multinational organizations.

For advertising managers and creatives:

- web/net will be the biggest advertising medium in the world;
- web/net is a country with a population of over 350 million consumers;
- web/net is growing at more than 100 per cent a year;
- web/net will combine television, radio, press, direct mail and point-of-sale advertising in one medium;
- find out about the new e-commerce value chain;
- web/net is a direct one-to-one marketing medium;
- web/net integrates corporate promotion, product information, catalogue publishing and direct selling in one medium;
- web/net is the future of advertising.

For business managers and executives:

- web/net communications mean huge saving in telecoms costs;
- access to a global marketplace;
- web/networking means secure, low-cost virtual private networks;
- networks for internal company administration;
- networks of dealers and suppliers;
- networks of ustomers and retailers;
- web/net is a country with a population of over 350 million consumers;

- web/net is growing at more than 100 per cent a year;
- web/net will be the biggest advertising medium in the world;
- web/net allows low-cost publishing of corporate information;
- savings in call-centre operations;
- low-cost, one-to-many publishing and advertising;
- savings in print costs;
- savings in postal costs.

For educationalists:

- net will be the biggest education machine in the world;
- web/net allows free access to more than 1 billion pages of information, on all subjects;
- access to a large pool of courseware, reference material, information, resources;
- create distance-learning courses, offering training and education online;
- learn from the collected experience of thousands of teachers worldwide;
- join specialist newsgroups and online conferences;
- access the latest papers and articles on education and subject specialisms;
- publish details of courses, seminars, lectures, etc.

For politicians:

- net is a powerful tool for democracy;
- net allows better communications with people, organizations and parties;
- net allows online polling and electronic voting;
- net provides access to latest news and information from official and unofficial sources;
- net allows secure private communications between individuals, government departments and local government;
- net provides access to government information and services.

B2B Business-to-business services have always looked promising. There are many convincing reasons why businesses should be online, and once you join the 120 million companies already internet-connected, it makes further sense to use the web/net to talk and trade with them. The B2B market is forecast to grow rapidly, and illustrates some of the more radical philosophical implications of the web/net: an understanding of the co-evolution of the networked business community, co-opetition, stakeholder thinking, the law of increasing returns, and much more besides. It's been called the future of *all* business.

In 1999, B2B was the next big thing (by the end of 1999 the B2B market was worth $145 billion). In 2000 it *was* the 'big thing', with highly credible

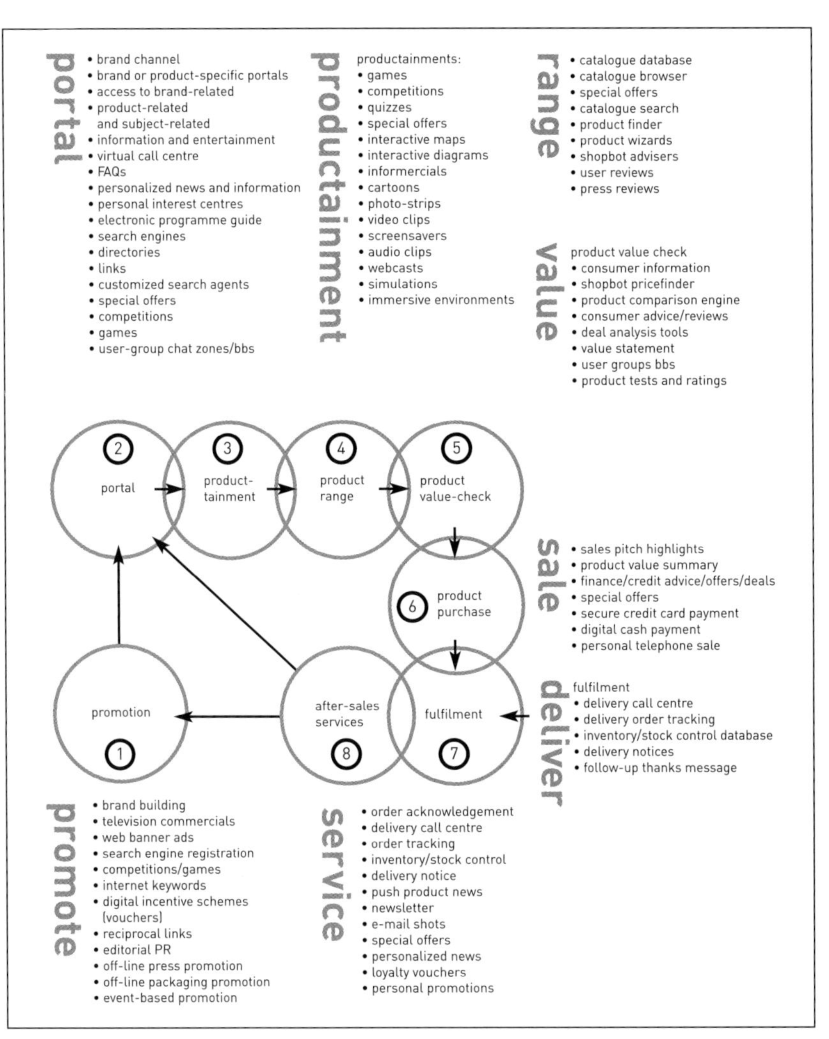

This is part of the value-chain visualized as a seamless e-commerce experience, where consumers are guided toward a particular range of products or brands, become immersed in the entertaining exploration of choice and identification of what they want, are able to summon critical reviews, consumer-organization help, financing advice, and absorb the views of other consumers, are able to compare prices and the whole value-offer, arrange financing if necessary, make the purchase (with human hand-holding if necessary), track delivery and benefit from 'joined-up' after sales service and ongoing relationship-building.

forecasters such as Gartner predicting that the B2B market would grow to a staggering $7.29 *trillion* by 2004. The less bullish Forrester Research predicted a $2.7 trillion market by 2004. The B2B market was hailed as the 'B2B Big Bang'. All this gung-ho enthusiasm from what suck.com calls 'Wall Street's chattering class' is of course typical of the hype and spin that surround the early stages of a next big thing, but with 120 million companies using the web/net in 2000, and online business traffic doubling every year, it looks like Andy Grove was not being too apocalyptic with his 1999 forecast:

'In five years all companies will be internet companies, or they won't be companies at all.'

Andy Grove, CEO, Intel

So exactly what does B2B mean? What can it do for businesses? There are several strands to this. B2B is impacting on almost every level of conventional business practice, from procurement to fulfilment, and at all stages in between, and vertically too, in flattening the pyramidical hierarchies on which so many businesses have traditionally been structured.

Unlike the first generation of B2B network products, such as virtual private networks and electronic document interchange (EDI), the web/net B2B solutions are easier and cheaper to implement, they use open standards such as XML, and span a range of corporate tools from simple company websites (electronic brochureware) to industry-wide electronic markets. B2B includes every level of corporate communications from online catalogues of products and services, virtual call centres, virtual media centres, and other company-specific online applications, through to intra- and extra-nets that extend the company's reach to include suppliers and customers, manufacturers, distributors and marketers, and specialists in PR, advertising, consultancy services and other relevant stakeholders. Extending outwards, both vertically and horizontally, B2B is exploring new, faster, more transparent, and more efficient ways of bridging the gap between buyers and sellers, between supply and demand, between manufacturers and wholesalers and retailers.

On a global level, marketplaces such as the Worldwide Retail Exchange, announced in March 2000 – a $100 million investment by 11 king-size retailers including K-Mart, Safeway, Tesco, Kingfisher and Marks & Spencer – is designed to facilitate and simplify trading between the 11 founders and the 30,000 stores they own, and more than 100,000 of their suppliers, partners and distributors.

The idea is to aggregate publicly available data with private price and promotion information and make this available to buyers and sellers in the exchange. The aim is to let users 'have visibility into the supply chain', allowing them access to manufacturing data, inventory, goods in transit, and even shelf stocks.

Typically, such exchanges handle and standardize requests for tenders and quotations (RFTs and RFQs); the electronic posting of bids and offers; real-time auctions and reverse auctions; and offer members transaction security, reputation verification, and real-time negotiation channels. By nurturing competition and transparency in the supply chain, such exchanges have produced savings of up to 15 per cent – even for buyers who thought they were already getting bedrock prices.

Similar exchanges are emerging for other industrial sectors, including energy, automobiles, paper, chemicals and oil, but there is still considerable resistance to such co-opetition in the more conservative industries. While the advantages of B2B are evangelized by key players and B2B service providers such as Ariba, Commerce One, Freemarkets, PurchasePro and VerticalNet, others worry about issues such as encouraging monopolistic practices, penalizing suppliers through commoditization and the loss of identity in price-comparison dealing, and the technological problems inherent in linking many different legacy IT systems into such exchanges.

The main development vectors in B2B include more specialist B2B exchanges, with more sophisticated buyer-seller matching tools (not just price but quality, reputation and other value-added signifiers); security (encryption, protection, surveillance, digital signatures, trust and verification services); virus-protection services; multi-party, low-cost, multimedia video conferencing (and mobile conferencing too); virtual conferences; recruitment auctions; and the like. But this entire area is a maze of development vectors. Look at the interstices and overlaps between every component part of the supply chain and value chain and you will discover that someone somewhere is dis-intermediating or re-mediating something or someone.

MP3

The lesson here is one that resonates through the history of the web/net: that in a self-organizing system, radical change is an emergent property, and often appears first at the grass-roots level. The web/net is bottom-up, not top-down. MP3 is widely heralded as the 'people's solution' to inflated CD prices, and to the perceived price fixing in the music distribution and publishing cartels. As an illustration of this process, look at the genesis of MP3 and the phenomenon of music sharing as personified by Napster.com.

MP3 was a standard that emerged from the second generation of digital video standards established by the Motion Picture Experts Group, called MPEG. The audio standard in MPEG2 was called MPEG2 level 3, or MP3 for short, and defined the file structure and compression ratio for sound files that offered near-CD quality from dramatically smaller data files – and this was the secret of MP3's success on the web/net. It rapidly became the format of choice for downloading music tracks – CD quality, at a fraction of the download time.

MPEG

The Motion Picture Experts Group was formed in 1988 as part of the joint technical committee of the International Standards Organisation and the International Electrotechnical Commission. They had a mandate to develop standards for the 'coded representation of moving pictures, associated audio, and their combination when used for storage and retrieval on digital storage media'. Before MPEG, several large companies had developed workable proprietary algorithms for highly compressed digital video, notably Philips with the Compact Disk Interactive (CD-i) system, and Intel with its DVI (Digital Video Interactive) process. These and other algorithms had been designed to solve the problem of squeezing movie-length video sequences onto the compact-disk format, and to retrieve, decompress and display this digital video at 'full screen size' and full motion video (FSFMV) rates (ie 25 frames/sec in the UK and 30 frames/sec in the US).

Originally MPEG planned three coding methods – MPEG1 to deliver FSFMV digital video at a rate of 1.5 Mbits/sec (ie suitable for CD-ROM); MPEG2 – up to 10 Mbits/sec (for digital television and broadband disk systems, such as DVD); and MPEG3 – 40 Mbits/sec, for broadband cable and fibre systems. MPEG3 was dropped in 1992 because MPEG2 developments made it redundant. This also avoided confusion with the emerging MP3 digital audio format, which was originally and confusingly described as MPEG2 level 3 audio encoding.

MPEG2 was constructed to deliver the optimum video image quality (it has subsequently become the broadcast quality standard for DTV). MPEG4 was proposed in mid-1991 to develop a standard for audio-visual coding at very low bit rates (that is, suitable for consumer internet applications), and to carry interactive functionality too. MPEG's aim was and still is to deliver all its standards in advance of market needs in order to encourage a smooth and uninterrupted take-up of new media, and to stay abreast of the rapid development of hardware technologies. To speed up the otherwise lengthy standardization process, MPEG evolved new administrative processes which proved very successful.

MPEG1-2 use various compression techniques to achieve their desired data rates for FMFMV, included Discrete Cosine Transform, Quantization and Huffman-encoding. MPEG1-2 store only complete data for 'key' frames in the movie, with successive frames described by the differences in the frame compared with the key frame.

MPEG4 is in development and is designed to create a standard for very low bit-rate files combining video, video conferencing, audio and multimedia (starting as low as 2 kbps and up to about 64 kbps). It is likely to feature embedded hyperlinks, as well as copyright management and protection. Many of the characteristics of Apple's Quicktime media format will be built into MPEG4.

Future MPEG developments include MPEG7 (the 'multimedia content description interface'), and the development of standardized methods of describing audio-visual content so that non-text searches can be performed on vast networked collections of stored video and broadcast data. Such a standard would dovetail perfectly with Tim Berbers-Lee's notion of the semantic web – a web of data that 'knows' more about its content data. MPEG7 would enable more precise image, video and other media searches, better EPGs and more effective personalized push and filtering applications.

The combination of high-quality sound and small file sizes meant that MP3 became the format of choice for wired music fans: tracks could be downloaded very quickly, stored on the hard disk and played through juke box-style software players, or alternatively copied through a serial or other cable to a portable, solid-state, hardware player for mobile listening.

MP3 came to public attention in the late 1990s when the music industry woke up to the fact that kids were downloading near-CD-quality tracks of their favourite bands free from various web/net sites. MP3 wasn't the first file format used for encoding music tracks, but it was a quantum leap in quality and download speed over previous formats such as MIDI and WAV. What's more, the software tools necessary to convert music tracks from CDs to MP3 were also available online. There were even free software MP3 players, 'virtual jukeboxes' in which to store your MP3 collections. The final salt in the wound for Tin Pan Alley was the emergence of the portable, hardware MP3 players signalled by the launch of Diamond Corp's Rio player in 1998. Many more hardware mobile MP3 players were available by 2000, with others in development (including a Memory Stick Walkman from Sony, others from Samsung, and Philips). By mid-2000, MP3 was

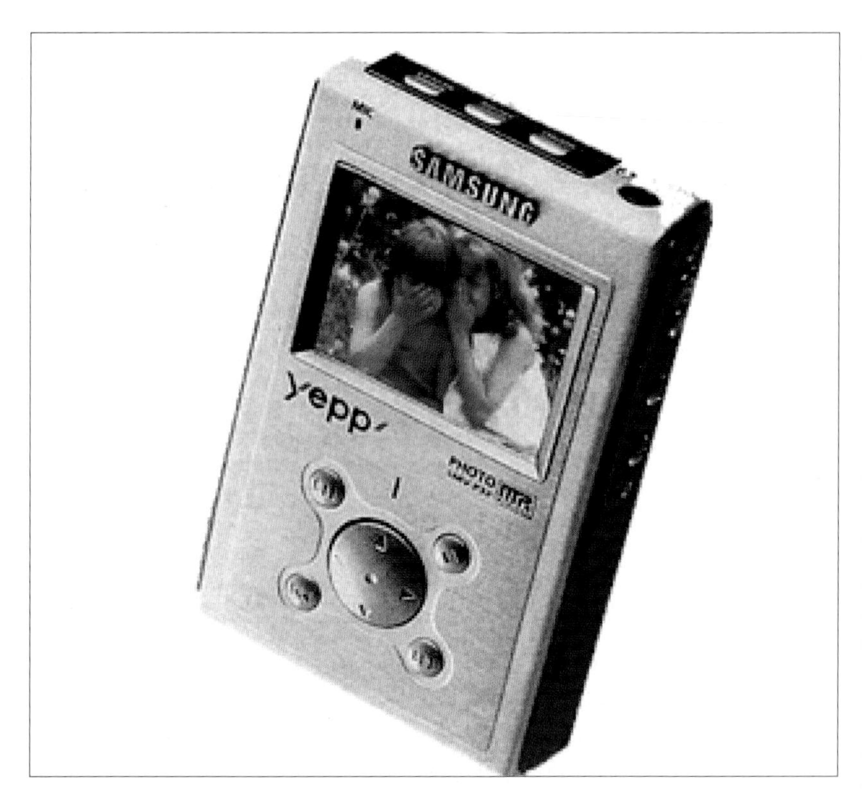

With a 16-bit full colour LCD screen, the Photo-Yepp is more than just an MP3 player – it could point to the future of multimedia music devices, displaying album graphics, band photos, video clips and other multimedia information as well as storing favourite MP3 tracks.

mainstream: there were 23 standalone MP3 portable players, 10 in-car players and 25 computer-peripheral players available. These players have a really big advantage over similar-sized tape or CD players. With no moving parts (they are solid-state), their batteries last many times longer than drive-based machines *and* you suffer no generation loss as MP3 data files copy perfectly from web/net to PC to MP3 player. By June 2000, Forrester Research estimated that there was an installed base of more than 10 million MP3 players, both hardware and software versions, and predicted continued rapid growth.

Real innovation in music distribution is emerging from the web/net, not just in MP3 itself but also in the means of distributing MP3 files, and that is threatening the very foundations of the music industry. Take Napster.com and its innovative music-sharing concept – a downloadable application that searches for the MP3 files you want on the hard disks of all participating Napster users. Effectively, you share your collection of MP3 tracks with all other Napster users through an interface that includes a search facility, a messaging service, and streaming audio player. Napster argues that it is not infringing copyright, but the music industry claims it is providing tools that allow others to do so. At the beginning of 2001, Napster was in litigation with the Recording Industry Association of America over this issue.

> “REAL INNOVATION IN MUSIC DISTRIBUTION IS EMERGING FROM THE WEB/NET, AND IS THREATENING THE VERY FOUNDATIONS OF THE MUSIC INDUSTRY”

The music industry is fighting back in other ways, first through its failed injunction to stop production of the Rio player, and in its support of a new file format for selling music through the web/net: the Secure Digital Music Initiative. Proposed by the RIAA, this allows the online sale of copyright-protected music. To many observers, this looked like a belated attempt to bolt the stable door, and they say this is typical of an industry that is inherently conservative about multimedia, for example, missing the opportunities of optimizing its investment in promotional videos, in letting MTV create a mass pop-video market, and even letting the small marketing company K-Tel introduce it to the radical idea (!) of TV advertising.

The wider implication of client-to-client* file sharing of course threatens all copyright holders and publishers. Already by mid-2000, products such as CuteMx and Wrapster extended the Napster idea by providing the means

*The web/net comprises many millions of client computers, connected through the net with several tens of thousands of servers. Normal data transactions take place between client and server. Client-to-client (or peer-to-peer) file sharing effectively means that anyone's personal (client) computer can become a server, and you can allow others to copy files from your hard disk to theirs.

for users to locate and download *any* files (e-books, software applications, images, videos and music) from the personal computers (clients) of participating users. Many argue that this kind of sharing and co-operation is not only a central characteristic of the web/net but is the reason it came into existence in the first place. Others maintain that they have a right to swap music, just as they are free to give or lend a book or record to a friend.

e-books

E-books, like MP3 players, are indicative of a new form of consumer electronics, the 'media access device'. E-books will eventually threaten the paper-publishing business just as MP3 is threatening the disk-publishing business. All the signs are that media will inevitably graduate from atoms to bits.

Just as MP3 has focused attention on music products as 'tracks' – individual songs or instrumental pieces – rather than albums or entire CDs, so e-books separate out the content of a book from the physical medium that carries this content – the printed paper, covers and binding. The content of books, the actual text, can be represented in digital form with very small data files. The idea of the e-book is that it is a solid-state 'reader', a machine into which the user can download or copy book contents from publishers or authors on the web/net. At about the size of a paperback, a single e-book could have the storage capacity for several, perhaps dozens, of 'books' – we could carry entire book collections around in our pocket, erasing books no longer needed and replacing them with new ones direct from the web/net.

Of course, people have been speculating about e-books for some years, and some have argued that such machines will never catch on, will never surpass the simplicity and ease of use of the traditional printed paper book. Printed books don't need a power source, they say, they are high-resolution, easy to use, cheap to produce, highly portable, and can be very beautiful too.

Now, I am a bibliophile myself, and own several hundred books, and I am fairly knowledgeable about the history and aesthetics of print, but I still believe in the potential of the e-book. Essentially, this is an NBT that is one to watch. I would argue that there will come a time within the next few years when all the conditions for a commercially successful e-book will be met. These conditions are:

- very high-resolution, paper-like, back-lit screen, preferably 24-bit (full-colour);
- large amount of downloadable texts available at the right price;
- cheap, high-capacity, solid-state storage media;
- software that allows easy indexing of book collections and retrieval of particular volumes, search engines for multi-volume searching; the control of text and font display size, speech-synthesis options, and enhancements such as hyperlinking, electronic bookmarks, margin notations, glossaries and dictionaries;
- a stylish, ergonomically designed hardware case, no larger than a standard paperback;
- a sub-$100 price tag.

Given these conditions, and taking into account the paper and materials savings, vast savings in the production process, virtually zero distribution costs, and therefore much higher margins – or much cheaper products! – the e-book will inevitably replace its printed ancestor. (Besides, just think how many books really don't need to be on paper. Not just the average novel, but most school textbooks, all books with a limited lifespan in terms of temporal relevance (including this one), that is, most computer books, most science books, in fact most books). And think of all those books that would benefit enormously from the digital format – all reference works, course-books, manuals, all those books where hyperlinked cross-references, or online updating, animations, sound and video enhancements could add value and increased functionality to the standard text. E-books will also have a further social benefit – digital talking books (a new standard proposed by NISO, the US National Information Standards Organization) will be a boon to handicapped people, and to toddlers learning to read.

The e-book will become a meta-book, storing our personal libraries, a boon for travellers who need several books. Of course, the e-book will also be able to download your favourite newspaper, or indeed your personal newspaper/magazine, every time you dock it for recharging and downloading. Electronic books will be much cheaper to purchase, with authors (hopefully) receiving a higher percentage of the 'cover' price, and with everyone benefiting (that is, apart from paper-makers, printers and book distributors, unless they are already planning for this 'atoms to bits' shift).

In his lecture at Imperial College in London a few years ago, Alan Kay (the inventor of the dynabook concept) referred to the dangers faced by major industrial sectors of ignoring technological developments, pointing to the fate of the US railways – content and profitable in the 1930s, 1940s and 1950s, but choosing to ignore those little silver areoplanes flying overhead. Both the music business and the publishing sector are ripe for the kind of disintermediations and new routes to market made possible in the networked economy.

e-book hardware developments Of course, there is already a market for e-books. As we have seen, much web/net access will be through handheld mobile devices, and these units, such as the Palm, the Psion, Casio and other handhelds, can download and display texts already. New generations of WAP and 3G phone/PDAs are also potential e-book readers. But this decade will see a variety of new technologies impact on this market, from new light-emitting polymers to electrophoretic inks, and these new technologies promise e-book hardware that will look and feel much like a 'real' paper book, with flexible 'pages', and very high-resolution displays. The market for e-books is vast, when the price/value conditions are met, and will have repercussions way outside of book publishing.

> “THIS DECADE WILL SEE A VARIETY OF NEW TECHNOLOGIES IMPACT ON THIS MARKET, FROM NEW LIGHT-EMITTING POLYMERS TO ELECTROPHORETIC INKS”

m-commerce Mobile commerce takes the web/net from the confines of the office or home PC and puts it out there in the street – it's the meeting of clicks and bricks, another model of e-commerce, one that is not based on mail-order fulfilment chains (the mobility of goods) but on the mobility of customers.

M-commerce is the mobile version of e-commerce: the provision of business and transaction services through wireless application protocol; and from 2000–2002, 3G broadband cellular radio networks. According to Durlacher Research's projections, the number one m-commerce application by the year 2003 will be, guess what? Advertising. In its (Q1 2000) report it called m-commerce 'an unrivalled one-to-one marketing capability'. Durlacher estimates that after 2001, no mobile phones will be manufactured that are not 'internet-enabled', and by 2003 no less than 200 million mobile owners (Strategic Analytics estimates 525 million) will be accessing those internet services, generating $23.6 billion in annual revenues in Europe alone.

Apart from advertising ($5.4 billion by 2003) and one-to-one marketing, it's likely that financial services will be the second largest m-commerce market, with mobile broking, m-banking, m-payments and related services. Following these, at £3.5 billion, Durlacher suggests that actual mobile shopping, via micro-browser e-commerce retailing, auctions, reservations, etc, will be the third largest revenue generator.

location-specific m-commerce Of course, these figures (like all early NBT projections) must be taken with a pinch of salt, based as they are on the piggy-backing of growth extrapolations from both mobile phone sales and from internet access take-up. Put the two together and, the industry forecasts, you've got the killer app. A movable feast of customers, all waiting to buy, sell, exchange and absorb advertising, while chatting and messaging and browsing the web/net. And we've only just started: the real interest in m-commerce comes from the potential of new technologies (such as GPS devices and location-position systems) to pinpoint mobile phones and PDAs geographically within a few metres. From October 2001, the US Federal Communications Commission (FCC) is stipulating that all mobile service providers will be required to identify the location of emergency (911) calls to within 125 metres. So there are several competing technologies around to do just that, and with even greater accuracy than the FCC demand. For example, SnapTrack's GPS-based system is good down to between 5 and 75 metres, while Cell-Loc Inc's Cellocate system has a claimed 15-metre accuracy. When these technologies mature, there is no doubt that mobile service providers worldwide will build them into their products, offering a wide range of location-specific services (and marketing channels!) to their customers.

Location-specific m-commerce will mean that a plotted cellular position can be cross-refererenced to a geographical map, and so to a geographical information system containing databases of local shops, restaurants, pubs, clubs, cinemas, car parks and other services. This information can then be made available to the m-user walking down a particular high street, along with (of course) the local special offers, events announcements, ticket availability, and other time/location-specific offerings.

Add to this mix the new Motorola/Trinitech virtual credit card and you've got a mobile e-commerce or m-commerce system. The virtual credit card (VCC) is a software configuration of any standard GSM handset, and offers a one-click solution to all payment forms at online merchants. With a voice-activated mobile, users will be able simply to say 'buy' or 'pay' and the secure transaction will be made. The VCC is much easier to implement on a mobile than the smartcard-based solutions on offer from Ericsson, Visa and Mondex, which require hardware upgrades to the handset. And of course, small payments can simply be added to the phone bill.

digital cash and smart cards This first decade of the 21st century looks like the decade when we finally make the switch from analogue to digital. And I'm not just talking television, books, magazines and newspapers here. I mean money too. Several R&D programmes and successful large-scale user trials in smart cards and other digital cash, cyber cash and micro-payment systems are culminating in the global introduction of this new form of money. Digital cash has been a next big thing for more than a decade, and smart cards even longer. The great vision here is of a seamless transaction medium that can be used as well in the high street as online. Such cards should allow both macro and micro credit and debit transactions, as well as easy top-ups and cash transfers, from DTV or set-top box swipe-card mechanisms, ATMs, POS terminals, PC or laptop, and vending machines. And the vision doesn't stop there. One of the great characteristics of digital cash is that it can be spent in all kinds of tiny increments, even from a tenth of a cent and up. Micro-payments like this promise to catalyze new business models for all kinds of online digital publishing ventures. When customers can easily buy a photo or a paragraph or two of text for just a few cents, perhaps even with permission to reproduce built in, so the argument goes, they will do so, and suddenly the web will become a gigantic global cash marketplace – an online street market that will encourage the development of new business models for publishing, information services, and other low-level transactions.

All the large credit-card companies are developing smart-card 'digital wallets' – plastic cards with embedded microprocessors and memory chips. The first of these is the Amex Blue Card, but cards from Mondex, Mastercard, Visa and other card services are also available. Smart cards offer several advantages over magstripes – they can store much more data, can 'read' as well as 'write', can input and store data as well as output it.

Many of the new smart cards utilize a global operating system standard called MULTOS (Multi-Application Operating System), originally developed by Mondex, and now an open standard administered by a consortium ingeniously called MAOSCOM. MULTOS can run several individually firewalled applications, and deploys industrial-strength encryption to the ITSEC LevelE6 standard. The kind of applications currently written for MULTOS include credit/debit, electronic wallets and purses, airline ticketing, bus or rail season tickets, medical records, loyalty programs and incentive points, national ID cards, driving licences, telephone cards, and security and access control functions.

MULTOS faces competition from Microsoft's Windows for Smart Cards, Visa's OpenCard, and Sun's Javacard. MULTOS is programmable in C, Mel and Java.

future developments in m-commerce Look for a lot of activity in this area, especially in the 'location, location, location' arena. The idea is that your mobile could be a really useful information tool, not for general browsing (you can do this better on the larger screens of laptops or desktops) but for information you need on the hoof, answers to questions like where shall we meet in Les Halles? Where's the nearest tube? Has my flight been delayed? Where can I get a burger? Where's the best pub locally? What time's the next train home? Where can I get a cab? What's on at the cinemas locally? What's the traffic like on the M40? How do I get to the Tate Modern? Where's the nearest petrol station? What's the score? Is there a jazz club near here? Where can I get a room for the night? Of course, services that provide this location-specific information will be able to offer commercials and special offers tied to location and/or projected routes as well, but it's the information you need most, preferably tied to a map of where you are, and a timeline of what's happening now, or soon, in your vicinity.

> WHAT IF EACH SHOP, DINER, HOTEL, BAR, CLUB AND PUB WERE TO ESTABLISH AND MAINTAIN THEIR OWN WEBSITE

So what if someone aggregated all the relevant information you would need to provide such a location-specific service? It would be a non-trivial task to say the least, linking yellow pages, retail information systems, hotels, pubs, clubs and bars, street names and other geographical information *plus* all the time-based, highly volatile information you would need to make such a service useful (and the problems of updating this from many hundreds of thousands of different sources). It doesn't really look feasible yet, does it?

But take a look from another perspective. What if each shop, diner, hotel, bar, club and pub – and everyone else who had something to offer the m-customer – were to establish and maintain their own website (working to some common template), then all that would be needed would be a geo-

Mondex Smart Card. Smart Cards like that introduced by Mondex promise to be the hardware 'interface' with our bank account in future. Acting as a 'digital wallet' smart cards like this will be unbiguitous and as acceptable in vending machines as in ATMs and by retailers both online and on the High Street. Smart cards proffer the opportunity of making 'micro-payments' in sums from one-tenth of a cent up to $10 – both online and off – this will create a 'cash web/net'. (image courtesy of Mondex)

graphical (position) grid reference, so that all m-services within 200 metres or so of the m-user would be polled in real time, and their WAP URLs posted to users' mobiles by SMS (short messaging service). Using Rich-Site Summary (RSS) formatting, the m-user would receive compacted information (location, opening times, the special offers and other notable volatile information, even current price lists) from stores in their location.

P2P communications and online communities Online communities have developed ever since the first internet connections were made in the late 1960s, and P2P (peer-to-peer, or people-to-people, or person-to-person – take your pick) communications, virtual worlds and online communities remain a staple next big thing as we enter the 21st century. Why? Because the web/net is a people-to-people medium *nonpareil*. From the earliest ARPANET connections to today's globe-encircling web/net, person-to-person communication via e-mail was the big bonus that emerged as a kind of by-product of a network designed to let computers 'talk' to each other. E-mail is by far the most popular web/net application – by 1999, there were no fewer than 569 million e-mail accounts worldwide, and researchers were predicting that there might be as many as 1 billion by 2002 (Messagingonline.com). And e-mail was just the first of an increasingly diverse range of communication tools, including messaging, chat, net voice telephony, voice chat, online communities, virtual worlds, and video chat, all of which exploit increasing bandwidth and processing power to provide ever more realistic person-to-person connections.

Because these tools encourage one-to-many and many-to-many (as well as one-to-one) communications, the web/net has fostered community building almost from the outset. Howard Rheingold has catalogued the history and development of online communities in his excellent book *The Virtual Community* (1994). From bulletin-board systems (BBS) and list-servers (e-mail lists) to subject-specific discussion groups (UseNet), MUDs and chat rooms, there are many who argue that the phenomenal success of the web/net is not due just to the amount of information that is available but to its ability to foster online communities.

List servers, chat rooms and UseNet groups share more or less the same principle: one person sends or posts a message to the server (computer) managing the list, chat room or discussion group, and that computer relays the message to the people on the e-mail list, in the chat room or in the discussion group. Each new message is added to the string of others to create a real-time discourse. A MUD or virtual world extends this idea by creating an entire environment within which the user can navigate, and providing the means to chat to other users who happen to be in the same place. In such 'worlds', the environment may be represented by 2D or 3D images, and the individual is able to signal his or her presence by means of a graphical representation (again in 2D or 3D) called an avatar.

But an online community can be much less structured than this. It may just be a collection of people who share the same server and generic URL, such as Geocities, a community that is comprised of lots of personal web pages organized into communities of interest. Other online communities may be geographically based, such as the WELL (Whole Earth 'Lectronic Link), which primarily (although not exclusively) links people living in the San Francisco Bay area, creating what Rheingold called a 'virtual village', where conferencing and e-mail provide a means of nurturing relationships that may be developed further in real-world, face-to-face contacts.

Typically though, online communities span the world, linking people of similar tastes and interests in affinity groups that transcend geographical location. Of course, the concentration of many hundreds or thousands of like-minded people in one 'space' has considerable commercial potential – marketers can target their advertising much more precisely and effectively. Geocities realized this from the start, and grew into a community of 2.4 million users by trading free web space and e-mail, free design and web-page construction kits in return for the right to place adverts on each member's site. Now a $1.2 billion business, Geocities has had to cope with complaints about intrusive advertising and the release of members' personal data to advertisers, but despite this, Geocities, and other online communities such as Lycos Angeltree and Tripod, continue to grow. Everyone knows there is no such thing as a free lunch, and to many people an arrangement where they swap personal information and advertising space for these various 'free' services and facilities is a good deal.

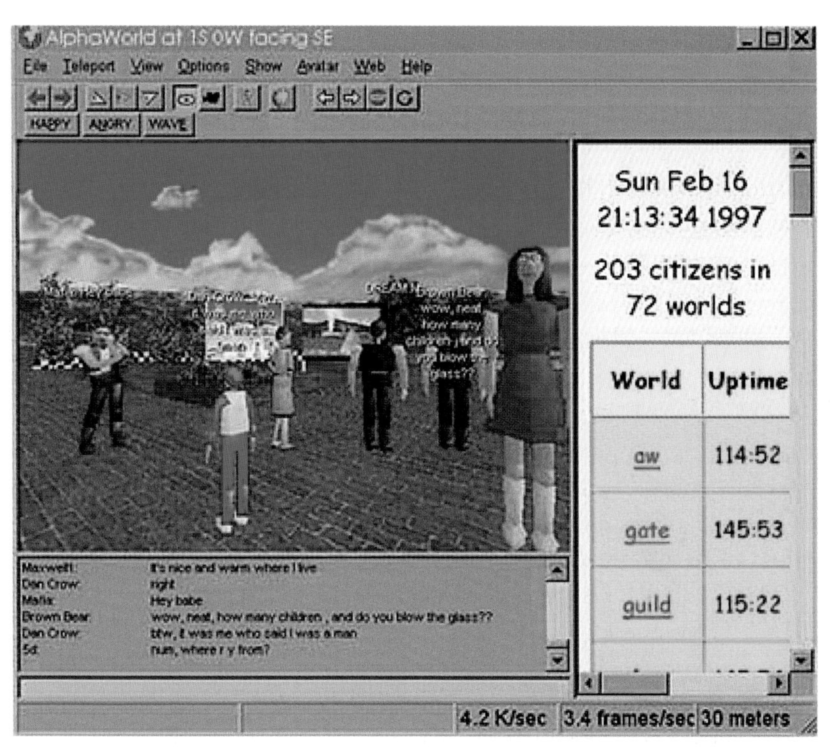

The ActiveWorld's browser (here looking into Alphaworld), begins to explore the nature of the interface between multiple users and the 3D world they are choosing to inhabit or to visit. Free text 'sound bytes' appear beside speakers as well as in the scrolling chat window. The technologies that will transform graphical chat worlds like this within the next few years, include: more realistic avatar creation and control, voice input and output (IP multi-party telephony), AI in 'native' (non-human) residents, Artificial Life (in the flora and fauna of the world), international standards governing laws of decency, security, privacy and rights in such virtual worlds, universal digital cash standards for virtual world and e-commerce interoperability, and facial expression (emotion)-capture and transcription to avatars.

Indeed this is a very strong development vector. Increasingly sophisticated community and communication tools will be offered in return for increasingly detailed personal information, and the licence to use this as a marketing tool. This is the basis of the ideas for 'really useful advertising' and the 'personal meta-shop' described in 'Portals' (above). To maintain the trust between community-service provider and individual members, such arrangements must be completely transparent and open and, of course, individuals anxious to maintain their privacy can join any of the host of other, less commercial communities.

Because the web/net fosters all kinds of mutual-aid and self-help communities, from family genealogies to farming co-operatives, single-parent support groups to consumer groups and fan clubs, many observers, including Rheingold, suggest that virtual communities may be the means by which we are able to regenerate the sense of community and social discourse absent in so many of our metropolitan lives. Others suggest that the web/net represents the triumph of the kind of syndicalism and mutual aid central to the anarchist philosophies of Godwin and Kropotkin (for an absorbing discussion of these issues, see *Anarchism and the Cybernetics of Self-Organising Systems,* by John D. McEwen at *www.tao.ca/~freedom/cyb.html*).

People-to-people communications through the web/net will continue to grow and develop as new access devices present new opportunities for those of us who don't have, or don't like, personal computers. For instance, in Japan in 2000 there were nearly 7 million people using cell-phone e-mail (DoCoMo I-mail), and new users are adopting this kind of non-computer e-mail at the rate of 25,000 a day!

Many people prefer to talk rather than type, however. By 1999, 2.5 billion VoIP (voice over IP) calls were made annually. An estimated 4 billion VoIP calls will be made in 2000. Voice over IP is considerably cheaper than using the standard telephone, indeed, they are sometimes free (well, 'advertising-supported' free). And, of course, the same kind of web/net voice technology is beginning to transform other previously text-based media, such as chat rooms and MUDs. Using *excite@home* voicechat (voicechat.excite.com) users can chat in public rooms with up to ten participants, or set up a private room with selected correspondents.

As the web/net becomes broadband, the potential for full multimedia participation in online communities will be realized, first in social or personal video conferencing, and later in the kind of scenario described below.

Personal video conferencing is dominated by CUSeeMe software, with cuseemeworld.com as the site to sign up to, download your software, buy your webcam (between $45 and $100), and for high-resolution colour images, pay $70 for the CUSeeMe Pro software (which also offers groupware, whiteboard-sharing and other collaborative applications). CUSeeMeworld video chat rooms handle up to 25 simultaneous visitors. You can chat via text or voice, and see the personal profile of anyone in the room.

Other video-chat software such as freewebphone or i-visit is available free on the web/net. In 1998 the pioneering i-visit team demonstrated i-visit work in progress to the designers and creatives at AMXstudios, and it was 'awesome'. You could summon a screen showing thumbnail still images of all those video-chat users currently online, click an image to zoom into it, open a two-way channel, or chat with several users simultaneously – all over a standard modem and ordinary phone-line connection.

a scenario for future multimedia online communities

So how might online communities develop as we enter the broadband millennium? Well, there's no doubt that audio and video will become the interface of choice for many people. Webcams are still dropping in price and increasing in resolution and ease of use. Software is freely available and will no doubt deploy MPEG4 standards, so that true, hyperlinked video and other multimedia documents can be exchanged in real time. Factor into this scenario the mobile videophone (Orange and other mobile specialists are developing handsets with built-in video cameras), and you have the potential of virtual worlds that hybridize with real-world locations to create flowing, real-time worlds that marry actual locations, live participation from desktop and mobile users, 3D virtual worlds, *and* real world, face-to-face meetings.

“FACTOR INTO THIS SCENARIO THE MOBILE VIDEOPHONE AND YOU HAVE THE POTENTIAL OF VIRTUAL WORLDS THAT HYBRIDIZE WITH REAL-WORLD LOCATIONS”

ubiquitous computing As processors develop with built-in sensors and switching devices, and as they become 'as cheap as sand', so called smart-dust chips will be embedded throughout our real environment, turning the world into an 'intelligent' and responsive place, and extending cyberspace to embrace and integrate the real world.

9 main trends in the digital decade

'THE FUTURE OF THE FUTURE IS IN THE PRESENT.'

John McHale

Why the digital decade? Because this is the decade when both Britain and the United States *go digital* – make the switch from analogue television broadcasting to digital television. It's also the decade in which we will see mobiles and the internet – the two fastest-growing technologies in history, far faster than electric light, railways, telephone or television – really take off. The web/net hasn't really got started yet. Its combination of digital computing, wireless communications, consumer electronics and digital content will come to characterize this decade, and these technologies and the information they will carry become ubiquitous and truly global. It is in this decade that most of the important decisions regarding the future of our media – some say of our planet – will come to be made. It's important for us all to understand the implications of the standards and protocols that are being proposed, as they will determine the shape of our media for several decades. And also, as these new media permeate every aspect of our lives and our environment, it's important for us to realize where these technologies are taking us, and for us all to participate in the debate as to where we would *like* them to take us – towards an omniscient and out-of-control artificial intelligence, or towards a world brain that is made up of all of humanity and all of humanity's collected knowledge networked together? Towards a Big Brother dominated by ECHELON and SKYNET, or towards an international co-operative effort to make the world a sustainable environment fit for us all?

In this section I collect, collate and review some of the prognostications made for media technology developments in these next ten years, review some of the possible scenarios, and summarize some of the main trends in technology development.

As we have seen, many of the development vectors in new media technology are guided by the visions of a few singular individuals. And developments this decade will continue to echo these great seminal ideas of man-computer symbioses, global networking, memory extension, augmenting the intellect, and the liberating power of really personal, mobile computing and communications. We will be gradually perfecting the technologies dreamed of by Vannevar Bush, Joseph Licklider, Ted Nelson, Tim Berners-Lee, Alan Kay and others.

We will see major developments in computing power, in bandwidth, in access devices, in memory and display, and in content and software. By 2010 we are each likely to own a dozen or so computers, and perhaps 100 (some say 1000!) or more additional processors embedded in the artefacts we own – in our house, in our cars and other transport, and in our clothes, in our bodies themselves, even in our food. We will integrate and interface with all these processors and sensors by means of personalized software running over a body-area wireless network. These devices will also be wireless web/net access devices. We may prefer to have several separate such devices, for example an e-book reader as well as a mobile internet access device as well as an MP3 player and a digital camera. But many of us will own devices that include all this functionality, and more, in one hybrid machine. By the end of the decade, automatic language translation for all but the most obscure minority languages will be taken for granted, and will be a standard feature of telephone and web/net communications. We will also all be used to creating, customizing and manipulating personal software avatars and agents, each of us having several or several dozens of these digital doppelgangers to do our bidding in the global network.

On what do we base these predictions? Only on our knowledge of the present, and the vectors of development that persistently shape our global network. We extrapolate from the now using three 'laws' of technological development: Moore's Law (governing the exponential increase in computing power), Metcalfe's Law (the exponential increase in the power and value of networks), and Gilder's Law (the exponential increase in bandwidth). From these, here are the trends to watch.

twelve trends for the digital decade

processing power will continue to increase exponentially

'Moore's Law is speeding up': in 1965, Intel co-founder Gordon Moore predicted transistor density on microprocessors would continue to double every two years (while the price would remain stable). This prediction has so far proven amazingly accurate, but now, according to *Scientific American's* 150th anniversary issue in September 1995, Moore's Law is accelerating: 'The rate of improvement in microprocessor technology has risen from 35 per cent a year only a decade ago to its current high of approximately 55 per cent a year, or almost 4 per cent each month. Processors are now three times faster than had been predicted in the early 1980s; it is as if our wish was granted, and we now have machines from the year 2000.'

Experts reckon Moore's Law is good for another 20 years or so. (Actually, Intel predicts that silicon scaling will reach its physical limit by the year 2017.)

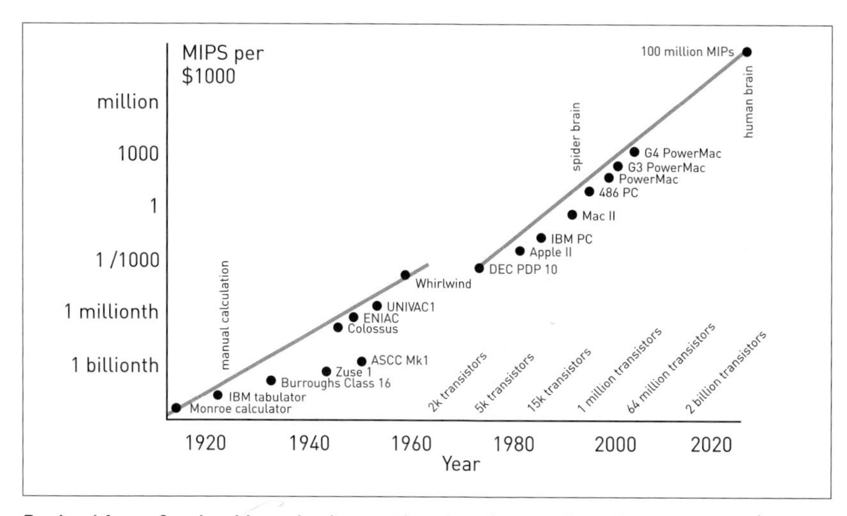

Derived from Gordon Moore's observation that the number of components (eg transistors) in an integrated circuit doubled every 18 months, while prices remain relatively stable, Moore's Law has become the 'industry standard' for extrapolating developments in microprocessors. And Moore's Law is speeding up – components double every year or so now. Moore's Law is the reason that computers always seem to cost roughly the same, although their capabilities increase immensely every year or so.

the web/net will be broadband and ubiquitous Bandwidth enough for good-quality web video and other streamed media will be available to anyone who wants it, albeit expensive at first. Most pundits forecast that bandwidth will become cheaper and cheaper through this decade. Gilder's Law states that bandwidth will double every 18 months while prices remain steady. In this decade four main technologies will service this drive to broadband: DSL through telephone wires, cable modems through cable TV networks, satellite through dish, PC or set-top box, and 3G wireless through cellular networks.

Broadband DSL (digital subscriber loop) through the telephone wire, and cable networks, will service most of the populations of the UK and the US, with satellite broadband providing coverage for rural communities and homes. Satellite internet access is just about to be reborn as AOL/Hughes and MSN/Gilat satellite services come online. These services will provide broadband access to AOL's 23 million subscribers and MSN's 4 million. In mobile communications, 3G standards will offer broadband from 2002.

any time, any place, anywhere During the early years of this decade, really small-scale local-area networking will be a major player in the digital home-office, home entertainment, and consumer electronics marketplace. Personal-area networks, desk-area networks, home networking, even 'body-area' networks, will emerge as highly functional extensions of wireless network technologies currently in development, and in some cases already in prototype. IBM's Almaden Research Centre has already demonstrated some of its really 'personal' computers. No, not those bland boxes and towers with flashing LEDs (light-emitting diodes) and ergonomic keyboards that haven't changed substantially in size or looks since the early 1980s. What IBM and other developers are producing is real *personal* computing devices – wearable devices doubling as digital jewellery. For example, they have described digital jewellery modules that could separate out the mouth-piece and earphone components of mobile phones and embody them as entirely hands-free, voice-activated ear-rings and brooches.

With built-in Bluetooth wireless networking, a built-in GPS positioning system receiver, and interface devices reading the user's biometrics, IBM says the possibilities are endless. Apple has shown that desktop and laptop personal computing can be stylish – brilliant product design breaking new markets for sophisticated processors with good-looking operating systems. This digital decade, the stage is set for even more of an accent on the *style* of really personal computing; the *substance* of these devices will be taken for granted. Bluetooth and other wireless small-area networks will offer a wide variety of telematic remote control of household implements and infrastructure, as well as the multimedia networking of web/net, DTV, digital radio and other information and entertainment channels throughout the home.

Supported by industry heavyweights such as Intel, Toshiba, IBM, 3Com, Motorola, Ericsson, Nokia, Lucent and Microsoft, Bluetooth will allow mobile devices and wearables to connect to and synchronize with stationary devices in the home and office. Interoperability with mobile devices such as phones means that intimate control over household equipment, lighting, heating, security and other monitoring equipment can be exercised on the move. Nokia, Ericsson and other cell-phone manufacturers are promising to turn the mobile phone into 'all-purpose terminals'. Toshiba and Sony plan to integrate Bluetooth into their consumer electronics devices, things like toasters, coffee machines, fridges, video recorders and microwaves. Look for WAP and GPRS 'remote cookery' recipes in 2002. 'We're putting the mobile phone at the centre of the consumer's universe,' says Jorgen Nordin, Product Management Director at Ericsson. 'It will store your calendar, open your garage door, and connect to your land-based telephone line.' Many experts see e-commerce as the main driver of Bluetooth, storing credit information on the mobile device, and sending it wirelessly to the Bluetooth-enabled cash register or customer checkout. (However there are unresolved security issues in Bluetooth.)

“NOKIA, ERICSSON AND OTHER CELL-PHONE MANUFACTURERS ARE PROMISING TO TURN THE MOBILE PHONE INTO 'ALL-PURPOSE TERMINALS'”

range of access devices Access devices – TV STB, DTV, PDA, handheld, mobile phone, e-book, MP3, games consoles, wearables, embedded devices, microservers, etc – will be the most visible signs of our transition to the networked economy. Devices from Apple, Nokia, Motorola, Ericsson, Philips, Sony, Sega and many, many others will impact on popular mobile culture just as the Walkman and Gameboy did in the 1980s, and the cell phone did in the 1990s. In the home, new HDVRs and smart STBs, as well as networked, broadband-ready games consoles and wall-size flatscreens and electronic pigments, will change the television into a new exciting medium (again).

The three main strands of development in e-media access devices are in the home (DTV, consoles, home-area networks, etc), in the office (PCs, pads, readers, PDAs, smart cards, etc, and on the street – mobile access devices like MP3 players, e-books, media pads, handhelds, 3G mobiles and the like. The Compaq I-paq pocket PC (top) is one of the new generation colour PDAs that offer extensive software and connectivity. Sony photoframe (bottom) offers instant viewing of memory-stick stored digital photographs. (Images courtesy of compaq at www.compaq.com and Sony at www.sony.com)

range of sensors and interface devices MEMs, webcams, security CCTV cams, personal mobile video phones, body-motion and expression capture, avatar building, voice-user-interface, personality-user-interface, automatic language translation and 3D worlds will affect how we interact with each other, with machines, and with our real-world environment. As early as 1994, the technical writer John Dvorak predicted: 'This is the future: TV cameras everywhere – all accessible over dial-up lines.' (Now read 'all accessible via wireless and unique IP address'.)

Little Sister: Cybernetic artist Andrea Zapp's CCTV/webcam drama or 'surveillance soap' winks at Orwell's (and Endomol's) Big Brother, and Bentham's Panopticon. Zapp is an artist dedicated to exploring the potential of new networked media technologies. Little Sister projects our eyes into the mundane and the bizarre – mixing images from webcams all around the world in a kind of 'object trouve' art-form that indicates the possible direction of surrogate travel and networked drama. Image courtesy of Andrea Zapp (www.azapp.de/littlesister/)

open-standards, open-source futures, free software Open-source software and open standards are well on the way to becoming the dominant player in the computing/internet world, and look set to eventually topple the mighty Microsoft. An open standard is a published standard that is owned by no one and can be used by anyone, and in which updates and evolution of the software happen by consensus. The web/net was built on open standards – the internet on IP and TCP, the web on HTML and HTTP. The European single open digital cellular standard, GSM, means that Europe is far in advance of the US in the take-up of mobile communications. Open standards provide an open, transparent way for companies to interact in a co-operative and competitive way, to co-operate to create markets quickly and then to compete for market share. According to open-source vendor Michael Tiemann of Cygnus Solutions: 'Open standards are not only better, but they are also getting better faster.'

There are two key characteristics of open-source software: it is designed to be studied and improved upon by other programmers, and all such improvements must be made public and submitted for inclusion into the developing open standard by its guardians. The advantages of open standards? They are inexpensive or free, they encourage 'vendor-neutral' standardization across the industry, they undergo continual testing and redevelopment, and therefore they are more robust.

Netscape publishes its browser source code; the common server (CGI) programming language Perl is open; Linux, 'technically the best OS in existence', is open, and it is the first OS to include Java capability – every increase in Java programming increases Linux functionality. Corel WordPerfect Office 2000 applications are available for Linux OS. Lotus announced Linux versions of its Domino and Notes products. Java is Sun's elegantly 'portable' proprietary programming language, is widely used by developers, and is open in the sense of developers sharing large resources (libraries) of code (Java 'beans' and 'applets'). Another example of widely used open-source software is the Apache web server. Originally developed as open-source, public-domain software in 1995, it became the most commonly used web server a year later. Apache now commands 61 per cent of the server market, delivering more than 5 million active sites.

24/7 access Both cable modems and DSL connections offer 24-hours-a-day, seven-days-a-week internet connection. You pay when you use it, but you are always connected. 'No delay' means that the web/net can flourish at last as an instant information and reference tool. I believe we will see the re-emergence of server push services as 24/7 access means there could be truly real-time, personalized news and information services, everything from general and technical news services, stock tickers, and sportscasts, to agent-based web trawling and just-in-time delivery of subscription media – the latest single from Blur, the latest Gloria video, etc. 24/7 broadband connectivity may also mean there's some more mileage in the idea of the network computer. With no wait states, network computers become a reality for the first time, and the advantage of only paying for software when you want to use it, and always getting the latest version to use, will be decisive for many people.

encryption In the era of ECHELON, the Bloomberg hackers, and other privacy threats, private encryption technology seems more and more like a good idea. About 15 years later than George Orwell predicted, ECHELON is the global interception system operated by the intelligence agencies of the US, UK, Canada, Australia and New Zealand. It is capable of intercepting and processing many types of transmissions around the globe. The crusading journalist Duncan Campbell estimates that ECHELON intercepts as many as 3 billion communications every day (phone calls, cellular calls, microwave packet radio, e-mail messages, web/net downloads, satellite transmissions, etc), gathering them indiscriminately, then filtering them for target meanings (keywords, key concepts and so forth) using AI techniques.

Some people reckon ECHELON filters 90 per cent of web/net traffic, though this seems improbable. Using speech-to-text translation, ECHELON applies 'semantic forest' techniques to retrieve information. This means that everyone's communication, via wire or wireless, is subject to random checks by ECHELON, and may then be classified and filed in some Big Brother-style relational database against your name and whatever subject ECHELON caught you mentioning in your correspondence. So one significant trend during this decade will be in the further development and 'productivization' of personal and corporate encryption software. If you're feeling ever so safe and secure using PGP* software now, I suggest you read Neal Stephenson's brilliant cryptographical novel *Cryptonomicon* and his cryptanalyst subject expert Bruce Schneier at *www.counterpane.com* for sceptical enlightenment. Note that the American Civil Liberties Union is arguing that 'the best way to protect privacy and safety in a digital environment is by encouraging the development of the strongest encryption products, for both domestic and international use'.

*Pretty good privacy – powerful enough encryption for everyday use.

peer-to-peer networks Napster pointed the way here, and we can expect to see all kinds of peer-to-peer activities in all kinds of media distribution and sharing networks. Some P2Ps will be ad hoc networks, others virtual private networks or intranets set up by mainstream publishers and media distributors. You will pay a premium for legitimacy, and if the publishers get it right, you will get the value-added rewards by way of digital enhancements (extra multimedia add-ons to the product you're buying or licensing) and digital packaging or merchandise.

the smart semantic web The web will get more 'intelligent', that is, it will 'know' more about itself, effectively becoming more like a relational database. When new web protocols are developed to classify and categorize the information contained in each HTML document (indeed *all* digital documents) and make them suitable for analysis by machine – make them machine-readable and processable – then the web/net will become a much more powerful resource for us all, and agents and search engines will be able to deliver much more of their promise. Together with the Berners-Lee W3C tentative proposal for the semantic web, agents and search engines, and other AI applications, such as real-time content filtering, collaborative filtering, user profiling, monitoring agents, recommendation engines, and knowledge-management systems, all of which are in various stages of development, the web/net will become a smarter, more 'self-aware' information space over the next few years. Companies and organizations to watch are Autonomy (*www.autonomy.com*), Firefly (*www.firefly.net*), Agentware (*www.agentware.com*) and InfoMagnet (*www.compassware.com/products/infomaglink.htm*).

the read/write web Berners-Lee conceived the web as a read/write medium. His first browser was a reader as well as a composer and editor of HTML, and you can expect to see many more easy-to-use read-write tools becoming available as the webDAV (distributed authoring and versioning) extensions to HTTP take off. The key to the kind of shared conceptual spaces and groupware envisaged by Licklider and Engelbart in the 1960s, webDAV applications will impact on work practice, socialware and hobbyware, opening up a wide range of dispersed group P2P activities.

the personality-user-interface This is my private speculation: I think personality-user-interfaces (PUI) will be really big. But I mean much more than the standard cellular phone definition of PUI, which is currently applied to the process of personalizing the menu on your mobile or PDA by choosing the options and functions you want. The area that I think is really important is the 'personality' – the personification of the user-interface in anthropomorphic form – in a computer generated talking head. The PUI would simply be a virtual character that you would talk to. It would use speech recognition to convert your commands into actions, making connections, launching applications, retrieving information, and use speech synthesis to provide feedback for you. I imagine PUIs along the lines of Digital Animation Group's Ananova virtual newsreader. Your PUI character could be customized to your exact requirements, or modelled on a real character of your choice (at a price!). Enhancements of the PUI might include the incorporation of custom expert systems – downloadable rule-based systems providing various functions such as subject-specialist mentors, companions, teachers, trainers, social secretaries, etc. Your PUI could be a 'perfect' digital companion, a 'friend' as well as an 'aide de camp'.

> “YOUR PUI CHARACTER COULD BE CUSTOMIZED TO YOUR EXACT REQUIREMENTS, OR MODELLED ON A REAL CHARACTER OF YOUR CHOICE”

How soon can we expect to see these trends emerging as products and services? In the following digital decade timeline, I've tried to indicate, through a collection of predictions and forecasts from a wide range of sources, when the experts think the future will happen.

the digital decade timeline This timeline is compiled from many sources, but importantly including BT Technology Timeline – Towards Life in 2020 at *www.bt.com/bttj/vol18no1/tomorrow.htm*; David Cary Futures at *www.rdrop.com/~cary/html/future_history.html*; OECD 21st-century technologies: a future of promise at *www.oecd.org/sge/au*; Sunday Times Chronicle of the Future at *www.chronicle-future.co.uk*; *The Age of Spiritual Machines* by Ray Kurzweil; and J.R. Mooneyham's gloriously titled *An Illustrated Speculative Timeline of Technology and Social Change for the Next One Thousand Years* at *www.kurellian.tripod.com/spint.html*.

But most of it is collected by me trawling through various site links. The intent? To provide a rough timetable of when to expect the kind of developments discussed in this book, and to provide a planning tool on which to base your strategic concept maps and timelines.

2000: the year zero in the digital decade

'In the next decade, some **1700 satellites** will be launched in space, creating the potential for more than 3 billion people to view CNN, make a phone call, tap into the information highway, or watch reruns of **Seinfeld** and the **X-Files**. Assimilation will be swift. Our modern communications system is the result of more than half a century of planting copper wires in the ground, over our heads, and in our walls. The 21st century's infrastructure of satellites, ground stations and wireless networks is being put in place in a fraction of that time.' **Source**: Regis McKenna, **Real Time**, Harvard Business School Press, 1997, courtesy Professor John M. McCann, 'Technology Cybertrends' at **www.duke.edu/~~mccann/q-tech.htm.**

bandwidth 2000

2.5G (halfway to 3G) – **GSM upgrades to GPRS** – up to 80 kbps on a mobile access device.

In June, CellNet UK offers GPRS.

US home users unable to get high-speed internet connectivity via DSL or cable modem will have the option of **two-way satellite broadband access** by the end of 2000, with services from MSN/Gilat and Hughes/AOL.

June: BT launches **OpenWorld,** the first national UK DSL service. Installation is £150, service is £39.99 per month.

Bandwidth: data capacity of fibre optics is doubling every six months.

May: Sony announces plans for its new wireless broadband '**bit-drive**' service, initially aimed at corporate users; bit-drive provides 1.5 Mbps networking for video conferencing, media distribution and other services. From July, bit-drive will operate in Tokyo, Yokahama, Nagoya, Kyoto and Fukuoka, going national in Japan in December.

RealNetworks and Ncube announce joint venture to provide VOD and other **multi-party streaming media-on-demand services** for broadband internet users.

processing 2000

The Apple G4 easily matches the performance of the £30 million 1985 Cray II Supercomputer – for $4000. In 15 years, the cost of processing has fallen almost four orders of magnitude.

Sony launches **Playstation 2** – a 128-bit high-speed CPU and media processor offering phenomenal computing power for around £300 – the trend here is that the cheapest computers will be the fastest, and the companies that make the fastest computers will also be consumer electronics companies.

Intel Pentium III operates at 800 MHz.

Mid-2000: **VM Lab's Nuon graphics chip** is chosen by Samsung, Toshiba, Motorola and others for their DVD-player hardware and set-top boxes. Nuon will provide games-resolution graphics and other real-time digital enhancements for DVD-stored and broadcast movies, music and games.

By November Sandia labs will install a **new Intel machine**, a $46 million computer 'capable of cracking the long-time fantasy speed of 1 teraflops. That's computer speak for a trillion calculations per second'. That machine may actually manage 1.8 teraflops (the US Accelerated Strategic Computing Initiative).

memory 2000

A 10 Gb hard disk costs approximately $100. In 1981 a 10 Mb hard disk cost $1000 (John Markoff, 'Trends: Smaller, Faster Cheaper', **MacWorld**).

Seagate CTO observes that for the past two years, storage has been doubling every nine months – that is **twice as fast** as Moore's Law predicts.

stats 2000

According to NUA (**www.nua.ie**) there are **332.73 million people online** in July.

ITU estimates basic cost per minute of circuit-switched (conventional) voice telephone call at $0.06. Voice-over IP (internet telephone call) costs $0.018.

access devices 2000

BT forecasts **washing machine** capable of issuing distress calls to engineers over internet, fridge-front internet access (including e-mail – Philips delivered), screen phones and wristwatch camera (Casio delivered).

Forrester Research predicts that by year-end, 34 million US households will use **interactive TV guides**, 5 million will interact with programmes and commercials, and 750,000 will use HDVRs like Tivo and ReplayTV.

Sony to launch Palm-like handheld device, autumn 2000.

March, Microsoft unveils plans for its **X-box games console** – three times more powerful than Playstation 2 with 3 Gb hard disk, and has set up a new sector within the Home and Retail division Microsoft Games.

Various infrastructural deals are made relevant to **digital cinema distribution** – secure networks, digital projection devices and servers.

Casio launches wristwatch MP3 player and a wristwatch digital camera: **wearable computing** is a reality already.

Sharp launches **MPEG-4**, internet-ready camcorder.

Sony launches '**digital photo-frame**' – a digital photo viewer, a memory-stick digital photo album/viewer for stills and videoclips.

99.7 per cent of US households have a TV set.

July, Sony plans release of **portable Playstation console**.

Japan's DoCoMo I-Mode service has 7 million subscribers out of DoCoMo's 31 million mobile subscribers.

Sony Playstation 2 launched in UK and US, autumn 2000

software and content 2000

Gartner predicts B2B market to be worth $403 billion.

BT forecasts the creation of a visual, **virtual computer personality** (a high-band Ananova?).

Forrester Research predicts that between 2000 and 2002, cable and satellite TV operators will create '**walled gardens**' – captive collections of commerce and ad-supported content – generating more than $3 billion in commerce by 2002.

KPMG predicts that **HDVRs,** like Tivo and ReplayTV will have a significant negative impact on television advertising revenues over the next five years, perhaps by as much as 10 per cent.

Strategic Analytics forecasts that, by year-end, 16.5 million homes around the world will have access to **TV-based interactive shopping**, e-mail and banking services.

Forrester predicts that next-generation TV devices (such as HDVRs, personalized STBs and other TV players) will drain $18 billion in ordinary TV advertising revenues over the next five years.

bandwidth 2001

During 2001, Sony will 'establish its revolutionary computer entertainment system **Playstation 2**, as an platform for internet-based distribution of digital content'. With an ethernet connection to a broadband network such as digital cable, Playstation 2 users will be able to download data-intensive computer entertainment content to hard disk drives (Sony Computer Entertainment, America, 1999).

US' Federal Communications Commission may give unlicensed clearance for **ultra wide-band wireless networks** – UWB has very low energy emission and opens opportunities for applications in radar tracking, precise positioning and short-range computer networking. UWB detects movement through walls, can be used as a collision detector in cars, and for high-speed internet access home-area wireless networks (**www.uwb.org**).

Spring, Japan's DoCoMo will launch **W-CDMA** (broadband) mobile service – up to 384 kbps.

One-third to one-half of US net users upgrade to access 35 times faster than typical 1997 performance (BT estimate).

Dish Networks launches Open TV.

processing 2001

Early 2001: **1 gigaHertz PC** chips the norm.

The $400 Sony Playstation 2 console will outperform a 1994 specialized military flight simulation computer costing $300,000.

The NSF plans its **Terascale Computing System** (supercomputer) to come online by February – initially performing at 426 billion operations per second, it is expected to reach 6 trillion operations per second (6 teraflops) by end-2001.

access devices 2001

Nintendo plans to launch 128-bit games console codenamed **Dolphin** in Japan.

Mooneyham estimates digital PC-TV sets break the sub-$1000 barrier and free network computers become available.

Mooneyham estimates that **$200 PCs** become widely available.

BT forecasts 3D LCD screens with XGA resolution.

Mid-2001, Hughes DirecTV and AOL launch AOLTV with Philips set-top box incorporating Tivo hard disk video recorder technology.

Microsoft X-box games console due autumn 2001.

BT forecasts wireless home-area networks (using **Bluetooth**, Jini or Piano).

DataQuest predicts that 100 million Bluetooth-enabled devices will be shipped. The first Bluetooth products should ship 'mid-2001' – these are likely to be PC-card devices for laptops and handhelds. Integration with mobile phones is likely by 2002.

BT forecasts **'emotional jewellery'** – jewellery that responds and reacts to biometric feedback (as demonstrated in prototypes at the Royal College of Art in 1998).

Orange may release its 1999-announced **mobile video phone**.

BT predicts a **'robotic kitten interface'** – presumably a follow-up to Sony's AIBO?

Microsoft will launch its dot.NET network computer service and TabletPC reader device late in 2001.

software and content 2001

Nokia Spatial Location Protocol (SloP) due June: catalyzes location-specific WAP and similar services.

Mooneyham predicts '**vicarious virtual immortality** options emerge online'. I think he means the increasing popularity of memorial sites where the deceased are celebrated with multimedia biographies and epitaphs.

BT forecasts '**portable voice translators**' – but I think this is too early by at least three years.

Steve Jobs predicts 'early 2001' release of **Mac OSX** – O.S. 10.

BT forecasts the 'first **Robo Olympics** in Japan'.

Personality-user-interfaces this year or next – embody a computer-generated head and shoulders 'personality construct' that uses discrete speech recognition and voice synthesis to handle most in-out (i/o) operations, especially designed for small handheld devices such as mobile phones and PDAs. Personalities use considerable user profiling and rule-based systems to deliver a 'smart' personal digital assistant service.

BT predicts the use of **fingerprint recognition access** for mobiles and handhelds – the beginning of biometric user-interfaces.

Cyveillance in its market research report 'Sizing the Net', predicts 4 billion web pages in web/net by early 2001.

BT forecasts that television will be available on mobile phones (this is surely more likely after 2002/3 using 3G?).

Multi-user video conferencing reaches consumer-level prices as bandwidth and PC processing power – and MPEG-4 compression – encourage widespread use of group 'video e-mail' and social video conferencing.

Lucent markets a range of IP Exchange products – integrated messaging including voice, data, fax, SMS, video and multimedia.

IBM launches its Walkman-style clip-on wearable computer, with monocular head-up display and voice-user interface.

bandwidth 2002

3G services due to be available, offering outdoor connection speeds of 384 kbps, car access at 144 kbps, and indoor or static access at 2 mbps.

i-Sky launches **Ka-band** 2-way satellite services.

According to Microsoft: '**Teledesic** is scheduled to go into operation with a network of 288 satellites in low-earth orbit providing high-speed data connections to anywhere in the world.'

BT forecasts **multi-channel 100 Gbits** on single fibre optic.

Broadband services are accessible to all households in US and UK – via DSL, cable, cellular, microwave or satellite networking.

'Imagine information travelling **a million times faster** than today's modems. The National Aeronautics and Space Administration (NASA) and five other US government agencies are doing more than imagining, working on a "new" internet that will operate at these speeds within five years. NASA's Ames Research Center here is leading the research and development efforts on the Next Generation Internet (NGI) initiative that could, by 2002, result in information flowing a million times faster than today's modern home computer modems and 1000 times faster than a current standard T1 business computer line, they say.'
Source: Bill Pietrucha, 'Internet – The Next Generation A Million Times Faster', Newsbytes News Network article, February 24 1997, courtesy Professor John M. McCann, 'Technology Cybertrends' at **www.duke.edu/~~mccann/q-tech.htm.**

processing 2002

Data networks will also deliver new clout to the desktop – clout some think can change the balance of power in industries. Under a contract from the National Science Foundation, MCI is building **Internet 2** – a next-generation, very-high-speed data network. Today it links five supercomputing centres in the US, enabling them to pool processing power for work on complex problems like drug design and weather forecasting. Within two years, 100 universities will be able to tap into the system. In four to five years, anyone will. Says MCI chief engineering officer Fred Briggs: 'Imagine you're at your desk. Your PC is the equivalent of a mainframe, you have unlimited bandwidth and can time-share into a virtual supercomputer network. What kind of capabilities will that bring to thousands of entrepreneurs around the world?'
Source: Andrew Kupfer, 'Transforming Telecom: The Big Switch', **Fortune**, October 13 1997, pp. 105–116, courtesy Professor John M. McCann.

Mid-2002: **2 GHz PC chips** become the norm.

Rich Templeton, senior Vice-President of Texas Instruments' Semiconductor Group, committed to providing us with a $1.50 400-MIPS DSP by 2002. It will run on 40 mA.

Low-cost and **'free' network computers** (aka set-top boxes) and appliances become widely available.

Gartner Group predicts that the **'era of contextual computing'** will begin, and 'will be characterized by a proliferation of devices in the home, office, car and on the person, with different functions and interfaces optimized for their physical and logical context'.

Low-cost **'desktop servers'** with broadband network capability become available.

By 2002 or 2003 a **100-teraflops supercomputer** is expected (the US Accelerated Strategic Computing Initiative.)

George Gilder predicted (in 1995): '**A billion-transistor chip** – equivalent to the processing power of 16 Cray YMP supercomputers, or 42 telephone companies' central office switches – that would cost some $300 million – is manufacturable on a single chip for less than $100. This technology is just six or seven years away.'

access devices 2002

Ericsson predicts that there will be more than **55 million handheld** and notebook-style information devices in the world.

BT predicts availability of 1.5m flat screens for £2000.

BT forecasts **personal display tablets** for TV, magazines, etc.

BT forecasts **electronic notebook** with contrast as good as paper.

MEMs devices (less than 1 cubic millimetre in size) are available on the industrial and business market. These provide sensors and effectors for all kinds of industrial, surveillance, news-gathering, agricultural and environmental monitoring and telematic control.

Low-cost networked sensors embedded in remotely operated vehicles – miniature helicopters and planes, for example – start to be used for news and information gathering (surveillance) in hazardous environments.

Nissan is due to launch **sideways-looking video cameras** for cars, with built-in image-processing collision-warning software.

software and content 2002

Deloitte and Forrester forecast $**1.2 trillion in e-business revenues** this year.

Probe Research estimates that IP (internet) phones will have captured 10 per cent of total long-distance traffic.

International Data Corp forecast e-commerce market to be worth £265 million by 2002.

Hackers crack ECHELON encryption using distributed network processing involving 2 million computers.

BT predicts unmanned and **remotely-piloted aircraft** (UAVs and RPVs) will expand the scope of news and information gathering for the media and others.

In US, FCC 911 mandate will require mobile service providers to identify the location of a 911 caller to within 125 metres. GPS can currently operate to within 5 metres – this opens path to location-specific e-commerce.

BT predicts **3D whole-body scanners** in use in clothing stores.

BT forecasts **automatic music composition** in any style, from R&B to rock, etc.

Michael S. Malone of Intel forecasts the beginning of an **'e-lance' work culture**, where independent practitioners co-operate on single projects with many different people in widely dispersed geographic locations. E-lance practices begin to transform business methods and recruitment.

Broadband groupware and shared workspaces, multi-user concept mapping and other 'groupware' become the standard mode of working.

Industrial – even military-strength – **encryption** is available to all.

processing 2003

1 Mb of hard disk storage costs $0.958.

1 Mb of DVD RAM costs $0.007.

BT forecasts supercomputer speeds exceeding 1 fetaflop – 1 floating-point operation every quadrillionth of a second (a thousandth of a trillionth of a second!).

Andersen Consulting predicts that **networked microprocessors** will begin to appear everywhere – in clothes, notebooks, medicine cabinets, and fridges.

bandwidth 2003

3G EDGE (Enhanced Data rates for Global Evolution) adds voice-over IP capability.

BT forecasts 10 terabits on single fibre. A terabit is a thousand gigabits or one trillion bits per second.

access devices 2003

Wireless access devices expected to overtake PCs as most popular web/net access devices.

One terabyte **(1 TB) disk drives** are normal in desktop PCs – large enough to store 400 movies at MPEG1 (VHS-quality).

BT forecasts domestic appliances with remote (networked) intelligence.

TechTrends forecasts that US shipments of integrated **set-top boxes and hard disk video recorders** will grow to more than eight times the number of stand-alone HDVRs.

BT forecasts holographic animated or video advertisements.

Sony intends to have a cell phone with memory stick and personal stereo functions 'providing easy access to music, film and other content via the internet, especially in 3G market from 2003 on'. Kuritake Ando (President, Sony Corp).

BT forecasts **roaming displays** (accepting input from many different mobile sources).

BT forecasts net access using touch-sensitive displays in kitchen appliances.

BT forecasts **cybersphere 'holodeck'**, using giant 'hamster ball' on air bearings.

BT forecasts **electronic paintings**.

Expect to see the first MEMs consumer products.

BT forecasts **chips on foods** to tell when food is at its best.

BT forecasts **hydraulic chair** for VR games.

BT forecasts devices registered in home that won't work if stolen.

Strategic Analytics forecasts 525 million WAP-enabled phones globally by 2003.

DataMonitor forecasts 63 million interactive TV consoles globally by 2003.

BT forecasts 600 million mobile access devices worldwide.

This year or next, video cameras will be compressed to microchip level and become cheap enough to install (wirelessly) everywhere we want a third (or fourth, fifth or nth) eye. '**A world of ubiquitous video** is not a world of people looking at each other via video conferencing. Rather it is a world of cameras aimed at everything everywhere, watched over by machines, and only occasionally examined by people.' Paul Saffo, Institute for the Future.

software and content 2003

BT forecasts chat **'video jewellery'** – presumably jewellery that responds to personal profile matching body-area network, low-power, wireless transmissions – matching profiles in the local area.

Forrester Research predicts that this year will see the dawn of the **digital TV era** proper – by now, the industry will have agreed on global standards for 'metadata', the information about programmes and commercials that are embedded as links in the video stream (see Chapter 7, Enhanced television content). According to Forrester, metadata standards will unlock the true potential of DTV – creating new TV viewing and usage patterns, and opening up DTV to embedded enhancements, e-commerce, personalization and other possibilities. Such patterns could create up to $7 billion in new subscriptions, $17 billion in marketing and advertising fees, and $23 billion in e-commerce streams, between 2003 and 2005.

BT forecasts software agent '**personal shoppers**'.

Durlacher predicts **m-commerce** revenues in Europe to grow to €23 billion by 2003.

BT predicts a TV chat-show hosted by a robot (Max Headroom Jnr?).

Prosumer-level whole body-surface scanners drive '**avatar boutique**' services: the creation of personalized, designer-styled corporate and institutional call-centre interfaces.

The confluence of extremely powerful 'desktop servers' at consumer-level prices, broadband networks, low-cost digital camcorders, still cameras, webcams, MP3 recorders, and easy-to-use desktop publishing and editing tools will create the conditions for the growth of **desktop webcasting** – home 'publishing' and 'narrowcasting' will become a major growth area.

bandwidth 2004

'Everyone agrees that by 2004 there will be around 26 million homes in the US who will not have a way to be connected (via broadband). Satellite two-way broadband services will fill this gap.'

'We'll have **infinite bandwidth** in a decade's time.'

Source: Bill Gates, Microsoft CEO, quoted in **PC Week**, October 11 1994.

processing 2004

DataQuest predicts that **1 billion Bluetooth-enabled devices** will be on the market.

'While today's ICs (integrated circuits) typically contain 5 million transistors with line widths between 0.35 and 0.5 um, the semiconductor industry predicts that by the year 2004, silicon foundries will be able to create ICs containing **more than 100 million transistors**, built with structures less than 0.15 um wide.' – 'DAC issues: co-design of hardware, software, and formal specification', **Source**: Article by Linda Geppert in 'The Institute', August 1996.

Gigabit RAM chips expected (Microsoft Research).

RAM costs approximately $0.005 per megabyte.

access devices 2004

BT forecasts displays with image quality comparable to paper.

BT forecasts **virtual retina displays** on spectacles.

software and content 2004

BT forecasts real-time language translation.

This is a likely year for the emergence of real-time **translating telephones**. DSP processing power for handhelds could make portable automatic translators a possibility this year, at least for the most popular language pairs (English/Japanese, English/Chinese, for example).

BT forecasts **children's toys** with 'network-based intelligence'.

Gartner Group forecasts that by 2004, more than $4 billion in revenues will be generated by **TV portals**. Gartner suggests that TV companies will attempt to replicate the successful internet models such as those of AOL, Yahoo! and MSN by means of TV-based portals. The heart of these will be the combined EPG profiling engine and web-search engine. The majority of revenues from such portals will be from VOD, PPV, EPG-sponsorship and advertising, e-commerce and internet access provision.

processing 2005

2005–2010: 'With the power that's coming down the pike, by the year 2005 (and certainly by 2010) **state-of-the-art virtual reality** will be like going into the holodeck on **Star Trek**. It will be everything but Smellivision – and if there's enough demand, you'll probably get that too.' **Source**: Clifford Meth, 'Invisible Computing', in **Electronic Design**, January 1996.

A 500-teraflops supercomputer may be possible by 2005 (US Accelerated Strategic Computing Initiative).

access devices 2005

Ericsson predicts that the number of handheld information devices shipped will exceed the shipments of personal computers.

BT forecasts **polymer screen advertising** billboards.

Strategic Analytics forecasts 179 million households worldwide will access a variety of enhanced and interactive online services by means of their television sets.

BT forecasts **video walls** – single screens 2 metres across.

Strategic Analytics forecasts for 2005 that:

- the average US online home will have 2.7 online devices;
- 91 per cent of US homes will be online;
- 90 per cent will be using an internet PC;
- 73 per cent will also use other access devices.

software and content 2005

BT forecasts machine use of common-sense inference.

BT forecasts **behaviour alarms** based on human mistake mechanisms.

Forrester Research predicts that 'smarter TV will add $25 billion to TV industry revenues by 2005'. Forrester predicts that while smarter personal TV devices like HDVRs will drain away $18 billion in advertising revenue, at the same time over these five years from 2000 they will create $25 billion in revenues.

BT forecasts **computers that write** most of their own software.

BT forecasts **intelligent robotic pets**.

Home **3D body-surface scanners** available at consumer-level prices: facial expression-capture WALDOs and whole-body motion-capture software.

Continuous speech recognition is widely used for human-computer interaction – with PCs, PDAs, mobile phones.

Forrester Research predicts that there will be 87 million US households using **electronic programme guides**, 65 million households with interactive TV access, and 53 million HDVR owners.

access devices 2006

US intended **analogue television cut-off date** (UK will probably shut down analogue TV broadcasting '2–3 years after 50 per cent market penetration' – but 2006–2010 have been mooted).

software and content 2006

BT predicts **'first artificial electronic life'.** (But what about Tamagotchi, and Norns?)

Forrester Research estimates that by 2006, voice traffic will be less than 1 per cent of worldwide total telecoms traffic.

bandwidth 2007

'Within 10 years, the **all-optical network** will be thousands of times more cost effective than electronic networks. Just as the electron rules in computers, **the photon will rule the waves** of communication.' **Source**: George Gilder, 'Fiber Keeps its Promise', **Forbes**, April 4 1997.

access devices 2007

BT forecasts domestic appliances with personality and **talking-head interface**.

Sky Report predicts 25 million US DBS (**direct broadcast by satellite**) households by 2007.

Gartner Group forecasts the beginning of the '**era of spontaneous computing**', 'providing anytime, anywhere access to information and messaging through highly portable or wearable systems'.

BT forecasts that all new cars will have GPS fitted as standard.

software and content 2007

BT forecasts systems to understand text and drawings (eg patent information).

BT forecasts that people have some **virtual friends**.

Avatar creation will become increasingly realistic – chat-bots and software agents may begin to approach Turing test pass levels in their specialized knowledge of their human owners.

access devices 2008

Market researcher Jakob Nielson predicts that the **last US paper newspaper** will be printed this year.

Electronic multimedia **readers and players** are now ubiquitous – mostly comprising flat pads with extensible paper-quality screens or 'electronic' ink pigment displays, several gigabytes of solid-state memory, supercomputer-power microprocessor, voice-user or personality-user-interface, and the ability to wirelessly connect, automatically locate and download video, television programming, movies, audio, digital radio, e-books, e-newspapers and magazines, according to the personal profiling data driving the software.

software and content 2008

Virtual reality webcasts of 3D stadia and sports sims from Olympic Games.

Expo 2008 is the **first global virtual expo**: a 3D real-time, net-based expo that accurately maps the real Expo – including 3D avatars of all body-scanned visitors.

BT predicts that 10 per cent of UK shopping is electronic.

Personality expert systems are widespread. Advantages? You can clone your personality to deal with all kinds of run-of-the-mill daily transactions: to fill in forms, to pay small bills, to locate and collate information, to programme media recorders and players, to provide written responses to mundane queries, to order routine groceries and repairs, etc.

Mooneyham: 'The internet permeates our lives and begins radically reshaping our institutions, even as breakthroughs in other fields promise fundamental changes in living standards and all future human endeavour; personal computing gets still more powerful even as costs drop; net users in the developed nations are becoming increasingly isolated in physical terms; the first crude "second skin" applications arrive; some forms of insanity prove to be literally contagious; the danger of biochemical weapons use peaks for most developed states; the wealthy enjoy "perfect" organ replacements; there are significant increases in the numbers of people taking to the sea to live and work; vigilante organizations rise in prominence and influence.'

processing 2009

$1000 computer can perform about 1 trillion calculations per second (Kurzweil).

Chips are really ubiquitous by now – **embedded processors** are found in almost every type of product – in fresh-fruit tags and labels, in 'paper' books (with wireless database access to search tools), in clothes (they talk to the washing machine and tumble dryer), even sub-cutaneous tags for hospital and healthcare tracking. These embedded chips use wireless network technologies like Bluetooth to communicate with each other. Some of the most obvious examples of embedded networking are biometric health sensors linked to paramedic and emergency healthcare networks, cars networked to avoid collisions, traffic clustering and traffic jams, booking inner-city parking, and calling public-cab transport on the move.

'Computers will come with video cameras, and the ability to **recognize their owner's face**' (Kurzweil).

software and content 2009

Most routine business transactions take place between a human and a **virtual personality** (Kurzweil).

The majority of text is created using **continuous speech recognition** (Kurzweil).

Translating telephones are in wide general use (Kurzweil).

'The graphical user-interface will be replaced by the language user-interface' (Kurzweil). When talking to their computers, he says, people will interact with an **'animated personality'** or a simulated person.

access devices 2009

BT forecasts **'electronic wallpaper'.** (I think this is rather late; in 2000, E-Ink in Massachusetts had already developed the monochrome pigment 'screens' for e-wallpaper, and was working on the full-colour version.

processing 2010

'10 to 20 per cent of all power today is used by computers. By 2010, it could reach 60 per cent.' – 'Disasters in the Making', article by Ray Alderman in **OEM** magazine, October 1996.

BT forecasts AI models used extensively in business management.

Artificial nervous system for autonomous robots.

CEO Andy Grove predicts Intel will deliver 100,000 MIPs, 10 GHz chips next year (2011). Moore's Law predicts **128 GHz by 2011**.

Kurzweil predicts that the average home will have **more than 100 computers**, as well as its own server.

Processing next year? 'Software mogul Bill Gates says computers like Hal in the movie **2001: A Space Odyssey** – able to talk, see and listen – could be developed by 2011. Faster, more powerful microchips, combined with breakthroughs in software, will allow personal computers to recognize and converse with people, Gates said at the annual meeting in Seattle of the American Association for the Advancement of Science. 'When people look back on the computers of today, they'll say: what did they do?' says Gates. 'They couldn't see, they couldn't listen, they couldn't speak.'

Source: Bill Gates: 'Hearing Hal, talking computers', United Press International release, February 17 1997, courtesy Professor John M. McCann.

access devices 2010

Bob Metcalfe predicts in 2000 that by 2010 PCs 'will be the exception rather than the rule (as network access devices), with Wintel machines only a bit more important than punched cards today'.

Paul Saffo (Institute for the Future) predicts that MEMs and other inexpensive analogue and digital sensors will collect all kinds of data, and diffuse it around pervasive wireless networks, changing personal, professional, social and industrial practices in all kinds of ways, paving the way for mass-customization of goods and '**consumer connectivity** like you never imagined'.

software and content 2010

BT forecasts that the '**highest paid star is synthetic**'.

BT forecasts a '**smart Barbie** with personality chip and full sensory input'.

Kurzweil predicts that at least half of all business will take place online.

Esther Dyson predicts that issues of quality of service, security and authentication (digital and biometric signatures) on the web/net will all be resolved by 2010 and 'the internet will be the basis of everything'. She also predicts that constant wireless connectivity will be the norm.

I predict that many kinds of expert systems will be available – everything from **digital mentors** for almost any subject, to **entertainment gurus** – experts in music, art, jazz, movies, books, antiques ... these will be software plug-ins that users can add to their own 'personality user interfaces' (Kurzweil's 'Language User Interface'). We will hire the knowledge-mined wisdom of real people and real collections of people on a pay-as-you-work basis, accessing continuous upgrades and latest data from the web/net. **Everyone's knowledge will be everyone's knowledge.**

sample scenarios for 21st-century media development

Scenario planning is one of the means that forecasters use to help make sense of the myriad decisions facing us in this fast-moving, real-time economy. According to one of its pioneers, Pierre Wack of Royal Dutch Shell: 'Scenario planning is a discipline for rediscovering the original entrepreneurial power of creative foresight in contexts of accelerated change, greater complexity, and genuine uncertainty.'

According to Lawrence Wilkenson of Global Business Network, a consultancy specializing in the holistic approach to strategic planning (*www.gbn.org*):

'Anything that can help make a decision in the midst of uncertainty will be valuable. One such tool is scenario planning. A growing number of corporate executives are using scenario planning to make big, hard decisions more effectively. And it's not just for bigwigs: scenario planning can help us at a personal level as well.

'Scenario planning derives from the observation that, given the impossibility of knowing precisely how the future will play out, a good decision or strategy to adopt is one that plays out well across several possible futures. To find that "robust" strategy, scenarios are created in plural, such that each scenario diverges markedly from the others. These sets of scenarios are, essentially, specially constructed stories about the future, each one modelling a distinct, plausible world in which we might someday have to live and work.

'Yet the purpose of scenario planning is not to pinpoint future events but to highlight large-scale forces that push the future in different directions. It's about making these forces visible, so that if they do happen, the planner will at least recognize them. It's about helping make better decisions today.'

> “A GROWING NUMBER OF CORPORATE EXECUTIVES ARE USING SCENARIO PLANNING TO MAKE BIG, HARD DECISIONS”

Scenarios are stories we tell ourselves about the future in order to help us understand the nature and impact of the forces that are driving our society. With the right spread of possible scenarios – from the worst that is likely to happen, through to the best, from distopia to utopia, you might say – we can devise a range of strategies that will cope with all eventualities, and by focusing on the commonalities in these diverse strategies, we can plan the most economical 'best-bet' route for whatever it is we want to accomplish. The act of developing and working through the scenarios is as vital as the finished scenarios, and it's important to understand that scenarios aren't 'forecasts' – they are strategic planning tools.

Here's a summary of just one scenario from a set of four created by the Global Business Network:

'The world fragments into a working pandemonium of individuals, organized by jobs rather than geography. Communication is pervasive and focuses on personal empowerment. The net becomes the chief exchange medium for decentralized work, personal gratification and global commerce. Physical infrastructure in North America stagnates, while personal spaces thrive. Art and attention are turned inward, as personal expression flourishes in new media and old public spaces crumble. Technology is the global culture. The have-nots become the have-lates. Ethnic or group differences give way to a homogenized patchwork of unbridled individual variety. Europe is wracked with civil strife as its socialistic civilization unravels. Russia rebounds. Japan lags. China and the developing countries become huge flea markets where just about anything goes.'

Scenario 1: the media industry in 2010 – the Creative Review scenario (May 2000) This was prepared in response to a request from *Creative Review,* a monthly magazine aimed at creatives in art and design and advertising, to write about the kind of new media environment that would exist by 2010. What would the creative studio look like? What kind of jobs would the 2010 creative director be working on?

By 2005 the wave of corporate collisions that characterized the start of the new millennium – the AOL-Time Warner-EMIs, the Viacom-Nintendos, the Vodafone-Mannesmanns, the age of megacorps – was coming to an end. By mid-decade, most of these broadcast media dinosaurs were in the throws of demerger or dissolution – for several reasons:

1 They realized that their legacy talent rosters weren't being refreshed or updated by new talent from within the corporation. The industry had polarized: on the one hand giant global conglomerates with a stifling hand on mass promotion and marketing; on the other, independent creative bou-

tiques inventing, nurturing and packaging new entertainment talent and content, creating entertainment brands, labels, products, personalities.

Worse still for the global corporates …

2 … their media philosophy was still entrenched in the one-to-many broadcasting paradigm. The digital switch from broadcast to networked narrowcast and many-to-many interaction was a paradigm-shift too far. With their size and their inertial lurching, unresponsive momentum mitigating against change, the global media giants just never really got the new net philosophies of bottom-up participation, co-opetition and co-evolution. They were still fighting for 20th-century market share in a shareware 21st century.

3 More fundamentally, the global-local dichotomy (always a difficult area for multinationals) had become a defining issue for world youth. Just as the WTO needed Seattle 99 to remind it that it was dealing with real people and actual communities, so the 'soft' protests that reverberated like Mexican waves through the media-net during 2004 – crashing servers, hacking corporate intranets, virus-bombing e-commerce media stores, mass spamming call centres – this breaking of electronic windows forcefully reminded the global media giants that the global teenager didn't want a US-centric diet of heavily pre-processed media. Identifying brand with bland, kids were busy not only generating their own garage cyberpunk art and entertainment but creating the social networks – the street-hip, floating, swarming, out-of-control, libertarian flux of virtual social life in which fashions and tastes were ephemeral 15-minute meme events – like neurons firing and networking out into the brain.

4 As a result of this increasing alienation of their primary market, and taking into account the increasing media-savvy of kids who were maturing entirely in the digital domain, by the end of the first decade entirely new patterns of media production and consumption had emerged. The kids had begun to reclaim their media: forget TV and one-way, top-down media, the kids wanted interactive to *mean* interactive – equal media rights! – you make, you publish, you buy. Symmetrical Bandwidth, Open Systems and Universal Access became the clarion calls of the digital generation.

5 Local political pressure, expressed as anti-trust legislation, forced mega-corps into demerger and fragmentation. Audiences too – especially the young – wanted media that specifically addressed their own cultures – in form, in content, in style, in their own vernacular …

screen-age digerati Alongside these issues, two other major factors began to emerge in the early noughties: first a range of new mediators – brand guardians, new product development agencies, new media boutiques, digital-art studios, advertising hot-shops, rights and marketing agents; and secondly, and importantly, a first wave of media-creation talent nurtured and matured in the net began to deliver the 'street-smart' media that captured the zeitgeist perfectly, just as 20 years earlier cyberpunk had for the pre-web digerati. By 2003, the first generation of truly net-centric designers and artists began to impact on the medium. Kids who had matured in the 128-bit webbed multimedia world, who thought broadband thoughts in networked cyberspaces, and were both entrepreneurially proactive and socially highly interactive, and who were globally cultured and highly mobile, began to create the entertainment that came to characterize the decade: global social-ware or 'globalware'. Provided for, and created by, a majority world audience of global 'screenagers', these broadband, televisual, social networks linked media, people and information in high-resolution simulations and wireless city-street networks that were concoctions of audio-visual-haptic immersive experiences and real street life. Produced by artists who married skills in *mise en scène* and MPEG2, Flash and funk, catwalk and computer-animation, movies, MIDI and montage, real-time 3D and DTV, grunge and graphics – all those new and old media skills that crunched together as soon as the magic ingredients were assembled: broadband networks; 24/7 connectivity; set-top and handheld supercomputing power; highband mobile cell-nets; a mass market of 2.5 billion screenagers, and universal access to the digitally aggregated cultural products of their ancestors.

the jobs So the current projects in Studio 2010 reflect the dynamic growth vectors within the media business – but for the media creative, they essentially come down to deploying the same timeless creative and communication skills, albeit in very different ways: global promotions and brand-building programmes for the multinationals, and similar streetwise exercises for the newly emergent independent cultural producers. For example:

- Designing and managing the information architecture of *3D multi-user worlds*.
- The conceptual flowcharting of *interactive soaps* and *fly-on-the-wall webcasts* or *surveillance soaps*.
- The creation of an *AD-venture ride* for Apple-Wintel in the latest virtual theme park: Expo2010 in Beijing.
- Designing *in-situ virtual adverts* – commercials embedded in virtual environments, and responsive to the personal profile of any avatar that wanders by.
- Art directing and profiling personas for AI-driven *celebrity avatars* – descendants of Ananova – the synthetic anchormen and women, and virtual vee-jays and MCs that are the presentational interface between fragmented audiences and equally fragmented content sources – the friendly face of the EPG, an essential item in a 5000-channel, 10 million-website world). The central persona can be subtly modified in real time as a response to the user's profile and tastes, and as a result, the virtual veejay morphs between users, presenting an ideal infotainment companion for each user.

“THE VIRTUAL VEEJAY MORPHS BETWEEN USERS, PRESENTING AN IDEAL INFOTAINMENT COMPANION.”

- Designing *wearable interface idents* – personal and corporate idents that play in varying degrees of subtlety over your T-shirt and other vestments. Look-ahead job-seekers are wearing their multimedia portfolio, presented as detailed full-motion stitch-maps, complete with career-summary interstitials. If you've got it, flaunt it.
- Wearables are fun, because the fabrics can respond to your biometrics – and to the biometrics of nearby strangers. *Profile-matching software* reads the wireless output of that girl across the bar, checks for a match – and bingo! – you both glow or ripple in matching colour-waves. In 2010, you can wear your heart on your sleeve.
- Branding a *surrogate travel agency* that has the largest network of webcams, satellite cameras, CCTV and security cams in the world.

Users can travel around the world in 80 clicks, hopping from cam to cam – from wing-mounted jet-cams to bonnet-mounted car-cams to panoramic view-cams and café-cams in every major city on earth. You can hitch a ride with a local guide, take the grand tour 2010-style, or check out the street life with a wannabe celeb or local-style guru.

- Creating sponsors' idents for *high-band cellular broadcasts* and multimedia music-messaging, chat, and deejay services, to the 95 per cent of global teenagers who have mobiles, digital radios, wireless games consoles, old MP3 players or multi-media pagers. (These guys are offering real-time clubbing, chat-line and dating services based on cellular location, SMS, GPS position, personal profile and avatar-handshakes. Radio Luxembourg was never like this.
- A launch for Sony-Nikon's pioneering *holographic TV* – yes, like video phones, it's back-to-the-future time again.
- Branding an *artificial-life desktop rain forest kit*. Designed to inform kids about the intricate ecologies of the biosphere – those really complicated real-world networks – the ALs include digital DNA for some 100,000 distinct species – there's a promotional global competition with a $1 million prize for the most diverse, sustainable forest. You have to sell it to parents scared of their tender offspring becoming a digital Dr Moreau.

the studio technology The top-of-the-range creative studios of 2010 vary in style and content from minimalist conceptual spaces where the only hardware is software – you and your media access tools sewn into your clothes – to the responsive immersive environments described below. Here are some pointers as to what to expect – most of them on the drawing board, in prototype, or production already:

- *Computer(s) everywhere.* The drivers of all the digital technologies described in this spread (all of which are in development – or already available – in 2000), are of course microprocessors – computers. In 2010, they won't just be on the desk or in the mobile, they will be everywhere. Some will be sewn into your clothes or built into your rose-tinted glasses (see 'wearables'), some implanted in our bodies and on our fingernails (let your fingers do the walking – see 'body-area networks'), some in the walls ('immersive screens'), in furniture (see 'active desktop'), and some even in the palm-tops, laptops, desktops and mobiles we've been used to for the past 30 years. By 2010, we will have gone through a cycle of at least ten generations of Moore's Law (yes, it's speeding up!), so for around £1000 we can buy personal computers that will perform 1 trillion calculations per second. This is not Year Zero supercomputer performance – it's ten times more powerful.

- *Bandwidth.* By now, all the constraints imposed by bandwidth scarcity on high-resolution, real-time media have gone. Broadband is ubiquitous, and as a result is really cheap. Competition between suppliers has driven down prices while at the same time providing broadband access everywhere on the planet. Mostly, broadband is wireless – progressive refinements to the 3G GPRS telecoms standards introduced in 2000–2002 have resulted in cellular-radio broadband networks worldwide, supported and (up- and down-) linked by global satellite systems such as Microsoft's Teledesic, InMarSat's 'businessband', Hughes WorldCast, Motorola's Iridium2, and many others. These global-area networks mesh seamlessly with smaller networks right down to body-area network level, which is also wireless, using extensions of Bluetooth, AirPort and other technologies. Other broadband comes wired – not only xDSL-adapted copper wires but switched-circuit cable, optical fibre, and the ubiquitous home, office and factory Powerline (datastreaming through the electromagnetic fields surrounding all electricity transmission cables) – 'you want bandwidth, just plug and play'.

  (R&D and product announcements from Symbian, Avio, Apple, Epigram, Sony, Motorola, Intel, Microsoft, Sun, Energis, etc.)

- *Immersive screens.* Studio/office walls coated with electrophoretic paint (digital 'ink') become an immersive virtual environment, reprogrammable to any function or view – ie virtual conferencing, chilling out in Antarctica, brain-storming on the neural net … sharing quality time with the family, or absorbing café society atmosphere in Tribeca, Montparnasse, or wherever you fancy from the webcam network (linking CCTV, webcam, satellite, tourist and surveillance cameras worldwide).

- *Electrophoretic paint*. Contains millions of microcapsules of electro-sensitive pigments. Passing electric current through these 'pigment pixels' causes a change in colour – initially these were just black or white (the electric charge flipped a micro-sphere the size of a toner particle, that was black on one side, white on the other). The processor to drive these pigment images is also printed on to the paper – the diodes, transistors, insulators, all the bits you need to make a processor, can be printed on to the substrate, along with the electrophoretic pigment. This technology will revolutionize surface printing: billboards, screen technology, books, magazines, clothes, cars, anything with a printed surface interface. Anything can become a screen – every artefact an interface. Since 2005, we've been able to print entire consumer-electronics components on substrates too – so the electrophoretic surface displays TV, digital radio text and images, and VOD as well as stills and video phone input. Alongside the processor we print its power supply – a solar cell – too. And remember, this is 1000dpi resolution! What colour car do you want today?

  (Electrophoretic ink at MIT and E.Ink Corp.)

- *3DTV*. Based on the principles described by Neil Gershenfeld of MIT in 1999: a computer calculates the light that would be reflected from a 3D object (say, in the middle of our studio), then modulates a laser beam to produce exactly that pattern for us. It does this 60 times a second, using the ubiquitous broadband net to pump the motion-3D data. The major downside? 3DTV is not as good as reality – never will be – as Gershenfeld points out: 'The problem is that reality is just too good. The eye has the equivalent of many thousands of lines of resolution, and a refresh rate of milliseconds.' Add to this the fact that data from the eye is being processed through a 500-billion-node neuronal network (our brain), and cross referenced to millions of 'stored' images (our memory) – and you realize it's not all going to be roses selling 3DTV. Initial consumer disappointment may be offset by selecting or developing the kind of programming that optimizes this new communications technology – football games and athletics for example – where action speaks louder than resolutions.

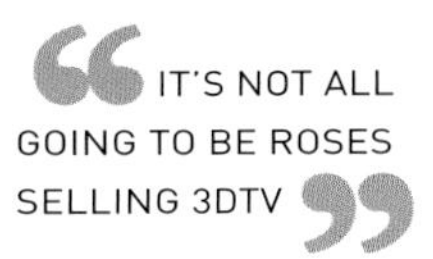
IT'S NOT ALL GOING TO BE ROSES SELLING 3DTV

  (Holographic TV at MIT.)

- *Gaze-tracking, motion capture and voice-user-interface.* Wandering through studio 2010, your position is tracked against the datum of the studio fixtures, fingertip sensors (fingernail pads), return xyz and motion data, and eyeball sensors mounted in your Gucci shades track your gaze. The wall-screens are totally responsive (you can adjust the refresh rate to non sick-making rates), and react to voice commands, gestures (pointing, pulling/pushing – you train your own software), and eyeball tracking.

(By 2000, motion analysis and motion capture, voice-user-interfaces, continuous speech recognition, gaze tracking and other technologies alluded to here were already either in production or in R&D.)

- *Design media-mentor expert system.* A software assistant (rule-based system) that happens to know everything about design – with access to databases throughout the web – every campaign, every poster, every commercial, every movie, every magazine, every CD cover, every brand identity – with dedicated software picture-research agents working a 24/7 shift. And it also knows all about media-creation expertise (the best people for the job), media technologies and production methodologies. With a voice-user-interface, gesture and gaze tracking, design problems can be mapped out spatially on the electrophoretically-painted wall-screens – ideas compared with historically similar problems and their solutions, colleagues can be video-windowed to share the brainstorm. Media-mentor also project manages: critical paths, budgets, diary synchronization and workflow organization are second nature.

  (We've had expert systems since the early 1980s, and the 1990s saw an increasing availability of commercial image- and media-databases, and the growing use of groupware. Broadband access is likely to accelerate services in this sector, making low-cost multi-participant video conferencing and multimedia groupware a reality. Continual speech recognition (voice-user-interface), gesture and gaze-tracking and motion-capture input were all more or less sorted by the end of the 1990s.)

- *Active desktops*. I'm not talking user-illusion here, I'm talking smart furniture – desktops like those that Xerox PARC and MIT have been developing – with built-in electronic sensors, electrostatic paper handling, paper coding and filing mechanisms. You won't need a mouse – your finger will do the pointing. Smart desks with their own agendas, meetings diaries and to-do lists, with digital-paper pads and smart markers – felt-tips that record the graphics you sketch. No intellectual output is lost in

Studio 2010. And, just as Andy Warhol's Factory was full of tape and video recorders, desks like this compliment your wearable armoury of sensors, scanners and recorders, automatically capturing your precious ideas. When you sit down, you automatically and wirelessly dock your wearables into your real desktop, synchronizing your diary and file version updates, and backing up your latest ideas. And the Herman Miller Aeron2010 will be smart enough to know you prefer more lumbar support, and like a lumbar massage after an hour of answering e-mails. In fact, the biometrics built into your wearables and your furniture really do look after you, monitoring heart-rate, muscle-tension, temperature, EEG brain activity, blood pressure and other indicators, and subtly adjusting themselves to suit your requirements.

(Developments in embedded processing (Motorola, Intel, etc), and current R&D at Xerox PARC.)

- *Automatic language translation software.* Phones and other voice-coms are routed through a dedicated DSP and processor that stores lots of language databases and can translate many different pairs of languages. The essential components of this de-Babelizing technology – continual speech recognition (speech to text), text-to-text translation, and speech synthesis (text to speech) – were all around in 2000. Now, in 2010, we have plenty of cheap processing power to perform these functions in real time, for hundreds of language pairs. Really cool creatives have a video phone that displays their personal avatar, and generates all the facial expressions and mouth movements in synch with the foreign language version of what they are saying. Of course personal avatars don't have to be hyper-realistic …

  (From Ray Kurzweil's projections of language translation technology: he points out that most of the elements of automatic language translation are already available or in advanced stages of development in 2000 – continuous speech recognition, text-to-text translation for some language pairs, and speech synthesis. Kurzweil suggests 2003 as the likely date for a real-time translating telephone. Lip-synch avatar design at Paul Allen's Interval Research, avatars and agents at BT Martlesham, and MIT. Automatic translation at Alta Vista, Lernout & Hauspie.)

- *Hybrid portable media capture/player*. People like hardware gizmos – so our 2010 creative will probably have the latest hybrid access device. On the desk you'll see a pocket-size media capture device, an integrated solid-state device offering the following capture/publishing/web access/player functions:
  - digital still camera – 32 gbyte flash-card/mini-HD memory – 10,000 JPEG photo-resolution images, auto webcam facility;
  - DV camera – 10 hours MPEG2 video;
  - MPEG2 player – stores five full-length features;
  - voice-recorder/digital audio solid-state recorder 50 hours MP3 audio files;
  - Symbian OS with WAP web access – e-mail and web;
  - e-book digital text storage and display – 5000 e-books – a pocket library;
  - 256-bit Nuon-powered games engine;
  - DVD – backward compatibility to old optical disk standards. DVD is still the biggest tangible distribution media because it's cheaper to press a disk than fabricate a chip. DVD replaced VHS for both home recording and media distribution after the analogue TV cut-off in 2006. DVD interactive movies use Nuon-generated real-time multiple overlays on the MPEG2 datastream, and feature live online windows of mobile-video phone input;
  - time-slice lens adapter – makes camcorder time-slice 3D movies.
- *VM Labs' $20 (1999 price) Nuon chip*. A combination MPEG2 codec and graphics-engine DSP that can add real-time video effects to the MPEG movie datastream it is decoding. Fabricated by Motorola, by 2000 Nuon had been chosen by Samsung, Toshiba, Motorola and others for their DVD-player hardware and set-top boxes. By 2010, Nuon had scaled up from 128-bit to 1024-bit (1 Kbit), become a major games platform, rivalling Playstation 4 (the much-vaunted 'thought-processor') and becoming the primary means of delivering interactive movies. Nuon has the ability to drive high-definition TV screens, to texture map in real time, to play games, to video-composite, to carry overlays of live video from mobile video phones or camcorders, and to provide set-top digital

FX to any broad- or narrow-cast datastream. So as Nuon technology transformed DVD from a movie-player into an interactive movie-game console, it also transformed the humble set-top pizza box into an arcade games-engine, and went on, after analogue TV cut-off, to become the CPU of digital television sets.

(Memory-capacity based on likely doubling of chip capacity and flash-card technology from 64Mb (1999) every year to 2010, giving a likely 16–32 Gbyte solid-state memory by 2010, but also factoring in the likelihood of further development in the miniaturization of hard disk technology. Other projections: VM Labs, Motorola, Samsung, Toshiba, Sony.)

“LIKE A SELF-WINDING WATCH, YOUR BODY MOVEMENTS RECHARGE THE BATTERIES THAT POWER THIS REAL BODY-AREA NETWORK”

- *Wearables*. Personal biometrics, reality-capture, profile handshakes: why carry all those consumer electronics around when you can wear them? Well, one reason is that Sony-Nikon makes it very desirable to own its latest hardware – and to flaunt it. But if you need to be discreet, or are just naturally sly, then wearables – sensors, memory and processing sewn into (or fabric-printed on to) your Comme des Garçons jacket – are just fine. Like a self-winding watch, your body movements recharge the batteries that power this real body-area network – a network that links:
  - spectacle-mounted stereo webcamcorders – tiny webcams mounted in your Cutler & Gross rose-tinted shades, they record everything you see and file it against SMPTE time-code that is shared by your voice-capture lapel-mounted microphones. Your designer-shades also contain inward-looking gaze-tracking sensors, and feature polarized ‘augmented reality’ interface projectors – your shades become the graphical user-interface to your suit. The under-side of your jacket’s sleeve is a high-resolution scanner, while the back of the jacket is software-switchable to an HDTV Teletubbies screen.
  - personal biometrics – heart, lung, brain, blood pressure and other sensors – monitor your health and stress levels.
  - output is by voice, body movement and gesture: mini position-sensors that decorate your fingernails, or embellish the rings you wear, enable you to type, paint, or play music, on virtual keyboards, virtual canvasses, and virtual instruments.

- personal profile publishing interface – streams your profile data to any Bluetooth-equipped device. Any computer you use automatically becomes yours – your desktop preferences, your web favourites, your most recent files – and uploads the personal public consumer profile that defines you on the network. This includes an only slightly exaggerated personal synthespian avatar – equipped with the voice-projection lip-synch algorithms developed by Interval Research in the 1990s.

▶ *Networks GANS, WANS, LANS, DANS, PANS and BANS*. By 2010, cyberspace is as deeply layered as a Martin Lambie-Nairn ident – and the planet's culture is defined by these layered networks of people, information, machines and media-networks within networks, starting from the top:

Global-area networks – low-earth orbit satellite constellations and geo-stationary satellites, along with our wire, cable and fibre infrastructure, provide the wrap-around IP-based communications for the global village. In orbit, include GPS position-fixing, mapping, emergency response, and remote-sensing satellites too. Low-latency LEO satellites service Teledesic-style global phone networks. The world wide web is really worldwide by 2010 – available absolutely anywhere and everywhere, so this GAN supports global access to around 10 million (broadband) websites, hundreds of thousands of online databases – downloadable e-book libraries and bookshops – (no more mass-printed books!), downloadable music, video and other media – so it's an information network and a media network too. Added to this is the webcam network – all kinds of video surveillance, CCTV, securicam, tourist-cams, picture-cams and mobile camcorders and video phones, even humble $5 webcam golfballs – all around the world, providing a network of live, real-time imaging from everywhere interesting. You can browse the world now, not just the web.

National-area networks – this is the infrastructural wire, cable and fibre backbone that interconnects the wired world, and provides IP-based national broadband networks. By now, we've realized that localization isn't just a geographical issue, so NANs are less territorially defensive –

cyberspace knows no borders, so why bother? NANs are where the weather, traffic, air-quality, national news and sports and entertainment thrive. The big surprise in the last decade was the meteoric emergence of China as the leading online nation. Leapfrogging the wired west, China went straight to wireless – 3G cellular and LEO-satellite networks, a much lower infrastructural investment. Mobile phone ownership in China reached 500 million by 2008, and 90 per cent of those phones were internet access devices. China Online is now the world's largest subscription ISPortal.

Wide-area networks – down to cellular-radio cell level now, these are the mix of IP-based radio and wired networks that provide broadband access to local communities, offices, universities, etc, through broadband mobile and broadband cable access.

Local-area networks – these are the familiar building-wide networks linked by a mix of wire and wireless, including ethernet, firewire, Bluetooth, Airport and Sony i-Link, these nets bring IP-based comms down to office scale. All co-evolved collaborators (knowledge 'workers') are interconnected through smart badges, their wearables, or their other (hybrid, laptop, palm-top, wristwatch) mobile access devices.

Home-area networks – these are broadband wire and wireless systems that provide media and computing access everywhere in the home, and potentially link all electrical and mechanical servo-mechanistic functions (doors opening, locking, heating, lighting, air-conditioning, etc) into a telematic system cleverly responsive to the occupants' requirements, but which also saves money by intelligent and economic use of utilities. By 2000, several home-area network systems were in development, including Avio's Mediawire home-area net, Sony i-Link and others such as the Home PNA system.

Mediawire (for example) uses ordinary phone wire (twisted pair) to carry up to 100 Mbits/sec, in a packet-switched network linking up to 100 devices over a chain up to 2.5 miles long. According to Avio, this capacity would enable it to handle 18 separate video streams, 132 CD quality audio channels, 16 ISDN-quality telephone lines, and 12 separate computer channels.

> *Body-area networks* – these wrap-around meshes of fabric and electromagnetics, of printed processors and solar cells – of printed consumer electronics – give 'body language' a new digital twist. Pheronomes are clumsy compared with body-area network communications. BANs expedite that perennial human search for other people who share our tastes, humour and interests – they low-power broadcast to the immediate vicinity (and to the web if you wish), your personal profile avatar – a software agent capable of interrogating other people's agents, and of being interrogated in return – electronically acknowledging, avoiding, handshaking, saluting, cutting-dead, and even flirting, inside the wireless avatar-space of social engagement.

'Scientists at IBM's Almaden Research Center (San Jose, California) are perfecting a new personal-area network technology (PAN) that uses the natural electrical conductivity of the human body to transmit electronic data. Using a small prototype transmitter (roughly the size of a deck of cards) embedded with a microchip, and a slightly larger receiving device, the researchers can transmit a pre-programmed electronic business card between two people via a simple handshake. What's more, the prototype allows data to be transmitted from sender to receiver through up to four touching bodies.'

Source: 'Hi Tech, hi touch: Personal-Area Networks', IBM Research.

scenario 2: WhichWorld? 'MarketWorld' scenario

This scenario is one of several from *Which World: Scenarios for the 21st Century: Global Destinies, Regional Choices* by Dr Allen Hammond (Island Press), available to order online at *www.amazon.com.* Courtesy of Dr Allen Hammond, copyright 1998: Dr Allen L. Hammond, World Resources Institute. By permission of Island Press. Parts of this book are reproduced online at *http://mars3.gps.* What had begun tentatively towards the end of the old century exploded in the new. Country after country adopted what was now almost a formula: privatize, deregulate, rein in public spending, and unleash competitive market forces. Join the global market by dropping tariffs, promoting exports, and seeking foreign investment. Build up financial capital by encouraging savings and

> “COUNTRY AFTER COUNTRY ADOPTED WHAT WAS NOW ALMOST A FORMULA: PRIVATIZE, DEREGULATE, REIN IN PUBLIC SPENDING, AND UNLEASH COMPETITIVE MARKET FORCES”

entrepreneurship. Build up human capital by emphasizing education and health. Create a modern infrastructure for transport and communications. Modernize the state by containing corruption, cutting red tape, and revamping the legal framework to protect property rights and facilitate commercial transactions.

The strategy championed by the United States and pioneered initially by the Asian tigers exported well. First China, then Chile and other Latin countries, then Uganda and a clutch of other African countries made it work. Southeast Asia, too, recovered and began to boom again. Russia, once its political situation stabilized, also proved adept at turning its educated workforce and huge natural resources into an economic powerhouse. The transition took longer in India, with its massive central government, and in the mullah-dominated, xenophobic Middle East. But India eventually began to grow rapidly, its low-wage but well-educated workforce giving it a huge advantage, and Iran and a few other Middle Eastern countries found ways to preserve a conservative Islamic culture while joining the global market.

The result was a worldwide economic boom of unprecedented breadth and longevity. Two decades into the new century, economic integration was well advanced. Trade had grown twice as fast as economic output and was now central to the economic fortunes of even the largest countries. The Free Trade Zone of the Americas, the South Asian Free Trade Zone, the integration of Russia and most of Central Europe into the European Union, the African Common Economic Market – all were thriving. Financial integration was even further along: effectively, there was only a single, global, financial market with daily volumes measured in tens of trillions of dollars, larger than the annual output of any single country. Indeed, its fluctuations have occasionally been damaging, which is why a Global Reserve institution was created some years ago to provide stabilizing and regulatory features. There is even talk of a global currency, modelled after Europe's euro. But by its sheer size and speed, the global financial market had become the de facto regulator of national economic performance, imposing instant financial penalties in the value of currencies and in interest rates on countries perceived to be less competitive. Moreover, economic integration had already begun to transform political and security relations: nations competed for share of market, not for territory, and many military forces had been sharply cut back.

One of the factors that facilitated economic and financial integration and rapid economic growth was the spread and continuing refinement of information technology. We take for granted now, at the mid-point of the century, the extensive network of fibres, satellites and cellular phone links that connect any place on earth instantly to any other, but this global information infrastructure was already well established by 2020. It not only tied the global market together but enabled novel types of organization and new forms of co-operation and commerce; it even made possible leapfrogging patterns of development. Who would have guessed that Sri Lanka would emerge as a key financial centre, the Switzerland of Asia, managing huge portfolios and investment services – and providing its people with a very comfortable lifestyle without ever developing an industrial economy? And of course the huge amount of commercial activity built directly on these information networks was itself a major source of new jobs in virtually all countries. But other technologies – biotechnology, molecular engineering – have proved important as well, generating successive waves of innovation and economic expansion.

A second key factor underpinning this new era of prosperity was the transnational corporation. There are so many transnational companies now of all sizes that we scarcely notice, but in the first few decades of the century large transnational corporations played a critical role as conduits of technology and expertise and as sources of patient investment capital that helped jumpstart economic growth in many developing regions.

With global economic integration has come convergence in consumption patterns and in production methods. Advertising has in part driven the first; competitive pressure and the rapid spread of new technology the second. There has also been convergence in forms of government, with democracies predominating.

It's true that not every country has managed the full set of reforms, and there have been a number whose leaders have foolishly tried to ignore the global market – and those countries have paid an enormous price. A few are backwaters yet, living on the raw materials they can sell and on the money that their expatriate workers send home; others are making progress but are decades behind. But there is very little sympathy for such places. The way to succeed is clear – it's their choice.

Some have decried the materialism of our global society, others the fact that huge inequities, even a small amount of abject poverty, persist. But they overlook what has been achieved – more than a fivefold expansion of economic activity over the past half century; unprecedented and widespread prosperity, with a sizable middle class providing an anchor for social and political stability in most countries. The world's population peaked nearly a decade ago, never having reached 9 billion, and is now declining slowly. There have been enormous advances in science and medicine – vigorous health at 80 and 90 years of age is common. Pollution has been sharply reduced almost everywhere, thanks to more efficient technology and competitive pressures – after all, wastes are a sign of inefficiency and poor management. Not that all environmental problems have disappeared: the climate is changing, although modern societies can easily adapt to the changes. But everywhere we see evidence of what human ingenuity and enterprise, once unleashed, can achieve. We have great universities and research institutes, endowed by private benefactors. Numerous foundations underwrite scholarship and cultural endeavours. The arts, sports, virtually every form of entertainment, are all flourishing – testimony to the wealth and leisure time that economic prosperity has provided.

> “THERE HAVE BEEN ENORMOUS ADVANCES IN SCIENCE AND MEDICINE – VIGOROUS HEALTH AT 80 AND 90 YEARS OF AGE IS COMMON”

©*Whichworld?: Scenarios for the 21st century* (Island Press) 2000 by Dr Allen Hammond, senior scientist and director of strategic analysis at the World Resources Institute in Washington DC, at *http://mars3.gps.caltech.edu/whichworld//explore/scenarios/scenmw.html.*)

Postface: Tuning-in to the zeitgeist

Futurecasting the web is a non-linear task and can become an absorbing, interactive and participative activity in itself. 'Tuning-in to the zeitgeist' involves staying abreast of the most exciting intellectual developments of our time (of all time?) by recording, cataloging and forecasting the extraordinary cultural and technological achievements of our 21st-century 'wizards' – the artists, hackers, product designers, producers, entrepreneurs, programmers, programme-makers, games designers, directors, writers, engineers, business people, computer scientists and information architects – who together create and engineer the infrastructure, products, content and software that constitute e-media.

I have spent some time building a 'big picture' of the web/net and other e-media, and I have included considerable historical perspective primarily in order to indicate the strength and continuity of the various vectors of development that we have examined. So this 'big picture' isn't just relevant for this year and maybe for next – it is for the foreseeable future of e-media.

The big ideas that are driving these developments include the world as a global village linked by ubiquitous communications technologies; the web/net as a global free market; the web/net as a global encyclopaedia/library; hypermedia as a natural extension of human memory; the web/net as a 'world brain'; e-media as augmentations of our intellect; e-media global networks as mankind's noosphere; and e-media networks as planetary management systems. The web/net is also seen as the largest entertainment machine ever created (ergo as the largest education machine); and e-media as the next stage in our cultural evolution (as a sustainable global community); as an expression of a perfect anarchy or a perfect democracy; or as the marriage of mind and technology or *technoetics*. All these ideas will continue to resonate through developments in e-media as we seek solutions to the problems of ignorance, inequity, iniquity and intolerance, and try to steer ourselves through an evolutionary transformation into a successful and sustainable planetary species – towards the Global Village.

All these utopian urgings and visions that percolate and project e-media developments are, I would argue, the key to futurecasting the web. You need a big picture and you need to know what sparked these developments. You must understand what's driving them, so you need to know what to look for, how to determine what's important and how to update your big picture, in order to make sense of this chaotic and breathless roller coaster ride into the future.

So this book will, I hope, provide you with enough of a 'concept map' and 'guide book' to both map the territory and to indicate the various vectors along which it may develop. While staying abreast of these rapidly changing techno-cultural developments is, of course, not what books are for, it is preeminently what the web/net is for. The web/net is itself a futurecasting machine and provides access to all the sources we need to dynamically update our big picture and to 'tune-in to the zeitgeist'.

Bibliography

3G Partnership Project www.3gpp.org

Advanced Television Enhancement Forum (ATVEF) www.atvef.com

Alderman, Ray, 'Disasters in the making' in *OEM* magazine, October 1996.

Amara, R. and Salanik, G. (1972) *Forecasting: from conjectural art torwards science.*

Ananova at www.ananova.com

Ascher, W. (1979) *Forecasting: an appraisal for policy-makers and planners*, Johns Hopkins University Press.

Ascott, Roy (ed) (1999) *Reframing Consciousness*, Exeter, Intellect Books.

Axelrod, Robert (1984) *The Evolution of Co-operation*, New York, Basic Books.

Bagdikian, Ben H. (2000) *The Media Monopoly*, Beacon Press.

Barry, Dave (1996) *Dave Barry on Cyberspace*, New York, Crown Publishers Inc.

Beacham, Frank (25/03/93) 'An interview with Nicholas Negroponte' at www.beacham.com

Bennahum, David S., 'The biggest myth of the new economy' at www.strategy-business.com/opinion00102/page1.html (1996) 'The Myth of Digital Nirvana', *Educom Review*, September/October, www.educause.edu

Benedetti, Paul and DeHart, Nancy (eds) (1998) *McLuhan: Forward Through the Rear-view Mirror*, Ontario, Prentice-Hall Canada.

Benedikt, Michael (ed) (1992) *Cyberspace: First Steps*, Cambridge, Mass, MIT Press.

Berners-Lee, Tim and Fischetti, Mark (1999) *Weaving the Web*, London, Orion Business Books.

Best, Steve and Kellner, Douglas, 'Kevin Kelly's Complexity Theory: the politics and ideology of self-organising systems' at www.uta.edu/huma/illuminations/best7.htm

Best, Steve and Kellner, Douglas (1991) *Postmodern Theory: Critical Interrogations*, Guilford Press.

Brand, Stewart (1987) *The Media Lab: Inventing the Future at MIT*, New York: Viking Penguin.

Brandenburger, Adam M. and Nalebuff, Barry J. (1996) *Coopetition: 1 A revolutionary mindset that redefines competition and cooperation; 2: The Game Theory strategy that's changing the game of business*, New York, Doubleday.

Bringsjord, Selmer (2000) *Artificial Intelligence and Literary Creativity*, Lawrence Erlbaum Assoc. Brutus website at www.rpi.edu/dept/ppcs/BRUTUS/brutus.html Personal website at www.rpi.edu/~brings/

British Telecom, BT Presentation for Agenda for Action in the UK (House of Lords, 1996) at www.dti.gov.uk/hol BT Technology Timeline: Towards Life in 2020 at www.bt.com/bttj/vol18no1/tomorrow.htm

Brunner, John (1975) *The Shockwave Rider*, J.M. Dent.

Bumgardner, Jim, 'History of the Palace' at www.jbum.com/history

Bush, Vannevar (1945) 'As we may think', *Atlantic Monthly*, August. Reprinted in *Macintosh Hypermedia Vol 1* by Michael Fraase, Scott Foreman & Co, 1990.

Buzan, Tony and Buzan, Barry (1996) *The Mind Map Book: how to use radiant thinking to maximize your brain's untapped potential*, Plume Publishing. mind maps at http://www.buzancentre.com/mm_desc.html

Cairncross, Frances (1995) 'The death of distance', *The Economist*, September 30. (1997) *The Death of Distance,* (Harvard Business School Press.

Cameron, Andy and Barbrook, Richard, 'The California Ideology' at www.wmin.ac.uk/media/HRC/ci/calif6.html

Cary, David, 'David Cary Futures' www.rdrop.com/~cary/html/future_history.html

Case, Steve, Speech to Superhighway Summit, 11/01/94, at Craig Birkmaier's website, www.digitaltelevision.com/future14.shtml

Cotton, Bob (1999) *You Ain't Seen Nothing Yet*, London, ICA.

Cotton, Bob and Oliver, Richard (1993) *Understanding Hypermedia*, London,

Phaidon Press. (1994) *The Cyberspace Lexicon*, London, Phaidon Press. (1998) *Understanding Hypermedia 2.000*, London, Phaidon Press.

Druckrey, Timothy (ed) (1999) *Ars Electronica: Facing the Future,* Massachusetts, MIT Press.

Dyson, Esther, 'Release 1.0' 1998 at www.edventure.com/release/1198.html (1998) *Release 2.1 A Design for Living in the Digital Age*, London, Penguin Books.

Electronic Frontier Foundation www.eff.org

Franco, Gaston Lionel (ed) (1983) *World Communications: new horizons, new power, new hope*, Le Monde Economique International Publications.

Fuller, Richard Buckminster (1970) *I Seem To Be A Verb*, New York: Bantam. (1971) *World Game Series: Inventory of World Resources*, Carbondale, Illinois.

Garud, Raghu, Jain, Sanjay and Phelps, Corey, 'A Tale of Two Browsers' at www.stern.nyu.edu/~~regarud/browserchat/strat.html

Gates, Bill (1995) *The Road Ahead*, London, Viking Penguin.

Gelernter, David (1991) *Mirror Worlds* (Oxford, Oxford University Press.

Gershenfeld, Neil (1999) *When Things Start to Think*, London, Hodder and Stoughton.

Gibson, William (1984) *Neuromancer*, London, Grafton. (1987) *Count Zero*, London, Grafton. (1998) *Mona Lisa Overdrive*, London: Grafton. (1988) *Burning Chrome*, London, Grafton.

Gilder, George 'The Gilder Technology Report' (archive) at www.gildertech.com (1990) 'The technology of liberation' in Raymond Kurzweil, *The Age of Intelligent Machines*.

Global Business Network www.gbn.org

Global Internet Liberty Campaign www.gilc.org

Greiman, April (1990) *Hybrid Imagery*, London, Architecture, Design and Technology Press.

Hafner, Katie and Lyon, Matthew (1996) *When Wizards Stay Up Late*, Simon & Schuster.

Hammond, Allen 'Whichworld? Scenarios for the 21st Century' at http://mars3.gps.caltech.edu/whichworld/explore/scenarios/scenmw.html

Hammond, Ray (1996) *Digital Business*, London, Hodder and Stoughton Coronet.

Hawkins, Trip (1983) 'Shaping Consumer Software', interview with Phil Lemmons and Barbara Robertson in *Byte*, October.

Herz, J.C. (1997) *Joystick Nation*, London, Abacus Books.

Hirschfeld, Thomas P. (ed) (1993) 'Interactive Multimedia: When Worlds Converge', Investment Report, New York, Salomon Brothers, June.

Hughes, Bob (2000) *Dust or Magic: Secrets of Successful Multimedia Design*, London, Addison Wesley.

Institute of Electrical and Electronic Engineers www.ieee.org

International Standards Organisation (ISO) www.iso.ch

International Telecommunications Union (ITU) www.itu.int

Interval Research www.interval.com

Irwin, Roger, 'Management Guide to SS Tactics' at www.geocities.com/SiliconValley/Hills/9267/sstactics.html

Jones, Jon Chris (1988) 'Softecnica' in *Design After Modernism*, edited by John Thackara, London, Thames and Hudson.

Kahn, Herman 'Choosing a perspective on the Future', Hudson Institute at www.hudson.org

Kay, Alan C. (1991) 'Computers, Networks and Education', *Scientific American*, September. (1984) 'Computer Software', *Scientific American*, Vol 257, No 3, September. (1990) 'User Interface: A Personal View' in *The Art of Human-Computer Interface Design*, edited by Brenda Laurel, Reading, Mass: Addison-Wesley.

Kelly, Kevin (1994) *Out of Control: The New Biology of Machines*, London, Fourth Estate. (1998) *New Rules for the New Economy: 10 ways the Network Economy is changing everything*, London, Fourth Estate.

Kurzweil, Raymond (1990) *The Age of Intelligent Machines*, Reading, Mass, MIT. (1999) *The Age of Spiritual Machines*, London, Orion Business Books.

Laurel, Brenda (1991) *Computers as Theatre*, Menlo Park, Calif: Addison-Wesley. (1990) 'Interface Agents: Metaphors with Character' in *The Art of Human-Computer Interface Design* edited by Brenda Laurel, Reading, Mass, Addison-Wesley. (1989) 'On Dramatic Interaction' in *Verbum* 3.3, San Diego.

Laurie, Peter (1980) *The Micro Revolution*, London, Futura Publications.

Leary, Timothy (1990) 'The Interpersonal, Interactive, Interdimensional Interface' in *The Art of Human-Computer Interface Design* edited by Brenda Laurel, Reading, Mass, Addison-Wesley.

Levine, Rick, Searle, Doc, Locke, Chris and Weinburger, David (2000) *The Cluetrain Manifesto*, London, Pearson Education/FT.com. www.cluetrain.com

Licklider, Joseph (1960) *Man-Computer Symbiosis*. (1968) 'The Computer as a Communications Device', with Robert Taylor, downloadable as PDFs from http://www.memex.org/licklider.html

Lodge, David (1990) 'Narration with Words' in *Images and Understanding*, edited by Barlow, Blakemore and Weston Smith, Cambridge, Cambridge University Press. 'The Novel as Communication' in *Ways of Communicating*, edited by Mellor, D.H., Cambridge, Cambridge University Press.

Malone, Michael S., 'One Digital Day' at www.intel.com/onedigitalday/explore/intro.htm

Martin, James (1978) *The Wired Society*, New Jersey, Prentice-Hall.

McCann, John M., Technology Cybertrends' at www.duke.edu/~~mccann/g-tech.htm

McCorduck, Pamela (1991) *Aaron's Code Meta-Art, Artificial Intelligence and the work of Harold Cohen*, New York, WH Freeman and Co.

McEwen, John D., 'Anarchism and the Cybernetics of Self-Organising Systems' at www.tao.ca/~freedom/cyb.html

McKenna, Regis (1997) *Real Time*, Harvard Business School Press.

McLuhan, H. Marshall (1964) *Understanding Media*, New York, New American Library. (1968) *War and Peace in the Global Village*, New York, Bantam Books.

Meth, Clifford (1996) 'Invisible Computing' in *Electronic Design,* January.

Michie, Donald and Johnston, Rory (1984) *The Creative Computer Machine Intelligence and Human Intelligence*, London, Viking Penguin.

MIT Software Agents Projects
http://mevard.www.media.mit.edu/groups/agents/projects

Mooneyham, J.R., 'An Illustrated Speculative Timeline of Technology and Social Change for the Next One Thousand Years' at
www.kurellian.tripod.com/sprint.html

Moore, Gordon, 'Moore's Law' at
www.intel.com/intel/museum/25anniv/hof/moore.htm

Moore, James F. (1995) *The Death of Competition: Leadership and Strategy in the Age of Business Ecosystems*, New York, Harper Business.

Morningstar, Chip and Farmer, S. Randall (1992) 'The Lessons of Lucasfilm's Habitat' in *Cyberspace: First Steps*, edited by Michael Benedict, Cambridge, Mass, MIT Press.

Motion Picture Experts Group (MPEG) www.mpeg.org

Negroponte, Nicholas (1991) 'Products and Services for Computer Networks' in *Scientific American*, September. (1970) *The Architecture Machine*, Cambridge, Mass, MIT Press. (1975) *Soft Architecture Machines*, Cambridge, Mass, MIT Press. (1990) 'The Noticeable Difference' in *The Art of Human-Computer Interface Design*, edited by Brenda Laurel, Reading, Mass, Addison-Wesley. (1995) *Being Digital*, New York, Alfred A. Knopf. 25/03/93 'An Interview with Nicholas Negroponte' at www.beacham.com

Nelson, Ted (1987) *Computer Lib – Dream Machines*, Redmond, Washington, Tempus Books of Microsoft Press, originally published 1974. (1989) 'The Crime of Wizzywig' in *Mondo 2000,* August. (1990) The Right Way to Think About Software Design, in *The Art of Human-Computer Interface Design*, edited by Brenda Laurel, Reading, Mass, Addison-Wesley. (1982) *Literary Machines*, Mindful Press.

Neumann, John von and Morgenstern, Oskar (1944) *Theory of Games and Economic Behaviour*, New Jersey, Princeton University Press.

Newman, Nathan, The Origins and Future of Open-source Software' at www.netaction.org/opensrc/oss-whole.html

OECD, 21st-century technologies: a future of promise for all at www.oecd.org/sge/au

Open-Source Organisation, www.opensource.org

Pask, Gordon (1968) 'The Colloquy of Mobiles' in *Cybernetic Serendipidy*, Studio International special edition, edited by Jascia Reichardt.

Pask, Gordon and Curran, Susan (1982) *Microman: Living and growing with computers*, London, Century Publishing.

Pierce, Mark Stephen (1989) 'Making Fun' (Videogame Design) in *Verbum* 3.3, San Diego.

Raymond, Eric S., 'Open-Source Software – a new development methodology at www.opensource.org/halloween1.html

Reichardt, Jascia (1968) *Cybernetic Serendipity: the computer and the arts*, London, Studio International Special Edition.

Rheingold, Howard (1991) *Virtual Reality*, London, Secker & Warburg. (1994) *The Virtual Community*, London, Secker & Warburg.

Ridderstrale, Jonas and Nordstrom, Kjell (2000) *Funky Business*, London, Pearson Education/FT.com.

Russell, Peter, Mind-mapping website www.peterussell.com/mindmap1.htm

Schneier, Bruce, cryptography website www.counterpane.com

Schwartz, Peter (1991) *The Art of the Long View*, New York, Doubleday.

Senge, Peter (1990) *The Fifth Discipline*, New York, Doubleday.

Small, Peter (2000) *The Entrepreneurial Web*, London, Pearson Education/FT.com.

Stephenson, Neal (1992) *Snow Crash*, New York, Bantam. (1999) *Cryptonomicon*, New York, Avon Books.

Sterling, Bruce (1999) 'The Future of Cyberspace: Wild Frontier v. Hyper-real estate', 1990 in *Ars Electronica: Facing the Future*, edited by Timothy Druckrey, Massachusetts, MIT Press.

Sunday Times, Chronicle of the Future' at www.chronicle-future.co.uk

Systems Dynamics Society, www.albany.edu/cpr/sds/

Turoff, Murray (1993) *The Network Nation*, Massachusetts, MIT Press (first published 1978).

Vallee, Jacques (1982) *The Network Revolution: Confessions of a Computer Scientist*, Berkeley, And/Or Press.

Vinge, Vernor (1981) *True Names,* first published in Dell 'Binary Star #5.' (1987) *True Names and Other Dangers*, New York, Baen Books.

Wack, Pierre, quoted at www.gbn.org/public/gbnstory/origins

Weisberg, Robert (1992) *Creativity – beyond the myth of genius*, London, W.H. Freeman and Co.

World Wide Web Consortium (W3C), www.w3.org

Wright, Will (1992) quoted from S. Reeder in 'Making Sense of Software: Computer Games and Interactive Textuality' at www.duke.edu/~tlove/simcity.htm

Youngblood, Gene (1970) *Expanded Cinema*, London, Studio Vista.

Index